The
Neo-Orthodox
Theology
of
W. W. Bryden

Princeton Theological Monograph Series

K. C. Hanson, Editor

Recent titles in the series

Richard Valantasis et al., editors
The Subjective Eye: Essays in Honor of Margaret R. Miles

Stephen Finlan and Vladimir Kharlamov, editors
Theōsis: Deification in Christian Theology

Sam Hamstra Jr.
*The Reformed Pastor: Lectures on Pastoral Theology by
John Williamson Nevin*

David A. Ackerman
*Lo, I Tell You a Mystery: Cross, Resurrection, and Paraenesis
in the Rhetoric of 1 Corinthians*

Paul O. Ingram, editor
Constructing a Relational Cosmology

Caryn Riswold
Coram Deo: Human Life in the Vision of God

Byron C. Bangert
*Consenting to God and Nature:
Toward a Theocentric, Naturalistic, Theological Ethics*

Michael G. Cartwright
*Practices, Politics, and Performance:
Toward a Communal Hermeneutic for Christian Ethics*

Philip Harrold
*A Place Somewhat Apart: The Private Worlds of a Late
Nineteenth-Century University*

Mark A. Ellis, translator
The Arminian Confession of 1621

The
Neo-Orthodox
Theology
of
W. W. Bryden

JOHN A. VISSERS

Pickwick *Publications*

An imprint of *Wipf and Stock Publishers*
199 West 8th Avenue • Eugene OR 97401

THE NEO-ORTHODOX THEOLOGY OF W. W. BRYDEN
Princeton Theological Monograph Series 56

ISBN: 1-59752-513-8

Cataloging-in-publication data

Vissers, John A.
The neo-orthodox theology of W. W. Bryden / John A. Vissers.

     xii + 284 p. 23 cm.
     Princeton Theological Monograph Series; 56
     ISBN 1-59752-513-8   (alk. paper)

     1. Bryden, Walter Williamson (1883–1952). 2. Theologians—
Canada. 3. Neo-orthodoxy. 4. Theology—History—20th century. I. Title.
II. Series.

BX4825 V58 2006

Manufactured in the U.S.A.

For my wife, Lynn

"The heart of her husband trusts in her . . ."
Proverbs 31:11

Photo courtesy of the Presbyterian Church Archives

Contents

Preface and Acknowledgments / ix

Introduction: The Word of God and the Words of Walter W. Bryden / 1

1 The Making of A Presbyterian Mind / 27

2 The Emergence of A Neo-Orthodox Voice / 71

3 The Judging–Saving Word of God / 130

4 A Theology of the Spirit / 176

5 A Church Reformed and Reforming / 219

6 The Witness of W. W. Bryden and the Neo-Orthodox Legacy / 249

Bibliography / 270

Preface *and* Acknowledgments

A MONG the pictures of past principals to be found in the Caven Library of Knox College in Toronto hangs the portrait of Walter Williamson Bryden. Owlish in appearance, eyes that pierce in eager encounter, a facial expression marked by solemnity and wisdom—Bryden's image represents what many undoubtedly imagine a Presbyterian divine to look like. For twenty-seven years, from 1925 until 1952, Bryden taught most of the clergy who served in The Presbyterian Church in Canada. This was a critical period in that church's history. As the sixth principal of the College, from 1945 until he died in 1952, Bryden left an indelible theological imprint on many of the church's ministers. Through them he influenced the faith and life of Presbyterianism for a generation to come.

When it was suggested a number of years ago that I should explore and document the theological legacy of Walter W. Bryden in Canadian Protestantism, I was, it has to be admitted, somewhat skeptical. I knew little about Bryden, and what I did know did not immediately convince me that a thorough theological study was warranted. At the time, a few of Bryden's students had written papers and articles on his thought and influence, but little else, despite good intentions, had been done. However, as I studied Bryden's material, interviewed his former students, read what had been written about him, and delved into the history of Protestant theology in North America, Britain, and Europe in the nineteenth and twentieth centuries, I soon became convinced that there was indeed a theological story to tell. I trust that this effort, therefore, will contribute to the understanding of a pivotal figure and an important era in the development of Canadian Protestant thought.

The sources upon which I have drawn, in addition to the published material, are those housed primarily in the Knox College Archives and the Archives of the Presbyterian Church in Canada. The materials upon which I have focused set out Bryden's theological views as expressed in published books, articles, and pamphlets, as well as in unpublished lectures, sermons, and correspondence. References to these sources and the secondary literature that have shaped my interpretation of Walter Bryden's thought and the character of neo-orthodox theology can be found in the notes and the bibliography.

Several institutions and people are to be thanked for their contribution to this book. The Board of Governors of the Presbyterian College, Montreal granted me a five-month sabbatical leave from my responsibilities as principal and professor of theology in order to complete the final draft of the manuscript. The Association of Theological Schools, through its Lilly Theological Research Grant Program, and The Priscilla and Stanford Reid Trust for Reformed Theological Education in Canada, provided financial support. Knox College and Tyndale Seminary, both in Toronto, provided resources, at an earlier stage, that allowed me to pursue the research and writing which forms the basis of this book. I should also like to acknowledge the resources of The Presbyterian Church in Canada Archives and archivists Kim Arnold and Bob Anger.

The list of those who entered into this project at various stages is so long that I am sure to omit some. Nevertheless I should like to begin by thanking a number of Walter Bryden's students who have shown a keen interest in this project and kindly spent time with me discussing his life, ministry, and theological contribution. They include a number who died before this book was completed: Arthur Cochrane, Charles Cochrane, Donald Wade, J. Charles Hay, George L. Douglas, and Walter Bryden's son Kenneth Bryden. I want to thank Joseph C. McLelland, whose work on Walter Bryden has shaped mine, and Robert Anderson, for his unflagging commitment to seeing that Bryden's theological work remains before the Canadian Protestant church.

A number of Canadian historians and theologians have provided assistance at critical points. I should like to thank David Demson and W. James Farris who supervised an earlier version of this work as a doctoral thesis at The Toronto School of Theology, University of Toronto. Although the material has been expanded considerably and the scope of the argument widened, a good deal of the original research done under their direction has found its way into the book. As far as I can remember, it was Brian Fraser, formerly of the Vancouver School of Theology, who first suggested to me that I pursue research into the theological contribution of Walter W. Bryden. The Roman Catholic scholar Harry McSorley of St. Michael's College, University of Toronto also read an earlier version of this manuscript and encouraged its publication. Harold Wells of Emmanuel College did likewise.

Numerous friends and colleagues have read all or part of the manuscript at various stages and offered helpful comments and corrections. Among them I would like to thank Glenn Smith, Barry Mack, W. J. Clyde Ervine, Glen Scorgie, Douglas John Hall, Ian S. Rennie, and John Moir. William Klempa and A. Donald MacLeod reviewed the manuscript carefully and offered many helpful suggestions.

I should like to thank Donald McKim of Westminster John Knox Press for his interest in this project, and K.C. Hanson and Jim Tedrick of Wipf & Stock Publishers who have guided the book through to publication. I am grateful to Denise Allen who did the copyediting and proofreading.

To be sure, not all those named will be satisfied with every aspect of my interpretation of Bryden's thought and influence. It is to be hoped, however, that those who may see things a little differently will nevertheless conclude that I have sought to explicate Bryden's thinking clearly and fairly in the context of European and North American theology. It goes without saying that any and all errors of commission and/or omission are the responsibility of the author alone.

My wife Lynn, and my children, Grant, Jennifer and Joel, have lived with Walter Bryden as an unseen member of the family for as long as they can remember. I thank them for their role in making Walter Bryden's theological story more widely known.

Introduction

The Word of God and the Words of Walter W. Bryden

---

*We must take the best and most irrefragable of human doctrines, and em-
bark on that, as if it were a raft, and risk the voyage of life, unless it were
possible to find a stronger vessel, some Divine Word on which we might
journey more surely and securely.*[1]

---

*The Gospel is therefore not an event, not an experience, nor an emo-
tion—however delicate! Rather, it is the clear and objective perception of
what eye hath not seen nor ear heard. Moreover, what it demands of [us]
is more than notice, or understanding, or sympathy. It demands participation, comprehension, co-operation; for it is a communication which presumes faith in the living God, and which creates that which it presumes.*[2]

D R. Stuart C. Parker, the influential liberal minister of St. Andrew's
Presbyterian Church (Simcoe Street) in Toronto, was beside himself
with rage, and had to be physically restrained. Walter Bryden, Knox College's
professor of church history and the history and philosophy of religion, had
just delivered a one hour and fifty minute address on the significance of
the Westminster Confession of Faith to the General Assembly meeting in
Hamilton, Ontario. The year was 1943, and Parker assumed that by now
most Canadian Presbyterians, especially those teaching in the church's colleges, considered the seventeenth-century statement of Reformed theology
as having not much more than historical significance. Yet here was Bryden,
one of the church's leading theological professors, extolling the virtues of the

---

[1] This quote from Plato's *Phaedo* was cited by Bryden in the opening lines of his unpublished
manuscript "After Modernism, What?" (1934). Bryden noted that he was indebted to Richard
Birch Hoyle, *The Teaching of Karl Barth: An Exposition* (London: SCM, 1930) 267 for the
quote.

[2] Karl Barth, *The Epistle to the Romans*, trans. by E. C. Hoskyns (London: Oxford University
Press, 1933) 28.

Westminster Confession for the continuing Presbyterian Church in Canada. To be sure, he pointed out its limitations as a confessional standard, and he resisted any and all attempts to adopt it as a statement of faith which set out eternal truths once for all time. But when it came to making his main point, Bryden was unapologetic: the Westminster Confession of Faith represent-ed the enduring witness of a generation to its faith and life in Jesus Christ, and continuing Presbyterians in Canada were under the same obligation of the gospel to confess their faith in God's Judging-Saving Word. Fortunately, Parker was intercepted as he made his way down the aisle of St. Paul's Church to speak to the slight and soft-spoken Walter Bryden. Nevertheless, Parker's response represented the increasing impatience on the part of some Canadian Protestant church leaders with the emergence of a new and distinct theo-logical witness in the second quarter of the twentieth century. What kind of theologian and what kind of theology could possibly provoke such a strong reaction, especially in Canadian Protestantism? These are the questions to be explored in this book.

Canadian Protestant theology during the 1930s was rife with the mood of crisis. It was a time, in the words of one Canadian church leader, "of the seeming failure of liberal theology, a time of theological perplexity, of the lost radiance of Christianity, of the dominance of secularism, of optimism about man and the world though this has faded in the face of the world crisis [and] of the decay of worship."[3] Idealism, which had provided the major philo-sophical paradigm for Protestant theology in Canada since about 1870, had floundered. Two-party Protestantism, divided by the fundamentalist/mod-ernist controversy, bedeviled the mainline churches and, for all its ecumeni-cal promise, the church union movement did not fulfill its hope of renewing the church to confront the forces of secularism. Indeed, as David Marshall has argued, the emergence of such movements as the Oxford Group and the Fellowship of Reconciliation were band-aid measures.[4] To the extent that the crisis being felt in the churches belonged to the wider mood of disillusion-ment in Canadian society, it was fed by the economic uncertainty of the Great Depression and the threat of another cataclysmic war in Europe.

Despite the mood of crisis, or perhaps precisely because of it, a revived Protestantism in the spirit of Luther and Calvin appeared during this pe-riod to challenge the dominant Canadian theological ethos and ecclesiasti-cal establishment. The uncertainty and ambiguity which characterized much of the preaching in Protestant churches in the first quarter of the twentieth

---

[3] J. G. Berry, Review of W.W. Bryden's *The Christian's Knowledge of God* in *Presbyterian Record* 66.2 (1941) 45.

[4] David B. Marshall, *Secularizing the Faith: Canadian Protestant Clergy and the Crisis of Belief, 1850–1940* (Toronto: University of Toronto Press, 1992) 184ff.

century generated a protest by a new generation of clergy who believed that the Christian faith had something significant to say in the midst of troubling times. J. G. Berry, writing in the *Presbyterian Record* in 1941, noted that this new Protestantism took its stand firmly on the Word of God, which it affirmed as the revelation of the living God.[5] It drew sharp distinctions between time and eternity and it emphasized "the infinite qualitative difference" (Kierkegaard) between God and humanity. It railed against the teachings of nineteenth-century liberal Protestantism and yet it refused to retreat behind the Biblicism of conservative orthodoxy. It pointed again and again to the Divine Word which it believed had been spoken decisively in God's crucified Messiah. The mood of crisis, it argued, had to be understood in terms of God's judgment.

Among the voices raised in this protest none was stronger in Canada than that of Professor Walter Williamson Bryden. During the 1920s Bryden had already been tenaciously burrowing to the foundations of modern theology in order to find a different basis for Protestant faith and life than the idealist version of Christianity to which he had been introduced as a student. By the early 1930s, when the mood of crisis set in, he was in a position to offer an incisive critique of Canadian church life and the theology which supported it to a new generation of theological students who believed that liberalism had been tried and found wanting. The importance of the Swiss theologian Karl Barth for this movement soon became apparent, and Walter Bryden was one of the first Canadian theologians to understand the radical challenge Barth's protest posed for the modern church.

Karl Barth was a young Reformed pastor in Safenwil, Switzerland when, in 1919, he startled the European theological world with the publication of his commentary on Paul's letter to the Romans. Dominated by the language of paradox, crisis, and dialectics, Karl Barth's book was an astonishingly brash challenge to the hegemony of nineteenth-century liberal theology and *Külturprotestantismus* (Cultural Protestantism). Unsatisfied with the first edition, Barth rewrote the book leaving, as he said, no stone unturned. The second edition, published in 1922, erupted with even more volcanic power as Barth pointed to the centrality of the Word of God which touched time and history in Jesus Christ, and which continues to touch humanity again and again as the original Word is heard, "leaping across the distances of time which are no barrier or hindrance to the running of the communication from eternity."[6] Barth spoke passionately about a word of judgment which contradicted and condemned human pride and its manifestation in ethics, politics, and religion. Religion, Barth argued, far from being the point of closest con-

---

[5]   J. G. Berry, *Presbyterian Record* (1941) 45.
[6]   Alasdair I. C. Heron, *A Century of Protestant Theology* (London: Lutterworth, 1980) 77.

tact with God, is the house human beings build in order to hide themselves from God, to convince themselves that God is within their grasp and under their control. "The hurricane of the Word tears away the flimsy structures of our pretensions, the altars of our false gods, the artificial securities to which we love to cling, all that Paul describes as the 'righteousness of the Law.'"[7] The cross of Jesus Christ is God's final and decisive 'No!' to all that: it leaves us literally nothing of our own on which we can rely. But God's 'No!' is spoken to create faith so that human beings may trust solely in God and hear behind and beyond this 'No!' the even deeper, more profound, and final promise of God's 'Yes!' The affirmation is the real purpose of the negation as God's Word of judgment makes real and radical faith possible, inviting humanity into the saving purposes of God.

At about the same time that Karl Barth was ringing a bell that sounded throughout Christendom,[8] a youngish Walter Bryden, an ocean away in "a quiet little village in the heart of Old Ontario,"[9] was working his way through Paul's Corinthian correspondence with many of the same theological questions. Like Barth, Bryden knew what it was to mount the pulpit steps each week to speak to his congregation in "the infinite contradiction of their life, but also to speak the no less infinite message of the Bible."[10] Passing largely unnoticed at the time, the book that resulted from Walter Bryden's study did not contain the sharp language that characterized Barth's work. But *The Spirit of Jesus in St. Paul* showed, as James D. Smart noted, "a mind moving abreast of the most vital developments in Christian theology" at the beginning of the twentieth century and "already grappling with the questions which dominated the attention of the church's leading theologians in the second quarter of the twentieth century." More importantly, "when one reads this book, written before much had been heard of Barth or Brunner, one realizes why Dr. Bryden immediately felt a community of interest with them. They were asking the same questions as he had been and were struggling to find the way forward to a Church that would recover its roots in the Scriptures and in the Reformation."[11]

Even though he was uneasy about the ecclesiastical and theological climate within which he found himself, Walter Bryden assumed the starting-

---

[7] Karl Barth, *The Epistle to the Romans*, quoted by Heron, *A Century*, 77.

[8] Later in his life Barth compared the experience of writing his commentary on Romans to a man who, tripping in the darkness of the church tower, had accidentally caught hold of the bell-rope to steady himself and alarmed the whole countryside. See Heron, *A Century*, 78.

[9] Bryden, "The Triumph of Reality," in *Separated Unto the Gospel*, edited by D. V. Wade (Toronto: Burns and McEachern 1956) 131.

[10] Karl Barth, *The Word of God and the Word of Man*, trans. Douglas Horton (Boston: Pilgrim, 1928) 100.

[11] James D. Smart, "The Evangelist as Theologian," in *Separated Unto the Gospel*, x.

point of modern theology at the end of the nineteenth century: Divine Spirit. He made the claim that the essential thing in religion "is a real *apprehension of God* which is neither a purely intellectual or moral, nor yet an emotional experience of life."[12] Such a real apprehension of God, he argued, cannot be experienced but through the Spirit of God as the most important and most present factor in this realistic world. The Spirit is "an unobtrusive Presence, easily grieved away and sometimes quenched, but it waits at the door of every soul and is quick to enter at the behest of the slightest need."[13] The problem of the church in his day, he contended, was that "the fact of the Spirit had been so modified in so-called Christian circles (if not altogether dismissed from the category of real things), as to make it practically identical with the natural evolution of the laws of moral progress."[14] The Spirit of God, as Bryden understood it, had been separated from the revelation of God in Jesus Christ and attached to the rational ideals of the modern world. This was precisely the antithesis of the New Testament gospel, a message which emphasized that there was a need for revelation in history and a need for revelation in every individual soul, "if that soul is to know truth—God. Revelation in the individual's life is that light which breaks upon personal labor and patience, and courageous and obstinate adventure in the sphere of the Spirit, and which reveals itself in a knowledge ear-marked of God."[15]

Walter Bryden was reacting to the idealism and rationalism that dominated Protestant thought and life in the opening decades of the twentieth century. Canada's leading idealist philosopher of the time, John Watson of Queen's University, Kingston, for example, appealed to Paul's Athenian address in order to shore up a Hegelian and Darwinian worldview: "In God 'we live and move and have our being,'" Watson told a Kingston meeting of the Y.M.C.A. in 1901. "We are spirits capable of communion with the Spirit of all things; the meanest as well as the highest object within our reach witnesses of this universal spirit; and living in it, we may become worthy members of the family, the community, the state, the race. To realize this spirit in all its forms is our true life work."[16] The spirit about which idealism spoke gathered up all humanity as one in the progressive unfolding of history. Watson's conception of the spirit, however, was too domesticated for Bryden. In the hands of politicians and ecclesiastical bureaucrats it had been used to prop up the status quo and to justify a society and a church that appeared to have little

---

12 Bryden, *The Spirit of Jesus in St. Paul* (London: James Clarke, 1925) 237.

13 Ibid., 237.

14 Ibid., 238.

15 Ibid., 253.

16 John Watson as quoted by A. B. McKillop, *A Disciplined Intelligence: Critical Inquiry and Canadian Thought in the Victorian Era* (Montreal: McGill-Queen's University Press, 1979) 207.

in common with the faith of the New Testament. The Spirit of Jesus, Bryden argued, created longings, passions, paradoxes, and even uncertainties in the midst of real life. The Holy Spirit, it seemed to him, raised questions about God, human beings, and the world, before it created a knowledge of God. The Spirit, when it stirred in the human soul, caused people to labor under the burden of their sins and long to hear a divine word.

Bryden sensed that there was something profoundly wrong with the idealist bent of Canadian Christianity, yet he also knew that he could not simply embrace the old orthodoxies. Already between a rock and a hard place, Bryden's dilemma was exacerbated by the church union movement where appeals to the principles of idealism and rationalism were rampant. Though sympathetic to the need for church unity, he remained aloof to the debate in the years leading up to church union "because he was alarmed by the indifference to theology displayed by both sides."[17] When required to make the decision, however, Bryden opted for the continuing Presbyterian Church in Canada because the case for union had left him unconvinced. But it would take Karl Barth's radical and clarion call to reorient Walter Bryden to the theology of Word and Spirit at the heart of the Protestant Reformation. In the wake of Barth's influence, and within a few short years of writing *The Spirit of Jesus in St. Paul,* Bryden talked paradoxically and prophetically about God's Judging-Saving Word, and launched his own protest against the worldview of the dominant ecclesiastical establishment. Along the way, he became one of the most important and articulate post-union voices in the continuing Presbyterian Church in Canada.

Four years after Walter Bryden's death in 1952, James D. Smart, then a professor at Union Theological Seminary in New York, and one of Bryden's former students in the 1920s, gave the following assessment of Bryden's theological significance:

> A future historian who attempts to understand and evaluate the development of the Presbyterian Church in Canada in the half century following 1925 will find himself very clearly confronted with the fact of Walter W. Bryden. He will not find the name appearing often in the minutes of the General Assembly nor among those serving on important committees which are supposed to wield great power in the shaping of the church's life. But as he examines the convictions which have moved men to action and asks why the ministry of this Church has moved in certain directions and not in others, he will come upon innumerable trails all leading back to the classroom of this one man.

---

17   Robert Wright, "The Canadian Protestant Tradition 1914–1945," in *The Canadian Protestant Experience 1760–1990,* edited by George A. Rawlyk (Burlington, Ont.: Welch, 1990) 152.

It can be said that he has moved the Church at the level of its faith and
its deepest thinking as has no other man in its history.[18]

An exalted estimate, to be sure, but it is safe to say that outside Canadian
Presbyterian circles Bryden's name has never been widely known, let alone
acclaimed. Over the years a few United Church theologians have commented
on Bryden's legacy in passing. W.O. Fennell, for example, noted in his anniversary retrospect of the Canadian Theological Society that there were fore-
runners to the present association of Canadian theological scholars, among
them Walter W. Bryden and the Trinitarian Society which met at Knox
College during the 1930s and 1940s: "the Trinitarian Society, founded by
ministers graduated from Knox College, much under the influence of the
Barthian scholar, Principal Bryden, and including a few non-Presbyterians
in its membership, met regularly to discuss classical theological themes with
vigour and scholarly acumen."[19] Some of Bryden's books were published and
reviewed outside Canada but for the most part his influence was exercised
within the Presbyterian Church in Canada in the two decades following
church union. These were the years he mounted a rigorous defense of the
Reformed faith for a church that had gone through a major crisis. He did so
by appealing to the increasingly influential dialectical theology of Karl Barth
and his colleagues. As a result, Bryden became the conduit through which
many Canadian Presbyterians were introduced to neo-orthodox theology.

Born on September 12, 1883 on a farm near Galt, Ontario, to a family of Scottish immigrants, Walter Bryden studied philosophy, psychology,
and modern languages at the University of Toronto before proceeding to
theological studies at Knox College, Toronto in preparation for the ordained
ministry of The Presbyterian Church in Canada. During the course of studies
in divinity, Bryden spent a year abroad at the United Free Church College
in Glasgow where he was exposed to theological teachers who were to have a
decisive influence on his thinking. Following graduation in 1909 he served
successively as the minister of Presbyterian congregations in Alberta, Ontario
and Saskatchewan before being called in 1927 to a professorship at Knox
College, where he taught church history and the history and philosophy of
religion. In 1945 he was appointed by the General Assembly as principal of
the college, a position he held until his death on March 23, 1952.[20]

---

[18] James D. Smart, "The Evangelist as Theologian," in Bryden, *Separated Unto the Gospel*,
vii.

[19] W. O. Fennell, "The Canadian Theological Society: An Anniversary Retrospect," *Studies in
Religion* 14 (1985) 409. See also the more recent article by Gordon Harland, "God's Judging
Saving Word: The Legacy of Walter W. Bryden," *Touchstone* 13.3 (1995) 43–51.

[20] "Death of Principal of Knox College," *The Presbyterian Record* (May 1952) 9.

In five books, numerous articles and book reviews, correspondence, sermons, and more than ten volumes of unpublished lecture notes and manuscripts, Bryden almost single-handedly set forth an approach to Christian theology that was to reposition Presbyterianism within Canadian Protestantism after church union.[21] Bryden's contribution as a Presbyterian minister, theological professor, and college principal is essentially twofold: first, he was one of the earliest and most influential interpreters of Barth and Barthianism on the Canadian scene; and second, he was one of the ablest and most articulate critics of church union in Canada in the post-union era. The main purpose of this book is to examine both dimensions of Bryden's theological contribution and their interdependence. On the one hand, Bryden marshaled the new Reformation theology of Barth and Brunner to launch a broadside against Canadian Protestantism in general and the church union movement in particular. At the same time, his increasing disillusionment with the idealism of modern Protestant theology and church life, especially as it was expressed in church union, had already prepared him to embrace wholeheartedly the witness of the neo-orthodox theologians.

The Neo-Orthodox Protest and Canadian Protestantism

The story of the reception of Karl Barth's theology in Canada and neo-orthodoxy's subsequent influence in Canadian Protestantism, as historians have long recognized, is bound up with the life and thought of Walter W. Bryden. In his *A History of the Church in the United States and Canada*, R. T. Handy identified "Professor (later Principal) Walter Williamson Bryden of Knox College, a Presbyterian seminary" as one of Karl Barth's chief interpreters in North America. Bryden, in fact, was the only Canadian interpreter of Barth mentioned.[22] Similarly Mark Noll's *A History of Christianity in the United States and Canada* isolated but a single figure, "W. W. Brydon (sic) of Knox College, Toronto" as a significant neo-orthodox thinker in Canada.[23] Canadian church historian John Webster Grant noted that the works of the Swiss theologian Karl Barth "had first been drawn to the attention of

---

[21] Bryden's books and articles are introduced throughout this book. His six main books, in the order of writing and publication, are: *The Spirit of Jesus in St. Paul* (1925), *Why I Am A Presbyterian* (1934), *After Modernism, What?* (unpublished, 1934), *The Christian's Knowledge of God* (1940; republished in 1960), *The Significance of the Westminster Confession of Faith* (1943), and *Separated Unto the Gospel* (published posthumously, 1956).

[22] R. T. Handy, *A History of the Church in the United States and Canada* (Oxford: Oxford University Press, 1976) 409.

[23] Mark A. Noll, *A History of Christianity in the United States and Canada* (Grand Rapids: Eerdmans, 1992) 522.

Canadians through the enthusiastic sponsorship of W.W. Bryden of Knox College."[24]

Beyond initial and isolated acknowledgement, however, no one has really examined the nature and substance of Bryden's thought and influence as a neo-orthodox theological professor in the Canadian context. In fact, Canadian historians and theologians have generally ignored the neo-orthodox movement in twentieth-century Canadian Protestantism. The studies that do exist have gotten the movement quite wrong, either because they fail to examine the thought of Canadian theologians in detail or because they force neo-orthodoxy to fit a preconceived argument concerning the development of religious thought in Canada. For example, Robert Choquette summarizes neo-orthodox theology in Canada by describing Barth's influence during the 1930s as providing "conservative evangelical Christians with a refreshing alternative to the overly simplistic and literal reading of the Bible that all too frequently prevailed in fundamentalist circles."[25] One looks in vain, however, for any mention of a Canadian theologian or thinker who actually appropriated Barth in this manner. In an otherwise illuminating study of Canadian religious history, Michael Gauvreau dismisses "Barthian neo-orthodox theologians" as modernists, relativists, and existentialists who, "rather than returning to the sources of evangelical tradition, broke decisively with its theology of history."[26] The distinctive tenets of the emerging "theology of crisis" were characterized by what Gauvreau describes as a "sense of absolute contradiction between the uncertain, constantly changing record of human civilization, and the eternal, unchanging, incomprehensible revelation of God."[27] Though his instincts may well be correct, Gauvreau says all this without examining the thought of even a single Canadian neo-orthodox thinker. Similarly, in his argument for secularization, David B. Marshall contends that neo-orthodoxy was a brief and unsuccessful detour on the road that led inevitably from Victorian Christianity to secular modernity.[28] To his credit, Marshall takes a few pages to examine the reception of Karl Barth's theology and the emergence of neo-orthodox themes in John Line, D. L. Ritchie, Walter Bryden, and E. H. Oliver. But the overall impression remains the same: neo-orthodoxy had little currency in Canadian Protestantism during the 1920s and 1930s.

---

[24] John Webtser Grant, *The Church in the Canadian Era* (Burlington, Ont.: Welch, 1988) 152.

[25] Robert Choquette, *Canada's Religions* (Ottawa: University of Ottawa Press, 2004) 320.

[26] Michael Gauvreau, *The Evangelical Century: College and Creed in English Canada from the Great Revival to the Great Depression* (Montreal: McGill Queen's University Press, 1991) 268.

[27] Michael Gauvreau, *The Evangelical Century*, 268.

[28] David B. Marshall, *Secularizing the Faith: Canadian Protestant Clergy and the Crisis of Belief, 1850–1940* (Toronto: University of Toronto Press, 1992) 4, 181–204.

Most interpreters have also failed to distinguish between the theology of Karl Barth and the influence of so-called Barthianism that was transmitted to Canada via other representatives of the dialectical school of theology, especially Emil Brunner and Reinhold Niebuhr. One notable exception is Robert A. Wright who has pointed to the crucial role played by Reinhold Niebuhr of Union Seminary in New York in transmitting Barth's influence to Canadian Protestantism during the depression. But again, aside from passing references to Walter Bryden, J. King Gordon of the Canadian Fellowship for a Christian Social Order, and John Line of Emmanuel College, there is no serious attempt to understand Canadian expressions of neo-orthodox themes, nor precisely how it was that Niebuhr became so influential in the reception of neo-orthodoxy in Canada.[29]

A careful examination of Walter Bryden's thought and influence, as I intend to show, raises serious questions about the assumptions concerning neo-orthodoxy with which Canadian historians and theologians have worked. For example, Walter Bryden's early reception of Karl Barth's early theology indicates that neo-orthodoxy began to emerge in Canadian Protestantism by the late 1920s. There is also evidence to suggest that the interpretation of Barth embraced by Canadian theologians owed as much, if not more, to Brunner and a number of English interpreters in Britain and the United States, as it did to their reading of Barth himself. Furthermore, Walter Bryden was not interested in adopting the themes of Barth's theology wholesale and transplanting them to Canadian soil. Rather than parroting Barth or borrowing idly (as many of Barth's followers were known to do), Bryden tried to work out the implications of Barthian insights for the Canadian churches in the second quarter of the twentieth century. And perhaps most important of all, although Walter Bryden was one of the first on the continent to see the significance of Barth, he came through to his basic theological position on his own. He developed his own thought, primarily in reaction to the idealism which dominated Canadian Protestant thought in the first part of the twentieth century, and largely through the influence of the moderating Calvinism espoused by theologians like James Denney and P. T. Forsyth. The reception of Barth by Bryden was also prepared by the influence of Albert Schweitzer's deconstruction of the search for the historical Jesus, and accompanied by the *Formgeschichtliche Schule*, of which Rudolf Bultmann's book *Jesus* was representative. Bryden's version of neo-orthodoxy, then, had roots that went deep in Canadian and British intellectual soil as well as those that reached out to continental European theology.

It is in this context, then, that Barth's decisive influence on Bryden is to be understood. By the late 1920s Bryden was sounding the themes that were

---

29   Wright, "The Canadian Protestant Tradition 1914–1945," 179–80.

to signal his lifelong engagement with Barth whom he referred to as "the stern new prophet of Europe" and "the modern scion of the Reformation spirit," and whose theology he described as "real Calvinism in a modern dress."[30] Bryden's formative teachers had introduced him to a mediating and moderate form of Calvinism which combined critical scholarship with evangelical piety, but it was Barth who provided the categories with which Bryden framed his protest against both confessional Calvinism and progressive Protestantism.

The term 'neo-orthodoxy' demands particular explanation since it figures so prominently in this account of Bryden's thought and influence. Despite the fact that it is, as Douglas John Hall notes, a highly ambiguous term that defies categorization, and always has been, the term 'neo-orthodoxy' has been used to describe the development of twentieth-century theology for so long now that it seems unimaginable to tell the story without it.[31] Neo-orthodoxy has usually been identified with the theology of the schools of Karl Barth and Emil Brunner, and sometimes Reinhold Niebuhr, which reasserted the principles of Reformation theology in a protest against the continuing influence of late nineteenth-century culture on Protestantism. In fact, the story of how Barth rebelled against his eminent liberal teachers and became the leader of a revolt against a liberal Protestant theological establishment is, as Gary Dorrien has noted, "the founding narrative of twentieth-century theology."[32] In the 1920s Barth and his chief theological collaborators were known as "theologians of crisis" or "dialectical theologians." Initially Barth's allies included Eduard Thurneysen, Friedrich Gogarten, Emil Brunner, Rudolf Bultmann, and Paul Tillich. By the 1930s these thinkers and others, including Dietrich Bonhoeffer, Reinhold Niebuhr, H. Richard Niebuhr, Regin Prenter, Gustav Aulen, Helmut Thielicke, and Suzanne de Dietrich, were working out their own forms of theology beyond liberalism while emphasizing their differences from Barth and each other.

Nevertheless, their initial protest against liberalism was marked by a number of common themes including the transcendence and holiness of a wholly other God, human sinfulness, the doctrine of grace, the centrality of Christ, the strange new world within the Bible, and justification by faith alone. They objected to liberal Protestantism's emphasis on the immanence of God, the optimism which characterized liberalism's view of humanity and the progress of history, the authority of religious experience, the identifica-

---

[30] Bryden, "The Triumph of Reality," in *Separated Unto the Gospel*, 134; see also "The Presbyterian Conception of the Word of God," unpublished manuscript, 49.

[31] Douglas John Hall, *Remembered Voices: Reclaiming the Legacy of "Neo-Orthodoxy"* (Louisville: Westminster John Knox, 1998) 5.

[32] Gary Dorrien, *The Barthian Revolt in Modern Theology* (Louisville: Westminster John Knox, 2000) 3.

tion of revelation with rational and ethical ideals, and the gradual coming of the Kingdom of God on earth through social means. As modern thinkers, however, they accepted biblical criticism and were concerned to work out a social ethic in the industrial order that took social criticism of religion seriously. Initially launched as a protest against liberalism, the so-called neo-orthodox theologians soon trained their sights on the older forms of orthodoxy as well—confessional Protestantism, scholasticism, and fundamentalism—rejecting what they perceived as the reduction of Reformation insights to static scholastic principles and the identification of revelation with the words of a verbally inspired and infallible Scripture. They also pressed their critique to include Roman Catholic theology prior to Vatican II because it allowed, they believed, that human beings could gain a knowledge of God prior to and apart from the revelation of God in Jesus Christ. The movement in which these theologians found themselves as allies of a sort earned such tags as neo-supernaturalism, theology of encounter, existential theology, kerygmatic theology, theology of paradox, theology of the Word of God, Christian realism, dialectical theology, crisis theology, neo-Reformation theology, and Barthianism. Although ambiguous and problematic, the most prominent and persistent title given to the theological protest represented by this web of theological trajectories was neo-orthodoxy.

The giant figures, as Gary Dorrien notes, "compel later generations to explain them. To the extent that they have any say in the matter, they also usually resist the labels assigned to them." [33] The fact that Karl Barth offers a striking example on both counts is an important point for understanding the shape of neo-orthodoxy in Canada. The movement that grew up around Barth's initial theological protest soon took on a life of its own. Increasingly, Barth felt the need to distance himself from the others and sharply denied that he was a neo-orthodox theologian. He wanted no part of a movement to create a new or modernized orthodoxy. Furthermore, he rejected almost every other label used to describe the theological work with which he and his colleagues had been engaged, partly because he insisted that he did not want any school of followers, and partly because major rifts began to appear between them in the late 1920s. By the time the periodical *Zwischen den Zeiten* ceased operations in 1932, Barth and Bultmann had parted company over hermeneutics, and a dispute over natural theology was heating up between Barth and Brunner that led to their acrimonious split in 1934. Aware of this, and writing much later, James Smart lamented the confusion surrounding the term neo-orthodoxy:

---

[33]   Dorrien, *The Barthian Revolt in Modern Theology*, 1.

Who and what does it signify? Is this the theology of either of the Niebuhrs, or of Paul Tillich, or of Karl Barth, or of Emil Brunner? It cannot be the theology of all of them since they differ from each other not in superficial but in basic aspects of their theologies. Lumping them together as proponents of a "Neo-Orthodox Theology" misrepresents every one of them. Yet a surprising number of authors use this term, undefined, chiefly as a way of putting behind them a number of significant theologies of the immediate past.[34]

The theology of Barth and his colleagues which reached Canadian shores in the late 1920s, therefore, was already a theology in transition. Whatever consensus had existed among the crisis theologians was in the process of breaking up. And the differences between them were real theological differences. What frequently went by the name of Barthianism represented positions Barth had already repudiated. The reception of Barth and Barthianism in the English-speaking world, including Canada, facilitated by secondary interpreters, often exacerbated the confusion. Perceptively, Walter Bryden was one of the first Canadian interpreters of Barth and Barthianism to see the distinctions, although he was not always consistent in applying the insights. For this reason, Bryden sharply denied on more than one occasion that he was a Barthian. Like Barth, Bryden saw himself as a church theologian in the ongoing tradition of Calvin and Luther who sought to express the faith of the Reformation in ways that were adequate to the twentieth century. Like Barth, he wanted to be categorized under no other marker than church theologian of God's free and sovereign Judging-Saving Word.[35]

Regrettably, then, the term neo-orthodoxy has often been used to paper over the differences between any and all post-liberal options without examining the distinctive theological character of each and the unique theological contributions of those who espoused them. Even more disconcerting, this has been done in and under the name of Karl Barth. It is one of the purposes of this book, therefore, to examine a specific example of neo-orthodox theology in Canadian Protestantism, in order to correct this gross generalization of Canadian religious history. Theological neo-orthodoxy was a diverse and contentious movement, and the term itself was disowned by Barth and most of his theological collaborators. It is time for scholars to recognize neo-orthodoxy for what it was: a series of theological trajectories which emerged from a common theological protest. Rather than using the term neo-orthodoxy to describe a monolithic position, it is better to speak about "neo-orthodoxies."

---

[34] James D. Smart, *The Past, Present, and Future of Biblical Theology* (Philadelphia: Westminster, 1979) 24–25.

[35] Dorrien, *The Barthian Revolt in Modern Theology,* 1.

Walter Bryden, in this sense, represented one of those trajectories in North American theology.

It might be argued, of course, that the continuing use of the term neo-orthodoxy is no longer justified if it fails to illumine the theological thought of those it is intended to represent. If the term is meant to describe a new form of orthodox confessionalism or scholasticism, then neither Karl Barth nor Walter Bryden deserve the label, and the term should be mothballed. But few, if any, interpreters use the term neo-orthodoxy in this way any longer. The neo-orthodox impulse, as I intend to argue, was a complex and creative blend of Reformation theology with modern thought, reformulated to overthrow liberal Protestant Christendom; not retreating behind the modern world or seeking to go around it, but going through it. As such, it was a thoroughly modern option in twentieth-century theology. Furthermore, the continuing use of the term acknowledges a basic historical reality: a theological trajectory emerged in the first half of the twentieth century that was perceived, rightly or wrongly, to provide a third option beyond two party Protestantism in North American Christianity and, for better or worse, the name by which it became known was "neo-orthodoxy."

The Nature of Bryden's Neo-Orthodoxy

Walter Bryden's role in this movement in Canada compels an explanation. He provided leadership to a particular post-liberal, anti-modernist protest against idealism and rationalism in the second quarter of the twentieth century and one of the main tasks of this book is to explain the nature and function of that protest in Canadian Protestantism. The explanation is guided by the following thesis concerning the character and function of his neo-orthodox theological contribution: Walter Bryden pointed Canadian Presbyterians to a neo-Reformation theology of Word and Spirit at a critical moment in their history. Three distinctive features of this neo-orthodox theological witness are to be noted: (1) it was a theology of revelation, (2) it was a critical retrieval of Reformation theology and (3) it was a self-consciously post-Enlightenment theology.

First, it was a theology of revelation, or more particularly a neo-Reformation *theology of Word and Spirit*. Bryden's forte, as Joseph C. McLelland has noted, was "theological epistemology—a theory of knowledge which accepts as a primary datum the novelty of a Word from God."[36] Bryden focused on the question of revelation and the knowledge of God because

---

[36] Joseph C. McLelland, "Walter Bryden: 'By Circumstance and God,'" in *Called to Witness: Profiles of Canadian Presbyterians*, edited by W. Stanford Reid (The Presbyterian Church in Canada, 1980) 2:123.

these constituted, for him, the central issues of the Christian faith. Already in his first book, *The Spirit of Jesus in St. Paul*, published in 1925, Bryden identified this question as one of fundamental importance: "'What do you mean by Knowledge of God,' is probably the most difficult question that may be asked of a religious man; but the fact of its attainability is the most fundamental and universal, if least definable, of religious convictions."[37] Similarly, Bryden's most important book, *The Christian's Knowledge of God* (1940), was an attempt to explore the meaning of Christian revelation by challenging the modern focus on rational, historical, ethical, and philosophical ideals, and positing in their place what he argued was a realistic conception of revelation centered in the self-disclosure of the God who shares self-knowledge with human creatures. The result, for Bryden, was a Trinitarian theology of the Word and a dialectical, christocentric reconstruction of the doctrine of revelation, which he described as the Judging-Saving Word of God.

Walter Bryden shared this concern for revelation with other Protestant theologians in the first half of the twentieth century. As Wilhelm Pauck has noted, they stood over against the strategy of theological liberalism, from Schleiermacher-forward, to base theology on human religious consciousness. Defiantly in the place of theological liberalism, theologians like Barth and Brunner interpreted the Christian faith on the basis of God's revelatory Word in Jesus Christ. As a theological strategy, "instead of asking: 'What has modern man to say about the gospel?' the theologians now concerned themselves with the question: 'What does the gospel say to modern man?'"[38] Accompanying this focus on revelation was a new emphasis on the Bible. Pauck argued that, in contrast to the modernist view of the Bible, Barth and Brunner's view differed from "that which can be obtained by the use of the historical method for the interpretation of historical texts and documents," because it took "the books of the Bible as bearers of kerygma, a message of salvation that must be believed."[39] On the other hand, Pauck insisted, their view had "nothing in common with the view of the fundamentalists," who stressed "the literal inerrancy of the Bible as if this were the foremost article of the Christian faith."[40] The Christian message, the kerygma, the gospel of Christ, in the view of the dialectical theologians, represents "a scandal and a provocation" to the contemporary world because the revelation of God, revealing as it does the radical message of the cross, calls into question all human efforts at self-salvation. It offers human beings "renewal through the forgiveness of

---

37 Bryden, *The Spirit of Jesus in St. Paul*, 152.
38 Wilhelm Pauck, in Kegley and Bretall, *Theology of Emil Brunner*, 35. See also Hall, *Remembered Voices*, 126.
39 Pauck, 35.
40 Ibid., 35.

their sins." This was the conception of revelation and faith that Bryden shared with the theologians who came to be described as neo-orthodox.[41]

In his use of the concept of revelation, Bryden was particularly driven, as we shall argue, by the concern to isolate and identify the nature of the Christian's encounter with God. "What was the nature of faith?" and "What constituted the Christian's knowledge of God?" were questions of paramount importance to him. Barth's startling comments in the Second Edition of the *Epistle to the Romans* were mirrored in Bryden's own theological anxiety. What was the participation, comprehension, and cooperation which the revelation of the gospel demanded? In what sense did the revelation of the gospel presume faith in the living God, and create the faith which it presumed? Long before he heard anything about the theology of Karl Barth, Walter Bryden had already been wrestling with questions about the life of God in the souls of men and women. But with the assistance of Barth and the neo-orthodox theologians he began to develop a dialectical conception in which there was a relation of correspondence between an act of God and an act of the human subject, the act of divine self-revelation and the human act of faith in which the revelation of God is apprehended. This was the existential position he pursued over against conservative and liberal forms of Protestant theology.

Second, Bryden pointed to a *Reformation* conception of Word and Spirit. In all his theological work Bryden sought to recover, re-appropriate, and reassert the Reformation insights of Calvin and Luther. When one reads Bryden's lectures, books, and sermons, it is difficult to disagree with John Godsey who argued that the term 'neo-Reformation' might be a more apt descriptor for the theological movement known as neo-orthodoxy.[42] The Barthian revolt in modern theology, as Gary Dorrien has described it, effected a stunning reorientation of the field of Christian theology by insisting that modern Protestantism could recover its authentically Christian basis only by returning to the Reformation's conceptions of revelation and faith. This conventional definition of neo-orthodoxy suffices as long as one bears in mind that a neo-orthodox theologian like Walter Bryden took modern forms for granted and took his "orthodox" elements from Luther and Calvin, not from later Protestant orthodoxy. Assuming that a recovery of authentic Reformation teaching was both possible and desirable, Bryden believed that the church of his day had to reach back beyond post-Enlightenment modernism and scholastic Calvinism to the theological renewal which had taken place with Luther, Calvin, and Zwingli.

---

[41]   Hall, *Remembered Voices*, 126.

[42]   John Godsey, s.v "Neo-orthodoxy," in *Encyclopedia of Religion*, edited by Mircea Eliade (New York: Macmillan, 1986) 10:360ff.

Calvin's theology in particular played a decisive role in shaping Bryden's thought. As a Reformed theologian Bryden pointed to Calvin's theology of Word and Spirit as the source of renewal for Canadian Protestants. "If, however," Bryden wrote, Protestant Christians can "learn to discern again what John Calvin meant by God" and "if they can grasp what he meant by the Word of God" they will "have secured for themselves a substantial basis for a higher and more fruitful Christian unity than has been."[43] Along the same lines, Bryden argued that "if we are to possess any convictions worthy of a truly Christian faith—we must get back to something of that understanding of the Word of God which created both Calvin and the Reformed faith."[44] "It is not too much to hold," he argued, that it was "a completely fresh and living apprehension of the Word of God which constituted the primal inspiration of the Reformation movement as a whole," and for Calvin in particular.[45] When Reformed Christians today speak about revelation and the Word of God, they must mean by it what Calvin meant.[46]

Not only did Bryden explicitly and self-consciously seek to re-appropriate Calvin's conception of the Christian message, he also stood within Luther's tradition of a theology of the cross, sounding a great "No!" against all theologies of glory. The term *theologia crucis* was used by Martin Luther to describe the early period of his Reformation theology. The term referred not simply to the Christian doctrine of the atonement, but to an entire theological method in which the cross is seen as the focal point of God's revelation and the organizing principle of all theology. In Luther's words, "the cross is the criterion of all things" (*Crux probat omnia),* and "the cross alone is our theology." In the Heidelberg Theses (1518) Luther contrasted the *theologia crucis* with the theology of glory *(theologia gloriae).* The theology of glory summed up Luther's objections to late medieval scholastic theology and its approach to the knowledge of God. Like Luther, Bryden rejected a theology of glory *(theologia gloria)* as he saw it manifested in the modernism and fundamentalism of his day. Modern idealists and rationalists, he believed, perceived the glory of God—God's power, wisdom, and goodness, manifest in the works of creation. Instead, Bryden turned to a theology of the cross *(theologia crucis)* in which the church places its faith in the God hidden in the suffering and humiliation of the cross. Like Luther, Bryden believed that the natural knowledge of God to be gained from the created order, when left in the hands of sinners, even sinners redeemed by grace and called to be the

---

[43] Bryden, *Why I Am A Presbyterian* (Toronto: Presbyterian Publications, 1934) 165.
[44] Bryden, "The Presbyterian Conception of the Word of God," in *Separated Unto the Gospel,* 178.
[45] Ibid., 179.
[46] Ibid., 218.

church, resulted in attempts at self-justification by moral, intellectual, cultural, social, political and economic achievement. A theology of glory, Bryden believed, creates a church that domesticates the Word and the Spirit of God. In Luther's terms, a church that looks at the invisible things of God as they are seen in the visible things does not deserve to be called a church. But the church that looks on the visible rearward parts of God as seen in suffering and the cross does deserve to be called a church. A theology of the cross creates a church in which all human preconceptions of deity and human perceptions about how God may be known and how God may act in the world are shattered. For Walter Bryden, "the Word of God is Jesus Christ, and Him crucified, with nothing to be added or subtracted from simply that."[47] In the cross of God's crucified Messiah, God's judgment and salvation are revealed, not in the power and glory which human beings usually associate with the Absolute, but in poverty, suffering, and death.

Walter Bryden was not a lone voice in bearing witness to the enduring value of Reformation insights for his day. He lived and taught at a time when a "Luther-and-Calvin Renaissance," to quote Wilhelm Pauck, was taking place. The new work on Luther and Calvin allowed the great Protestant Reformers, it was believed, "to speak in their own name as they have not been able to do in any previous period of Protestant history."[48] It would be a mistake, to be sure, to describe Walter Bryden as a Calvinist as if he were concerned to defend some ecclesiastical or denominational distinctive. Nevertheless, Bryden's theological witness is incomprehensible apart from the tradition of Calvin and Luther.

Third, Bryden's theological protest, for all of its blistering attacks against modernism, remained importantly rooted in the tradition of nineteenth-century theological liberalism. It was a decidedly *neo*-Reformation and modern option in theology. But it sought to use the modern insights illuminated by liberal Protestantism in order to overturn rather than advance idealism and rationalism in theology. The great essentials of the Reformed faith, Bryden believed, could be re-appropriated without violating modern ethical and religious sensibilities.[49] Many of Bryden's critics argued that his neo-orthodoxy deviated too much from the orthodoxy of the Reformation theologians and the classical Protestant confessions to be a thoroughly Reformed theology, while others argued that it was too narrowly conservative and orthodox to sustain Christian faith in the modern context. Both failed to recognize that neo-

---

[47]   Bryden, *The Christian's Knowledge of God.*, 173.

[48]   Pauck in Hall, *Remembered Voices,* 127.

[49]   Bryden, Review of *The Organism of Christian Truth* by John Dickie in *Canadian Journal of Religious Thought* 9.1 (1932) 81.

orthodoxy, for all its problems, was a sophisticated synthesis of Reformation theology with modern thought.

The neo-orthodox theologians, as Wilhelm Pauck and David Tracy have argued, shared the liberal and not the orthodox understanding of the task of theology. Despite its critique of liberalism and modernism, neo-orthodoxy was indebted to many of the practices established by liberal Protestant theologians, including the use of historical criticism, the acceptance of the social criticism of religion, the conception of revelation as the self-revelation of God, and the importance of cultural analysis in theology. David Tracy draws a parallel between the 'neo-orthodox' theologians and Marx, Freud, and Nietzsche, in their affirmation and negation of liberal modernity, and their rejection of both orthodoxy and liberalism as adequate for contemporary needs. The neo-orthodox theologians were compelled to challenge their liberal forbears not out of lack of regard for the theological relevance of cultural analysis, but out of a different postmodern analysis. This analysis found its roots in disillusionment with the optimism of the evolutionary theory. In their critique of the liberal enterprise, neo-orthodox theologians emphasized the radical nature of sin and evil, and rejected liberalism's Christological formulations. They argued that only the unique gift of the Word of God and faith could provide an adequate foundation for a truly Christian theology. Tracy notes that on this point the neo-orthodox joined the orthodox theologian in "insisting upon the theologian's own faith as an existential condition of the possibility of theology."[50] The difference, however, existed in the fact that the neo-orthodox theologian's faith, unlike that of the orthodox, was radically experiential and claimed to illumine all human existence since "the subject-referent of the neo-orthodox theologian is not really the "believer" as for the orthodox, but the more radical model of the human being of authentic Christian faith."[51]

At the same time, Walter Bryden stood within a tradition of Canadian Presbyterian orthodoxy of sorts. In his recent history of Knox College, Brian J. Fraser has argued that the faculty there has always taught a basic, if somewhat varied, orthodoxy. The argument is that they were committed to what Fraser describes as "the great evangelical truths" which "included the doctrines of creation, fall, redemption, atonement in Christ, justification by faith, sanctification through the work of the Holy Spirit, and eternal life."[52] Fraser argues that "the ways in which these affirmations were expounded and interpreted

---

[50] David Tracy, *Blessed Rage For Order* (New York: Seabury, 1979) 27. See also Tracy, *The Analogical Imagination* (New York: Crossroad, 1981) 193ff.

[51] Tracy, *Blessed Rage For Order*, 28.

[52] Brian J. Fraser, *Church, College, and Clergy: A History of Theological Education at Knox College, Toronto, 1844–1994* (Montreal: McGill–Queen's University Press, 1995) 14.

by different generations of faculty changed four times between 1844 and 1994. The changes from conservative orthodoxy, to progressive orthodoxy, to neo-orthodoxy, to divergent views of orthodoxy, reflected the different ways of interpreting the central truths of the gospel to the culture in which the church found itself."[53] As one of the new faculty members appointed to Knox following church union in 1925, Fraser notes, Walter Bryden set out an approach to the theological heritage of Presbyterianism in the form of neo-orthodoxy:

> Influenced by Scottish theologians James Denney, P. T. Forsyth and German theologian Karl Barth, both confessional orthodoxy and progressive orthodoxy failed to understand the true nature of the gospel and the church. Confessional orthodoxy reduced the gospel to a system of thought and progressive orthodoxy reduced it to a system of morals. The church needed to recover the full heritage of the Protestant Reformation and recognize the transcendent, unique and mysterious nature of Christ's encounter with humanity at the centre of the church's life and witness. Knowledge of God grew out of this transforming encounter with the person of Christ, in whom God's self-revelation was complete and by whom God redeemed the world.[54]

In short, Bryden employed a modern theological method to protest against both modernism and fundamentalism and to reassert the great evangelical truths of the Reformed faith. Neo-orthodoxy, as we intend to demonstrate, was a theologically complex movement. Its expression in the Canadian context, as Bryden's theology reveals, was highly ambiguous. It betrays quite appropriately, as Douglas John Hall has described it, a certain Kierkegaardian contrariety which defies categorization.[55]

Bryden and the Identity of Post-Union Presbyterianism

Bryden's neo-Reformation theological witness emerged and functioned within a particular ecclesial context. In the aftermath of 1925, approximately one-third of the membership and one-quarter of the clergy of The Presbyterian Church in Canada decided not to enter church union, and to continue as Presbyterians. Walter Bryden emerged as a theological leader among this group and marshaled a neo-Reformation theology of Word and Spirit in the service of continuing Presbyterianism. As N. Keith Clifford has noted in his

---

[53] Ibid.
[54] Ibid., 15–16.
[55] Hall, *Remembered Voices,* 6.

book *The Resistance to Church Union in Canada 1904–1939*, those who opposed church union and constituted the continuing Presbyterian Church "did not bind their church to any theory of biblical inerrancy, premillennialism, or dispensationalism, and they did not insist that their church adopt an anti-ecumenical stance. Consequently, after 1925 the Presbyterian Church in Canada was completely free to follow Walter Bryden, their new young theologian at Knox College, beyond modernism and fundamentalism to neo-orthodoxy."[56] Through his influence as a theological teacher Bryden exercised more power than might at first be recognized from an analysis of the formal constituency of his thought. The theology of the majority of a generation of Presbyterian ministers was forged by listening to Bryden's voice in the classroom and the pulpit. The theological themes enunciated by Bryden became, in the hands of his students, a post-union apologetic for the continuing Presbyterian Church in Canada. As Joseph C. McLelland has argued, in this context Bryden's influence was considerable:

> The quarter century and more during which Bryden taught the theologues of Knox was the most critical in the history of the Presbyterian Church in Canada. Behind lay mixed motives and traditions, ahead an uncertain future, no clear theological position emerging, but rather a struggle over the Church's relationship to its subordinate standard, the Westminster Confession of Faith. This was Bryden's hour. Occupying one of the highest and most influential positions in the Church, he brought his considerable gifts to bear on the practical issue of theological education—the teaching of those 'teaching elders' who must minister to a Church undergoing a crisis of identity.[57]

In an essay on The Presbyterian Church in Canada after 1925, Neil Gregor Smith agreed: "The long association of Dr. W. W. Bryden with Knox College, first as Professor of Church History and History and Philosophy of Religion, and later as Principal, contributed a great deal to a theological awakening in the church."[58] In the official history of The Presbyterian Church in Canada, John Moir notes that in the years after 1925 "Within Knox College and Presbyterian College the majority of faculty members were older men who showed little interest in theological trends and seemed to repeat well-worn lectures," the notable exception being W. W. Bryden, who

---

[56]   N. Keith Clifford, *The Resistance to Church Union in Canada 1904–1939* (Vancouver: University of British Columbia Press, 1985) 4.

[57]   J. C. McLelland, "Walter Bryden: 'By Circumstance and God,'" in *Called to Witness*, edited by W. Stanford Reid (The Presbyterian Church in Canada: Committee on History, 1980) 2:120. For Bryden's influence see also John Moir, *Enduring Witness* (Hamilton, Ont.: The Presbyterian Church in Canada: Bryant, 1975) 235.

[58]   Neil Gregor Smith, "1925 and After," in *A Short History of The Presbyterian Church in Canada* (Toronto: Presbyterian Publications, 1966) 97.

"through his classes and writing did much to shape and challenge a generation of younger ministers."[59] As Walter Bryden introduced his students to the
new European trends in Protestant theology in the early 1930s, a generation
of younger Presbyterians began to see their church's destiny "as that of being
the instrument through which in Canada Protestantism might be recalled to
its heritage as a church reformed and ever anew reforming according to the
Word of God in Scripture."[60]

The question arises as to why Bryden's voice was so influential in such
circumstances? This was a period of crisis, to be sure, and Bryden passed
on to his students what many considered to be a compelling new form of
theology. But in such circumstances why was Bryden's influence so decisive
while others were overshadowed? The competing factions in the post-union
church included those who advocated Machen's Princeton orthodoxy, others
who emphasized John Watson's progressive ideals of liberal Protestantism,
and still others who expressed a sentimentalism for the Scottish identity of
Canadian Presbyterianism. At the same time, the theological direction of the
new United Church seemed somewhat unclear as it dealt with the convergence of Wesleyan, Holiness, and Reformed theologies accompanied by liberal ideals and a passion for the Social Gospel. In this context, the Word-cen-
tered Reformed tradition of Canadian Presbyterianism was naturally more
hospitable to the neo-orthodox vision embraced and espoused by a man like
Bryden. The content and context of Bryden's message, therefore, were very
significant factors, to say the least. Bryden was in the right place at the right
time and he had something important to say.

But Walter Bryden's influence is also explicable in terms of who he was
and how he comported himself. Bryden offered his students not simply a
theology but also a credible model of the minister as confessing, prophetic
theologian, one who strove to put faith into words and actions and who
sought to embody the message he proclaimed. The profound personal effect
that Bryden had upon students is clear in their testimony: "In that company
and in those circumstances Dr. Bryden shone with a brilliance to that of
the star of Bethlehem directing the footsteps of the shepherds unerringly to
the Christ-child. It would be impossible to exaggerate the debt students of
that era owe to Walter Bryden."[61] Hagiographic to be sure, but it reflects the
high esteem in which Walter Bryden was held by those who were profoundly
shaped by his teaching. In Bryden's case, the prophet himself was decisive
in the reception of the message. In short, Bryden was a passionate and ar-

---

[59]   John Moir, *Enduring Witness*, 235.
[60]   James D. Smart, "Canadian Presbyterianism Since 1925," *Presbyterian Record* 79.2 (Feb.
1954) 19.
[61]   Charles Cochrane, "Personal Memoir," unpublished, 17.

ticulate theological professor who cared deeply about those he was educating for the ministry of the continuing Presbyterian Church in Canada. They, in turn, received the Christian message in terms of Bryden's neo-Reformation conception of God's Judging-Saving Word, and delivered it to a church trying to find its ecclesial and theological bearings in the second quarter of the twentieth century.

Conclusion

The theological contribution of Walter W. Bryden will be examined by arguing that his dialectical christocentric conception of revelation as the Judging-Saving Word of God is the center of his theological thought; that this conception of revelation was an attempt to recover Calvin's doctrine of the Word of God, reaching back behind both modernism and Protestant scholasticism; that it was initially shaped by the liberal evangelical Scottish Calvinist theology of the late nineteenth and early twentieth centuries, also by Schweitzer and Bultmann, and then decisively by the theology of the early Karl Barth and the neo-orthodox movement; that it was driven by the theological critique to be found in Luther's theology of the cross; and that it functioned to provide a post-union theological vision for Canadian Presbyterian theological students and clergy, largely through the profound personal influence of Walter Bryden himself.

This examination of Walter Bryden's theological contribution, therefore, is primarily a study in historical theology. As such, my concern is to set forth a thorough exposition of the main themes of Bryden's texts, published and unpublished, within the context of the prevailing theological, ecclesiastical, and religious issues of his day, in order to document what Bryden believed about revelation, why he believed it, and how he understood its significance for Canadian Protestantism. My purpose, therefore, is not to provide a detailed biography of Bryden's life, intellectual or otherwise, although a good deal of historical and biographical material is included in order to understand the origin and genetic development of Bryden's thought and influence. By genetic I mean an understanding of Bryden's development taken from a standpoint within Canadian Protestantism rather than from the endpoint of Barth's decisive influence.[62] The neo-orthodox theology of revelation, if it is to be understood properly in the Canadian context, requires more than the general appeal to Barth's thought and influence which has characterized the studies to date.

---

[62] I am indebted to Bruce McCormack of Princeton Theological Seminary for this concept. See his seminal study of the origins and genetic development of Karl Barth's theology, *Karl Barth's Critically Realistic Dialectical Theology* (Oxford: Clarendon, 1995).

It must also be stressed that I do not intend to give a purely theoretical account of certain Christian doctrines as espoused by Walter Bryden. Rather, I propose that a study of Walter Bryden's theological contribution opens a window on the entire Reformed Protestant tradition in Canada in the first half of the twentieth century, enabling us to examine how and why certain theological trends prevailed, while others receded. In particular, this study reveals that Walter Bryden was an able and vigorous participant in a period of dramatic theological challenge and change; that neo-orthodox theology had real currency in Canadian Protestantism by the early 1930s; and that Bryden's form of neo-orthodoxy played an increasingly important role in the continuing Presbyterian Church. This book is the story of the development of a particular doctrine as espoused by a particular theologian in a particular context. It differs, on one hand, from the works of Canadian historians who examine religious history with reference to institutions and intellectual movements, but pay little attention to the details and nuances of doctrinal development. On the other hand, it differs from the works of Canadian theologians who examine Christian doctrine with little or no reference to the Canadian intellectual tradition within which it is embedded. There is, I have discovered, a lively Canadian theological tradition to be documented, explored, and appropriated, and the thought of Walter Bryden is a case in point.

In this study I am chiefly concerned, then, with the modest task of describing the various positions taken by Walter Bryden, in a manner that is both fair to him and clear to readers. My hope, therefore, in writing this book is threefold. First, I hope that my readers will discover the thought of a relatively unknown Canadian theologian, and will be inspired to read his books for themselves. Readers of this book are often introduced to Bryden's theology in his own words. The systematized manner in which Bryden's theological contribution is presented, however, is not a substitute for a direct reading of Bryden himself. Second, I hope that my readers will come to understand how Bryden's thought represented the early reception of Karl Barth's early theology and the neo-orthodox movement in Canada, and how these ideas came to function, flourish and fade at a particular moment in Canadian Protestantism. Third, I hope that my readers will come to appreciate the significance of a Christian tradition which emphasizes a theology of Word and Spirit. Walter Bryden believed that in revelation God shares divine self-knowledge with human beings in the person of Jesus Christ through the witness of the Holy Spirit. The Christian's knowledge of God, therefore, is rooted in a past act and a present reality: the decisive self-disclosure of God in Jesus Christ and the ongoing action of a personal, relational God who creates the faith by which the God revealed in Jesus Christ is encountered. As a theologian of Word and Spirit, Bryden did not force a choice between a theology of the Word and a theology of experience. One may be permitted the observation that, given the fragmentation of much contemporary theology, a tradition that holds Word and Spirit together is surely worth preserving, not only because it illumines the past, but also because it offers lessons for the future. A theology of Word and Spirit, framed within a theology of the cross, offers words of judgment and salvation that are vital for the ongoing renewal of the Christian movement.

The argument proceeds as follows. The first chapter examines the origins and development of Bryden's theological mind as a Reformed theologian, and sketches the ecclesiastical, intellectual and theological ethos within which he was raised and educated as a Canadian Presbyterian (1883–1909). The second chapter examines the development, emergence and dominance of Bryden's neo-orthodox voice within the context of his work as a Presbyterian minister, theological professor, and college principal (1909–52). Chapters one and two set the stage for the exposition of Bryden's theology of revelation in chapters three through five. Chapter three sets out the central themes of Bryden's theology of the Word, including his critique of modern idealism and rational orthodoxy, and his constructive proposal for a dialectical christocentric re-conception of revelation, identified as the "Judging-Saving Word of God." This chapter explores Bryden's theological contribution against the background of Calvin, Schleiermacher, and Barth. In the fourth chapter I examine Bryden's doctrine of the knowledge of God in terms of Bryden's theology of the Holy Spirit and his understanding of faith. We see how his thought converges with Luther's theology of the cross. Here we move from doctrine to experience, from theological affirmations and negations to existential realities in Bryden's thought. The fifth chapter sets out Bryden's ecclesiology on the basis of the doctrine of revelation and knowledge of God in the previous two chapters, noting the emphasis Bryden placed on the church as a confessing community. The church, he argued, is created, built up and sent out into the world by Word and Spirit. In the conclusion, I assess Bryden's theological legacy in relation to the succeeding generation which followed him into neo-orthodoxy, the subsequent decline and fall of neo-orthodoxy in the twentieth century, and the ongoing significance of Bryden's theological witness.

Karl Barth once advised a younger theologian that truly profitable research in theological history is motivated by something more than dispassionate interest. Throughout this book I have tried to heed his advice:

> For me it would be the canon of all research in theological history, and perhaps in all history, that one should try to present what has engaged another person, whether in a good way or a less good, as something living, as something that moved him and that can and indeed does move oneself too; to unfold it in such a way that even if one finally

takes some other route, the path of this other has an enticing, or, if you like, tempting attraction for oneself. Disregard of this canon can only avenge itself by rendering the attempted historical research unprofitable and tedious.[63]

Since the theology of Karl Barth plays such a significant role in this study of Bryden's theological contribution to Canadian Protestantism, heeding Barth's advice appears to be the better part of wisdom. Hence, this book seeks to present what engaged Bryden as something living, as something that moved him, and as something which, as it moved him, moved others through him. James D. Smart said that it was impossible to understand Walter Bryden's theological contribution except as the fulfillment, in a special sphere, of the task of an evangelist. Bryden's concern, in even the most involved intellectual consideration, was that the Gospel might be heard and believed. We would do well to remember, Smart concludes, "that the response the evangelist covets is not an elaborate eulogy but that his gospel should be heard and believed and that the decisions with which it confronts the Church should be faced without evasion."[64]

---

[63] Karl Barth, *Letters, 1961–1968,* trans. Geoffrey W. Bromiley (Grand Rapids: Eerdmans, 1981) Letter 239; cited in John Webster, *Eberhard Jüngel: An Introduction to His Theology* (Cambridge: Cambridge University Press, 1986) 5.

[64] James D. Smart, "The Evangelist as Theologian," in *Separated Unto the Gospel,* x, xi.

1

The Making of a Presbyterian Mind

There is no such thing as Reformed Theology . . . only a continual refer-ence to the Word of God in Scripture . . . . A hankering after tradition is a sign that the living thing in faith has been lost.
—Walter Bryden

I stand firmly by the Reformed faith, subject to Scripture which I believe cradles God's living Word for those who have ears to hear it. That about sums me up, whatever lies before.
—Walter Bryden

IN lectures delivered to students in the early 1930s at Knox College on the nature of Presbyterianism, Walter Bryden spoke about denominational-ism and ecclesiasticism as insufficient reasons for rejecting church union. "It has often been assumed that, being born and nurtured in the Presbyterian Church," he said, "it is something like a moral and religious duty to die in it."[1] Aware that loyalty to a denomination and a church tradition might blind one to the truth of the Christian message and the importance of church unity, Bryden rejected the conviction that there was something sacred, ab-solute or final about Presbyterianism, "the simplicity of its worship and the democratic character of its government, the purity of its doctrine and the evangelical nature of its gospel."[2] Ecclesiasticism, he argued, was "the attempt to substantiate the validity of a Church upon purely ecclesiastical grounds, or by its ecclesiastical credentials."[3]

---

[1] Bryden, *Why I Am A Presbyterian* (Toronto: Presbyterian Publications, 1934) 23.
[2] Ibid., 30.
[3] Ibid., 29–41. See also Brian J. Fraser, *Church, College, and Clergy: A History of Theological Education at Knox College, 1844–1994* (Montreal: McGill–Queen's University Press, 1995) 176.

27

His concerns notwithstanding, Walter Bryden was a Presbyterian, by birth and by choice. Like many of his contemporaries, he was nurtured and shaped by the ecclesiastical culture and ethos of The Presbyterian Church in Canada, and he labored within its bounds all his life. In 1925, unlike many of his contemporaries, he made the difficult decision to remain a Presbyterian minister, and he died in a church that was less than one third the size of the church into which he had been born. What was the nature of the Presbyterianism to which Bryden remained committed throughout his life? The purpose of this chapter is to examine the ecclesial ethos that shaped Bryden's formative years. This will provide a basis for understanding his faith and life, his theological instincts, his influence as a theological teacher, his enthusiasm for Barth and the neo-orthodox theologians, his conception of revelation and the knowledge of God, and the decisive role that he played, at a critical moment in the history of the Presbyterian tradition, in reshaping the Church within which "he lived and moved and had his being."

Church and Family, 1883–1902

The eldest of three children in a Scottish Presbyterian family, Walter Bryden was born in 1883 and raised on the family farm on the banks of the Grand River at Blair, just outside Galt in rural southwestern Ontario. An aptitude for study, accompanied by his mother's desire to see her elder son pursue formal education (leading, perhaps, to the Presbyterian ministry) was confirmed by circumstance. Through either illness or accident Bryden's right arm was disfigured. According to a family friend, Bryden's father reluctantly agreed, "We shall have to give Walter a schooling; he will be no good now for the farm."[4] Bryden's students remember the permanent disability as a distinctive feature of his presence in the classroom. "In appearance slight, one delicate arm held close, movements denoting energy—and eyes that pierced in eager dialogue."[5] It certainly added to the burden of his work, as he noted in the preface to *The Christian's Knowledge of God.* He acknowledged his wife's assistance in preparing the text: "It would be nothing more than just to say that this book could never have come to the light of day without the unrelenting labour of my wife. Because of a physical disability of my own, it was necessary for her to write practically all of the original manuscript."[6] A memorial tribute by the convener of the Knox College Board of Management in 1952 said much the same thing: "The untiring assistance and care of Mrs. Bryden

---

4   W. I. McKeown, "Memoirs of Dr. Bryden," *Presbyterian Record* (October 1975) 8.
5   J. C. McLelland, "Walter Bryden: 'By Circumstance and God,'" *Called To Witness*, 2:119.
6   Bryden, *The Christian's Knowledge of God*, xii.

undoubtedly helped to make possible the effectiveness of Dr. Bryden's work in those years when his physical infirmities rendered such help imperative."[7]

Despite the physical disability he lived an active life. As a student at the University of Toronto he was a member of the track team and captained a championship soccer team. As a Presbyterian minister he organized sports activities for young people. As a professor he coached Knox College teams in intramural sports, and Presbyterian legend has it that because he was such an ardent fan he was granted regular season passes to watch the Toronto Maple Leafs play baseball. The task to which he devoted the majority of his energy, however, was the life of the mind in the service of the church.

The Free Church Tradition. The Bryden family attended Knox's Church, Galt, where Presbyterianism had flourished since the early nineteenth century through immigration from Scotland. Late in his life, Bryden recalled that as a teenager in high school he had read all kinds of old national Scottish history, as well as the history of the Kirk. "Indeed," he said, "there was a time when I verily believed Scotland was God's throne and the rest of the world His footstool."[8] Further historical study, he acknowledged, happily disabused him of this notion.

Among the various aspects of Scottish Presbyterianism that shaped Bryden's thought, one left a deep imprint. Knox's Church, Galt had been organized as a congregation of the Free Church in 1844 under the leadership of The Rev. John Bayne. The Free Church congregations exercised a robust form of Presbyterian polity with a particular understanding of church-state relations. Presbyterian polity was shaped by the conviction that the role of the elder (presbyter) in the New Testament was essential to good church order. This conviction resulted in a system of church government in which ordained ministers (as teaching elders) and ordained lay people (as ruling elders) participated equally. The church's governing structures consisted of a hierarchy of courts (sessions, presbyteries, synods, and general assemblies), each appointing representatives to the higher courts. As Bryden later noted critically, for many Presbyterians this meant that the constitutive principle of Presbyterianism "is held to inhere in the Presbyter, or in the corresponding order of the Presbytery."[9] The system rested upon two equally-held principles. First, all those who participated in the government of the church, whether clergy or lay, were to be elected to their offices, making the system in some

---

[7]   R. M. Sedgewick, "Report of the Board of Management of Knox College," *The Acts and Proceedings of the Seventy-Seventh General Assembly of The Presbyterian Church in Canada,* 1952, 122.

[8]   Bryden, "Address Delivered to the Presbyterian Congress" (5 June 1950). See also Gordon Harland, "God's Judging-Saving Word: The Legacy of Walter W. Bryden," *Touchstone: Journal on the United Church of Canada's Theology and Faith* 13.3 (1995).

[9]   Bryden, *Why I Am A Presbyterian,* 32.

sense democratic. At the same time it was believed that this form of church government was divinely ordained by Jesus Christ who ruled the church as its only king and head, giving the system a theocratic character. Holding these two principles in tension, ministers and elders were not only representatives elected to their respective offices with an authority derived from the people, but they were also called by Jesus Christ and set apart by the courts of the church to govern God's people. The implication was that the church (particularly the presbytery) functioned not merely as an elected representative body of the people, but under a divine right which was not, under any circumstance, to be infringed upon by other church bodies or by the state. Thus, Presbyterian polity had implications which went far beyond ecclesiastical organization.[10]

In Scotland, where Presbyterianism had been established since the sixteenth century, the church frequently came into conflict with governing authorities over these principles. When the monarch or local laird attempted to dominate the church, for example, by appointing a local minister, many Scottish Presbyterians resisted in the name of "The Crown Rights of Jesus Christ" or "The Crown Rights of the Redeemer."[11] Christ alone, they argued, ruled the church as its king and head. Resistance to government intrusion, aided and abetted by aristocratic patronage, was not only justified, it was demanded. In the course of Scottish church history, some Presbyterians rejected the principle of establishment altogether and moved towards voluntarism. In the Canadian church, to cite a later example of this argument, opposition to church union in 1925 was justified by the argument that the new church was being created through parliamentary legislation, The Church Union Act of 1924. In the eyes of those who resisted the proposed union, this was viewed as an illegitimate usurpation of ecclesiastical authority by the state. The parliament, they argued, had no right whatsoever to create and establish a church, and the churches had no right to ask them to do so.[12] Furthermore, this emphasis on the "kingship of Christ" was limited not only to ecclesiastical matters. If Jesus Christ was king, his sovereign lordship extended over all of life, his will was to be the concern of Christians in every sphere of society, and his moral law was to be obeyed by all. Presbyterians, therefore, not infrequently found themselves at odds with the civil authorities.

---

[10]   W. S. Reid, "The Scottish Protestant Tradition," in *The Scottish Tradition in Canada,* edited by W. S. Reid (Toronto: McClelland and Stewart, 1976) 118–19. See also Richard W. Vaudry, *The Free Church in Victorian Canada 1844–1861* (Waterloo: Wilfrid Laurier University Press, 1989) 2–4.

[11]   Reid, *The Scottish Tradition in Canada,* 118–19.

[12]   Ibid., 119.

This was the spirit of Presbyterianism within which Walter Bryden's understanding of church and society was shaped at Knox's Church, Galt. The congregation had been founded as a direct result of a major division in Scotland over just these principles. The pressure had been building in the years leading up to 1843. Then Scottish Presbyterians, representing the strict Calvinist evangelical party within the Church of Scotland, charged that the church had denied the headship of Christ by allowing the church to become subject to the governing authorities in matters purely ecclesiastical. Although there had been increasing tension between the evangelicals and the deistic and latitudinarian moderates in the Church of Scotland on a variety of theological emphases, the matter was brought to a head around the patronage appointments of ministers to parishes by lay patrons, whether individual landowners or the state itself, thus negating the congregation's call.[13] As Canadian historian John Moir notes, these developments within Scotland found support in Canada. The disruption was reduplicated in the colonies: "Even before that fateful day, 18 May, 1843, when Dr. Thomas Chalmers led 202 other commissioners out of the General Assembly of the Church of Scotland to found the Free Church, considerable colonial sympathy had been expressed for the cause of these protesters."[14] Moir also notes that this was entirely explicable because "in the wake of the Napoleonic wars a flood of Scottish immigrants fled depressed conditions at home to settle in the colonies," particularly in western Ontario, and most of these immigrants supported the Evangelical party in the Church of Scotland. Although the issues of "patronage" and "intrusion" did not yet exist in British North America, the Disruption in Scotland called for a sympathetic response on their part.[15]

In the colonial context the Free Church tradition fuelled protests against clergy reserves and a public education system dominated by one church. It pushed for responsible government in Upper Canada. Free Church Presbyterians resented and resisted the family compact system, spoke out against the social privileges and economic interests of the governing classes, and lobbied for a more equitable societal structure. The Presbyterianism of southwestern Ontario within which Bryden was raised "was closely allied with the political liberalism of one of its most prominent laymen, George Brown, proprietor of the powerful Toronto *Globe* and its publishing empire."[16] What

---

[13] John S. Moir, "'Who Pays The Piper . . .': Canadian Presbyterianism and Church-State Relations," in *The Burning Bush And A Few Acres of Snow: The Presbyterian Contribution to Canadian Life and Culture,* edited by William Klempa (Ottawa: Carleton University Press, 1994), 68.

[14] John Moir, *Enduring Witness: A History of the Presbyterian Church in Canada* (Hamilton, Ont.: Presbyterian Church in Canada, 1987) 101.

[15] John Moir, "'Who Pays the Piper,'" 72.

[16] Brian J. Fraser, *The Social Uplifters: Presbyterian Progressives and the Social Gospel in Canada,*

was known in Canada as the Grit reformist tradition, later absorbed by the Liberal Party, provided a focus and forum for the marginalization felt by many.

Walter Bryden's life, theology and influence, to a great extent, stood in continuity with these traditions and principles. He argued that "the preponderating spirit of Canadian Presbyterianism during its entire history has been that of increasing freedom from any meticulous ecclesiastical emphases, or from any particularized claims for sanctity, privilege or authority."[17] For Bryden, theology and preaching were as much about protest as they were about proclamation. His lectures and his books reflected a passion for social justice manifested in what students and clergy heard as prophetic, sometimes almost revolutionary, pronouncements. Ever exhibiting a sense of contrariety, Bryden did not shy away from questioning the way things were in theology, the church, and society, even when he himself became a part of the ecclesiastical and academic establishment. "Scholars, when they cease to be prophetic," he proclaimed, "and thus fail to be theologians, possess a significance little more than that of scribes."[18] He objected to the alignment between Christianity and capitalism and despised the "banker mentality" which had been insinuated into the churches, transforming them into religious reflections of economic, social, and political self-interest. "The real threat to Christian faith," according to Bryden, "lies not in science, even though it may appear to have slain the gods, *but in the domestication of the radical faith of Jesus Christ in the middle-class society.*"[19] In short, Bryden embodied the principles of critical judgment and prophetic protest that were an integral part of the tradition he inherited.[20]

Calvinism and "Common Sense." As part of its dissenting Free Church heritage, Knox's Presbyterian Church, Galt was also strongly Calvinistic and evangelistic. After Bayne's death in 1859 the congregation was served by The Rev. A. Geikie, a Dr. Thompson, and The Rev. James K. Smith. The congregational history records "a significant revival" which took place in 1869. On October 4, 1888, The Rev. Alexander Jackson of Pittsburgh was inducted as the minister. Jackson continued the tradition of Calvinist theology and evangelical preaching that had become characteristic of the congregation, and under his leadership the church flourished. During Bryden's formative years

---

1875–1915 (Waterloo: Wilfrid Laurier University Press, 1988) 23. See also F. Landon, *Western Ontario and the American Frontier* (Toronto: McClelland and Stewart, 1967) 267–68; and J. M. S. Careless, *Brown of the Globe* (Toronto: Macmillan, 1959) 1:20–23 and 33–35.

[17]   Bryden, *Why I Am A Presbyterian,* 32.

[18]   Bryden, *The Christian's Knowledge of God,* 26.

[19]   Donald Wade, "Preface," in Bryden, *Why I Am A Presbyterian,* reprint ed. (Belleville, Ont.: Essence, 1997) 9.

[20]   W. Kenneth Bryden, "Interview," May 27, 1986.

as a young person, the congregation was vibrant and growing. In 1889, the Sabbath School enrolled a record number of 679 students, with 52 teachers and officers. In 1894, a record 159 new members were added to the rolls of the church, and in 1895 five students from the congregation were preparing for the Presbyterian ministry at Knox College in Toronto.[21]

The Presbyterian tradition's emphasis on its form of government may be "one of the great strengths of the Reformed or Presbyterian tradition." Nevertheless, "some would say ... its greatest strength, is its emphasis on theology."[22] Knox's Church, Galt was steeped in the Reformed and Calvinist theology characteristic of many late nineteenth-century Canadian Presbyterian congregations. The term "Reformed" refers to that Protestant tradition which emerged during the sixteenth-century European Reformation under Ulrich Zwingli in Zurich, John Calvin in Geneva, John Oecolampadius in Basel, Martin Bucer in Strasbourg, John Knox in Edinburgh, and Peter Martyr Vermigli. Belonging to the so-called magisterial Reformation, their followers shared much in common with Lutherans and Anglicans. They experienced a number of points of tension with late medieval Roman Catholicism, especially as the latter was set out in the Counter-Reformation by the Council of Trent in the 1540s, and also from various Radical and Anabaptist movements. With Lutherans, Reformed church leaders emphasized the doctrines of salvation by grace alone, justification by faith alone, Scripture alone, Christ alone, and the glory of God alone. By 1590, however, a theological distinction between Lutheran and Reformed teachings was clear, characterized by differences in Christology, the sacraments, ecclesiology, and the relation of law and gospel. Accordingly, Queen Elizabeth I spoke of the Calvinist strand as "more reformed" than Lutheranism.[23]

The dominance of Calvin's thought in this movement resulted from the influence of his major work, *The Institutes of the Christian Religion*, once described by the well-known nineteenth-century theologian Albrecht Ritschl as "the masterpiece of Protestant theology."[24] Although interpreters of Calvin's theology have agreed that his thought may not easily be characterized, a number of key motifs have been noted, including the glory of the sovereign God, the centrality of Christ as mediator, and the authority of Scripture. First, for Calvin the beginning and end of true and sound wisdom consists in the

---

21 "History of Knox's Church, Galt," *The Presbyterian Church Archives.*

22 William J. Klempa, "Presbyterians and Canadian Theology," in *The Burning Bush and a Few Acres of Snow*, 183.

23 Ibid., 183; see also Philip Schaff, editor, *The Creeds of Christendom* (New York: Harper, 1877) 2:389–90; William Stacy Johnson and John Leith, editors, *Reformed Reader: A Sourcebook in Christian Theology* (Louisville: Westminster John Knox Press, 1993) 1:xx; and John H. Leith, *Introduction to the Reformed Tradition* (Atlanta: John Knox, 1977).

24 Cited in Klempa, "Presbyterians and Canadian Theology," 184.

knowledge of the majesty of God, a true piety expressed in love, reverence, and obedience. Secondly, Calvin's theology was centered on the role of Christ as mediator, who by the course of his obedience in life and death and by his resurrection achieved salvation for humanity, a salvation by grace which is appropriated through faith alone. Calvin also emphasized the Christian life as a life lived in union with the ascended Christ whose ongoing ministry as prophet, priest, and king shapes the ministry of the church. Thirdly, Calvin was committed to the authority of the Bible, the written Word of God, which, through the internal testimony of the Holy Spirit, is the ultimate standard of faith and life. The doctrine of predestination, with which Calvin's name is often associated, was, as William Klempa has noted, "simply the ascription of the whole of salvation to God."[25]

With the death of Calvin in 1564, and the spread of Calvinism to France, Scotland, the Netherlands, eastern Europe, and England, a continuing doctrinal refinement occurred, particularly in the doctrine of predestination. In the early seventeenth century the dispute between the Calvinists and the Arminians over the doctrine of predestination was resolved for a time by the Synod of Dort (1618-1619) with a statement that emphasized five key points in the form of what became known as TULIP theology: total depravity, unconditional election, limited atonement, irresistible grace, and perseverance of the saints. In the seventeenth and eighteenth centuries, the concept of the covenant became an important emphasis in Reformed theology as another way of mitigating the harshness of the doctrine of predestination. The Westminster Confession of Faith and Catechisms (1643-1648) became the major statement of Reformed theology in the English-speaking world, replacing—in Scotland—the Scots Confession as the church's subordinate standard. As Calvinism was transplanted to the United States and British North America, the Westminster Confession became the dominant doctrinal standard of English-speaking Presbyterian churches.[26]

The Calvinism which arrived in British North America, however, was a theology transmitted and transformed by the Scottish church. Initially shaped by John Knox, who described Calvin's Geneva as "the most perfect school of Christ on earth," and Andrew Melville, who had studied on the continent, it was also influenced by Scottish Calvinist theologians like Robert Baillie and Samuel Rutherford who had served as commissioners of the Scottish church to the Westminster Assembly. By the time this Scottish Calvinist theology was exported to the colonies by Scottish immigrants from 1763 onwards, however, it had also been shaped by the Common Sense Philosophy of the Scottish Enlightenment, especially during the nineteenth century.

---

[25]   Ibid.
[26]   Ibid.

This school of Scottish realism was led by the Scottish philosophers Thomas Reid (1710-1796) and Dugald Stewart (1753-1828) and, in the nineteenth century, by Sir William Hamilton (1788-1856). It attempted to combat the philosophical skepticism of David Hume by beginning with a universal moral sense, independent of God and revelation. Refuting Locke's notion of ideas as representative substitutes for an external reality, Reid appealed directly to the data of consciousness in order to develop a realistic theory of perception based on an empiricism of the mind. The great truths of humankind and the small truths of everyday experience were accessible to all people, i.e., they were matters of common sense. Resting upon a faculty psychology, the Common Sense philosophers argued that the many senses of the mind were not simply analytic constructs, but were in fact true descriptions of the actual physiology of the mind. Included among these faculties was a capacity to arrive at moral truths, a "moral sense" or "moral nature," which everyone possessed. Reid divided the faculties into "speculative" and "active" while Sir William Hamilton later divided mental phenomena into "knowledge" (cognition), "feeling" (pleasure or pain), and "will" (or desire). Assuming that such faculties existed, the Scottish philosophers appealed to the process of introspection in order to observe the data of one's consciousness. These insights constituted a significant contribution to the history of philosophy because they led philosophy to psychology.[27]

Scottish Common Sense Philosophy functioned in two distinct ways in relation to Christian thought. In Scotland, the movement tended to be liberalizing and heterodox while in the United States and British North America it was used as an apologetic for Calvinist orthodoxy. As an apologetic, it used the appeal to the faculties as a means of shoring up the first and fundamental truths of orthodox theology, and it did so while being able to show some sympathy for science. The basic truths of the Christian faith, it argued, were accessible to "common sense" and demonstrable as the data of human consciousness. Common Sense Philosophy assumed a clear and inviolable distinction between subject and object by maintaining "that the principles of common sense, imposed upon us by the constitution of the human mind, are principles by which our cognition is conformed to its objects, to things as they really are in themselves."[28] In short, Common Sense Philosophy provided the philosophical constructs to support a natural theology which could in turn be used to support Calvinist orthodoxy and piety. It made Calvinism appear intellectually rigorous, philosophically sophisticated, and scientifically

---

[27] A. B. McKillop, *A Disciplined Mind: Critical Inquiry and Canadian Thought in the Victorian Era* (Montreal: McGill–Queen's University Press, 1979) 26–27.

[28] S. A. Grave, *The Scottish Philosophy of Common Sense* (Oxford: Clarendon, 1960) 3.

justified.[29] Indeed, it was not so much a technical philosophy as it was a mode of thought that infused the Calvinist worldview of the eighteenth and nineteenth centuries, and as Sydney Ahlstrom has argued, in America and Canada it "was free enough from subtlety to be communicable in sermons and tracts" and "came to exist… as a vast subterranean influence, a sort of water-table nourishing dogmatics in an age of increasing doubt."[30] In Canada, as A.B. McKillop has shown, "Common Sense was one of the defining characteristics of the Scottish mind" and the moral philosophy it spawned operated magisterially as an integrating system rather than as one discipline among others.[31]

More recently, Michael Gauvreau's work has helped us understand the particular manner in which Common Sense functioned in Canadian Presbyterianism in the nineteenth century. Gauvreau's thesis is built upon Mark Noll's threefold analysis of Common Sense in the American context. First, Common Sense involved an epistemology, derived from the writings of Thomas Reid, "which posited that human perceptions reveal the world as it actually is." Second, it included a moral philosophy "which asserted that just as humans know intuitively some basic realities of the physical world, so they know by their own being certain fundamental principles of morality." And third, it worked with a developed methodology, or scientific approach, "closely connected with an exaltation of Francis Bacon, which stated that truths about consciousness, the world, or religion must be built by a strict induction from irreducible facts of experience."[32] The evangelical creed of nineteenth-century Calvinism in Canada, Gauvreau argues, was affected most by the third aspect of Common Sense. The Baconian ideal was particularly suited to assist Calvinists in nineteenth-century Canada who had experienced neither revolution nor Enlightenment directly, and who absorbed the influence of the great revivals. "First, the Baconian ideal was based on inductive methodology of current science, which derived its general laws of nature from a meticulous survey of particulars. Second, exponents of the inductive method propagated an emphatically empiricist approach to all forms of knowledge and greatly preferred objective facts to theories or hypotheses.

---

[29]   A. B. McKillop, *A Disciplined Mind: Critical Inquiry and Canadian Thought in the Victorian Era*, 28–30.

[30]   Sydney Alhstrom, "The Scottish Philosophy and American Theology," *Church History* 24 (1955) 268.

[31]   McKillop, *A Disciplined Mind*, 30–31.

[32]   Michael Gauvreau, *The Evangelical Century: College and Creed in English Canada from the Great Revival to the Great Depression* (Montreal and Kingston: McGill-Queen's University Press, 1991) 17. See Mark Noll, "Common Sense Tradition and American Evangelical Thought," *American Quarterly* 37 (1985) 216–38.

Finally, clergymen and scientists who subscribed to these beliefs indicated a distrust of hypotheses and even of reason itself."[33]

The Baconian vision of theology, therefore, as Gauvreau understands it, entailed due reverence for the biblical text because it contained divinely revealed "facts" disclosed by God which were prior to and superior to the facts of nature, philosophy, or science, which were discovered by human reason. Presbyterian scholars believed they had discovered a scientific and rational method that ostensibly acknowledged the supremacy of divine revelation. The application of the Baconian ideal was used, therefore, to buttress the social and cultural supremacy of theology by escaping the influence of the Enlightenment with its demands that all experience be interpreted according to human reason. The revealed data of faith provided the basis for certainty, and ironically, a method of rational, inductive study was used to limit the exercise of reason.[34] Gauvreau's argument helps explain how and why Common Sense in general functioned as an apologetic for Calvinist orthodoxy in British North America rather than as a threat to faith. Furthermore, if Gauvreau is correct he has explained, at least in part, why the Canadian Presbyterian church did not suffer great tension when it encountered Darwinism and the historical critical method. Its leaders and scholars simply subordinated the new insights to a theological interpretation of history, assuming all the while that revelation and reason should live in harmony, changes to the understanding of reason notwithstanding.

Among the proponents of Common Sense and the Baconian vision in Canada were Henry Esson, the first professor of mental and moral philosophy at Knox College, George Paxton Young, his successor who later became professor of philosophy at the University of Toronto and espoused the idealism of T. H. Green, James George of Queen's Theological College in Kingston (which had been founded as an Auld Kirk, i.e., Church of Scotland, Presbyterian university), and William Lyall, initially of Knox College and later a professor at Dalhousie. The peak of the influence of the Scottish Common Sense Philosophy upon the Anglo-Canadian mind occurred during the 1850s and 1860s when it provided a grand moral vision of a Christian civilization and was invoked as an authority on behalf of orthodoxy. By the fourth quarter of the nineteenth century in Canada the main elements of Scottish Common Sense vanished quickly, to be replaced by idealism. In the end, the insights of Common Sense Philosophy had been stretched so thin, to support a whole set of theological presuppositions, that they proved insufficient to meet many of the challenges of evolutionary science and the developing critical mind of Anglo-Canadians. At the same time, the Baconian vision of biblical history

---

[33] Gauvreau, *The Evangelical Century*, 41.
[34] Ibid., 38–45.

allowed Presbyterians to begin to absorb the increasing influence of German and British idealism on theology.

As a Canadian Presbyterian born in the late nineteenth century Walter Bryden stood, then, in a Calvinist theological tradition that had developed an impressive legacy. It included not only the theologians of the Reformation era and its confessions (i.e., The Scots Confession 1560; The Heidelberg Catechism, 1563; The Second Helvetic Confession, 1566), but also the continental systematicians of the seventeenth century, The Synod of Dort (1618-1619), The Westminster Confession of Faith (1647), and the Puritans of Old and New England. It also extended to the theology of America's theologian Jonathan Edwards and his inheritors of the eighteenth century. And, it included the confessionalists of the nineteenth century, represented by the initial faculties of New College, Edinburgh and Assembly's College, Belfast; along with the neo-Calvinism of Abraham Kuyper in the Netherlands, and the longstanding Old School tradition in America (represented but by no means exhausted by Princeton Seminary). But in particular, Bryden inherited the Scottish legacy of Calvinist theology, and the way in which that heritage had been transplanted to British North America, with its emphasis on Common Sense, Baconian induction, realism and natural theology.

As a born and bred Calvinist in this tradition, it stood to reason that he would find himself wrestling with many of the same questions about cognition, epistemology, revelation, and the knowledge of God. As we shall see, Bryden ended up rejecting the accommodation of Calvinist theology to both Scottish realism and British idealism. He felt both were too speculative and rational. In their place he sought to ground theology in particulars, not in the particulars of history as such, but in the particularity of the Christian's knowledge of God, the act of God in the soul of humans through the mediation of Word and Spirit. By so doing, Bryden understood himself as recovering and setting forth a sixteenth-century understanding of the gospel, i.e., Calvin's conception of revelation in Word and Spirit. Indeed, he believed that such a recovery was the urgent task of his day because nothing less than the true unity and authentic witness of the church was at stake. As a theologian of paradox, disjunction and radical discontinuity, Bryden may have rejected the options he saw before him, but he stood, for a time at least, in the Canadian tradition of "a disciplined intelligence" in his attempt to maintain the crucial equation of Christian orthodoxy and modern sensibilities through an appeal to biblical revelation.[35] In fact, Walter Bryden believed that a retrieval of the authentic tradition could fulfill the epistemological task at hand.

Evangelicalism. Another characteristic feature of the church tradition within which Walter Bryden spent his formative years was its evangelical-

---

[35]   Gauvreau, *The Evangelical Century,* 34.

ism. Brian Fraser described the Presbyterian church as emphasizing the great evangelical truths: creation, fall, redemption, atonement in Christ, justification by faith alone, sanctification through the Holy Spirit, and eternal life.[36] Evangelicalism as a term, however, was used more broadly than to designate a particular set of truths considered central to Christian orthodoxy. In its most basic sense, the Greek word "evangel" means "good news" and was translated into early English as "gospel." Thus, evangelicals were those who considered themselves as being committed to the proclamation of the gospel in word and deed. While it was a term, therefore, that could be applied to many Christian movements through history, from the Apostolic era to the present time, including the Reformation era, it came to be particularly identified with "a series of renewal movements which swept through Europe and America in the eighteenth and nineteenth centuries, and which encompassed Christians of various denominations and confessional positions."[37] Among this series of evangelical renewal movements were to be found the German Pietists, Moravians (led by Count Zinzendorf), the Great Awakenings of America, the Methodist movement under John and Charles Wesley, William Wilberforce and the Clapham Sect, and the Evangelical party within the Church of Scotland, personified by Thomas Chalmers. These various movements expressed different characteristics depending on their national and ecclesial contexts. Yet they had enough in common to infuse the term with meaning.

Church historian David Bebbington has described four common and essential marks of this evangelicalism, including that represented by the Free Church wing of Scottish Christianity: "*conversionism*, the belief that lives need to be changed; *activism*, the expression of the gospel in effort; *biblicism*, a particular regard for the Bible; and what may be called *crucicentrism*, a stress on the sacrifice of the cross."[38] Similarly, Kenneth Scott Latourette has noted that "It was characteristically Protestant and stressed the authority of the Scriptures, salvation by faith alone, and the priesthood of all believers. It made much of a personal religious experience, of a new birth through trust in Christ, commitment to him, and faith through what God has done through him in the incarnation, the cross, and the resurrection. . . . The awakening was intensely missionary. To employ technical terms, it was 'evangelistic' and emphasized 'evangelism.'"[39] In an evangelistic movement characterized

---

[36]   Fraser, *Church, College, and Clergy*, 14.

[37]   Vaudry, *The Free Church*, 6–7.

[38]   David W. Bebbington, *Evangelicalism in Modern Britain: A History from the 1730s to the 1980s* (London: Unwin Hyman, 1989) 1–20.

[39]   Kenneth Scott Latourette, *A History of Christianity*, vol. 2: *A.D. 1500–A.D. 1975* (New York: Harper and Row, 1975) 1019.

by missionary zeal, evangelicals sought to win an acceptance of their vision of the Christian faith among nominal and de-Christianized Christians in Christendom, and non-Christians throughout the world. In some ways the evangelical revivals were a reaction against the Enlightenment and therefore also shaped by it. Evangelicalism emphasized divine revelation over human reason, human sinfulness over human goodness, and conversion over polite morality. It also reacted against the cold, rational, and formal preaching in post-Reformation scholasticism and Enlightenment Latitudinarianism, turning instead to a faith that was strongly individualistic and intensely personal, imparting "to its followers zeal, enthusiasm, deep piety, great seriousness, and a strong sense of moral earnestness."[40] Rooted in pietism, evangelicalism was characterized by "its emphasis on becoming aware of God in the depths of the heart. Evangelicals were convinced that God was constantly rewarding, admonishing, and punishing individuals."[41] The doctrines of original sin and salvation by grace alone were compelling, experiential realities as one lived with a sense of God's abiding presence. As Richard Vaudry has noted, "The Canadian Free Church was, in particular, a child of the Evangelical revival in eighteenth and early nineteenth-century Scotland."[42]

The Presbyterian congregations of western Ontario were directly affected during the nineteenth century by the revivals of the Second Great Awakening in the United States. Initially the influence of the revivals was felt through Methodist and Baptist groups, and Presbyterian leaders were suspicious of, and often hostile toward, the theology and the methods of the early frontier revivalists. By the 1860s the revivalism of the Methodist and Baptist groups had been modified to make them more socially acceptable and stable, "while the Free Church split among Presbyterians had heightened the importance of evangelical experience among the majority of Presbyterians west of Toronto."[43] As a result, during the 1840s and 1850s a number of revivals were experienced within congregations of the Free Church of Scotland, including Knox's Church, Galt in 1869. In addition, western Ontario also proved to be a center for missionary enthusiasm in the nineteenth century, providing more missionaries for the home and foreign fields for Presbyterians than any other region of the country.[44]

In sum, Walter Bryden's earliest years were shaped by a Scottish family which belonged to a vibrant congregation of the Reformed tradition, with its

---

[40]   Vaudrey, *The Free Church*, 7.

[41]   David B. Marshall, *Secularizing the Faith: Canadian Protestant Clergy and the Crisis of Belief, 1850–1940* (Toronto: University of Toronto Press, 1992) 26.

[42]   Vaudrey, *The Free Church*, 8.

[43]   Fraser, *The Social Uplifters*, 24.

[44]   Ibid.

Presbyterian form of church government, its dissenting Free Church heritage, its strong Calvinism accompanied by Scottish Common Sense philosophy, and its lively evangelical heritage. By the late nineteenth century, to be sure, the tradition had undergone change, first by the union of the Free Church with the United Presbyterian Church to form the Canada Presbyterian Church in 1861, and then by the union of the Canada Presbyterian Church with the Synod of the Presbyterian Church of Canada (Church of Scotland), the Church of the Maritime Province (Church of Scotland), and the Presbyterian Church of the Lower Provinces, to create The Presbyterian Church in Canada in 1875. By 1883, therefore, the year of Bryden's birth, Knox's Church, Galt was a congregation of the recently formed Presbyterian Church in Canada. Furthermore, the Calvinist theology and evangelical piety which had been shaped by Common Sense philosophy had begun to be influenced by German idealism, mediated and moderated in Canada by its British interpreters and advocates. Nevertheless, during the 1880s and the 1890s Knox's Church, Galt provided Walter Bryden with a firm foundation in quite traditional Presbyterian theology, ecclesiology, and piety as he embarked upon a university and theological education that forced him to wrestle with the new intellectual changes that had been stirring in Canada since at least as early as 1870.

University of Toronto, 1902–1906

In 1901 Bryden matriculated from the Galt Grammar School where he received a formative high school education that stressed classical studies in Greek and Latin, and in 1902 he enrolled at the University of Toronto, studying moderns in his first year, and graduating in 1906 in Honours Philosophy and Psychology. During his undergraduate years at University College he served as treasurer of the Philosophy and Psychology Society.[45] In 1907 he earned the M.A. in philosophy and psychology, with honors standing, for a thesis on "A Verification of the Law of Weber, By the Method of Mean Gradations, With Reference to Great Differences of Light Intensities."[46] The thesis is a brief account and verification of an experimental method in the emerging field of psychology, and may well have been a piece of work that Bryden dashed off in order to fulfill the requirements for the degree. It might also indicate, however, a predisposition towards empiricism which fed his later suspicion of idealism.

---

[45] J. C. McLelland, "By Circumstance and God," 119.

[46] Bryden, "A Verification of the Law of Weber By the Method of Mean Gradations, With Reference to Great Differences of Light Intensities." Unpublished M.A. Thesis, 1907. University of Toronto Archives.

Idealism. Bryden studied philosophy, psychology and theology in Canada at the beginning of the twentieth century, a period during which the ideals of Enlightenment philosophy and post-Enlightenment thought had already deeply penetrated the philosophical and theological world, largely mediated through British scholars who taught in Canadian universities and theological schools. Idealism had replaced Common Sense as the integrating philosophical framework: the truth of the Christian worldview could no longer be assumed, and the theology of many church leaders appeared increasingly halting and uncertain.[47] During the nineteenth century, university education in British North America had been dominated by the presupposition that the pursuit of knowledge must also be a pursuit guided by the recognition and acceptance of universal moral principles. The purpose of such an education was to provide cultural leaders for the colonies who possessed a grand moral vision for western civilization. However, the explosion of knowledge that characterized the nineteenth century, accompanied by scientific advances, reinforced the ideals of the Enlightenment and increasingly challenged Christian thought.

The Enlightenment was a diverse intellectual European movement that created a major paradigm shift in the western Worldview. It has rightly been described as the revolutionary shift to a modern consciousness which set in motion the process of secularization, i.e., a growing tendency of human society to do without religion, or to try to do without religion.[48] It was no longer assumed that God and the supernatural were necessary to explain the natural world, history and the human person, and finally even religion. While the impact of this change in Western consciousness cannot be measured solely through the history of its emerging ideas, *Aufklärung, L'Illumination, or* "The Age of Reason," as it was variably described, was marked by a number of salient themes.

---

[47]   In 1877, when The Rev. George M. Grant became Principal of Queen's Theological College in Kingston, Ontario, he was mildly rebuked by a friend for the tone of his inaugural address: "I infer that your theology is somewhat halting and uncertain," he observed. See Ramsey Cook, *The Regenerators: Social Criticism in Late Victorian English Canada* (Toronto: University of Toronto Press, 1985) 18.

[48]   Owen Chadwick, *The Secularization of the European Mind in the Nineteenth Century* (Cambridge: Cambridge University Press, 1975) 17. For a discussion of the meaning of secularization in Canadian Protestantism see Ramsay Cook, *The Regenerators*, 3–25; David B. Marshall, *Secularizing the Faith*, 3–24; Gauvreau, *The Evangelical Century*, 3–12; Marguerite Van Die, *An Evangelical Mind: Nathanael Burwash and the Methodist Tradition in Canada, 1839–1918* (Montreal: McGill–Queen's University Press, 1989) 3–13. It is beyond the scope of this book to enter into the debate about whether secularization in Canada was a benign or a destructive process. Suffice it to say that the neo-orthodox theology of Walter Bryden and others in Canada shows that the journey from religious orthodoxy through theological liberalism to secularism was neither straightforward nor progressive.

Enlightenment thinking granted human reason absolute authority and elevated it to the place of an independent arbiter of all truth, thus transforming it into the framework within which all reality was to be interpreted. Although Immanuel Kant had recognized the limits of human reason, i.e., its inability to comprehend the infinite of which religion speaks, he did so in order to establish human reason as the supreme test of all human knowledge of sensory phenomena. In Britain, Reformed theologians since the eighteenth century, in response to the Scottish Enlightenment, had relied on the Scottish Common Sense philosophy of Thomas Reid to combat the influence of Hume's skepticism on Calvinist orthodoxy. By the nineteenth century, however, the influence of Kant's metaphysics was felt in British philosophy and theology. For Kant, knowledge was the product of subjective activities of the mind as it operated on the data received from without. Real knowledge, Kant argued, required some preliminary input from the natural world, and therefore made the transcendent closed to rational inquiry. Recognizing the challenge that this posed to metaphysics and theology, Kant moved beyond this critical judgment and proposed what he deemed to be a more secure basis for belief in God, freedom, and immortality. Kant's effort at reconstruction, however, for all its merit, fell somewhat short of shoring up the full corpus of orthodox teaching. In the 1840s and 1850s Sir William Hamilton of Edinburgh University began to interpret and mediate Kant's philosophy to the English-speaking world by developing an approach which integrated Kant's emphasis on the subjective elements in perception with Common sense realism's emphasis on the objective dimensions. This too, however, proved inadequate to sustain Calvinist orthodoxy.[49]

Common Sense philosophy and Kantianism were soon surpassed in Scottish theology by the influence of Hegelian idealism on British philosophy. By the 1870s many theologians were adopting idealism's affirmation of reason and spirit in order to protect religion from materialism and skepticism. The romantic idealism of Edward Caird, "Scotland's leading Idealist philosopher under whom many of the Free Church's most promising students studied moral philosophy in the 1870s," proved influential not only for theology in Britain, but also for theology in Canada.[50] Initially influenced by Thomas Carlyle to see the importance of idealist principles in German literature and poetry, Caird saw moral philosophy as necessary to produce an educated class of people capable of providing moral leadership in society. As he worked in the midst of the intellectual revival of Platonism in British philosophy Caird utilized the insights of Kant and Hegel to get past human sub-

---

[49] Glen G. Scorgie, *A Call For Continuity: The Theological Contribution of James Orr* (Macon, Ga.: Mercer University Press, 1988) 3–17.

[50] Fraser, *The Social Uplifters*, 2–4.

jectivity and individualism to the reconstruction of an intellectual and moral order grounded in an ultimate principle of unity. This rational principle unfolding in history was God. The highest expressions of this absolute unifying principle were human beings. If, as Hegel argued, the historical process was but the unfolding of a single principle, and that principle was spiritual, and it manifested itself fully in the life of human beings with their self-conscious intelligence, then Hegel's doctrine seemed to be the philosophical rendering of essential Christianity, the union or the identity of the human and divine.[51] Caird's brother John at the University of Glasgow specifically gave this idealist interpretation to Christianity, and through the work of Edward Caird's student John Watson this reconstruction of faith found its way to Queen's University in Kingston, Ontario where Watson served as Professor of Mental and Moral Philosophy.

According to Watson, Christianity was now useful in that it provided "a theology that affirmed that all forms of being were manifestations of a single principle, identification with which the true life of humanity consisted."[52] "Religion," Watson argued, "is the spirit which must more and more subdue all things to itself, informing science and art, and realizing itself in the higher organization of the family, the civic community, the state, and ultimately the world, and gradually filling the mind and heart of every individual with the love of God and the enthusiasm for humanity."[53] The Christian ideal synthesized the whole heritage of Western civilization by incorporating within it the Greek ideal of rationality and aesthetics, the Jewish ideal of righteousness, the Roman ideal of law and order, and the Teutonic ideal of freedom. The divine spirit of love of God and humanity in Christianity, he argued, unified all these ideals, and Jesus expressed the highest form of religious consciousness and morality. Jesus knew that nature and humanity were identical in their essence with God and based his moral teaching, not on external creeds and ecclesiastical structures, but upon the consciousness of this unity with God. While a good deal of Western thought had been plagued by a dualism of transcendence and immanence, Hegel had provided, Watson and others argued, a means to recover the spiritual and ethical monism of Jesus.[54] Hegelian idealism, Watson concluded, could resolve the issues that eluded the Common Sense school, without denying the fundamental moral nature of humans. It constituted a new conception of design and proper operating in the universe,

---

[51]   McKillop, *A Disciplined Intelligence*, 185.

[52]   Fraser, *The Social Uplifters*, 7.

[53]   John Watson, *The Interpretation of Religious Experience* (Glasgow: Maclehose, 1912) 2:327–28.

[54]   John Watson, *Christianity and Idealism* (New York: Macmillan, 1897) 216. See also Fraser, *The Social Uplifters*, 7.

one that could encompass, rather than capitulate to, or deny, evolutionary science. It had the ability to cultivate a pious disposition in the minds of students without belittling intellectual inquiry and critical thought. It showed the essential rationality of the universe and placed everything within the perspective of a new and modern interpretation of the Christian experience, even while defending the essentials of the faith. As A.B. McKillop argues, the secret of Hegel in the hands of Watson was a powerful tool in the Canadian context.[55]

At University College in Toronto Walter Bryden was introduced to the philosophical idealism of George Paxton Young, an erstwhile Presbyterian minister who began his career as a minister of the Free Church. After serving as Professor of Logic, Mental and Moral Philosophy at Knox College and as a superintendent of education, Young was Professor of Metaphysics and Ethics at University College from 1871. He set the intellectual tone, especially for the Free Church students who took their arts there before proceeding to theological studies at Knox College. In response to the skepticism of David Hume, and the Scottish Common Sense philosophy from which he turned having concluded that it was too bound up with Presbyterian theology, Young argued that human beings were free to shape their own destinies and that only reason could provide an adequate basis for belief and action.[56] With this commitment to reason Young believed in the ideal of self-realization, arguing that human beings could only grasp what reason opened up to them. At each stage in human development, in history and in the life of the individual, what must seem fitting and believable depended upon the state of self-development one had reached.[57] The ultimate truth might be attained through the development of the human mind. Young developed this philosophy along three lines of thought: metaphysical idealism, the doctrine of free will, and moral theory.[58] Above all, in Young's approach reason was not simply an impartial arbiter, a mere tool for apprehending reality, but reason was the development of the inner structure of the human being in the context of experience.[59]

Young died in 1889 and Bryden was introduced to Young's idealism primarily through his two successors at the University of Toronto, James Mark Baldwin and James Gibson Hume. "Baldwin," as McKillop notes, "the new professor of logic and metaphysics from the United States, was not in a tech-

[55] McKillop, *A Disciplined Intelligence*, 182.
[56] Leslie Armour and Elizabeth Trott, *The Faces of Reason: An Essay on Philosophy and Culture in English Canada, 1850–1950* (Waterloo, Ont.: Wilfrid Laurier University Press, 1981), 87.
[57] Ibid., 87.
[58] Ibid., 91.
[59] Ibid., 104.

nical sense a philosophical idealist; he was, at this early stage in his career, an exponent of experiential psychology and urged in his inaugural address in 1890 the development of laboratory facilities at the University of Toronto."[60] This likely explains Bryden's M.A. thesis. Baldwin was interested, however, in moral philosophy and recognized the need for a universal moral law as the basis for social community and the common good. Hume, on the other hand, the professor of ethics and the history of philosophy, had been a student of Young's and was an idealist through and through.

This exalted view of human reason as the inner structure of all reality, accompanied by the rise of critical inquiry, gained acceptance not only in philosophical and theological circles, but increasingly at the level of popular culture. Idealist rationalism seemed to work for many in an age of increasing intellectual restlessness. The progressive mood it cultivated led a man like Allen Pringle to write: ". . . The Rationalist may confidently look forward to the time when, in the higher and still higher development of man and the corresponding improvement of his environment, superstitious faith will have departed forever from the human mind, reason will sit supreme on its rightful throne, and a quietly superior practical morality will have attained the fruit of the awareness of Science and accumulated experience."[61] Such philosophical idealism was to have a decisive impact on Bryden's intellectual development, not only because it introduced him to the latest Anglo-Saxon thinking on questions of cognition, reason, human experience, and morality and their implications for religious faith, but also because it was the worldview he finally dismissed as inadequate and inappropriate. In hindsight Bryden could see that, in the late nineteenth century, theology was being ground up between the millstones of materialistic physical science and idealistic metaphysics. The residue proved intellectually indigestible. Many theological teachers and church leaders fled from the perceived threat of materialism to the welcome defense (or refuge?) offered by idealism. But this "idealist solution" turned out to be a snare as far as defending any type of orthodox faith was concerned. Bryden figured this out and spent the rest of his life spitting out the idealist metaphysics he was exposed to as a student at the University of Toronto. Idealist rationalism, especially disguised as modernist theology, was the enemy of authentic Christian faith as far as Bryden was concerned. It became the foil against which his later theology was forged.[62] But what

---

[60]   McKillop, *A Disciplined Intelligence*, 200–201.

[61]   Allen Pringle, *The 'Mail's' Theology: Being a Reply to the Saturday Sermons of the Toronto 'Mail,' including a Vindication of Charles Bradlaugh against the 'Mail's' Aspersions* (Toronto: Standard Book and Job Printing Office, 1882) 38–39, cited in Ramsay Cook, *The Regenerators*, 56.

[62]   I am indebted to Barry Mack for this insight.

were his philosophical and theological options in the early twentieth century? Neither fundamentalism nor high church ritualism appealed to him. By the time he wrote his first book in the early 1920s, as we shall see, Walter Bryden had embraced the revival of interest in Kierkegaard's existentialism in sharp contrast to the idealism of his university education.

Darwinism. The wave of idealism that swept over Canada was itself in part a reaction and response to the challenge posed by Darwinism to Calvinist orthodoxy and the Common Sense philosophy that underpinned it. The publication of *Origin of the Species* in 1859 and *Descent of Man* in 1871 signaled a fundamental shift in how human beings and the world were to be understood in their interrelatedness, and thus how they were to be understood in relation to God. Set within the explosion of knowledge and the scientific advances of the nineteenth century, the Calvinist orthodoxy which had relied upon the natural theology established by Common Sense now faced challenges to its cosmology and anthropology. Calvinism had spoken of all reality in terms of two levels—the natural and the supernatural, earth and heaven, the human and the divine. Science now spoke of the uniformity of natural laws and the ability of the scientific method to ascertain these laws. Traditional Calvinist thought had emphasized a sovereign God who providentially orders the world and who, from time to time, intrudes into it via miraculous interventions. Science now taught that the world could be explained as a closed system without any appeal to interventions from beyond. Reformed orthodoxy had appeared to confess the creation of the world in a literal six-day period. Darwin and his followers now talked about the evolution of the earth over hundreds of thousands and millions of years. And perhaps most devastating of all, it was now possible to account for humanity's physical, mental, moral and even religious origins on the basis of evolutionary theory. Explanations which appealed to human beings as unique creatures in the image of God were not only unnecessary, they appeared increasingly quaint. Through the influence of positivism, religion came to be understood as an elementary stage of human development through which humanity had now passed.

As one might expect, these assertions did not sit well with many Presbyterian theologians, ministers, and academics, among them Sir William Dawson of McGill University, one of Canada's most eminent scientists in the nineteenth century. [63] Until Darwin's challenge, scientific endeavor in British North America had been marked by the continuing presence of religious assumptions within the domain of science.[64] The natural theology of William Paley, in tandem with Scottish Common Sense and Baconian induction, allowed science to be wedded to Christian piety. Revealed theol-

---

[63] Cook, *The Regenerators*, 8–9.
[64] McKillop, *A Disciplined Intelligence*, 61.

ogy and natural theology existed in harmony. Natural theology provided the platform upon which revealed theology could be constructed, and revealed theology, for its part, pointed to the truths which science could not attain on its own. Darwin's hypothesis shattered this synthesis and William Dawson knew it. Dawson also recognized that the intellectual stakes were high because Darwinism, far from being a scientific hypothesis about one dimension of life, provided a comprehensive understanding of the world which challenged the Calvinist worldview. Darwinism marginalized the distinctions between the knowledge of God the creator and the knowledge of God the redeemer, between general and special revelation, between natural theology and a theology centered in supernatural revelation, basic to Calvinist orthodoxy. These distinctions had permitted Reformed theology to embrace Common Sense, Baconian induction, Paley's natural theology, and the pre-Darwinian scientific method espoused by James Beaven, James Bovell, and Dawson himself - within a thoroughly theistic framework. Science and religion had proceeded on the assumption that the two types of revelation stood in continuity with each other. A harmony between science and religion existed, which allowed both to proceed within their respective spheres of study. Darwin separated what had been only distinguished in Calvinist theology. He thereby made the world of nature accessible and explicable without reference to God. The need for a natural theology, at least of the sort proffered by nineteenth-century Calvinism, now seemed redundant.

Seeing that natural theology could no longer be shored up by Common Sense philosophy, Anglo-Canadian philosophers turned to idealism which they believed allowed them to accommodate the new scientific worldview while they continued to embrace the essential ideals of the Christian faith. As the Darwinian worldview gained acceptance and strength, the choice between a secular and religious explanation became sharper. There were some who opted to explain the origins of humanity without reference to God and followed Darwin into a thoroughly naturalistic worldview. There were others, to be sure, who opted to explain the origins of humanity without reference to Darwin and continued to affirm the older Calvinist orthodoxy, notwithstanding evidence to the contrary. For the most part, however, Canadian Protestants deployed a strategy of assimilation which embraced Darwinian science and Christian faith through the use of philosophical idealism. Their appeal to divine providence in universal and natural history made it possible for them to do so.

Social Criticism. In addition to idealism and Darwinism, Bryden's university studies introduced him to social criticism and the Marxist critique of the Christian religion and capitalism. As Ramsay Cook has noted, "... Marx's teachings played only a marginal role in the rise of Canadian social criticism," but "his point about the role of religion in society was widely accepted by conservatives and social critics."[65] Arguing that "the criticism of religion is the presupposition of all criticism," Marx contended that "The abolition of the *illusory* happiness of the people is the demand for their *real* happiness. The demand to abandon the illusions about their condition is the *demand to give up a condition* that requires illusions. Hence criticism of religion is in embryo a *criticism of this vale of tears* whose halo is religion."[66] There was no salvation for Marx other than the salvation to be found in this world, and historical materialism was the pathway to the classless utopian ideal which Marx believed was inevitable. The destinies preached by all religions were illusory. Marx's contention that religious faith sanctioned the social order was widely accepted in the late nineteenth century, even among those who rejected many of Marx's other teachings. Those who embraced Marx's teachings in whole tried to demonstrate that religion was false in order to discredit the established social order it supported.

In English Canada at the end of the nineteenth century, however, a more moderate, accommodating view prevailed. It proceeded on the assumption that a thoroughgoing criticism of society was rooted in criticism of religion but in contrast to Marx it did not advocate atheistic materialism. "Instead," as Cook has shown, "their aim was almost invariably a reinterpretation of Christianity to make it more relevant to the supposed everyday world of Canadians."[67] The social critics who emerged in late Victorian Canada, therefore, launched a critique of the Christian religion in order to overturn what they viewed as an inadequate orthodoxy, only to provide a reinterpretation as the basis for a new society. John Clark Murray of McGill University represented one such attempt in his book *Industrial Kingdom of God* in which he sought to demonstrate the application of Christian ethics to industrial society and argued that Christian doctrine and social action were inseparable. Christianity rightly understood, Clark Murray and others contended, provided the basis for a vigorous social criticism and the foundation for a new social vision. The social gospel in Canada was a powerful expression of this impulse. In the first decade of the twentieth century at the University of Toronto, the departments of philosophy and political economy introduced students, including Walter Bryden, to the writings of those who analyzed the inequities and conflicts of industrial society. The political instincts instilled in him by

---

[65]   Cook, *The Regenerators*, 7–8.

[66]   Karl Marx, "Towards a Critique of Hegel's Philosophy of Law: Introduction (1844)," in *The Essential Marx: The Non-Economic Writings,* edited by Saul K. Padover (New York: New American Library, 1978) 286–87. See Cook, *The Regenerators*, 7.

[67]   Cook, *The Regenerators*, 8.

Bryden's dissenting Free Church heritage in western Ontario continued to be nurtured by the social criticism of late nineteenth-century Canadian thought so that, as a Canadian theologian in the second quarter of the twentieth century, his "criticism of society was rooted in criticism of religion," in his case the idealism of established middle class Christianity in Canada. It was no accident that Bryden's son Kenneth became a social democrat, a political economist, and a politician.

Bryden began his formal theological studies in 1906 with these challenges to the Presbyterian tradition planted firmly in his mind. By the 1890s the old orthodoxies had been shattered. Common Sense had been dismissed as faulty in its psychology. Its inadequate conception of the mind was incapable of meeting the needs and challenges of an age of inquiry and analysis. The Paleyite natural theology had in large measure been replaced by an equally teleological, but more dynamic, Hegelian conception of social evolution. The Baconian ideal in science had also proved largely inadequate under the onslaught of the Darwinian method, although it provided for a continuing theology of history. In short, the hegemony of idealism had begun.[68] Idealism and Darwinism, accompanied by the insights of Marxist social criticism, presented considerable challenges to the Christian faith. Together, along with the emerging work of Freud, they provided the principles for a revolutionary new worldview. Hegel had convinced many that religion was the unfolding of universal absolute divine spirit in union with humanity, Darwin that it was an evolutionary phase, Marx that it was a sociological (and illusory and oppressive) phenomena, and Freud that it was a neurosis.

To be sure, the ideas of these thinkers had been modified by Canadian writers and teachers, and there was a decided effort on the part of many Christian leaders in Canada to accommodate the Christian faith to them. But a storm was brewing, exacerbated by even more changes that were taking place in Canadian society at the beginning of the twentieth century: consumerism, materialism, industrialization, urbanization, rapid progress in transportation and communication, and changing moral and social values.[69] The missionary encounter with other religions had raised questions about the uniqueness of Christ and the superiority of Christianity. Sports, recreation, trade unions, social clubs, political organizations, libraries, the theatre, and music and dance halls placed increasing pressure on the social hegemony of the church and the Calvinist theology which had been the stabling center of Presbyterian life in Canada.

Undoubtedly, there were many confessional Calvinists who argued the storm could be weathered by remaining faithful to the ship of orthodoxy.

---

[68]   McKillop, *A Disciplined Intelligence*, 205.
[69]   Marshall, *Secularizing the Faith*, 4–48.

Walter Bryden was not among them. At the same time, many theologians and church leaders were engaged in the project of hoisting overboard those elements of the Reformed faith which no longer seemed necessary for the voyage through the twentieth century. Bryden also had serious questions about their project. By the end of World War One, and for two decades after that, as the optimistic conclusions spawned by the idealist reformulation of the Christian faith were being challenged, Walter Bryden was among those who raised the most difficult and penetrating questions.

In the first decade of the twentieth century, however, Bryden's Presbyterian tradition and idealist education seemed irreconcilable. The price of Reformed orthodoxy, which appeared to be obscurantism, was not a price Bryden was willing to pay. At the same time, the price exacted by idealism was nothing short of a wholesale revision of Christian faith. As a minister and theological teacher standing in the aftermath of this intellectual and social transition in Canada, Bryden profoundly understood the need to relate the Christian faith to modern sensibilities. He had been thoroughly inculcated with modern values and he recognized that the church could no longer appeal to external authorities alone as the basis of faith for Anglo-Canadians. But he could not bring himself to turn the matter over to critical inquiry alone. Neither option, he would argue, justified the truly religious life.

In time, Bryden came to see the uncertainty of faith as a reality to be recognized rather than an obstacle to be overcome. It pointed, he came to believe, to a condition of crisis occasioned by the existential character of revelation and the paradox of faith rather than by the intellectual challenges of the culture. For now, however, he had to live with the tension. He was persuaded that the older Reformed orthodoxy, supported by Scottish Common sense, could no longer sustain the epistemological enterprise. The assessment of Professor Tracy in an article, "The Scottish Philosophy" in 1895 in the University of Toronto Quarterly made the case clearly: "However sincere their purpose, and however great their ability, they have not succeeded in... solving the epistemological enigma which has puzzled all modern philosophy. The question[s]: *How does the mind know its object? and what is the relation in which the mind stands to the material world?* are almost left where they were before."[70] While concurring, Bryden would have added that idealism also failed for the same serious reasons. But what, then, was the knowledge of God? And how could God be known? What conception of revelation was adequate for modern sensibilities and appropriate to the Reformed tradition? Were there other ways to negotiate between the Charbydis of confessional

---

[70]   F. Tracy, "The Scottish Philosophy," *University of Toronto Quarterly* 2 (Nov. 1895) 1–15; as cited by McKillop, *A Disciplined Intelligence*, 57 (italics mine).

Calvinism and the Scylla of liberal Protestantism? Bryden's theological studies opened up some possibilities.

Knox College, Toronto, 1906–1909

In 1906 Bryden began studies in theology at Knox College in preparation for pastoral ministry within The Presbyterian Church in Canada. With the death of Principal Caven, the College was in a period of theological transition and institutional reorganization.[71] William MacLaren acted as Principal from 1905 to 1908, when he was succeeded by Alfred Gandier. During the same period an internal reorganization took place which resulted in changes to the faculty, the facilities, and the curriculum. Due to the deterioration of the building, lack of space, and an inadequate library in the grand old building on Spadina Avenue, a decision was taken in 1906 to build a new college on the University of Toronto campus. In 1907, Knox College instituted a department of practical training; in 1908 courses on the social teaching of the Bible, Christian ethics, the conduct of public worship, and church administration were added; and in 1909 practical field experience in Christian or social work became a requirement of all students at the College. A new emphasis on missions also emerged with the organization of a Y.M.C.A. branch in the college in 1905.[72] These changes in theological education, with a greater emphasis placed on the practical training of ministers, reflected an awareness of the changing theological and social realities within the churches and the nation. Upon graduation Walter Bryden was awarded the prize in Calvinistic theology and three general proficiency scholarships.[73] The Calvinist theology which Bryden studied at Knox College during these years, however, represented a theology in transition.

Entering Knox College in 1906, Bryden discovered a theological school largely shaped by the powerful influence of William Caven whose long shadow continued to hang over its ethos in the years immediately after his death in late 1904. Caven had been appointed to the chair of biblical exegetics at Knox College in 1866, to convene the senate when Michael Willis retired as principal in 1870, and to the principalship in 1873. Born in 1830 in Scotland, he emigrated to Canada with his family in 1847 where he attended the United Presbyterian Divinity Hall in London before being called to the pastorate in St. Mary's, Ontario. After the union of the United Presbyterians with the Free Church in 1861, Caven rose to prominence in the life of the church, especially during his thirty-eight year tenure at Knox College.

---

71   Moir, *Enduring Witness*, 189.
72   Ibid., 189–90.
73   "Death of Principal of Knox College," *Presbyterian Record* (May 1952) 9.

In temperament and theology Caven represented a cautious and diplomatic approach. Although deeply committed to the Reformed tradition in theology, he was not uncritically committed to the confessional Calvinism of the nineteenth-century Princeton school because he had increasingly come to recognize that the presuppositions of Scottish Common sense and Paley's natural theology could no longer be sustained. At the same time, he was cautiously open to the insights of idealism and biblical criticism. In other words, Caven was conservative, but open to the progressive advance of knowledge and the application of critical thought to the Christian faith.[74] He had a firm faith in the reliability of the Bible's witness to the central facts of God's saving purposes. He believed that the minister was to be an interpreter of Scripture, a theologian, and an apologist, firmly grounded in the truth of the Christian message, able to communicate its meaning effectively in an age when the gospel was increasingly being assailed, and above all a teacher of the evangelical faith. He sought to instill in his students a balanced mind which was "conservative of everything good which comes down to us, while it seeks by careful investigation to enlarge the boundaries of ascertained truth and to purge away errors and mistakes."[75] In the words of Principal Gordon of Queen's University, Caven "did not readily accept new ideas or methods, for he was conservative in his habits of thought; and yet he was always open to new disclosures of truth, ready to receive them after careful and sufficient test."[76]

In affirming the inspiration of the Bible, Caven sought to harmonize the critical approach with the Presbyterian affirmation that the Bible was the Word of God. As Michael Gauvreau notes, by the mid 1880s "Caven had already charted a course that would mediate the preacher's need for inductive certainty in interpreting the Bible to the congregation, and the excitement of younger spirits who urged accommodation of evangelical theology with higher criticism and the idea of development."[77] Caven emphasized that theology was a progressive science grounded in the truth of the Christian message. "Theology is the same now that it has been in every age of the Christian era, so far as its central truths are concerned," he argued in a lecture at the opening of the academic year at Knox College in 1877, but it is also "continually changing by the growth of new truths, which an increasing knowledge of

---

[74]   Fraser, *The Social Uplifters*, 25.

[75]   W. Caven, "Clerical Conservatism and Scientific Radicalism," *Knox College Monthly* 14.6 (1891) 286. Cited in Fraser, *The Social Uplifters*, 25.

[76]   J. A. Macdonald, "Rev. Principal Caven, D.D.," *Knox College Monthly* 17 (Nov. 1891). Principal Gordon's observations were printed in *the Presbyterian* (10 Dec. 1904). Cited in David B. Marshall, *Secularizing the Faith*, 63.

[77]   Gauvreau, *The Evangelical Century*, 147.

the Bible has furnished."[78] By continuing to appeal to the inductive study of the Bible rooted in Baconian science, Caven had confidence that an alliance between evangelical Presbyterianism and the new historical-critical approach to the Bible was possible. He sought to foster what may be termed a reverent criticism of the Bible. William Caven, therefore, played a mediating role in shaping the Presbyterian response to both biblical criticism and evolutionary theory.[79] As a mediator, he helped to win acceptance for a compromise statement in the Macdonnell heresy trial in 1877, and also allowed that if the confessional standards of the church could be shown to be at variance with Scripture, they should be revised.

Caven's conservative mediating Calvinism also permitted him to build Knox College into a significant theological force at the turn of the century with a number of new faculty members, educated by Scottish evangelical liberal theologians, who represented a progressive orthodoxy. During his tenure, Knox College expanded its faculty, erected a new building, and increased its endowments, but perhaps his greatest legacy was the faculty he had been instrumental in putting into place by the time of his death in 1904. As Brian Fraser has argued, "Throughout the transition from confessional to progressive orthodoxy... Caven played the role of senior statesman and diplomat. While cautiously open to new understanding, he vigorously defended the centrality of the essential orthodox affirmations of evangelical Protestantism in the curriculum, the pious learning essential to effective ministry, and the importance of both to the mission of the church at home and abroad." Caven contributed to a great Canadian Presbyterian compromise which, in the end, "prevented the bitter and divisive battles that plagued Presbyterianism in the United States and Scotland. In a time of transition and trouble, William Caven guided Knox College through the treacherous deeps of theological change."[80]

At his death, Caven was succeeded by his aging colleague William MacLaren as principal of Knox College. MacLaren, the principal in place when Bryden entered the college in 1906, had been appointed to the chair of systematic theology in 1873 and was the first graduate of Knox to hold a chair in the college. MacLaren believed that the confessional orthodox interpretation of the Westminster Standards, especially as found in the Princeton theology, provided a comprehensive and persuasive case for the truth and power of Christianity. The best exposition of that faith, he believed, was that

---

[78] "'Theology and Religion,' A Review of Dr. Caven's Lecture at the Opening of Knox College," *Queen's Journal* (Q) 5.1 (20 Oct. 1877) 2. Cited by M. Gauvreau, *The Evangelical Century*, 147.

[79] Gauvreau, *The Evangelical Century*, 147–50.

[80] Fraser, *Church, College and Clergy*, 94–95, 105.

of A. A. Hodge in his *Outlines of Theology*, originally published in 1860, revised in 1878, and used by MacLaren as his basic text in theology throughout his teaching career. As a clear and articulate exposition of the system of revealed truth, it set out the substance, MacLaren believed, of the creeds and confessions of the Reformed churches and therefore provided the basic theological framework needed by Presbyterian theological students. The role of the clergy, he taught, was "to seek and save the lost, and then to train the saved for Christ through the faithful presentation of God's truth."[81] The best summary of that truth, he contended, was to be found in the Reformed faith. MacLaren conceived of theology as a science and believed that the proper method of constructing a system of doctrine was to apply inductive Baconian reasoning to the study of the Bible, thereby employing the methods pursued with success in modern times by the students of physical science. He was committed to the doctrine of plenary inspiration because he believed it was taught by Christ, affirmed the centrality of the penal substitutionary atonement, and was concerned about the question of future probation. He resisted the concessions being made to evolutionary theory in theology, criticized the speculative nature of historical criticism, and continued to affirm a thoroughly supernatural interpretation of the Christian faith. "If Christianity is anything," he argued, "it is not merely a supernatural revelation from God, but a supernatural revelation that a supernatural work has been accomplished by a supernatural person for man's salvation, and is applied by a supernatural agency to the human heart."[82]

At the same time, MacLaren did not abandon a dialogue with critical thought as he continued to reaffirm the essentials of confessional Calvinism. In his view, there was a place for biblical criticism, rightly employed, in separating the essential teachings of the Bible from incidental accretions to revelation. One had to admit, he conceded, that the Bible is couched in the scientific worldview of its day but it does not diminish the inspiration and authority of Scripture to acknowledge this. MacLaren affirmed the notion of progressive revelation in the Bible and drew a distinction between Christian and non-Christian approaches to evolution and historical criticism. Nevertheless, he vigorously resisted the reconstruction of the biblical worldview that resulted when evolutionary theory and historical criticism were employed as ideals rather than as methods. MacLaren's ability to maintain a deep commitment to confessional Calvinism, while also acknowledging (but not accepting) many of the changes that were taking place, was fuelled by his recognition of the practical task that faced the church. The Canadian church, faced with the

---

[81] Fraser, *Church, College and Clergy*, 71.

[82] William MacLaren, "The New Theology and Its Sources," *Canadian Presbyterian* (6 Oct. 1886) 663.

challenge of seeing that the gospel and its institutions were firmly established in a new land, did not have the luxury of indulging in speculative theology. A church focused on the work of saving souls and upbuilding the Kingdom of Jesus Christ, MacLaren believed, was not likely to wander from the fundamental verities of the Christian system.[83] When William MacLaren became principal, then, he inherited a faculty put in place by William Caven, and while MacLaren might have had serious misgivings about their theological formulations, he had no hesitations about their piety nor their commitment to the evangelical progress of the church at home and abroad. As a confessional Calvinist who was distinctly evangelical, he continued to hold fast to Reformed doctrine in the belief that it alone could sustain the practice and piety of the church.

MacLaren retired as principal in 1908 to be succeeded by Alfred Gandier. Born in eastern Ontario and raised in the Ottawa Valley, Gandier studied arts and theology at Queen's, where he was a gold medalist under John Watson, and where George Grant was a dominant influence. Watson provided Gandier with a spiritual conception of the universe and an intellectual basis for faith as a theological student facing the questioning of Christianity in the late nineteenth century. This conception seemed to provide a solution to the conflicts and tensions experienced in ideas and social conditions by positing that all reality originated in the Divine mind. All intellectual quandaries and social divisions, therefore, were to be resolved as all people were reconciled to God and the Kingdom of Heaven advanced on the earth. Idealism acted "as a sponge, absorbing all the complexities and contradictions of modern life and holding them together in a moral and religious whole."[84] The philosophical idealism taught by John Watson was modeled in practice by George Monro Grant whose theology and leadership ability in recruiting, fundraising, and building were to be an inspiration for Gandier. Grant was a formidable figure on the theological and ecclesiastical landscape in Canada. As Barry Mack has shown, "it was Grant who directed attention to theological developments in Scotland and who prevented Canadian Presbyterians from following the Princeton lead into a conservative defense of Calvinist orthodoxy."[85] Grant believed that Protestant theology had to be reformulated in the modern world and regarded Hodge's efforts at Princeton as nothing more than sophisticated obscurantism. He was not a liberal modernist, however, but rather a "Romantic evangelical who retained both a strong Calvinist awareness of

---

[83]   Fraser, *Church, College and Clergy,* 93–94.

[84]   Fraser, *The Social Uplifters,* 175.

[85]   Barry Mack, "Of Canadian Presbyterians and Guardian Angels," in *Amazing Grace: Evangelicalism in Australia, Britain, Canada, and the United States,* edited by George A. Rawlyk and Mark A. Noll (Grand Rapids: Baker, 1993) 273.

original sin and a belief in God's electing purpose in history even as he broke away from the Calvinism of double predestination and limited atonement that Robbie Burns had satirized so effectively in poems like 'Holy Willie.'"[86]

Having been shaped powerfully by the thought and example of Watson and Grant, Gandier graduated from Queen's in 1888 and did a year of post-graduate study at Edinburgh to complete the requirements for the B.D. degree. After ministries in Brampton, Ontario and Halifax, Nova Scotia, he was called, in 1900, to be the minister of St. James Square Presbyterian Church where William Caven and many Knox students were members. During these years he taught at Knox as a lecturer until he was appointed as principal, two years after his brother-in-law, Robert Falconer, had been appointed as President of the University of Toronto in 1906. Under Gandier's leadership the morale at the college improved immensely and the plan to relocate and rebuild the college building was realized. Throughout his years as principal Gandier supported the church union movement, believing that the basis of union provided a summary of the great saving truths which lay at the heart of the gospel. In revising the Knox curriculum, he sought to provide a much broader range of practical subjects to prepare students for exercising moral and social leadership in contemporary society. For Walter Bryden, this meant that the Knox College from which he graduated in 1909 was quite different from the college he entered in 1906.

In addition to three quite different principals whose influence and example he encountered at Knox College as a student, Bryden also sat under the teaching of professors who were to shape his developing theological mind. Foremost among them was John Edgar McFadyen, Professor of Old Testament Languages and Literature, who taught his students the newest insights of the historical-critical method of biblical interpretation. Later, McFadyen was instrumental in having Bryden's first book, *The Spirit of Jesus in St. Paul*, published in 1925, adding his own words of commendation in a foreword.[87] McFadyen had been appointed to Knox College in 1898 and just "as John Watson carried the thought of Edward Caird to Canadian shores, so John Edgar McFadyen disseminated the attitudes and teachings of his mentor, George Adam Smith."[88] MacFadyen had studied under Caird at Glasgow and Oxford. He took theology at Free Church College, Glasgow, under A.B. Bruce, Smith and other progressive Calvinists on the Glasgow faculty. After completing his studies with a semester in Marburg, Germany, he began his teaching appointment in Toronto. McFadyen later returned to Scotland

---

[86]   Mack, "Of Canadian Presbyterians and Guardian Angels," 277.

[87]   J. E. McFadyen, "Foreword" in Bryden, *The Spirit of Jesus in St. Paul* (London: James Clarke, 1925) 7–8.

[88]   Fraser, *The Social Uplifters*, 9.

where he served as Professor of Old Testament at the United Free Church College, Glasgow.

McFadyen was not the first, by any means, to introduce higher criticism to the Canadian scene, but he and John Campbell of Presbyterian College, Montreal, were the first prominent scholars to teach the newer views in Presbyterian theological colleges.[89] The influence of higher criticism on Calvinist theology became the controversial focus of diverging Reformed theologies at the end of the nineteenth century, when scholars (such as William Robertson Smith, A. B. Bruce, and Marcus Dods in Scotland, Charles Briggs and Henry Preserved Smith in the United States, and John Campbell in Canada) were charged with heresy by their churches. Behind these developments lay the application of Enlightenment scientific methodologies to the historical study of the Christian faith. A new historical consciousness made a distinction between bare historical facts (*Historie*) and historical interpretation (*Geschichte*) which meant that history could now be explained with reference to continuities and causalities without appeal to divine providence. The implications of this for Calvinist orthodoxy were far-reaching. The history of the church no longer needed to be interpreted with reference to divine sovereignty now that more convincing, natural causes and effects had been uncovered. Confessional statements could be interpreted as representative of a particular historical period rather than the record of eternal truths for all time. And most importantly, the historical critical study of the Bible appeared to challenge traditional conceptions of revelation and inspiration by establishing Holy Scripture as a record of human experience and reflection about God. Higher, or historical criticism, introduced methods of studying the texts of the Bible in their historical setting, raising new questions about the authorship and authenticity of particular biblical books. Having originally emerged in the German universities, higher criticism was adopted and adapted in Britain, the United States, and Canada where it met with substantial controversy, especially among Presbyterians.

McFadyen's commitment to biblical criticism was widely known and through a combination of scholarly study and evangelical piety he was influential in the acceptance of the new methods of biblical studies by Canadian Presbyterian theological students, including Walter Bryden. McFadyen was deeply committed to the view that the use of modern criticism would strengthen the genuine religious commitment of a generation raised on science and Enlightenment ideals. The proper use of criticism did not eviscerate the substance of revelation from the biblical text, he assured Canadian Presbyterians, but rather enabled the message of the gospel to be accessible and credible for the modern critical mind. His work on the Psalms demon-

---

[89]   Fraser, *The Social Uplifters*, 9.

strated just how much he stood in continuity with the experiential religion of Scottish evangelicalism. At the same time his work on the Prophets disclosed the extent to which he had been shaped by the social philosophy of the British idealists.[90] Although Walter Bryden later became idealism's antagonist, he shared the same commitment as McFadyen to the integration of evangelical theology with critical biblical scholarship. The method was entirely appropriate, Bryden would argue, while the conclusions reached by the critical scholars ought not to be accepted uncritically. Bryden owed a great debt to McFadyen for the training in biblical interpretation which the Canadian student received in the Scottish professor's classroom. It was likely McFadyen who encouraged Bryden to study in Glasgow, and it was the methodology of G. A. Smith and John Edgar McFadyen, forged by the fires of pastoral experience, which Bryden employed in *The Spirit of Jesus in St. Paul.* In 1910 McFadyen returned to Glasgow to succeed his mentor George Adam Smith. In McFadyen and others Bryden had continuing connections to theological scholarship in Scotland which he maintained throughout his life.

In October 1905 H. A. A. Kennedy and T. B. Kilpatrick were installed to the chairs of New Testament and systematic theology respectively. Harry Angus Alexander Kennedy, a student at New College, Edinburgh, and a classmate of Robert Falconer's in Berlin, had published *St. Paul's Conception of the Last Things* in 1904. He emphasized two things in this book with which Bryden later resonated in *The Spirit of Jesus in St. Paul.* Firstly, Kennedy emphasized the Hebraic nature of Paul's thought in continuity with the tradition of the Old Testament prophets, and secondly, he located the roots of Paul's eschatological hope "not in any vague speculations concerning human personality in the abstract, but in the relation of the individual soul to the risen Lord Jesus Christ."[91] Kennedy resigned in 1909 to assume the chair of New Testament studies vacated by his teacher Marcus Dods in Scotland.

Thomas Buchanan Kilpatrick was perhaps the most passionate and prolific proponent of progressive Calvinism on the Knox faculty during Bryden's student days. Graduating in 1877 from Glasgow University where he was reputed to have been one of Edward Caird's most brilliant students, Kilpatrick taught at Manitoba College before being appointed to Knox in 1905. Combining evangelical piety with an idealist worldview and a devotion to higher criticism, Kilpatrick quickly assimilated these with the spirit of optimistic nationalism and aggressive Protestantism that he found in Winnipeg in the first decade of the twentieth century. Having been convinced that the Christian faith provided a social vision, he emphasized the Christianization

---

[90] Fraser, *The Social Uplifters,* 10.
[91] H. A. A. Kennedy, *St. Paul's Conception of the Last Things* (London: Hodder and Stoughton, 1904) 341.

of civilization through his vision of a united Protestant church that could act as a national force for spiritual and moral regeneration. The ethical power of Christianity, he believed, was manifested through the creation of individuals and social organisms that had in them the mind of Christ. Such a vision, he argued, could sustain the challenge being faced by ministers in the twentieth century: the breakdown of external authority, the increasingly complex nature of society, and the emerging materialistic attitude to life. In short, Kilpatrick introduced Bryden to a socially progressive form of Calvinism largely shaped by the liberal Protestant mind at the beginning of the twentieth century. Bryden could not get out from under the crises identified by Kilpatrick, nor could he (nor did he wish to) deny the social nature of the Christian gospel. Nevertheless, there was something decidedly unsatisfying about the social gospel which Bryden was only able to identify in his later theological work.[92]

Two other professors served on the Knox faculty during Bryden's student years, James Ballantyne, professor of church history, and John D. Robertson, professor of apologetics, homiletics, and pastoral theology. Appointed to the college in 1896, Ballantyne succeeded William Gregg in the chair that initially covered both apologetics and church history. Born in Stratford, Ontario in 1857, he graduated from Knox College in 1883, and pursued graduate studies in Princeton, Edinburgh, and Leipzig. He was the minister of Knox Church, Ottawa when appointed to his teaching position, and he saw an important connection between apologetics and church history. The history of the church, when taught from the perspective of faith, provided a persuasive interpretation of the life of the Christian community in the modern world:

> The historian must exhibit this subject as the history of the Church of Christ—this history not of an isolated community with inferior and selfish ends in view, but of the most wonderful organization the world has known, maintaining itself as no other, and comprehending the vastest purposes possible to the grasp of man. God has made a revelation of himself to man. The object of this revelation is to meet man's need as a sinner by offering him redemption. It is centred in the person and work of Jesus Christ, in the facts of a divine-human life. For this culminating event of all history there was a long preparation, and the record of the society founded by Him is but the narration of the working out of the historical fact for which the world had been preparing.[93]

---

92 Fraser, *The Social Uplifters*, 27-43; idem, *Church, College, and Clergy*, 115–39.
93 James Ballantyne, "The Scope and Uses of the Study of Church History," *Westminster* (9 Oct. 1897) 280–81, cited in Fraser, *Church, College, and Clergy*, 100–101.

This is an important description of church history by Bryden's professor for at least three reasons. First, Bryden himself was to occupy the chair of church history at Knox College after church union. Secondly, Bryden offered a definition of church history in his own lectures which bears a striking similarity to that of Ballantyne in its emphasis on the theological character of church history. But thirdly, and most importantly, Ballantyne centered church history in the revelation of God in the person and work of Jesus Christ, which Bryden took as the starting point for all his own theological and historical work. Ballantyne was concerned to demonstrate to his students, through the study of church history, that there was indeed a gospel to preach in the twentieth century. In the post-union church Walter Bryden assumed as much. He used church history to preach the gospel of revelation to students in a church undergoing a crisis of identity. In short, building upon Ballantyne's emphasis on apologetics, Bryden developed an approach to church history which was both apologetic and kergymatic.

John D. Robertson was appointed to Knox College as professor of apologetics, homiletics, and pastoral theology in 1903. As a graduate in philosophy from Edinburgh University in 1880 he had a solid grounding in the evolutionary moral and religious worldview of idealist philosophy, the historical methods of the believing practitioners of higher criticism, and the movements among university students to spread the intellectual and social benefits of Protestantism throughout the world.[94] He studied theology at the Divinity Hall of the United Presbyterians under John Caird, and completed a Ph.D. from Edinburgh which included studies in France and Germany. Having served as the minister of the United Free Church of Scotland in North Berwick, he had written two books by the time of his appointment to Knox, *Conscience* and *The Work of the Holy Spirit in Christian Service*. Representing a form of progressive Calvinism, Robertson believed that the highest modern ideals of life and work were rooted in the Christian faith.

In sum, the Calvinism of Knox College in the first decade of the twentieth century represented a theology in transition with a number of diverging but moderate trajectories. Knox College, and the Presbyterian Church in Canada, which it served, had adapted to the theological challenges at the end of the nineteenth century without a great deal of division and turmoil, perhaps out of a continuing commitment to Baconian forms of reasoning, or perhaps simply out of practical necessity. In the words of Clarence MacKinnon, principal of the Presbyterian Theological College in Halifax (Pine Hill), Presbyterians had entered the twentieth century "with perhaps less irritation than any other part of Christendom." The harsh outlines of the Westminster Confession had been softened with a measure of evangelical piety, historical

---

94 Fraser, *Church, College, and Clergy*, 97.

consciousness, and social awareness. As Barry Mack has noted, MacKinnon attributed the smoothness of this shift to a special "spiritual tact… a peculiar practical instinct, [which] like a guardian angel, sifted for her what was eternal in the old and what was of advantage in the new, and enabled her to make the inevitable adjustments."[95] Knox's own John McFadyen also acknowledged the somewhat peculiar theological position of the Presbyterian Church in Canada at the turn of the century. In a memorial tribute to W. Halliday Douglas, who had died after teaching at Knox for only one year, McFadyen commented on the nature of theological teaching:

> The urgent pressure of the practical problems has left little time for speculative and scholarly pursuits, and the general temper of the Church has been not unnaturally conservative, though by no means obstinately so. At the same time many, especially though not exclusively among the younger men, some of whom have studied in Britain, have felt the growing importance and even necessity of keeping the Church in touch with the movements of modern theological scholarship. Thus the general conservative leanings of the Church are tempered by a distinctly progressive and growing influential element; and the occupant of the chair [of apologetics, homiletics, and pastoral theology] had to be, if possible, a man who could satisfy the hopes of both parties. He must neither be an obscurantist nor a radical; he had, on the one hand, to be able to reassure the conservative spirits, and on the other, he had to justify the hopes of those who believe that theology has a future as well as a past.[96]

Within this context, the live options for a bright young Presbyterian theological student like Walter Bryden in the first decade of the twentieth century were roughly four in number. First, there was a *confessional Calvinism* represented by William MacLaren who continued to rely on the Princeton theologians and the seventeenth-century Protestant scholastics, and who continued to employ Scottish Common Sense and Baconian inductive reasoning in theology. Secondly, there was a *conservative Calvinism* represented by William Caven who, while continuing to affirm the great essential truths of the Reformed faith, nevertheless was willing to accept the accommodation of others to the new challenges. Thirdly, there was a *progressive Calvinism* which emerged among the younger and newer faculty like McFadyen, Kennedy, Ballantyne, and Robertson, most of whom had been educated in Britain under Scottish liberal evangelical scholars, and who combined evangelical

---

[95]   Cited in John Thomas McNeill, *The Presbyterian Church in Canada, 1875–1925* (Toronto: General Boad Presbyterian Church in Canada, 1925) ix. See also Mack, "Of Canadian Presbyterians and Guardian Angels," 270–71.

[96]   John Edgar McFadyen, cited by Fraser, *Church, College, and Clergy*, 104.

piety with historical critical study of the Bible and an idealist and Darwinian worldview. This was also the Romantic evangelicalism represented by Alfred Gandier and George Munro Grant. Fourthly, there was the *liberal Calvinism* of T. B. Kilpatrick who moved slightly further in the adoption of liberal Protestant theology and the social gospel. In his later work, Bryden clearly rejected the first and the fourth options, referring polemically to confessional Calvinism as 'rational orthodoxy' and to liberal Calvinism as 'modernism.' The neo-orthodox conception of revelation which he later espoused stands closer to the second and third options, although as we shall see, there are discontinuities as well as continuities. But the options presented to Bryden at Knox College were to be refined further through his personal exposure to Scottish liberal evangelical Calvinism in Glasgow.

United Free Church College Glasgow, 1907–1908

Bryden spent his second year of theological study at the United Free Church College in Glasgow, an experience which was to be decisive in his theological formation. As important as Bryden's years at Knox may have been, they seemed to provide the prelude and postlude to what he considered to be his formative theological education. The Scottish teachers loom large in his later writings, and he was particularly fond of quoting Denney and Lindsay in his lectures. The connections between Knox College and the United Free Church colleges in Scotland were, of course, quite strong, especially in the persons of McFadyen and Kennedy, and Bryden's sense of swimming in the formidable theological stream they represented is entirely understandable. The United Free Church was formed in 1900 by the union between the United Presbyterian Church and the Free Church, and was a broadly evangelical body. As one historian has noted, "Its theological and practical ethos was that of liberal Evangelicalism, blending a moderate higher criticism, an acceptance of the findings of contemporary science, and a commitment to evangelism and missions."[97] One of the characteristic features of the United Free Church during this period was its attitude to confessions of faith, subordinate standards, and church constitutions. In 1906, after a period of conflict, the Church adopted the Act Anent Spiritual Independence of the Church, which gave its General Assembly plenary power "to alter, change, add to, or modify, her constitution and laws, Subordinate Standards, and Formulas, and to determine and declare what these are, and to unite with other Christian Churches." Within this framework of confessional theology,

---

[97] N. R. Needham, "United Free Church," in *Dictionary of Scottish Church History and Theology*, edited by Nigel M. de S. Cameron (Edinburgh: T. & T. Clark, 1993) 838.

the liberal evangelical spectrum was able to embrace varying doctrinal positions, as can be gauged from the presence of both George Adam Smith and James Orr within the United Free Church and its college in Glasgow.

George Adam Smith, McFadyen's mentor, represented the combination of evangelical piety and critical biblical scholarship that gained a wide hearing among many Scottish and Canadian Presbyterians. Born in 1856, Smith served as Professor of Old Testament Language and Literature at the United Free Church College in Glasgow from 1892 until 1909. Smith's defense of critical methods in biblical studies and their beneficial results were clearly set out in 1901 with the publication of his Yale lectures, *Modern Criticism and the Preaching of the Old Testament.* Following the W.R. Smith heresy trial in Scotland, Smith had set himself to "reconcile the outlook of an advanced scientific scholar with the spirit of devout reverence."[98] The use of critical methods, he argued, did not undermine the authority and inspiration of the Bible. Critical study was an important means of bringing the Bible to life for people because it helped them understand the experience of faith that produced the biblical record. The Old Testament was a record of progressive revelation and the highest form of ethical monotheism was to be seen in the Psalms and the Prophets. Smith's views, however, did not prevail in the United Free Church without a fight. In 1902, charged with heresy, Smith faced the possibility of censure, or worse, for his views. In the end, the General Assembly voted overwhelmingly 534 to 263 to dismiss the charge, at which point Smith's view became part of the accepted tradition within the United Free Church. The same view, as we have seen, prevailed within the Canadian Presbyterian church.[99]

Having studied under John McFadyen at Knox, Bryden had already been introduced to Smith's approach, but now in Glasgow he had the opportunity to experience it first-hand. The neo-orthodox theology which Bryden later embraced and espoused assumed that critical biblical scholarship was an appropriate method of biblical interpretation. In this sense, Bryden's later theology stood in continuity with the accommodation of Christian theology to the critical *method* of the Enlightenment, forged in the liberal evangelicalism of late nineteenth-century Scottish Calvinism. It also stood in continuity with this tradition in its insistence, at least for Bryden, upon the need for a living and authentic experience of God, a combination of evangelical piety with critical scholarship. Where it differed, and this became increasingly important, was that Bryden and the neo-orthodox theologians refused to accept the liberal *conclusions* of critical scholarship, and they rejected the assumption

---

[98]   C. G. Thorne, "George Adam Smith," in *The New International Dictionary of the Christian Church,* edited by J. D. Douglas (Grand Rapids: Zondervan, 1978) 910.
[99]   Fraser, *The Social Uplifters,* 9.

that the theological meaning of the biblical text could be guaranteed through critical study. Biblical criticism made the text more accessible, perhaps, and it was certainly a useful and appropriate tool, but it was not adequate in and of itself. The living Word of God in Jesus Christ attested to by Holy Scripture, Bryden would argue, was at the disposal of God, and God alone. The interpreter waited for God to manifest Godself in the text.

At the other end of the theological spectrum from George Adam Smith was James Orr, with whom Bryden also studied in Glasgow. Orr taught systematic theology and apologetics at the United Free Church College in Glasgow from 1901 until his death in 1913. While retreating from strict confessional Calvinism, he defended the central tenets of evangelical orthodoxy with wide-ranging scholarship and was one of the earliest and principal critics of Albrecht Ritschl's thought in Britain.[100] In *The Ritschlian Theology and Evangelical Faith*, Orr argued that Ritschl's theology was opposed to genuine Christianity, not only because it denied the truth of the Christian claim, but because it did so by limiting the role of reason in Christian thought and experience, making Christianity intellectually untenable. In his first book, *The Christian View of God and the World*, Orr offered an apologetic for what he considered to be an adequate and coherent interpretation of human existence inherent in the Christian faith.[101] In other books he tackled the challenge of biblical criticism in Old Testament scholarship, the doctrine of inspiration, the virgin birth, the resurrection of Jesus, and the Darwinian challenge to the Christian doctrine of sin. Through his books and lectures, Orr increasingly became recognized as a staunch defender of evangelical orthodoxy in the midst of the rising tide of liberal Protestantism on both sides of the Atlantic. In 1903 he gave the prestigious Stone Lectures at Princeton Seminary and also contributed to the series of books known as *The Fundamentals*. Nevertheless, Orr recognized the need for Calvinism to come to terms with the new realities. He campaigned for a modified subscription to the Westminster Confession of Faith within his church. He accepted the plenary inspiration of the Bible but regarded the Princeton school's insistence upon the inerrancy of the Bible as apologetically suicidal. Instead, he favored a doctrine of Scripture which he believed was in continuity with the Reformation, if not the whole history of the church, and with the Bible's witness concerning itself.[102] Orr's theological contribution "was decisively shaped by the convictions that evangelical orthodoxy is self-authenticating, that truth comprises a unity or interconnected

---

[100] Glen G. Scorgie, "James Orr," in *Scottish Dictionary of Church History and Theology*, 639. For a thorough study of Orr's theology, see also Scorgie, *A Call for Continuity*.

[101] Scorgie, *A Call for Continuity*, 48.

[102] Jack B. Rogers and Donald McKim, *The Authority and Interpretation of the Bible* (San Francisco: Harper and Row, 1979) 380–85.

whole, and that genuine Christian belief implies a two-storied supernatural cosmology."[103]

In many ways Bryden was less impressed with the more conservative Orr than with the liberal evangelical Calvinism to which he was being introduced in Glasgow. Nevertheless, two things stand out about Orr's theology in relation to Bryden. First, Orr represented a conservative Calvinism not unlike that espoused by William Caven, rather than the stricter confessional Calvinism represented by William MacLaren and the Princeton theologians. Orr was a Reformed theologian committed to defending Calvinist orthodoxy but not at the expense of theological integrity and clarity. In short, Orr was not an obscurantist. As an apologist he recognized that the challenges of biblical criticism, idealist philosophy, Darwinian thought, and Ritschlian theology could not be set aside, and he sought to meet them head-on. Secondly, Orr was probably the first teacher to introduce Bryden to a comprehensive and critical examination of Albrecht Ritschl's thought, fuelling the fire of Bryden's later polemic against modernism which he conceived of largely in terms of Ritschl's influence.

The leading lights at Glasgow for Bryden, however, were T.M. Lindsay and James Denney. Thomas Martin Lindsay was elected to the chair of church history in 1872 at the age of twenty-nine, and served until his death in 1914. From 1902 he was also principal. Making reference to "the things I learned in Principal Lindsay's classroom while a student in Glasgow,"[104] Bryden's own lectures in church history reveal an indebtedness to Lindsay's two main books, *Luther and the German Reformation* (1900) and the two-volume *A History of the Reformation* (1906–1907),[105] a substantial Scottish account of the Reformation with particular attention paid to the social and domestic aspects. Lindsay was involved in the labor movement, favored a more liberal approach to confessional subscription, and also actively supported William Robertson Smith in the heresy trial before the Free Church of Scotland (1877–1881) in which Smith's doctrine of Scripture was questioned.

On the issue of Scripture Lindsay's critique of the Princeton theologians in the first volume of his history of the Reformation is of particular significance. In a chapter titled "The Religious Principles Inspiring The Reformation," Lindsay set forth his understanding of the Reformation doctrine of Holy Scripture. In defense of W.R. Smith, Lindsay argued that Smith's doctrine of the Bible agreed with the Reformation doctrine and differed only

---

[103]   Scorgie, "James Orr," 639.

[104]   Bryden, *Separated Unto the Gospel*, 66.

[105]   Bryden, "Church History: Introductory;" "History of the Church of England;" "History of the Church of Scotland;" "Church History: The Period from the Great Creeds to the Reformation;" and "Church History: Post-Reformation History of the Church Up to 1648."

with the Princeton school's interpretation of it. In the course of the chapter Lindsay gave a lengthy critique of Hodge's doctrine of inspiration and argued that it stood in continuity with seventeenth-century Reformed scholasticism but not the Reformation. According to Lindsay the Princeton theologians had a purely intellectual apprehension of Scripture. They reduced the real distinction between the Word of God and Scripture to a formal difference. Their formal, as opposed to a religious, idea of the infallibility and authority of Scripture was problematic; and their still more formal relegation of the strict infallibility of the Bible to unknown and unknowable original autographs could simply not be justified.[106] This direct appeal to the Reformation, reaching behind the Reformed scholastic theology of the seventeenth and eighteenth centuries, rooted in historical study, left a deep imprint on Bryden's understanding of Calvinism.

"The prince of Scottish theologians" whose "terse observations, as the years go by, seem to become ever more pregnant with meaning."[107] That's the way Bryden referred to James Denney, upon whom he looked as a mentor and guide through the perplexities of theology at the beginning the twentieth century. After serving eleven years as the minister of the East Church, Broughty Ferry, Denney was appointed in 1897 to the chair of systematic theology at the Free Church College, Glasgow (after 1900 the United Free Church College). Denney was named professor of New Testament Language, Literature and Theology, in 1900, and principal in 1915. His works included *Jesus and the Gospel* (1908), *The Death of Christ* (1902), *The Atonement and the Modern Mind* (1903), *The Christian Doctrine of Reconciliation* (1917), *The Second Epistle to the Corinthians* (1894), *The Epistles to the Thessalonians* (1892), *Studies in Theology* (1894), and *The Way Everlasting* (1911). Denney had been schooled in strict Calvinism but increasingly came to embrace a broader historical understanding. He focused on the Pauline gospel of redemption and was passionately Christ-centered in his theology: "Christ is the whole of Christianity—Christ crucified and risen." He tried to shift the focus away from the quest for the historical Jesus to the reality of the risen and ascended Christ, present to the life of the Christian believer and the church. At the same time, he rejected all forms of speculative Christology and believed that Christ was known through what he had done. Denney refused to separate the incarnation from the atonement. Thus the atonement and the Pauline doctrine of redemption were central. Denney emphasized strongly that total depravity, human guilt and shame needed to be addressed by a brutal, costly

---

106 Rogers and McKim, *The Authority and Interpretation of the Bible*, 380–85.

107 Bryden, *The Significance of the Westminster Confession of Faith* (Toronto: University of Toronto Press, 1943) 27; "The Presbyterian Conception of the Word of God," unpublished manuscript.

atonement. In regard to the Bible, Denney had little time for arguments in favor of the verbal inerrancy of Scripture because he believed the focus was misplaced. The authority of Scripture, for Denney, lay in the infallibility of its power to mediate a saving word of grace in the power of the Holy Spirit, not in some abstract doctrinal formulation concerning its nature. While he was anti-Ritschlian, he resisted metaphysics in his Christology and argued that Christ could only truly be described with the language of religious faith. Firmly committed to the evangelical proclamation of the gospel throughout his life, he believed that "if evangelists were our theologians, or theologians our evangelists, we should at least be nearer the ideal Church."[108]

Denney's Christ-centered emphasis, his commitment to the gospel of redemption, and his approach to Scripture, pointed Bryden to a Calvinist theology which could be preached, a biblical theology rooted not in speculation but in history, a theology which was developed as "church dogmatics." Denney also helped Bryden to see that the knowledge of God which issued from faith was a paradox.[109] For a biblical theologian, faithfulness to the New Testament revelation required an acceptance of the dialectical, paradoxical, and even contradictory nature of the revelation and the accompanying Christian faith. Following Denney, Bryden came to see the centrality of the incarnation and the atonement together for Christian faith. The question of the relation between the finite and the infinite could only be addressed christologically, even though this was a paradox, rationally and ethically, which could never be fully apprehended by reason or experience.[110] Human beings, in creaturely finitude and in sin, were totally unable to apprehend this revelation in Jesus Christ apart from the gracious ministry of the Holy Spirit.[111] The resonance between Denney's insistence on the centrality of the cross in dealing with human sin and the later neo-orthodox reaction against liberal Protestantism's naïve optimism and humanism is striking. Holy Scripture, Denney argued and Bryden believed, is a means of grace by which, through the gracious testimony of the Holy Spirit, God communicates with human beings, making them know what is in God's heart towards them.[112] In this way, Denney did not follow the method of the Westminster Confession of Faith in which the Bible is first established as the epistemological basis for the Christian faith. Although he had a good deal of respect for the Princeton theologians, he diverged from them on this fundamental point: "Hence it follows that,

---

[108]   James Denney, *The Death of Christ.* Cited in Bryden, *Separated Unto the Gospel*, iii; see also K. R. Ross, "James Denney," *Dictionary of Scottish Church History and Theology*, 240.

[109]   Bryden, *The Significance of the Westminster Confession of Faith*, 27.

[110]   Ibid., 27.

[111]   Ibid., 29.

[112]   James Denney, *Studies in Theology* (London: Hodder and Stoughton, 1894) 202.

while the inspiration of the Scriptures is true, and, being true, is a principle fundamental to the adequate interpretation of Scripture, it nevertheless is not in the first instance a principle fundamental to the truth of the Christian religion."[113] Holy Scripture, as the record of revelation, must be known as the Word of God before doctrinal definitions may be set forth by the interpreter. Denney conceded that historical criticism had a limited usefulness but always emphasized what he considered to be a theological interpretation of the Bible which could be preached in the church. The theology of James Denney, in both its formal and material aspects, prepared the ground for Bryden's reception of Karl Barth some twenty years later. Denney's Calvinism was a theology with which Bryden resonated because it represented the re-appropriation of Reformation insights in the midst of Enlightenment challenges.

ooooo

After returning to Canada in 1908 Bryden completed his theological studies at Knox College and prepared for ordination and ministry within the Presbyterian Church in Canada. He had traveled a long distance, geographically, intellectually, and theologically, in the seven years since leaving the family farm on the banks of the Grand River in western Ontario to study at the University of Toronto. It is not difficult to imagine that he entered the Christian ministry in 1909 with some apprehension. His education had introduced him to new ways of thinking about the world, to a Calvinism in transition, and to a church both emboldened and intimidated by the optimistic and progressive ethos of Canadian society in the opening decade of the twentieth century. He had been shaped by the Presbyterian tradition of the nineteenth century in Canada, its democratic form of government, its simplicity of worship, its dissenting Free Church heritage, its Calvinist doctrine supported by Scottish Common Sense, its unifying spirit, and its evangelical piety. He was still a Presbyterian, to be sure, but what kind of Presbyterian? He had been challenged to re-examine the Reformed tradition by idealist philosophy (especially as espoused by George Paxton Young), by the increasing hegemony of the Darwinian worldview, by the social criticism of religion embodied in Marxism, and by biblical criticism.

He did not, however, face these challenges alone. Bryden's theological education at Knox College had introduced him to a variety of trajectories within the Reformed theological tradition, each seeking, in its own way, to map out a future for the church and for theology in light of the trends and transitions at the beginning of the twentieth century. Furthermore, the Canadian context moderated and mediated the differences that had created

---

[113] Ibid., 203.

serious rifts in the United States and Great Britain so that the choices were not so stark. But there were still choices to be made, and in Canada at least four options, not mutually exclusive, presented themselves: (1) confessional Calvinism (2) conservative Calvinism; (3) progressive Calvinism; and (4) liberal Calvinism.

The options were clarified through Bryden's formative experience at the United Free Church College in Glasgow, where he was given the opportunity to study with some of the leading liberal evangelical scholars in the Scottish church. There he found Reformed theologians who were seeking to recover and set forth the Calvinist faith while taking seriously the impact of the Enlightenment upon conceptions of reason, revelation, history, and religion. Modeling a combination of evangelical piety, historical and biblical scholarship, they affirmed the reality of revelation and yet employed critical methods. Self-consciously believing church theologians, they emphasized the centrality of Christ and his work of redemption. Rejecting both the confessional orthodoxy of the Princeton theologians and the liberal Protestantism of Schleiermacher and Ritschl, they pointed to the well-spring of faith and life to be found in the Reformation's recovery of the New Testament gospel, in its Pauline and Augustinian form, as the basis for Christian faith and life at the beginning of the twentieth century. They were theologians of Word and Spirit, who stressed the authority of the Bible as the Word of God, authenticated by the internal testimony of the Holy Spirit. Leery of undue emphases on either doctrine or experience, they advocated a knowledge of God grounded in the gracious acts of a gracious God. The intellectual roots of Bryden's Calvinism were nourished and developed through their influence. They prepared the ground for Bryden's theological development as a parish minister, and his subsequent reception of Karl Barth's theology. In short, they prepared the way for the emergence of Walter Bryden as a neo-orthodox voice in the Canadian church.

2

The Emergence of a Neo-Orthodox Voice

No I am not a Barthian but Barth did two things for me, he drove me back to the Bible and to my old teacher James Denney.
—Walter Bryden

IN his inaugural lecture on installation as principal of Knox College in October 1945, Walter Bryden referred to the resentment which had been aroused because "a certain challenging theology of the day" had been addressing the Church, Christians and people in terms that seemed "to diminish the significance of human personality and accomplishments."[1] By the end of World War II the theology of Karl Barth and the influence of the Barthian movement were well-known, and Walter Bryden had come to be regarded as one of the ablest and most articulate neo-orthodox voices in Canadian Protestantism. Students from the late 1920s and the 1930s recalled a provocative, polemical, prophetic type of teacher who was among the first church leaders in North America to see the significance of Barth. By the mid-1940s Bryden had become a senior theological statesman within the Presbyterian Church in Canada and to the extent that there was any serious theological discussion, the neo-orthodox position to which he gave voice tended to dominate the discourse of the denomination.

Bryden was nervous about theological labels, and he denied he was a Barthian as such. Indeed, his students argued that "he came through to his basic theological position on his own" hammering out the truth in "the forge of his own soul, in terms of his own flesh and blood struggle for faith."[2] Nevertheless, they also remembered that Bryden almost always quoted Barth

---

[1] Bryden, "The Church of God and the World," in *Separated Unto the Gospel*, 46.
[2] Donald V. Wade, "The Theological Achievement of Walter Bryden," unpublished paper presented to the Karl Barth Society of North America, 1974, 6.

approvingly, defended Barth against his critics, and sought to work out the implications of the continental theological renewal associated with Barth's name for Canadian churches. Bryden's students also insisted that he was neither a slavish nor uncritical interpreter of Barth's theology, and that he seemed fully sensitive to "the fact that Canada was not Europe, and transplants, theological or otherwise, were not wholly appropriate."[3] At the same time, what Bryden said in the 1930s and 1940s sounded strangely new and offensive to Canadian Protestants. It came as a word from beyond their situation, and it landed with great force on their ecclesial landscape. And that was largely due to Bryden's discovery of the theological protest in Barth's early theology. The more he read Barth's theology, the more Bryden came to see that Barth's formal theological method and his material interpretation of the Reformed tradition offered a way beyond idealism and rationalism. Barth's early theology confirmed and widened the grasp of biblical and reformed principles which had already been forming in Bryden's mind, and it gave him the categories to articulate with a fresh, strong voice the central themes of Presbyterian theology. This made him, at least in the eyes of his students, a rather rare person, an original Canadian theologian who sought to address the peculiarities of the Canadian scene in light of the new insights of European theology.[4]

The emergence of Bryden's mature theological voice on behalf of a neo-orthodox protest within Canadian Protestantism, however, did not take place overnight. It was forged in the fires of almost seventeen years of pastoral ministry, developed behind the lectern of a classroom in a theological college for two decades, and then used to exercise leadership for seven years as a college principal. The purpose of this chapter is to examine the emergence, development, and dominance of that theological voice within the Presbyterian sphere of Canadian Protestantism.

Presbyterian Minister, 1909–1926

Socialism, Idealism, and the Great War

After returning to Canada to complete his final year of theological study, Walter Bryden was ordained and appointed to be the minister of St. Andrew's Presbyterian Church in Lethbridge, Alberta, a ministry that he later referred to as "spade work in Western Canada" because it involved establishing a new congregation in the north part of town, an extension of Knox Presbyterian

---

[3] J. Charles Hay, "Allan Farris," in *The Tide of Time*, edited by John Moir (Toronto: Knox College, 1978), 16.

[4] Ibid.

Church.[5] During the late nineteenth century the Western Canadian frontier had emerged as an important missionary field for Canadian Presbyterians. Ralph Connor's early novels had romanticized the late Victorian missionaries who were able to overcome great hardships and challenges and successfully evangelize because of tremendous faith and unwavering dedication. James Robertson, the superintendent of missions for the Presbyterian Church in Canada, almost single-handedly established the presence of the Presbyterian Church in Manitoba and beyond. The missionaries of Connor's early novels embodied the Calvinist doctrine and evangelical piety represented by Robertson. They were evangelists and revivalists who encouraged people to profess faith in Jesus Christ as Savior and Lord in order to be received into the church. By the end of the nineteenth century, however, confidence in the value of the Western evangelistic missionary effort had begun to fade. Inadequate financial support accompanied by the influence of progressive Calvinism reoriented the churches toward the ideals of ecumenical cooperation and social Christianity.[6] It was this expression of Christianity that Bryden encountered in his first pastoral ministry in Western Canada.

In the early years the congregation which Bryden helped establish met in Redding's Hall and the Bailey Street School, but by 1911 construction of the first church building was undertaken with voluntary labor.[7] Lethbridge was a mining town and Bryden soon came to know the struggle of coal-miners for fair wages and safe working conditions. Many years later Donald Wade noted that Bryden's "experiences among the coal-miners of the west remind one of Reinhold Niebuhr's experiences in Detroit."[8] Another parallel, however, perhaps stronger, is to be found between Bryden's experience and Barth's involvement in the socialist movement during the years of his Safenwil pastorate (1911–21). Recent Barth scholarship has noted that Barth's theology was concerned for responsible action in the world and characterized by a commitment to democratic socialism. Refusing to divorce theology from ethics, Barth's early article "Jesus Christ and the Movement for Social Justice" set out the rationale for his vocal criticism of child labor and exploitative capitalism. At the beginning of his ministry Barth had worked to arouse the social conscience of the church on behalf of the workers, and saw democratic socialism as an ally. Following the outbreak of World War One, however, he feared the nationalist tendencies and narrow interests of the social democratic movement and developed a radical critique of Marxist-Leninist doctrine, arguing

---

5   Bryden, *Separated Unto the Gospel*, 131.

6   David B. Marshall, *Secularizing the Faith*, 99–126.

7   William Hay, *History of the Presbyterian Church in Lethbridge*, Presbyterian Church Archives.

8   Donald Wade, "The Theological Achievement of Walter Bryden," 3.

not that it was too radical but that it was not radical enough. The Christian, Barth contended, was engaged in permanent revolution while Leninism simply substituted one form of an oppressive state for another. Nevertheless, as Martin Rumscheidt has noted, Barth believed that a socialist *may* be a Christian, but that a Christian *should* be a socialist.[9]

Bryden's southwestern Ontario roots had already made him deeply sensitive to the exploitation of the working class by the family compact system, so it was no surprise that Bryden, like Barth, supported local efforts to organize the labor movement. In particular the young Canadian minister learned about the activities of the Industrial Workers of the World and the Western Miner's Federation, confessing later to his students that he learned a great deal about the meaning of the New Testament from the Marxist miners of Lethbridge. Bryden could see that the church in Canada had not only allowed itself to be used as a tool for exploitation, but that it had actually contributed to the creation of an entire system of oppression. The effective criticism of society, he concluded, began with the criticism of Christianity. Bryden stopped short, however, of embracing the increasingly popular Social Gospel, primarily because it seemed to him to reflect the progressive ideals against which he struggled.[10] On the one hand, he argued later, "a mere social gospel is never the Christian gospel, and the Kingdom of God is not to be equated with advances in social readjustment."[11] At the same time, his experience in Lethbridge made him merciless in his criticism of monopolistic capitalism: "The sober fact is that nothing has ever appeared among men which has been more cynically regardless of any ethic worth the name than the ruthless, competitive economic system which is known as Capitalism."[12] Capitalism, Bryden believed, despoiled the original intention of democracy and tended to secularize the Christian faith by making the success of the church dependent upon a consumer society. There was not a little truth in the statement, he believed, "that democracy as it exists in a capitalist society represents the best form of government ever devised for a privileged ruling class to exploit the

---

[9]   H.-Martin Rumscheidt has been responsible for making the theology of Karl Barth more widely known in Canada. See, for example, H.-Martin Rumscheidt, editor, *Karl Barth in Re-View: Posthumous Works Reviewed and Assessed,* Pittsburgh Theological Monograph Series 30 (Pittsburgh: Pickwick, 1981).

[10]   For Bryden's later references to the Social Gospel, see *Why I Am A Presbyterian,* 116; and *The Spirit of Jesus in St. Paul,* 160.

[11]   Bryden, "The Presbyterian Conception of the Word of God," unpublished portion of manuscript, The Presbyterian Church Archives.

[12]   Bryden, *The Christian's Knowledge of God,* 244.

masses."[13] Yet, he also insisted that he made these statements "without being either socialist or communist in any orthodox sense."[14]

All this began when, as a young Presbyterian minister in Western Canada, Walter Bryden found his theological education severely tried and tested by the ideals of socialism and capitalism. Only later would he be able to reflect clearly on the challenge and conclude that all earthly systems stood under the judgment of God, that humanity's existence was marked by a state of constant crisis, and that the Christian faith, rightly understood, demanded a state of constant revolution as the reign of God breaks into the world. Like Barth, Bryden continued to support democratic socialism but was neither a party theorist nor activist. Originally a Liberal, Bryden supported the Cooperative Commonwealth Federation after the 1930s and was known, according to his son Kenneth Bryden, to have voted Communist on one or more occasions. In short, Walter Bryden never developed a Christian social philosophy which he sought to implement, not because he thought that social ethics were unimportant, but precisely because he believed that the church's role in the social and political sphere was of such importance that a theoretical ethic would always miss the mark. What was required of the church in a world of crisis was an "occasional" and "ad hoc" protest against the domestication of the gospel and the exploitation of the marginalized. The Christian movement, at its best, created freedom for the declaration of the prophetic Word of God. Formal alignments between Christianity and capitalism, or Christianity and Marxism, undermined the gospel and the social vision of the New Testament. To be sure, this was not altogether clear to Bryden in the years between 1909 and 1912. Nevertheless, at this stage Bryden was willing to move beyond the constraints of the old orthodoxies while reserving the right to distance himself from the new ideals.

During his tenure as the minister of St. Andrew's, Lethbridge, Walter Bryden married Violet Nasmith Bannatyne (1884–1969). Born in Scotland, Bannatyne had trained as a teacher and taught for a time in the slums of Glasgow before emigrating to Canada. Her father, a supporter of Gladstone's Liberals in Britain, had worked in the Glasgow shipyards. The Brydens had two sons: William Bannatyne Bryden, who was born on August 10, 1911 in Lethbridge and died at the age of fourteen on August 25, 1925 in Woodville, Ontario; and Walter Kenneth Bryden, who worked as a civil servant in the Saskatchewan government of Tommy Douglas, served as a New Democratic member of the Ontario Legislature (1959–67), and taught political economy at the University of Toronto. He died in Toronto in 2002.

---

13 Ibid., 244–45.
14 Ibid., 247.

After three years in Lethbridge, the Bryden family moved east to Ontario. There, from 1912 to 1921, Walter Bryden served as the minister of Knox Presbyterian Church, Woodville—"a quiet little village in the heart of old Ontario."[15] Knox Church had been founded in 1848 as a congregation of the Free Church and represented the kind of congregation within which Bryden had been raised in Knox's, Galt. During the years in Woodville, Bryden gave himself to the task of preaching and, according to his parishioners and students, he was "like a flame in the pulpit."[16]

Within a few years, however, Western Canada beckoned Bryden again, this time a call to St. James Presbyterian Church in Melfort, Saskatchewan, the congregation where the well-known Presbyterian leader W.A. Cameron had ministered. St. James had been established in 1903. A new church building opened on April 30, 1905. In 1921, when Bryden became its minister, the congregation had a membership of forty and an annual revenue of $1,526.[17] After having ministered in an established Ontario congregation for almost a decade, Bryden once again found himself in a small, recently established, struggling, frontier church. He was remembered by the people there for his love of baseball and his work with the young people of the town. Ministry in a small western congregation afforded him time to write, and there he completed most of the manuscript of *The Spirit of Jesus in St. Paul* for publication.

At the same time, the movement for church union among Presbyterians, Methodists, and Congregationalists, which had originated in 1902 and drawn almost unanimous support in Western Canada, had gained the approval and momentum required to bring it to culmination in 1925. In 1924, for reasons that are not clear, Walter Bryden resigned as the minister of St. James Church and moved the family back to Galt, Ontario. According to Kenneth Bryden, the decision was precipitated by illness in the family. But was there more to it? Had there been difficulty in the relationship between the pastor and people of St. James, the kind of tension in pastoral ministry to which Bryden alluded in *The Spirit of Jesus in St. Paul*? Did Bryden see that the proposed church union was about to sweep across Western Canada and dramatically redraw denominational lines? At the age of forty-one did Bryden experience a crisis of faith and/or vocation? Did he anticipate the possibility of a teaching position if he were closer to the center of the church? Whatever the reason, it was a rather strange and dramatic decision which, as it happened, prepared the way for his subsequent appointment to Knox College. For a year Bryden

---

15   Bryden, "The Triumph of Reality," in *Separated Unto the Gospel*, 131.
16   Wade, "The Theological Achievement of Walter Bryden," 3.
17   B. Wittome and C. Bush, "St. James Presbyterian Church History," The Presbyterian Church Archives.

served as a supply preacher and immersed himself in the church union debate in preparation for the final vote at the General Assembly in 1925. As difficult as the decision was for him, he sided with the anti-unionists. Soon he was called by the continuing Presbyterians in Woodville, Ontario, once again to become their minister. He accepted the call while also agreeing to teach at Knox College on a part-time basis.

Bryden's pastoral experience was formative as he continued to find his theological voice. For one thing, the philosophical idealism he had imbibed as a university student was now creating waves among the rank and file membership of the churches in Canada. Idealism offered a powerful vision of an evolving Christianity in the progressive development of western civilization. Darwinism, Marxism, Freudianism, industrialization, urbanization, and consumerism had created a restless intellectual spirit across the country and a not inconsiderable challenge to Christian orthodoxy. Idealism initially provided a way of understanding and managing these changes and challenges. Christianity, it was argued, was evolving through the secular process of history. This religious progress was essentially spiritual in nature, and was nevertheless manifested everywhere in concrete terms. In this unfolding of human consciousness in history, religious faith could be better comprehended through rational and intellectual understanding. Piety and critical thought, therefore, were not at odds since faith could not be faith if it defied intellectual inquiry. Idealism provided for a universal union of opposites as the old divisions between the spiritual and the material, the sacred and the secular, God and humanity, were obliterated.[18] Idealism, therefore, inspired a compelling religious and social vision. But it was a philosophical achievement that also exacerbated religious uncertainty and created chaos and confusion among Presbyterians. Presbyterian ministers, Walter Bryden among them, were often forced to deal with the consequences in local congregations.

A. B. McKillop has described a very good example of this uncertainty as it existed in an exchange of correspondence between Mr. J. M. Grant, an otherwise anonymous Presbyterian Sunday school superintendent from Toronto, and John Watson of Queen's University. The correspondence took place between 1911 and 1918 during the period that Walter Bryden was the minister in Woodville, Ontario. Having read some of Watson's books, Grant was troubled by the religious difficulties created by idealism for orthodox faith. Was the orthodox doctrine of the Trinity now tenable? Did the resurrection of Jesus violate natural laws? Did it make sense to speak of God as absolute perfection? If God is perfect love, how is sin to be accounted for? Is the forgiveness of sin to be found in the atoning death of Jesus? What can be believed concerning immortality and eternal life? Grant's questions were not

---

[18] McKillop, *A Disciplined Intelligence*, 212.

motivated simply by intellectual curiosity. They represented the increasing anguish of a troubled soul struggling to come to terms with the meaning of Christian faith in the emerging modern world. The anguish was only exacerbated by the fact that he had been given the responsibility of passing on the Christian faith to the next generation in his church's Sunday school.

In his replies Watson tried to assure Grant that there was not only a way to reconcile Christian faith with the difficult questions he raised, but that idealism provided precisely the solution required and therefore the highest expression of Christian teaching. The Trinity, Watson explained, must be viewed in terms of the Self-Manifestation of God who, as an immanent deity, identifies with and is manifest in humanity. Christ is the perfect type of this manifestation and the Holy Spirit is the identification of that which binds humanity and deity together. The resurrection ought not to be interpreted literally and questions about the divinity of Christ, the forgiveness of sins, and eternal life should not detract from the essential message of Christianity. "Do you think," Watson wrote, "it really matters from the point of view of the essence of religion, whether one accepts what is called the divinity of Christ? What, to begin with, are we to understand by it? Does it mean that a man existed from all eternity, who yet was not a man but God? That, of course, is a thoroughly unthinkable thing."[19] Indeed, Watson wrote later to Grant, "No creed of any church can be accepted."

There is no evidence that Walter Bryden knew of this correspondence, and it is entirely possible that few, if any, members of his congregation in the small Ontario village of Woodville were plagued with the doubts that troubled Grant. But that is not the point. Walter Bryden knew John Watson's work; Bryden saw the impact of philosophical idealism on theology and church life in Canada; and as a Presbyterian minister who had been educated in idealism and who was required to preach weekly he struggled with the same questions. Bryden was astute enough to realize that Watson's approach, like that of Watson's mentor Edward Caird, was driven by a desire to rescue and reassert the moral and religious dimension of life which had been undermined by modern skepticism. Yet, as A. B. McKillop notes, the objective idealism adopted by Watson provided the basis for a form of belief that resembled evolutionary naturalism. In Watson's hands Christianity could absorb the evolutionary change and the fundamental unity of nature asserted by Hegel and Darwin. "The convergence between Hegelian idealism and the new naturalism . . . was one of the most important and distinctive results of Darwin's impact on British metaphysics."[20] It resulted, however, in a form of pantheism that was virtually indistinguishable from naturalistic and materi-

---

[19]   John Watson, cited in McKillop, *A Disciplined Intelligence*, 214.
[20]   McKillop, *A Disciplined Intelligence*, 215.

alistic atheism. This was precisely the critique that Bryden mounted against idealism during the 1930s. It was a criticism fueled by the failure of idealism to deliver a form of Christian faith appropriate to the Christian tradition as Bryden understood it in light of his pastoral experience. Idealism reduced the complexity and richness of the Christian tradition to the essence of Christian consciousness—the unity of humanity and God. But Bryden's concern was also driven by the conviction that the idealist form of Christianity was ultimately inadequate for modern sensibilities, especially when those sensibilities began to shift after World War I.

The Great War proved to be a difficult and disillusioning event for Presbyterian ministers like Walter Bryden, who tried to make sense of the suffering and slaughter in Europe from the perspective of parish life in Canada. At first, the ideals of progressive and liberal Calvinism persisted and the war was interpreted as a refining process in the evolutionary development of history. Advocates of the social gospel, which reached its apogee in Canadian Protestantism in 1915, appeared confident that the war experience would promote the redemption of Canadian society. As reports of the carnage and destruction unleashed by the war in Europe made their way back to Canada, however, Canadian Presbyterian clergy and teachers were forced to reassess many of the theological presuppositions with which they were conducting their ministries. Protestant ministers who served as soldiers and chaplains overseas often offered the most trenchant critiques of the theologies operative in the Canadian churches. Many of the issues enunciated during this period became critical themes in the theology which Walter Bryden would embrace wholeheartedly by the late 1920s.

The initial Presbyterian support for the war had been fueled by loyalty to the trinity of God, king and country, and the belief that "the war was part of a larger battle in which the forces of righteousness were combating evil and injustice."[21] But as the war unfolded it became apparent to many that culture Protestantism could be used to justify almost any and all national economic, social and military interests. The ineradicable evil and intractable suffering forced the churches to confront the reality of human sinfulness once again. Chaplains at the front discovered that a Christian message which emphasized individual moral righteousness and social moral reform fell on the deaf ears of soldiers whose existential concern was driven by fear in the face of death. The Presbyterian J. W. Falconer, for example, realized that many Christians in Canada were trying to come to grips with the meaning of the war for their faith. Writing for the Commission on the War and the Spiritual Life of the Church set up by the General Assembly, he noted the disillusionment with which many struggled:

---

[21] David B. Marshall, *Secularizing the Faith*, 158.

The war has uncovered the hideous features of evil. By its entail of calamity it has confirmed the Scripture, 'Sin when it is finished, bringeth forth death.' We had been flattering ourselves upon the progress of the world. . . . We were priding ourselves on our refinement, our ability, our humanism, thinking that culture was winning its way towards a human perfectability . . . . Even the Church had begun to forget that this is an evil world, where the children of the Heavenly Father cannot go on their way unmolested.[22]

The Calvinist emphasis on sin and the providence of God meant that Presbyterians should have had a theological framework within which to deal with the challenge of the war. However, the conceptions of sin and providence prevalent in both confessional and progressive Calvinism seemed somehow inadequate to address the horrific evil being perpetuated in Europe. Preachers like George C. Pidgeon of the Bloor Street Presbyterian congregation, and also a member of the General Assembly's commission, turned to the centrality of the cross and interpreted the sacrifice and suffering everywhere evident in the war in terms of the sacrificial and atoning death of Christ. His sermons overseas to soldiers in France focused on repentance, sacrifice, and salvation. Others emphatically declared that the idealism taught in the universities and theological colleges no longer applied.

David B. Marshall summarizes the apparent effect of the war on Canadian Protestant clergy in the following terms:

War had made apparent the inadequacy and outright sentimentality of much of the liberalism which had dominated thinking in Presbyterian and Methodist circles. The real presence of evil in human nature and Christian civilization was made clear. It seemed no longer possible to trust in progress and look exclusively to human nature as a means to understanding and reaching God. Salvation would not be brought about by some evolutionary process; there had to be fundamental redemption of the human personality. Although the war did not produce a religious revival, it did lead to a renewal of interest in theology . . . . The quest for a deeper theological understanding of the Word of God and Jesus Christ in the postwar era had its roots in the bloodied soil of the battlefields.[23]

Among the Presbyterian ministers who would pursue the quest for a recovery of Reformed theology focused on the Word of God and Jesus Christ in the postwar era was Walter Bryden. Indeed, his emphasis on the cross of

---

22   Cited in ibid., 162.
23   Marshall, *Secularizing the* Faith, 179. See also 156–80 for a summary of the effects of the war on Canadian Protestantism.

God's crucified Messiah as the locus of God's Judging-Saving Word resonated with the Canadian Protestant experience of the Great War.

Ministry, Preaching, and the New Testament

In addition to wrestling with socialism and idealism during this period, and the influence of the Great War on his thinking, Walter Bryden was confronted daily with the business of pastoral ministry and the task of Christian preaching. In a 1927 pamphlet called *The Christian Ministry*, written to support the continuing Presbyterian Church's efforts to recruit new ministers, Bryden reflected upon the nature of ministry within the Reformed tradition in general and upon his own experience in particular.[24] In three parts Bryden set out his understanding of the Presbyterian doctrine of ordained leadership, issued an appeal to young people to consider the benefits and motives of a vocation within the Presbyterian Church in Canada, and described the unique challenges and opportunities of the Canadian setting.

Bryden began by emphasizing that ministry is a gift of the risen and ascended Christ to the church, and not a professional service to advance civic and cultural ideals. In common with other Christian traditions Presbyterianism held that persons vested with church government derived their authority not from the people but from Jesus Christ. Presbyterianism, however, Bryden argued, made more room for the recognition of the people and the inner reality of Christian experience in the individual soul's sense of a divine call. The vocation of ordained ministry "came from God through a congregation and entailed responsibility to both." Bryden was realistic about the many mixed motivations for entering the service of the church, including the promise of adventure, the desire to serve, the opportunity of a reflective life, and the privileges of leadership. But he argued that mere human motives could never sustain the ordinary minister because there was too much perplexity, doubt, sorrow, seemingly useless labor and downright failure in every minister's life. Christian ministry, Bryden wrote autobiographically, was a burden because the work required the minister to deal with "the anxieties, insecurities, fears and sins of every individual under [the clergy's] care." The clergy encountered "troubles, perplexity, and opposition" known to few others. But God used mixed motives and heavy burdens to lead those truly called into their deeper selves as the tests and trials of ministry unfolded. It is a remarkable thing, Bryden noted, that "those who have once been tested and tried in the Ministry of Christ seldom find any other kind of work congenial." The hope

---

[24] Bryden, *The Christian Ministry* (Toronto: The Upper Canada Tract Society, 1927); also published in *Separated Unto the Gospel*, 120–30.

of the Christian minister is that an honest worker has never really failed, nor can such a worker possibly fail.[25]

Having labored for almost seventeen years in Lethbridge, Woodville, and Melfort, Bryden must have often wondered about the fruit of his own ministry, especially during a period when ministers spent their time engaged in work that appeared to have very little in common with what the church's ministers had done for almost two thousand years. On the one hand, Bryden knew that clerical identity could no longer be rooted in the minister's role as a teacher and defender of the church's doctrine, as Ephraim Scott, the erstwhile editor of the *Presbyterian Record*, and his confessional Calvinist colleagues seemed to emphasize. On the other hand, Bryden resisted the redefinition of Christian ministry by the exigencies of the times. Christian ministry entailed more than planning programs, administering institutions, and advancing ideals. It had to be rooted, he would come to understand, in the call of God centered in the Judging Saving Word.[26]

The focus of Bryden's struggle to come to terms with the nature of Christian ministry lay in what he considered to be its primary task, namely preaching. In 1929 he addressed the Spring convocation of the Presbyterian College, Montreal, on precisely this theme. Noting the modest and unusual nature of his own ministry, Bryden suggested that there were advantages to never having been the minister of an influential city pulpit: "I am persuaded, however, that this kind of ministerial career has its advantages and compensations. You get to know real life as other men do not know it, and your own life is tested by the inwardness of things rather than by the outwardness of conventions which after all do not matter. Besides, you are not so likely to be encompassed by exacting duties and if you have the will, you may train your mind and heart on those far greater things. As I see it now, my true student days began after I left the college halls; and had I to do it all over again, I surely would choose the same kind of ministry."[27] On the basis of his experience, he chose to speak about "those few things which have increasingly appealed to me in the course of my own ministry, as the essentials toward which one ought to strive" in order to make one's preaching effective, and to confine himself therefore to what he considered a simpler necessity, namely, "the need of first finding ourselves and then being steadfastly true to our highest selves at any sacrifice in all this work of preaching."[28]

Preaching, as Bryden defined it, was "the unveiling of one's soul as that soul in the course of life is being touched by God." Preaching was not to be

---

[25]   Bryden, "The Christian Ministry," in *Separated Unto the Gospel*, 120–26.

[26]   Ibid. See also Fraser, *Church, College, and Clergy*, 153–57.

[27]   Bryden, "The Triumph of Reality," in *Separated Unto the Gospel*, 131.

[28]   Ibid., 131, 133.

characterized by arguments and accents, but by thinking which had passed through the fire of the preacher's own experience as preachers searched their own faith to see what they truly believed. The preacher had to wrestle with true beliefs as "the issue of one's whole being as wrought upon by circumstance and God." The real test of ministry, Bryden advised future clergy, was what they would inwardly be "in the face of deepest disappointment and baffling frustration, in the face of those people you are sure to meet who never seem to get the real and greater meaning of the thing you believe and try to teach." Bryden sensed that there was a certain mystery to preaching which ought to instill awe and reverence in the preacher: "To see in the life around us, in the men and women we have known and in whose presence we have stood, humbled, and to see in this Christian religion, and in that unsearchable and indefinable person, Christ Jesus himself, *something* which eludes our grasp altogether and yet which haunts us as the ultimate reality, which we cannot ever give up, to see this is to possess the soul of a preacher who will be able to help his fellow men." Convinced that the church could no longer rely on its authority to impose its message on modern people, Bryden pointed to the self-authenticating and self-evidencing power of the gospel message. Preaching did not require rational arguments or rhetorical methods to commend the Christian message. The triumph of reality occurred when preachers sounded "the authentic note of that something '*Other*' in the soul and people heard in the preacher one who had surrendered truly and fully to God." Appealing to Barth, Bryden argued that a preacher must "recognize God." "It is easy," Bryden quoted Barth, "to say 'recognize,' but recognizing is an ability won only in fierce, inner, personal conflict. It is a task beside which, all cultural, moral and patriotic duties, all efforts in applied religion are child's play. For here, one must give oneself up in order to give himself over to God, that God's will may be done." To do God's will, however, means to begin with God anew. God's will "will not be a corrected continuation of our own. It approaches ours as *wholly other*."[29]

In short, during the course of his ministry Bryden had come to realize that neither dogmatic nor liberal thinking could sustain the task of preaching. Bryden knew that modernity's critique of Christian proclamation could not be evaded. It was no longer possible, as confessional Calvinists continued to insist, that preaching could proceed along the lines of dogmatic and traditional thinking. Preachers who refused to acknowledge the ethos of the modern world, who refused to be honest with themselves or with those they led, may have had a gospel to preach, but it was not *their* gospel. It had not passed through the fires of their own experience, and it had never been refined by the agonies of their own doubts. At the same time, the modern ethos pro-

---

[29] Ibid., 131–45; Fraser, *Church, College, and Clergy*, 153–57.

vided a new preaching ideal which Bryden equally resisted. During the late nineteenth century preaching had taken a decidedly psychological turn and theology had been transformed into anthropology. Preachers, Bryden had been taught by progressive Calvinists, were now supposed to provide rational insights into human experience in the service of a renewed social vision. Preaching was the art of communication rather than the call to proclamation. Such free and liberal thinking, Bryden argued, gave preachers something to preach, but it bore little resemblance to the church's gospel. In both cases, preachers were driven by the outwardness of conventions rather than the inwardness of convictions.

During his years in the pastorate Bryden continued to struggle with the pressures of weekly preaching in the midst of these competing claims. But after reading Karl Barth in the 1920s, and being reminded of his teacher James Denney, Bryden came to realize that there was a connection between theology and preaching that provided a more profound understanding of the preacher's experience of God. Furthermore, it forced him to rethink the character of theology itself. Barth had made an important claim: "that the possibility of a Christian theology is specifically conditioned by the fact that there is Christian speech." Bryden realized that the connection between theology and preaching is not simply important, it is essential, and he agreed that "there can be no Christian theology except through the task, the necessity in fact, and indeed through the recognition of the utter impossibility of Christian preaching." Theology not only grows out of preaching, it is also sustained by preaching at all times. "Theology is the issuance of that which precedes it, namely Christian speech." Barth's searching analysis of the meaning of Christian speech was, Bryden argued, "evidently the result of the perplexing problem imposed upon Barth as he labored to impart the Word of God to the humble people of a secluded Swiss parish in Safenwil. There is nothing about Barth which is of greater importance than the fact that his theology is so vitally and essentially related to his task as a preacher, that is to say, to the task of the Church. It is not enough, however, simply to recognize this fact. In order to understand Barth, to feel the power of his arguments, I am persuaded that we must also, in some real sense, have shared his peculiar difficulty."[30] Bryden understood Barth and felt the power of his arguments precisely because he had shared Barth's peculiar difficulty as a preacher in the second decade of the twentieth century.

As he continued to struggle with idealism, confront the challenge posed to Christian faith by the Great War, and wrestle with the ongoing challenge of Christian preaching during this period, Walter Bryden immersed himself in Paul's Corinthian correspondence and discovered 'the strange new

---

[30] Bryden, "After Modernism, What?" Unpublished manuscript, 179–81.

world within the Bible.' *The Spirit of Jesus in St. Paul*, written during the course of weekly preaching in Woodville and Melfort, shows that Bryden continued to think deeply about the meaning of ministry in the light of contemporary theological scholarship. In a generous introductory note the New Testament scholar William Manson recommended Bryden as "a young Canadian theologian whose attainments, while recognized in his own community, have not hitherto asserted themselves in any appeal to a more general audience."[31] Manson was Professor of New Testament at Knox College from 1919 to 1925, when he was appointed Professor of New Testament Language, Literature and Theology at New College, Edinburgh. Noting the connection between Paul's theology and the primitive Christian experience out of which it sprang, Manson pointed out how Bryden brought out the essential oneness of the ethical and emotional content of the theological system that resulted from the working out of ideas and motives already present and operative in the Christian soul. Bryden's insistence on the identification of the Holy Spirit with Jesus seemed to guarantee, Manson concluded, the unity of Paul's theology with the general historic witness of his time.[32] Manson commended Bryden's book because he brought this out in an analysis of Pauline teaching that was helpful both to religious experience and to practical life.

In the foreword Bryden's former teacher John McFadyen also commended the "literary first-fruits of my old Canadian pupil" as going to the root of the matter through a psychological study that brought readers nearer the center. McFadyen, by now teaching in Glasgow, noted that Bryden's discussion was not conducted in a speculative manner by a dispassionate observer, but by a Christian minister who was willing to be searched and tried himself by "the standards exhibited in that first and greatest of Christian ministers, and, amid all the chequered experience incidental to a faithful ministry, it is a summons to the perennial Source of refreshment and renewal."[33] In a review for the *Canadian Journal of Religious Thought* John Dow noted that although Bryden had "modestly sought two sponsors for his volume in Professor Manson and Professor J. E. McFadyen," readers "will welcome this book from what they know of the author himself."[34] Dow suggested that Bryden's work as a minister made him an ideal interpreter of Paul because he was "not the scholar who knows all the lore of the dictionaries, but the missionary on the field who has had fresh contact with the heathen heart, and the preacher who knows the vexations of congregational jealousies and

---

31 William Manson, "Introductory Note," in Bryden, *The Spirit of Jesus in St. Paul*, 6.
32 Ibid., 5.
33 John E. McFadyen, "Foreword," in Bryden, *The Spirit of Jesus in St. Paul*, 7–8.
34 John Dow, Review of Bryden, *The Spirit of Jesus in St. Paul* in *Canadian Journal of Religious Thought* 4 (Jan.–Feb. 1927) 89–90.

strange teachers." Bryden understood, Dow argued, that Paul was "not a master logician drilling all Christendom into a mechanically conceived creed, but a man on fire with Christ, pleading, exhorting, teaching a faith that saves."[35] Another reviewer noted that "the conception is original and the execution well done" but criticized what he considered to be "Bryden's loose views on Divine inspiration." The book, apparently, stirred some interest in England as well as in Canada.[36]

What was Bryden trying to do in this book? As the reviewers observed, *The Spirit of Jesus in St. Paul* was a psychological study of Paul's religious experience as that experience was revealed in the New Testament letters to the Corinthians. Assuming an analogy between the experience of the early church, specifically the experience of the Apostle Paul, and the experience of the modern church, particularly his own experience as a Christian minister, Bryden appealed to the Holy Spirit as the basis for such an identification. The Spirit of Jesus which inhabited and enlivened the soul of Paul was the same Spirit at work in the life of the church today. This appeal to the Spirit, Bryden believed, overcame not only the tendency in modern scholarship to draw a sharp divide between the religion of Jesus and the religion of Paul, or the experience of the primitive church and Paul's theology, but it also overcame the distance and discontinuity between Paul's time and our own. By studying "the 'soul of Paul' as his inner thoughts and feelings, his ethical appreciations and spiritual aspirations reveal themselves in these two letters," Bryden hoped that Paul's life would have some practical significance in understanding "the perplexities of our modern Church life, and in lending some guidance in the discharge of our important and difficult work."[37]

When Bryden examined Paul's rather strange religious experience in the Corinthian letters he had trouble reconciling it with the domesticated ideals of modern Christianity. Influenced by an eschatological reading of the New Testament, Bryden concluded that the thoughts and actions of the apostle were inexplicable apart from Paul's identification with Jesus and his belief that there was a continuity and spiritual unity between them. The basis of this belief for Paul, Bryden argued, rested upon Paul's conviction that his experience was the expression of the Spirit of Jesus operative in his life as a power and presence that created spiritual and ethical realities. The kingdom inaugurated by the life, death, resurrection, and ascension of Jesus continued to break into the world through the witness and work of Jesus' Spirit in the souls of his followers. Over against the prevailing tendency in modern scholarship to drive a wedge between Paul and Jesus, Bryden boldly asserted that a radical

---

[35]   Ibid., 89–90.

[36]   *The Globe* (January 9, 1926); *The Mail* (July 10, 1926). University of Toronto Archives.

[37]   Bryden, *The Spirit of Jesus in St. Paul*, 36.

discontinuity between the experience of Paul and the teachings of Jesus could not be sustained on the basis of a careful reading of the Corinthian letters. Wilhelm Wrede's 1906 book *Paulus*, for example, had sketched an apostle who attributed the features of a Gnostic master to Jesus thereby transforming Christianity into a Hellenistic cult. In a 1919 essay called "The Meaning of Paul for the Modern Christian" Johannes Weis had argued that Paul's doctrines of justification by faith, conversion by grace, and sanctification by the indwelling of the Holy Spirit were simply meaningless to modern people.[38]

Bryden would have none of it. Influenced by his former teacher H. A. A. Kennedy's careful reading of Paul, Bryden described an apostle whose heart and mind were inclined to a knowledge of God through the Holy Spirit. Paul's faith, therefore, consisted of more than knowledge about the historical Jesus, and Paul's experience could not be reduced to an ethical imitation of Jesus' life. Indeed, there was not only a continuity between Jesus and Paul, but an essential oneness between them. Paul believed that his experience of the Spirit of Jesus was an experience of knowing and being known by God. This was, for Bryden, an existential reality which transcended historical and ethical description, and it was the only adequate explanation, he concluded, for Paul's apostolic ministry. In short, through his study of Paul's theology in the Corinthian letters Walter Bryden found "a Christ-mysticism, a case of Christ's being formed in man by the energy of the Holy Spirit, and he reckons that this is authentic mysticism and the proper mystery."[39] The same Christ-mysticism, Bryden concluded, not only sustained the church throughout its history, but also provided the only authentic basis for Christian faith and life in the modern world.[40]

Bryden's exposition of Pauline theology in the late second and early third decades of the twentieth century was marked by a determined effort to cut away the tangle of philosophical, historical and theological weeds that he believed were choking out the life of the church in the modern world. Liberal Protestant theology had reduced Paul's theology to spiritual and ethical ideals to be understood and imitated. Conservative Protestant theology had refused to acknowledge the legitimate insights of historical criticism. Neither would do, and Bryden longed for a credible alternative to the rationalism, idealism, naturalism, and traditionalism of his day. Written before Bryden's encounter with Barth and Brunner, *The Spirit of Jesus in St. Paul* raised many of the same

---

[38] James D. Smart, *The Past, Present and Future of Biblical Theology* (Philadelphia: Westminster, 1979) 100–101.

[39] Joseph C. McLelland, "Walter Bryden: 'By Circumstance and God,'" in *Called to Witness*, edited by W. Stanford Reid (The Presbyterian Church in Canada: Committee on History, 1980) 2:125.

[40] Bryden, *The Spirit of Jesus in St. Paul*, 13–21.

questions that drove their reaction against the hegemony of liberal Protestant theology in Europe in the second decade of the twentieth century. One realizes why, as James Smart suggested, Walter Bryden was soon to feel a community of interest with them. They had been struggling as he had been to find a way forward to a church that would recover its roots in the Reformation.[41]

Bryden later reflected on the significance of this book for the development of his theological thought in an unpublished manuscript on modern theology. Following World War One, Bryden found his theological and practical difficulties as an active minister in a congregation coming to a focus. Before that time, he had passed through all the various phases of modern critical and theological thought. After studying Albert Schweitzer and H.A. Charles, Bryden came to the conclusion "that the whole outlook of the New Testament was eschatological in character" and "that the expectation of Jesus was distinctly so." Increasingly, Bryden was dissatisfied with the basis of authority for Christian faith in the "historic Jesus" of the historical-critical schools and while he appreciated the insights of such scholars as John Oman and Albrecht Ritschl, he could not reconcile how their views could be used to maintain adequately the particular claims of the traditional Christian faith.[42]

The work of John Wood Oman (1860–1939) particularly intrigued Bryden. Oman was a Presbyterian theologian who taught at Westminster College, Cambridge (from 1907), and served as principal from 1925 to 1935. Interested in the theology of Schleiermacher and Ritschl, Oman understood religion as the feeling of the supernatural or the sense of the infinite beyond the finite world. Oman wrote thirteen books including his most well-known books *The Church and the Divine* Order (1911) and *The Natural and the Supernatural* (1931). Bryden's encounter with Oman's theology was decisive in helping Bryden understand the nature of religious experience in modern theology. When, in 1931, James Smart inquired of Bryden where he should make a beginning at serious theological reading, Bryden sent Smart to read everything Oman had written.[43] By then, Bryden had been reading Oman for almost two decades. Principal Oman, Bryden believed, was "one of the most penetrating and incisive thinkers among modern scholars," and represented "the most challenging and convincing exponent of the modern religious viewpoint." Although Oman had been a product of philosophical and religious idealism, Bryden appreciated the fact that Oman never seemed to be in bondage to any school of thought.

---

[41]   James D. Smart, "The Evangelist as Theologian," in *Separated Unto the Gospel*, x.

[42]   W. W. Bryden, "After Modernism, What?" 181.

[43]   James D. Smart, "Lest We Forget," *The Presbyterian Record* 94.9 (1975) 6.

Bryden was pleased that Oman insisted on the fact that religion, to be genuine religion for the individual, must be such as is perceived by personal insight or experience. Oman's claim that the inner attitude of the soul to God alone constitutes the quality of a person's Christianity seemed fundamentally correct to Bryden. One of the distinctive features of Oman's work was his argument that the conceptions held of God, salvation and grace, are finally determinative of the character of religions, and are indeed the constitutive factors in the formation of the various institutional and ecclesiastical embodiments. His emphasis on the primary importance of the "inwardness" (religion as a personal possession and insight) of all true religion made Oman, Bryden contended, a prophet to his age. Oman did not, however, prove to be an encouraging apostle to those who longed for the union of the churches, Bryden noted, where the basis of that union was to be sought in things which Oman adjudged to be external to essential religion. Oman convinced Bryden that a good deal of religion was characterized by external factors which divide and which no ulterior necessity or well-meaning intent could unite, however much people may succeed in deluding themselves that unity could thus be achieved. The conception of God possessed by people; how God responds to the human act of faith; what God expects of people in enlightened insight and clear-eyed apprehension, decision and response: these were the things of paramount importance for John Oman that impressed Walter Bryden. Oman called Bryden to witness those deeper things of the soul upon which all true Christian fellowship is founded, and from which its permanency may alone be expected.[44]

Two other points in John Oman's *The Church and Divine Order* struck Bryden as important and found their way into *The Spirit of Jesus in St. Paul*. First, Oman had argued that the constitutive conception of the church was based solely upon the prophetic principle that God's rule comes not by might, nor by power, but by God's Spirit alone. Second, he had emphasized the apocalyptic character of the divine order that was always ready to break into the world wherever men and women were prepared to receive it in their hearts.

Bryden later raised serious objections to Oman's continuing indebtedness to idealism, but at this point Oman seemed to open the door for Bryden, if only a crack, to shed some light on a pathway which would ultimately take him back to his teacher James Denney, and forward to the theology of Karl Barth. Oman continued to be an important interlocutor for Bryden throughout his theological journey because Oman dealt with the nature of the Christian's experience of God in the human personality. In the end, however, Oman failed to explain what actually happens at the crucial point in which,

---

44   Bryden, "After Modernism, What?" chapter 7, par. 2.

what God the creator essentially is, meets with what a sinful human being is, in order to create what is known as Christian faith.[45] Despite Bryden's questions, it was Oman, a liberal Calvinist indebted to Schleiermacher and Ritschl, who alerted Bryden to the theological problems associated with the modern ecumenical movement.

Bryden would later admit that he was anything but consistent during this period of his development. "My thought," he wrote, "was oscillating between the modern and the traditional views." As a parish minister his difficulties became more acute and practical immediately after the First World War. He began to doubt the value of the many practical approaches to Christian ministry, the religious pedagogical methods, and the church programs that were becoming a characteristic feature of church life. He didn't see their purpose; he wondered what, if anything, was really being achieved, and he questioned whether anything of real spiritual value was being accomplished by all this bustle and activity. The anxiety created by this difficulty and disillusionment became the energy that propelled Bryden into the study of Paul. And while he had not yet arrived at a clear theological position, Bryden noted that by the time he wrote *The Spirit of Jesus in St. Paul* he had arrived at four distinctive and important positions which diverged sharply from the position of modern theology and from the basic principles which governed modern religious thought.

First, Bryden had "distinguished sharply between the customary method of speaking of the spirit of Jesus in terms of qualities of heart and mind" possessed and exhibited by Jesus during his life and ministry, and that those who follow Jesus were called to imitate—and the Spirit, which in the New Testament is always conceived as a creative source, or power, of new life. The Spirit of Jesus, Bryden had come to see, constituted the creative power of their membership for those who belonged to the early Christian community. In short, the Spirit of Jesus was not a way of life to be imitated, but a power of Jesus to be experienced.

Second, Bryden saw his first book as an attempt to address the problem of preaching in the modern world. He strongly advanced the claim "that the peculiar task of the Christian ministry could not be achieved by any kind of pedagogical instruction, however skillfully and sympathetically employed." Bryden contended that true preaching, at least as expressed by Paul in the Corinthian correspondence, was animated and authenticated by the Spirit of Jesus. Such preaching was made possible when preachers were conscious of their own bankruptcy in things which mattered to people. In self-abandonment preachers found their true freedom.

---

45   Bryden, *The Christian's Knowledge of God*, 152.

Third, Bryden had also come to the conclusion that the paradoxical nature of Christianity was something integral to the whole revelation of Christ and not only in certain phases incidental to Christian life and experience. The deep antitheses with which Paul expressed the incarnation, life, and death of Christ stood in complete and utter contradiction to the natural world. The unsearchable things of God, these paradoxes, Paul believed, were imparted to men and women by the Spirit of Jesus alone.

Fourth, Bryden asked the question in this book, as he saw it later, whether the modern church was real enough, earnest and true enough, noble enough in mind and spirit to acquire the courage to fail. Was the modern church prepared, together with the Apostle Paul, to be a fool for Christ? Was the modern church prepared to fail in the way that Jesus and Paul had failed in the eyes of the world? To borrow Luther's phrase, was the modern church prepared to forsake a theology of glory and embrace a theology of the cross, even a theology of weakness and foolishness? In sum, Bryden's thought was beginning to take shape as a theology of the Spirit, a theology of preaching, a theology of paradox, a theology of the cross, and what may be described as a critically realistic theology. His disillusionment with liberal theology, traditional theology, and modern Christendom, which was already acute, reached crisis proportions as 1925 approached.[46]

The Challenge of Church Union

Near what was to be the end of his years as a parish minister, Walter Bryden was confronted by the decision of whether to join the majority of his Presbyterian clergy colleagues in the new United Church of Canada. By the early 1920s many Canadian Presbyterians believed that The Presbyterian Church in Canada had had a good run since 1875 and that it was now time to throw their lot in with the proposed ecumenical venture involving Methodists and Congregationalists. Indeed, it was argued, the proposed union only continued the process of ongoing unions among Presbyterians in British North America since 1861 and mirrored the recent union among Presbyterians in Scotland. The proposal for what was to become The United Church of Canada originated in 1904. In a rapidly changing social and cultural context, church union appeared to provide a way to ensure that Protestantism would continue to be a major player on the Canadian scene, assuring institutional strength and social influence. By the time the union movement achieved its goal, years later than what had originally been envisioned, approximately two-thirds of the membership and three quarters of the clergy of the Presbyterian Church

---

46 Bryden, "After Modernism, What?" chapter 8.

voted in favor of the United Church of Canada. Walter Bryden found himself among the minority of resisters.

It could have been otherwise. In the years immediately prior to church union Walter Bryden lived and worked in Melfort, Saskatchewan. He had started his ministry in Lethbridge, Alberta. The churches of Saskatchewan and Alberta were virtually unanimous in their support of church union. There, the genie had already been let out of the bottle, long before 1925, with the creation of union congregations in towns that could not afford to support separate Presbyterian, Methodist, and Congregational churches. This practical impetus for church union was, as it turned out, unstoppable. Furthermore, many of Bryden's closest friends and colleagues, even theological kindred spirits, were among those who opted for union. The pressure was immense. But Bryden's misgivings about the whole venture were rooted in the suspicion that John Oman was right: true church unity could not be based on factors external to the essence of Christianity. And those misgivings ultimately determined his decision.

The problem for Bryden was that his reasons for opposing church union set him apart from most anti-unionists as well. Some had opposed church union because they believed that the Presbyterian tradition, especially its form of church government and its liturgy, was worth preserving. Others had argued in favor of a continuing Presbyterian Church that would defend the historic Reformed creeds and confessions. Still others, very conscious of social class, were threatened by the loss of social and political influence for Scots in Canada that might result from a union with Methodists and Congregationalists. At the same time, many of the anti-unionists were not anti-ecumenical. They were sympathetic with the unionist desire to reduce denominational competition in Canada and give fuller expression to the unity of the church, but saw federation, similar to the model of the Federal Council of the Churches of Christ in America, as the appropriate paradigm. Rather ironically, as it turned out, some liberal Calvinists even opposed the new church because they considered the Basis of Union too conservative, even fundamentalist. Bryden distanced himself from all these arguments.[47] The speeches made by fundamentalists, idealists, ecumenists, and sentimentalists alike failed to persuade him.

The main problem, as Bryden saw it, was that the ecumenical ideals upon which the United Church of Canada was being built rested on a liberal Protestant theology which was in the process of crumbling. The union movement reflected the late nineteenth-century mood of progressivism and

---

[47]   Allan L. Farris, "The Fathers of 1925," in *Enkindled by the Word: Essays on Presbyterianism in Canada,* edited by Neil G. Smith (Toronto: Presbyterian Publications, 1966) 59–82. See also Fraser, *Church, College, and Clergy,* 140–43.

optimism rather than the crisis and realism that signaled the twilight of western Christendom. While the mood had not yet shifted in North America, Bryden was aware that the churches of Europe were reeling from the shattering experience of World War One and its judgment upon all forms of culture Protestantism. The future of Protestantism in Canada, he believed, required Christian leaders to think deeply and act prophetically in relation to the inevitable demise of Christendom. The advocates of church union appeared to be oblivious to this. Their language signaled their belief that a stronger progressive Christendom church was precisely what Canada needed. Those who resisted the organic model of church union, Bryden argued, did not see things much differently. They worked with the same assumptions and pursued the same goals within the framework of culture Protestantism. The only real difference that obtained between the unionists and the anti-unionists concerned the institutional form of continuing Presbyterianism. The whole debate, he argued, was conducted on grounds that were primarily sentimental, expedient, utilitarian, and humanitarian, rather than ecclesiological and theological.

Perhaps not so strangely, then, Walter Bryden began to discover his changing theological voice in the midst of what was for him a crisis of epidemic proportions in Canadian Protestantism. The years in the pastorate had changed him. His engagement with Marxism had sharpened his instincts for social criticism and prophetic religion. Idealism increasingly appeared to be a chimera which was unable to sustain anything resembling classical conceptions of the Christian faith, while at the same time its advocates, though lionized (i.e., John Watson), remained oblivious to the fact that the philosophical and cultural ground beneath them was shifting. The Great War "had made apparent the inadequacy and outright sentimentality of much of the liberalism which had dominated thinking"[48] in Presbyterian circles. The task of preaching had forced Bryden to wrestle with, and for, the souls of his people, and had pushed him into 'the strange new world of the Bible.' As he studied Paul's Corinthian correspondence, he discovered conceptions of the Spirit and an eschatological worldview which, though startling, seemed to offer a form of Christian faith far more real and authentic than either the traditional orthodoxies or the modern ideals which dominated the Canadian Protestant landscape. In sum, Walter Williamson Bryden was ready, able and willing to speak, and after 1925 many within The Presbyterian Church in Canada were willing to follow "their new young theologian at Knox College beyond modernism and fundamentalism to neo-orthodoxy."[49]

---

[48]   David B. Marshall, *Secularizing the Faith*, 177.

[49]   N. Keith Clifford, *The Resistance to Church Union in Canada, 1904–1939*, 4.

Theological Professor, 1926–1945

Knox Faculty Member

In the aftermath of 1925, the continuing Presbyterian Church retained two theological colleges, Knox in Toronto and The Presbyterian College in Montreal. Since Principal Gandier and the entire Knox faculty had joined the United Church of Canada, the octogenarian Ephraim Scott, editor of the *Presbyterian Record*, and moderator of the continuing General Assembly, was appointed as interim-principal. This signaled the possibility that the confessional Calvinists might dominate the continuing church's courts and theological colleges. In addition to being a leading anti-unionist, Scott had close ties to Gresham Machen and the confessionalist wing that was at the center of the modernist-fundamentalist storm in American Presbyterianism. As it turned out, Scott exercised little control over the permanent appointments to the Knox faculty. The diverging trajectories of Calvinism in the pre-union church and the mixed bag of Presbyterians that had shared common ground as anti-unionists proved to be a considerable challenge to the establishment of a coherent theological and ecclesial ethos in the church and its colleges. The subsequent stormy history of Knox College from 1925 to 1945 bears ample evidence of the conflict and the struggle for a clear theological position to emerge in the midst of an uncertain future.

The continuing church moved quickly to appoint lecturers for 1925–26, three of whom would receive permanent appointments to chairs in 1926 and 1927. Among them was Walter Bryden who had accepted a call to be the minister again in Woodville, Ontario. Bryden commuted weekly by train in order to lecture part-time for one academic year while he continued his pastoral ministry, but in 1926 the Bryden family moved to Toronto so that Bryden could teach full-time at his alma mater. At the General Assembly in 1927 he was appointed professor of church history and the history and philosophy of religion, having received nominations from 24 of the church's 43 presbyteries. He was inducted to his teaching responsibilities at Knox College on Tuesday, October 11, 1927 and soon emerged as one of its most influential and revered teachers. The quarter century and more during which Bryden taught a new generation of Presbyterian theological students was, as Joseph McLelland noted, "Bryden's hour."[50] His theological contribution to the continuing church was far more significant than might first be evident from an analysis of the formal constituency of his thought. Indeed, he resisted the use of his platform as a theological teacher at Knox College to create his own theological system. Rather, he used his increasingly strong theological

---

[50]   Joseph C. McLelland, "Walter Bryden: 'By Circumstance and God,'" 120.

voice to point his students to the theology of Karl Barth and the recovery of Reformation theology to which Barth himself bore witness. At the convocation of The Presbyterian College, Montreal on April 12, 1928, Bryden was awarded the Doctor of Divinity degree (*honoris causa*).

Bryden's colleagues at Knox included Thomas Eakin, appointed in 1926 as principal and professor of Old Testament; J. D. Cunningham, professor of New Testament; and E. Lloyd Morrow, professor of systematic theology. Eakin had served as the minister of St. Andrew's Presbyterian Church, King Street in Toronto, and professor of practical theology at The Presbyterian College, Montreal, before his appointment at Knox. He represented a liberal and progressive Calvinism. Cunningham was closer to Bryden, having been educated at United Free Church College in Glasgow and exposed to the liberal evangelical theology of Scottish Calvinism. Morrow was a bit of a conundrum who finally resigned amid charges of incompetence after a decade of division and controversy in the college. In this entourage, Bryden's voice soon emerged as the one which caught the attention of students. He seemed willing to question and challenge his own theological roots more thoroughly than the others. Students of the 1920s and 1930s recalled Bryden as their sole source of intellectual stimulation. The other faculty members were older men "who showed little interest in theological trends and seemed content to repeat well-worn lectures despite student dissatisfaction with such uninspiring material."[51] In addition to inspiring students through his lectures, Bryden served as a mentor and model who formed close personal and pastoral ties to the students. He coached the Knox soccer team and spent time with students watching baseball at Maple Leaf stadium on the waterfront. In short, Walter Bryden represented, for students, the kind of prophetic pastor-preacher they themselves longed to be in the ministry of the continuing Presbyterian Church.

When Bryden began teaching church history and the history and philosophy of religion at Knox College in 1925, it was not at all evident that he was the most suitable candidate to do so. He did not possess an academic doctorate, his MA degree was in philosophy, and his only major publication was in the area of New Testament studies. At the same time, Bryden brought considerable intellectual gifts and personal skills to his new responsibilities. He knew the tradition and the institution well. He had learned theology at Knox College and the United Free Church College in Glasgow from theological teachers who combined evangelical piety with historical scholarship and pastoral experience. During almost seventeen years in the pastorate he had given himself to the life of the mind as well as his practical duties. Students recall how he introduced them to a sweeping history of Christian

---

[51] Moir, *Enduring Witness*, 235; See also Fraser, *Church, College, and Clergy*, 158.

thought chock full of incisive comments about contemporary theology and church life. Seldom a lecture went by without an aside that the students welcomed with eager anticipation. During an era when theological education was dominated by professors who mastered a whole range of theological disciplines rather than pure academicians who concentrated on one narrow field of study, Walter Bryden was, as it turned out, a natural church theologian behind the lectern.

Church Historian

Following his appointment Bryden set himself to the task of preparing lectures in church history. He focused on the history of Christian thought because he believed, like his teachers James Ballantyne and T. M. Lindsay, that the doctrinal development of the church ought to feed and correct the teaching and preaching of the contemporary church. The history of the church, Bryden argued, was "Word of God history" because "The Church is the 'body of Christ;' it is an extension of the Incarnation, i.e., of Christ's coming into the world. Great institutions are all established by God; some, however, grow out of the necessities of the natural life, while others rise out of the necessities of man's relation to God since God has come into the world." The Church (the believers of Jesus Christ as Lord) is "called" into being by God. Therefore, instead of man's "self" by nature, Christ is enthroned in the lives of Christians.[52]

While it may have sounded strange to hear a Protestant theologian speak of the church as an extension of the incarnation, Bryden was signaling his belief that church history was no ordinary business—it was rooted in the reality of revelation which he understood as God's self-disclosure. The study of church history, therefore, while it employed serious historical investigative methods, was a unique discipline. It was history defined in relation to the reality of God and God's dealings with a people called by God's name. From this perspective, Bryden lectured on the early history of the church introducing his students to the church fathers, the creeds, the heresies, the theological developments of the first five centuries, and the theology of Augustine. On this basis, he moved on to tackle the medieval period and the Reformation era with a focus on Calvin's theology which, he argued, had been hijacked by the scholasticism of the post-Reformation period and which, in turn, had lead to the tyrannical form of Calvinism against which the Enlightenment rightly reacted. The stark Scottish Calvinism parodied by Robbie Burns, with its emphasis on the sovereign decrees of God and the doctrine of double predestination, required, Bryden believed, a rethinking of Calvinism in light of the

---

[52]   Bryden, "Lectures on Church History: Introductory," 1.

renaissance of Calvin and Luther studies. Bryden also lectured on the post-Reformation history of the church up to 1648, accompanied by a detailed examination of developments in England and Scotland. Working diligently to stay ahead of his students Bryden immersed himself in the theological history of the church in order to establish the continuity of the Presbyterian Church in Canada after 1925 with the catholic and Reformation tradition. He chose to do this, not by focusing on the history of Presbyterianism in Canada, but by directing the attention of his students to the development of western Christianity as a whole. The little he did write and teach about Canadian church history focused, as one might expect, almost entirely on church union.

Philosopher of Religion. As if the teaching of an entire curriculum in church history was not enough, Walter Bryden was also assigned the task of lectures in the history and philosophy of religion. Despite persistent pleas from Knox College to the General Assembly for the funding of additional chairs, Bryden was saddled with a double load for over twenty years. If the teaching of church history provided an opportunity for Bryden to ground his students in the church fathers and the Reformed tradition, then his teaching of philosophy and comparative religions forced those students to engage the post-Enlightenment worldview within which Canadian Presbyterians found themselves. As a minister of the church, Bryden had seen the influence of idealism on Christian preaching and practice and he wished to deliver his students from its influence once and for all. He lectured on "The Reign of Naturalisms" and identified those views of life which assume "that Nature and Man are sufficient to themselves and are therefore self-explanatory."[53] After tracing the origins of naturalism in Greek thought, the Renaissance period, and the rise of the scientific method, Bryden examined a variety of philosophical schools and tried to demonstrate their significance for contemporary belief in God.

In another volume of lectures, Bryden spent some twenty-six pages setting forth the philosophy of Ludwig Feuerbach and its implications for Christian faith. Feuerbach, Marx, Freud, and Nietzsche offered compelling critiques of post-Enlightenment modernity that demonstrated, Bryden believed, the poverty of modern theology's accommodation to the new worldview. At the same time, their critique, fuelled by the renewal of interest in Kierkegaard, also made it clear that the old dogmatic orthodoxies would not do. Bryden felt compelled to challenge his progressive and liberal Calvinist forbears, then, not out of a lack of regard for the theological relevance of cultural analysis but out of a different post-modern analysis. As idealism

---

[53] Bryden, "Lectures on the Reign of Naturalisms," 1.

gave way to existentialism, a new theological response was required. This was Bryden's territory in the years following 1925.

By the late nineteenth century Canadian Presbyterian theological leaders, such as George Monro Grant, had recognized the burgeoning need to address the issues raised by the direct contact between western Christianity and the world's major religions. Admitting that his interest in the beginning had perhaps been "more academic than specifically Christian," Bryden began to penetrate into the heart of the great religions with his students, using whatever could be gleaned from history, sociology, psychology, anthropology, and theology to do so. He began typically with lectures on the philosophy of religion in which he dealt with the nature of religion; the relation of religion to morality, science, and art; the development of religion and the factors which entered into the development; and the general problem of religion and cognition. But soon he was grappling with the essence and significance of particular religions as he explored Buddhism, Confucianism, Taoism, and Hinduism. By the 1930s he had incorporated his study of religion into his overall theological approach:

> As a student for many years of the great religions of the world, it has become increasingly clear to me that no important "distinctiveness" on behalf of Christian faith and revelation can be either supported or maintained on the grounds offered by either Orthodox or Liberal apologetics. The characteristic miracles, for instance, in respect to virgin births, prognostications, visions and revelations, abound in all the great religions; doctrines in regard to saviour-gods, moreover, with the corresponding controversies (which are strikingly similar to those Christian), present themselves in some of those religions. What is more important, however, in view of the modern Liberal understanding of the Christian "religion" so-called, the New Testament offers nothing in ethical insight and responsibility, in human sentiment, or in religious appreciations or evaluations, to justify claims for uniqueness in these important respects. Some far more fundamental understanding of the Christian faith would seem to be necessary, if that faith is to become again a power among men, if it is to find an adequate warrant for its great assumption that it is under obligation to evangelize the "heathen" world.[54]

When Hendrik Kraemer's *The Christian Message in a Non-Christian World* was published in 1939 Walter Bryden discovered a theology of religions based on Barth's insights which resonated with his own instincts. Conservative and liberal Protestant theologies, while happily incorporating the Enlightenment's critique of religion in their apologetic strategies, had failed to incorporate

---

[54]   Bryden, *The Christian's Knowledge of God*, viii.

the same radical critique of religion in their understanding of Christianity. Bryden was one of the few theologians, along with Barth and Kraemer, who saw this.

The Example of P. T. Forsyth

By the late 1920s Bryden's relation to the progressive Calvinism which had dominated his theological formation was severely attenuated. The process of critically distancing himself from all forms of liberal and progressive Protestant thought continued with Bryden's discovery of P. T. Forsyth's theology. James Smart and Donald Wade recalled that Bryden grew increasingly fond of quoting Forsyth in lectures, often in asides where he urged students to read everything that Forsyth had written.[55]

P. T. Forsyth has often been described as a forerunner to neo-orthodoxy and a Barthian before Barth who, having been thoroughly educated in the nineteenth-century liberalism of F. D. Maurice and Albrecht Ritschl, worked his way back to a rediscovery of the doctrine of grace and God's holy love expressed in the person of Christ and his atoning work on the cross. Forsyth argued cogently that liberal Protestant theology had undermined any real authority for Christian faith by substituting for it the vagaries of subjective religious experience. The revelation of God, having become a category of the human conscience, was dominated by philosophical and psychological theories of cognition. But Forsyth argued that the Calvinist orthodoxy of post-Reformation scholasticism suffered from a similar weakness: it too relied on an anthropocentric method which obscured the primacy of grace. Forsyth recognized the need to find an authority for Christian thought which addressed the Enlightenment critique without capitulating to it. That authority, he contended, was to be found in Christ alone. Christian theology, if it was to reject all forms of anthropocentrism, had to begin where Christian faith itself began, namely, with God's movement toward humanity. Appeals to religious experience or the Bible as the basis of Christian faith were equally misguided, Forsyth contended, unless set within a proper understanding of God's decisive action in Jesus Christ. The Bible's authority, if one must speak of it, is derived from its role as a medium of the gospel of grace. The inspiration of the Bible, therefore, is a doctrine which describes the insight of the apostles into the person and work of Christ rather than the supernatural communication and preservation of information. Since the Bible functions within the soteriological purposes of God , Forsyth rejected any emphasis on inerrancy, and welcomed the findings of historical criticism. But above all else, and this

---

[55] Wade, "The Theological Achievement of Walter Bryden"; and James D, Smart, "Lest We Forget."

is a critical point for Bryden, the Bible's message was truly apprehended in the evangelical experience of regeneration. Religious experience was essential for Forsyth, and yet it provided neither the starting point nor the datum of revelation.[56]

It has to be said that this was precisely the theological point at which Walter Bryden found himself during the 1920s. Forsyth had used the new critical theological freedom of the early twentieth century to support and express the evangelical realities of the Christian faith in a way that appealed to Bryden. Forsyth helped Bryden to see that it might be possible for the human knower to have a genuine knowledge of God which was grounded, not in the knowledge of the knower established by the functions of human consciousness, but in the reality of God's gracious movement toward the knower in Jesus Christ. This was a logic driven by reconciliation and redemption rather than philosophical epistemology. And it was precisely the direction in which the theology of Karl Barth was moving when Bryden encountered it.

The Reception of Barth and Barthianism

Bryden's Encounter with Barth

Karl Barth was born in Basel, Switzerland, on May 10, 1886, to a family steeped in moderate Pietism. (Just three years earlier, Walter Bryden had been born in Galt, Ontario, to a family rooted in Scottish Presbyterianism.) After studies in Bern, where Barth's father Fritz was *Ordinarius* Professor of Early and Medieval Church History, Barth studied in Berlin, Tübingen, and Marburg, where he was influenced by the liberal theology of Adolf von Harnack and Wilhelm Herrmann. The first decade of the twentieth century was an auspicious and anxious time to be studying theology in both Europe and Canada. Bryden encountered, as previously noted, philosophical idealism and its manifestation in various forms of Scottish Calvinism, while Karl Barth was immersed in the neo-Kantianism and post-Ritschlian theology of Marburg. There, under Herrmann's influence, Barth discovered many of the themes and tendencies that were to survive his later break with the liberal theology of his teachers, including a definition of revelation as *Self-*revelation, an insistence upon the self-authenticating character of revelation,

---

[56] Rogers and McKim, *The Authority and Interpretation of the Bible*, 394. See also Haddon Willmer, "P. T. Forsyth," in *The New International Dictionary of the Christian Church*, edited by J. D. Douglas (Grand Rapids: Zondervan, 1978) 382–83; and Donald G. Miller, Browne Barr, Robert S. Paul, *P. T. Forsyth: The Man, The Preacher's Theologian, Prophet for the Twentieth Century* (Pittsburgh: Pickwick, 1981); Samuel Mikolaski, editor, *The Creative Theology of P. T. Forsyth* (Grand Rapids: Eerdmans, 1969); and John Rogers, *The Theology of P. T. Forsyth* (London: Independent, 1965).

and an opposition to natural theology and apologetics.[57] Barth and Bryden were both young bright theological students preparing for the ministry of their respective Reformed churches and both were ordained in 1909, Bryden in Lethbridge, Alberta, and Barth in Geneva, Switzerland. Barth began his ministry as a convinced liberal Protestant while Bryden wavered between the progressive Calvinism and the liberal evangelicalism of his most influential teachers. At about the time that Bryden moved to Woodville, Ontario Karl Barth was called to be pastor of the Reformed congregation in Safenwil (Aargau), Switzerland. From 1921 Barth served successively as a professor in Göttingen, Münster, Bonn and Basel while Walter Bryden began his teaching career at Knox College in 1925. Bryden (1883–1952) predeceased Barth (1886–1968) by some sixteen years. So far, their lives appear in outline to have paralleled one another. But there is, of course, more that must be said. By the late 1920s Bryden was working out his understanding of the Reformed faith in the shadow of Barth's enormous influence.

Karl Barth worked closely with his lifelong friend and colleague Eduard Thurneysen as they immersed themselves in the task of ministry and the issues of the day. Within a few short years Barth became utterly disillusioned with liberal theology. In the first place, soon after his arrival in Safenwil he became involved with "the religious socialists" (Herrmann Kutter, Leonhard Ragaz) and sought to organize the workers in his congregation. In addition to creating tension in the church, this placed Barth at odds with the liberal cultural Protestant theology of Germany which was politically conservative and socially bourgeois. Second, he was shocked by the virtually unanimous and unqualified support of his liberal theological teachers for the German side in World War One. And third, he questioned whether liberal Protestant theology had the theological substance and nerve to sustain Christian preaching. All this drove him to a study of Paul's letter to the Romans where he discovered "the strange new world within the Bible." Initially published in 1919, and revised and re-published in a second edition in 1922, Barth's commentary and subsequent public lectures established his reputation as a theologian with which to be reckoned. He proclaimed the "wholly otherness" of God and insisted, following Kierkegaard, that there was "an infinite qualitative difference" between God and human beings. Working with Thurneysen, Rudolf Bultmann, Friedrich Gogarten, and Emil Brunner, Barth founded the journal *Zwischen den Zeiten* (Between the Times) and continued to write theology that has been variously described as dialectical, realistic, and paradoxical. It was also characterized as a theology of crisis, a neo-Reformation theology, a theology of the Word, and neo-orthodoxy. By the 1930s Barth was engaged

---

57 Bruce McCormack, *Karl Barth's Critically Realistic Dialectical Theology: Its Genesis and Development 1909–1936* (Oxford: Clarendon, 1995) 68.

in the lifelong task of writing his major work, *Kirchliche Dogmatik* (*Church Dogmatics*), and because of his resistance to Nazism he was removed from his teaching post and expelled from Germany in 1935. He returned to the place of his birth, Basel, Switzerland, and its university, where he continued to write, teach, and exercise an influence as the most prolific Protestant theologian of the twentieth century. The development of Barth's massive theological project is complex and the object of continuing study, most of which need not concern us here. The important point to be considered is the reception of Barth's theology and the movement it spawned in Canada in the 1920s and 1930s through the work and witness of Walter Williamson Bryden.

As already noted, at about the time that Karl Barth was wrestling with Romans, Walter Bryden had immersed himself in the Corinthian correspondence. Although it was published in 1925, three years after Barth's second edition of Romans (1922), *The Spirit of Jesus in St. Paul* made no mention of Barth. It was four years later when Bryden, by then an established professor at Knox College, first gave notice that Karl Barth was a theologian to be reckoned with by Canadian Protestants. In his April, 1929 address to the convocation of The Presbyterian College, Montreal, Bryden wrote that Karl Barth was a "stern, new prophet of Europe" who described the existential angst involved in truly recognizing God. Knowing God means giving oneself over to God, to do God's will, to begin with God anew, and to recognize in the midst of fierce, inner, personal conflict that God approaches us as *wholly other*. Bryden saw Barth as a theological physician who offered a strong dose of doctrine to cure an ailing Protestantism. And in what appeared to be a parenthetical observation Bryden wrote: "and by the way this is real Calvinism in a modern dress. Indeed this is the heart and soul of Calvinism and that which will abide the changes of time and thought in that system of theology." Barth had recovered what was essential for Calvin: that the great Christian truths are not at our command. They cannot be ordered up and believed at will.[58]

Sometime in the early 1930s Bryden began to work on a manuscript called "After Modernism, What?" which included a major chapter on "The Challenge of Karl Barth." The book was never published and for the most part it contains material on Christology, eschatology, Schleiermacher, and Ritschl that can be found in Bryden's lectures, book reviews and other published works. The chapter on Barth, however, consists of material not found elsewhere. It is important, not because it provides an adequate and accurate account of Barth's theology per se, but because it describes Bryden's encounter with Barth's theology. In short, this material grants a glimpse of Walter Bryden as he wrestled with the insights of a theology that appeared to provide an alternative to Calvinist orthodoxy and liberal Protestantism. Barth's theol-

---

58   Bryden, "The Triumph of Reality," in *Separated Unto the Gospel*, 137.

ogy confirmed many of the instincts instilled in Bryden by Denney. At the same time, it forced him to question many of the presuppositions with which he had continued to work as a student shaped by progressive Calvinism.

Bryden gave no account of how he first came to be introduced to Barth's theology or with which of Barth's books he began. It is clear, however, that Bryden's reading of Barth was limited primarily to Barth's early theology. Bryden indicated that he had abandoned his initial intention to write a chapter called "The Significance of Karl Barth" because "I myself cannot profess to have read all that Barth has written." Given the scale, scope and steady pace of Barth's prodigious production Bryden would not have been alone. Very few at that time, especially in the English-speaking world, could have boasted that they had read everything that Barth had written. The important question is this: What of Barth had Bryden read? Here the answer seems clear. On the basis of works cited, Bryden had worked through the essays and lectures to be found in *The Word of God and the Word of Man* (English translation, 1928), the first volume of the *Christian Dogmatics* (German, 1927), the second edition of *Römerbrief* (1922 in German; 1933 in English), and *The Resurrection of the Dead* (c. 1933). In a footnote Bryden regretted that he had not had the opportunity to read the second edition of "The Dogmatik." (presumably he means Vol. I.1 of the *Church Dogmatics*, German 1932, English 1936) which Barth wrote when he determined that the earlier version (*Christian Dogmatics*) had to be set aside. Later, in the *Christian's Knowledge of God* (1940), Bryden indeed quoted from Vol. I.1. of the *Church Dogmatics* (*The Doctrine of the Word of God*) and *The Knowledge of God and the Service of God*. And in the work he produced for the Articles of Faith Committee of The Presbyterian Church in the 1940s Bryden showed familiarity with Barth's christocentric doctrine of election in Vol. II.2 of the *Church Dogmatics*. For the most part, however, Bryden focused on the stage of Barth's theology usually identified with the school known as "dialectical theology,"[59] and he was one of the first Canadian Protestant theologians to do so. In short, Bryden's reading of Barth was an early Canadian reception of Barth's early theology. Bryden himself was conscious of this fact: "I am disposed to think that any effort made, at present, to represent the final significance of Karl Barth and of those who are of like mind in regard to Christian theology must, in the nature of the case, be premature." Not only was Barth a pilgrim theologian whose work was still in

---

[59]   Bruce McCormack has recently demonstrated that the dialectical character of Barth's theology was a constant feature beginning with Barth's turn from liberalism in 1915 through to the *Church Dogmatics*. I do not dispute this. Bryden, however, received Barth's early theology in the context of its association with Gogarten, Bultmann, Brunner, Tillich, and Thurneysen who were known at the time as "dialectical theologians." See McCormack, *Karl Barth's Critically Realistic Dialectical Theology*.

progress, he was a witness to the *Truth* whose significance was undoubtedly much greater than any influence emanating from his work.[60]

Bryden and Barth's English Interpreters

Bryden interacted widely with the corpus of secondary literature in English that was emerging around Barth's theology in the 1930s. He admitted no first hand knowledge of Kierkegaard's writings, and of the essential relation that he felt existed between Kierkegaard and Karl Barth. Much of what he learned about Kierkegaard, Barth, and the dialectical theologians came from a number of early books in English which shaped the reception of Barth's theology in Britain and North America. He acknowledged that this was doubtless a rather hazardous course of attempting to understand the challenge or challenges which Barth brought. "Perhaps, were Karl Barth himself to see the result of my effort he would be tempted to declare (as I understand he has so declared in the case of other more ambitious attempts to evaluate his work) that he could have wished that the author had studied his own (Barth's) works rather than devoted himself to the things which had been written about him." Notwithstanding the hazard, Bryden felt it was important to admit that his understanding of Barth had been shaped by the community of interpreters that had grown up around Barth's theology and that, like many of them, he had been compelled "to bend before the difficult teaching and exacting and challenging thought of this man."[61] Furthermore, he believed that a critical assessment of the appraisals of Barth was also necessary. But there is an even more important point to be made here. Bryden presumed that he was writing about *the challenge which Karl Barth should constitute for the Church and the twentieth century.* He was not interested in Barth's theology for its own sake, but in what could be learned from it that would assist and enrich the church's proclamation of the Christian message, especially in Canada. The ways in which others in the English-speaking world were interpreting and applying Barth's theology, therefore, not only justified the procedure he followed; it required it.

Among the works cited by Bryden are R. Birch Hoyle's *The Teaching of Karl Barth: An Exposition*, first published by the Student Christian Movement Press in London in June 1930. Hoyle's explicit purpose was "to interpret the theological ideas of Karl Barth to English readers."[62] By the late 1920s numerous articles on Barth's theology had begun to appear in the religious papers and theological journals of Britain, including *The Expositor, The Hibbert*

---

60   Bryden, "After Modernism, What?"
61   Ibid.
62   R. Birch Hoyle, *The Teaching of Karl Barth: An Exposition* (London: SCM, 1930) 7.

Journal, The Expository Times, The Times Literary Supplement, and *The Review of the Churches.* Capitalizing on this interest in a theological movement un-like anything encountered in Anglican or Free Church circles in Britain, Hoyle sought to explore Barth's theology as something other than orthodoxy, liberalism, or any attempt to combine the two. Noting Barth's appeal to post-war conditions in Europe and the theological vacuum in the churches, Hoyle interpreted Barth as a theologian of crisis who emphasized the encounter between God and human beings which takes place when God speaks and human beings hear.

Bryden also referred to J. Arundel Chapman's 1931 book *The Theology of Karl Barth: A Short Introduction,* which appeared in London, England. Chapman came very near to the heart of Barth's experience, Bryden argued, when he directed readers to Barth's own words in *The Word of God and the Word of Man:* "Whoever can say 'Jesus Christ,' need not say 'It may be,' he can say 'It is.'" Then, citing Barth in *Römerbrief* directly, Bryden points to Barth's dialectical conception of judgment: "Those who have taken upon themselves the burden of the NO, are borne by the greater divine YES." For our purposes here it is important to note the manner in which Bryden moved seamlessly between the theology of Barth, the comments of Barth's interpreters, and his own thoughts. Chapman emphasized an aspect of Barth that became decisive for Bryden. Barth's theology provided a correction which countered every theology affirming or implying the divinity of humanity. Theology declared the judgment of God on human existence and therefore had to interpret the writing on the wall against an optimistic belief in progress and a cheerful acceptance of the essential goodness of human beings. The experience of faith for Barth, Chapman argued, and Bryden agreed, was the experience of being plunged into a crisis. The concept of crisis was vital to Barth's thought and its presence gave Barth's early teaching its tempestuous character. Faith may be understood as an agitated condition of negation which comes when we reach the end of ourselves and find, at the long end of the "No" the "Yes" of God waiting for us. Confronted by divine wrath and forgiveness, the human "I" is utterly broken.

The Scottish theologian John McConnachie, whom Bryden later referred to as "my dear old friend," wrote two books on Barth that were read by Bryden.[63] The first, *The Significance of Karl Barth,* was published in 1931. Even though, according to Bryden, McConnachie was regarded by Barth as his best English interpreter at the time, the book missed the soul of Barth because it tried too hard to systematize his theology in terms of a particular standpoint. McConnachie's second book, *The Barthian Theology and the Man*

---

63   Bryden, "Introduction to the Congress," in *Addresses from the Pre-Assembly Congress of 1950 and the 76th General Assembly* (Toronto: The Presbyterian Church in Canada, 1950) 11.

of Today, appeared shortly after the first and, according to Bryden, this time McConnachie had successfully captured the dialectical character of Barth's approach to Christian doctrine. The second book also had an earlier life in Canada as a series of lectures. It was dedicated "to the many kind and appreciative friends whom I met in Canada when I lectured on the theology of Karl Barth." Sounding the note of crisis, McConnachie suggested that Barth and Gogarten had rightly identified the judgment of God upon society and the church "in which none of us can play the part of spectator, for ultimately it is a crisis which sets each one of us before God."[64] American Protestant thought, McConnachie argued, continued to cling to a sentimental idealism in the post-war era and was therefore less open to Barth while Britain and Canada, conscious of the cataclysm that was shaking the foundations of western culture, had opened their doors to the Barthian theology of crisis.

In addition to the British publications which were decisive in shaping Bryden's reception of Barth, a number of American books also played a role. Emil Brunner's *Theology of Crisis* was particularly important, not simply for Bryden, but for the whole reception of Barth's theology in the English-speaking world. The European Brunner, like Barth, was Swiss and wrote primarily in German but this book consisted of lectures given in 1928 in America in English. Of all the dialectical theologians in the 1920s Brunner was the first to get his oar in the water "to introduce to the English-speaking world the theology of crisis."[65] The result was that a good deal of what passed for Barth's theology in the minds of many North Americans was in fact the theology of Brunner. During the 1920s the names of Barth and Brunner were identified closely by most interpreters who were unaware that differences between them on natural theology had already emerged, differences that finally led to their acrimonious split in 1934. In his assessment of Barth's dualism, Bryden quoted Brunner on a point concerning the transcendence of God that was to divide Barth and Brunner: "We are treating of an epistemological, but not of a cosmological transcendence. We hold, i.e., that God cannot be known by his active presence in the world. His presence in nature and history is not denied, but it is regarded as hidden so that, what God is, is not revealed." Such talk made Barth nervous and it was precisely the meaning of God's presence in nature and history within the context of German Christianity in the 1930s that caused the subsequent uproar.

The differences between Brunner and Barth notwithstanding, Brunner's interpretation of dialectical theology gained a wide hearing in North America under the guise of Barthianism, and for reasons that go beyond Brunner's

---

[64]   John McConnachie, *The Barthian Theology and the Man of Today* (London: Hodder and Stoughton, 1933) 13.

[65]   Emil Brunner, *The Theology of Crisis* (New York: Scribner, 1929) x.

early appearance on this side of the Atlantic. In the first place, unlike Barth, Brunner made a concerted effort to demonstrate the relevance of the theology of crisis for North American church and society. The word *crisis* for Brunner had two meanings: it signified the climax of an illness, and it denoted a turning-point in the progress of an enterprise or movement. Brunner argued that their theologies (i.e., Barth, Brunner, Gogarten, et al.) represented a turning-point in a liberal Protestant theology that had not only stalled, but was seriously ill. Brunner was aware that the impact of the crisis had not yet been fully felt in North America. In Europe since World War One, modern civilization was seen as having come to a really critical stage. The disintegration of western culture and the decline of western Christendom had led to a decisive point where the issue could only be new life or death. The economic prosperity and political security which led to a more optimistic assessment of the situation in North America, Brunner argued, did not diminish the actuality of the pending cultural and theological crisis. Brunner's analysis proved to be eerily prophetic. Within a year the stock market crashed and soon the entire continent was plunged into the Great Depression only to be followed by the international crisis in Europe. The same sense of cultural crisis that had engulfed Europe now prevailed in North America during the 1930s.

Secondly, Brunner also noted that the crisis was theological in nature and that this too expressed itself somewhat differently in the English-speaking world. Protestant theology, Brunner contended, was in a state of rapid dissolution. As in Europe, the churches in Britain, Canada, and the United States had become captive to a theology which had accommodated progressive, monistic, ethical, and optimistic ideals accompanied by naturalism and rationalism. But in the English-speaking world there were additional problems peculiar to the Anglo-Saxon intellect. "The idealistic-liberal worldview has been progressively undermined by a naturalistic positivism and pragmatism. The schools of radical psychology of religion offer incontrovertible evidence that all absolute values and all objective content of faith have been renounced."[66] The pragmatic, activist, and experiential tendencies of the English-speaking world, especially America, Brunner believed, also testified to the crisis confronting the church.

Thirdly, Brunner identified dialectical theology as a way through the divided mind of modern theology and the two-party Protestantism that had emerged in the modernist-fundamentalist controversy in North America. Brunner argued that the theology of crisis provided a third option, and a way in which a Christian could be truly critical and truly a Christian at the same time. Indeed, this was essential to Christian faith for Brunner: "A third thesis may be added with propriety, namely that only a Christian can be truly

---

[66] Ibid., 8.

critical, and only he who is truly critical can be a Christian. The principles of true Christianity and of true criticism are identical."[67] Modernism and fundamentalism, Brunner observed, are born of the same mother, that is, of the fear of sound critical thinking. All of this made sense to Bryden as he tried to appropriate Barth's insights, via Brunner, for the Canadian church. Brunner's analysis of the cultural crisis, the activist and pragmatic tendencies of a church in the shadow of idealism, and the modernist-fundamentalist controversy—these were themes that appeared time and time again in Bryden's teaching, writing, and preaching through the 1930s and 1940s.

Bryden also relied on Walter Lowrie's *Our Concern with The Theology of Crisis* to understand Barth's theology and the hearing that it received in the United States. Lowrie was an American Episcopal minister and theological liberal who was deeply influenced by reading the dialectical theologians and Kierkegaard's philosophy. Lowrie helped Bryden to see the importance for Barth of Christian proclamation as the basis of theological reflection and pointed Bryden to the significance of Kierkegaard's "infinite qualitative difference between time and eternity" for the whole Barthian movement. Lowrie's emphasis on Barth's radical antithesis between time and eternity confirmed Bryden's struggle to get beyond the domesticated eschatology of modernism. Eternity breaks into time when the speaking God, whose Word places the world in a permanent state of crisis, creates the existential moment in an individual in which an absolute "Either–Or" decision is exacted. Lowrie, however, was also concerned that Brunner, through his lectures in the United States and the subsequent publication of his book, had "hardly done more than give a sample of his own theology" and had "been made to loom too large in our view of the School of Crisis."[68] Nevertheless, Lowrie adumbrated many of the same themes as he sought to interpret and apply the theology of crisis in the United States by "determining the character it must assume in our environment, if it is to be assimilated at all."[69] Barth had sounded the trumpet against all theologies indebted to everything but the Word of God. It was now up to others to heed the call so that the theology of crisis could be acclimatized in the English-speaking world through original works of the same genre produced by English-speaking scholars.[70] Bryden's 1940 book *The Christian's Knowledge of God* was most certainly such a work.

If Lowrie's appreciative appraisal of Barth's theology represented a call to arms for Bryden, Wilhelm Pauck's *Karl Barth: Prophet of a New Christianity?* represented a more critical challenge to the adequacy and appropriateness of

---

[67]   Ibid., 14.

[68]   Walter Lowrie, *Our Concern With The Theology of Crisis* (Boston: Meador, 1932) 10.

[69]   Ibid., 25–26.

[70]   Ibid., 10, 81.

Barthian theology. Barth, according to Pauck, was really a philosopher of religion in disguise whose appeal to the phenomenology of existence was cloaked in the authority of the Christian tradition. While Bryden was sympathetic to Pauck's concern that it was difficult to discover what finally constituted authority in the Christian faith for Barth, Bryden had to confess that he did not understand the severity with which Pauck criticized Barth's theology.

By the late 1930s Walter Bryden was more than a little nervous about the way in which Barth's theology was being received and re-appropriated in some circles. Bryden believed that Barth's theology, rightly understood, constituted a powerful challenge to modern theology's tendency to synthesize utterly incompatible understandings of revelation. He was convinced that Barth was profoundly right "precisely at the point where he seems to be most offensive to many of the theologians of the day." Barth's modern critics, however, were adept at adopting the emphases and forms of his theology, "wittingly or unwittingly" adjusting themselves to it and frequently representing him "as saying what he has never said." They criticized "him on the basis of such misrepresentations, all the while patronizing him as being the prophet of a new theological era, though, to be sure, not to be considered seriously as a theologian of first rank." Ironically, Bryden contended, these theologians have accepted a "Barthianism," in whole or in part, without Barth's discriminating and essential contribution. In short, Bryden believed that there was a domestication of Barth's theology taking place, especially in the English-speaking world. Comparing Barth to Luther, and Barth's critics to Erasmus, Bryden argued that the radical antitheses of Barth's theology, disliked and dismissed by his critics, were essential to his theology. Apart from the radical antitheses, Bryden contended, what Barth had said theologically was not important.[71] It was no wonder, then, that Bryden often denied he was a Barthian as he continued to mine the theology of Karl Barth for the Canadian church.

In addition to Bryden's reading of Karl Barth's early theology, and his engagement with the community of English interpreters that emerged in the wake of Barth's theology, Bryden devoted three years "to rather intensive study of the Barthian and kindred schools of thought," and had "the privilege of addressing publicly students and ministers on this subject." He also studied with groups of students and ministers privately, and carefully observed different reactions to what he had endeavored to present as the Barthian theology. These conversations influenced Bryden's interpretations of Barth's insights. More importantly, his engagement with Barth's theology in this manner meant that he became the conduit through which Barthianism was mediated to the Canadian Presbyterian church. The material in the unpublished

---

71 Bryden, *The Christian's Knowledge of God*, 143–44.

manuscript represented not only the fruit of his own personal study, but also the testing of Barthian insights in the Canadian context.

The ways and means through which Bryden's reception of Barthianism was facilitated—Bryden's study of Barth's early theology, Bryden's engagement with the early English interpreters of Barth in Britain and the United States, and Bryden's interaction with students and ministers within The Presbyterian Church in Canada—shaped the scope and substance of the Barthianism he embraced. Many of the themes he identified as of significance in Barth's theology became critical pieces in his own attempt to fashion a theological response within and for the Presbyterian Church in Canada beginning in the late 1920s. The importance of Barth's claim that the possibility of Christian theology is conditioned by the actuality that there is Christian speech has already been noted. Bryden welcomed Barth's emphasis on the relationship between theology and preaching in the development of a theology for, in, and of the church. At the same time, Bryden raised questions about Barth's pneumatology, especially on what Bryden perceived as Barth's unwillingness to emphasize the Holy Spirit as the constitutive principle of the church or the positive aspect of the Spirit's work in the individual's heart. This was a problem, as we shall see, that Bryden sought to correct in his own account of the Christian's knowledge of God.

Dialectics, Crisis, and Existentialism

Bryden particularly noted the dominance of dialectical method in Barth's theology. In comparison to rational confessional Calvinism and idealistic liberal Calvinism, Bryden found Barth's early dialectical theology and its stress on paradox particularly attractive. As a classical form of argumentation, dialectical reasoning employed propositions, counter-propositions, and reconciling syntheses. In the nineteenth century Hegel, as noted earlier, incorporated dialectical reasoning as an essential component of absolute idealism. The progressive unfolding of absolute Spirit in history could be mapped by tracking the theses and antitheses, and the reconciling syntheses which transcended them. In the process history was constantly being elevated to a new level. In reaction to Hegel, Kierkegaard applied dialectical reasoning to individual existence which, he argued, could not be rationally comprehended or resolved. In the hands of Kierkegaard dialectical now referred to a way of reasoning in which contradictory and contrary assertions were held together in paradox. If one had to speak of a synthesis, resolution, or reconciliation of divergent positions, one could only do so in terms of faith.

In the second edition of his commentary on Romans, Karl Barth employed Kierkegaard's method and his infinite qualitative difference to emphasize the radical distinction between God and humanity, time and eternity, and infinite and finite. The revelation of this radical distinction occurred in the paradoxical veiling and unveiling of the Word of God in Jesus Christ. There was, therefore, no higher rational synthesis beyond the contradictions, only the two poles which remained in tension, revealed in Jesus Christ, and apprehended by faith. Idealism failed as a system of rational thought because the lives of human beings can never be summarized as a paragraph in a system. The basic question which confronts human beings is one of authentic existence. An authentic philosophy, therefore, is a philosophy for life, not for idle speculation at sunset when the owl of Minerva has made its appearance. Life as it comes to human beings is not neatly rational; it is paradoxical, and the Christian faith presents human beings with paradox at its very center—God and humanity, time and eternity, the infinite and the finite—in the person of Jesus Christ. The challenge, therefore, is not to find the truth but to live it, not to worry about what Christianity is but to ask how to become a person of authentic Christian faith. Bryden astutely observed that what lay behind Barth's dialectical method was his conviction concerning a human being's incapability of knowing and apprehending the infinite God. The antitheses and antinomies which Barth stressed were not primarily matters of concepts, ideas or even truths that belonged essentially to the mental problems of human beings. The contradiction and the paradox that constituted Barth's real problem had to do with life itself as it was understood over and against the wholly-other God, whom human beings did not know.

Dialectical method, therefore, as it was employed by Barth during this period in his theology, emphasized that if God was to be known at all, God must reveal the divine being. Bryden noted that both Barth and Hegel recognized a thesis and antithesis in the different aspects of life. Unlike Hegel, however, Barth refused to allow any synthesis that human beings might make. Human beings know an absolute "Yes" and an absolute "No." In neither of these, however, could human beings settle down and abide. Life in God's world is a journey "on the knife-edge of two opposing abysses." The truth is that the "No" is always concealed in the "Yes" and the "Yes" in the "No." Bryden emphasized that Barth never permitted a consummation of these in a static certainty.[72]

In addition to the dialectical character of Barth's theology, Bryden (along with Brunner) also noted its emphasis on crisis. The idea of crisis was taken in either of two senses. First, it referred to the proximate occasion prompting the theological movement in Europe: the outbreak of World War One and the consequent disillusionment of Barth, Thurneysen, Brunner, Gogarten and Bultmann with the optimistic view of society and culture espoused by

---

[72] Bryden, "After Modernism, What?"

liberal Protestant theologians. In North America the crash of the stock market in 1929, the continuing economic depression of the 1930s, and the political developments in Europe put an end to the optimism of liberal theology in American and Canadian Protestantism. As Sydney Ahlstrom noted, "it was in this time of crisis that a new theological epoch began to take shape, and for better or worse neo-orthodoxy is the term by which it has come to be known."[73] But as Wilhelm Pauck reminded readers in his 1931 book on Barth, it would be a mistake to see the theology of crisis as a mere expression of a war-psychology or particular cultural moment and therefore a temporary phenomenon. This crisis, first confronted in Europe and later felt in North America, provided the impulse for the development of a new interpretation of Christian thought.

Second, the theology of crisis also referred to the mode in which the neo-orthodox theologians expressed themselves, that is in critical categories such as: the negation of any power within humanity to reach God, the judgment of God upon all forms of self-righteousness, the absolute necessity of God's grace, and the crisis of faith, which demanded a decision in the confrontation of human existence by the Word of God. In this sense the crisis of culture, church and individual was an ongoing crisis under the judging Word of God. As William Hordern noted, the crisis theologians:

> taught that God confronts human beings and creates a crisis in which people must say yes or no to God. The purpose of preaching was to force human beings to face this crisis and to make a decision. Preaching could no longer appeal to human strength or consist of moral appeals; it had to preach to human weakness, confronting people with their creatureliness and sin, and point them to their only hope, the Word of God in Jesus Christ.[74]

Bryden noted this important connection between the conceptions of revelation and crisis in Barth's theology of the Word: Christian speech "is essentially a being apprehended by God in crisis." Bryden argued that Barth recognized the importance of a moment in the present: "It is the experience of the moment, of crisis, of revelation, of faith."[75]

Dialectics and crisis were accompanied by an emphasis on existential thought in Barth's theology as Bryden understood it. Barth's theology, however, according to Bryden, was not grounded in existentialist philosophy as such. Nor was it driven by a concern for individual, authentic experience. Rather,

---

[73]   Sydney E. Ahlstrom, *Theology in America: The Major Protestant Voices from Puritanism to Neo-Orthodoxy* (New York: Bobbs-Merrill, 1967) 78.

[74]   William Hordern, *The Case For A New Reformation Theology* (Philadelphia: Westminster, 1959) 22.

[75]   Bryden, "After Modernism, What?"

it was the means through which Barth sought to overturn the influence of idealism in the Christian thought of the nineteenth century and constituted, therefore, one of Barth's main challenges to modern religious thought and one of the most fruitful springs of his entire thinking. Existentialism, Bryden believed, was the vehicle of a new realism in theology which used idealism against itself in the development of a genuine alternative in modern theology.

In all this Bryden believed that, undoubtedly, Barth reflected the original attitude and spirit of the Reformed churches. Barth had truly grasped, Bryden argued, the motives and quickening impulses which inspired the sixteenth-century movement. Thus, Barth had no peer or equal as an interpreter of the earlier Reformation, and gave to it, as no other, its true significance. Barth even went beyond the Reformers, Bryden contended, to prevent the religious experience to which they gave expression from congealing into a pure intellectualism or dogmatism. The Word of God which may be spoken and heard in the sermon, the lecture, the written page, Barth claimed, can never be "possessed" by the preacher, the lecturer, or the writer. The presumption of human beings who claim that they know God, can speak or write about God, can impart knowledge concerning God, destroys the one condition by which God can be known and heard at all.[76]

This was the fundamental insight that finally turned Bryden, once and for all, against what he considered an uncritical, rigid, confessional Calvinism on the one hand, and a latitudinarian, liberal Protestantism on the other, and towards a neo-Reformation conception of the Word. As significant as dialectics, crisis, encounter, paradox, realism, and existence may have been for understanding Barth's theological witness, the important thing about Barth's theology for Bryden was that the Swiss Reformer had made it possible, once again, to speak of God with the awareness that it was impossible to speak about God unless God speaks first. Barth was preeminently a theologian of the Word. His Trinitarian conception of revelation, Bryden believed, represented the constructive theological expression of this fundamental insight. On this basis, and within this theological paradigm, Walter Bryden bore witness to the Judging-Saving Word of God within Canadian Protestantism. In short, Bryden began to understand the voice of the church in preaching, teaching and theology, and therefore his own voice, as a response to the voice of God in whose voice human beings hear much more than the echo of their own voices. The significance of Barth for Bryden in finding his theological voice was immense: "It can be affirmed at once . . . that Barth has proven already to have been the man who has struck the rock in the present-day wil-

---

[76] Ibid.

derness of doubt, perplexity and uncertainty, from which, it is acknowledged, are flowing living waters to refresh the souls of men."[77]

Canadian Protestantism on Barth

Walter Bryden was not the only Canadian Protestant theologian at the time who was interested in Barth's theology—but he appeared to be one of the few who was willing to follow Barth's "audacious and penetrating insights" through to their conclusions. A number of United Church ministers and theologians had recognized the need for a new theology to address the post-war period in Canada by the late 1920s. Among them was Richard Roberts who anticipated a good deal of the neo-orthodox critique of liberalism when he argued that the flaw of liberal Protestant theology rested on its overestimation of human nature. The failure to account for the transcendence of God and the reality of sin meant that liberal theology had produced a soft and sentimental faith, unable to sustain faith and life in the post-war era. Unable and unwilling to choose between the modernist's emphasis on immanence and the fundamentalist's disposition towards transcendence, Roberts argued that the church had to live with the dualism implicit in Christian faith.[78] He proposed "to be both a traditionalist and a modernist, in the belief that a frank dualism is a healthier state of mind than a premature and muddled synthesis."[79] Such an attempt, he recognized, would involve him in "inconsistencies and paradoxes." Sensing the same need, other United Church leaders soon began to note the thought of Karl Barth and the other leading proponents of dialectical theology. The English translation of Barth's *Der Wort Gottes und Die Theologie*, by Walter Horton in 1928, made Barth's theology directly accessible to Canadian Protestants who, until that time, had relied mainly on Brunner and Barth's English interpreters.

The new interest in the theology of crisis by Canadian Protestant theologians resulted in no fewer than four articles on Barth and Barthianism in the *Canadian Journal of Religious Thought* between 1929 and 1931. Published between 1924 and 1932 in Toronto as an ecumenical venture, the journal "was dominated by United Church ministers who contributed the most articles and held the greatest number of positions on the editorial board."[80] The first article on Barth was a review of *The Word of God and the Word of Man*, written by John Line of Emmanuel College. Line's response was generally positive, albeit cursory and cautious. Aware that Barth's theology was important and

---

77   Ibid.

78   Marshall, *Secularizing the Faith*, 195–201; Gauvreau, *The Evangelical Century*, 265–68.

79   Richard Roberts, "The Scope of Theology," cited in Gauvreau, *The Evangelical Century*, 265.

80   David B. Marshall, *Secularizing the Faith*, 201.

yet relatively unknown first-hand, Line spent most of the review quoting passages from Barth's text at length. No one interested in the church and its problems should be content to remain ignorant of Barth's theology, Line argued. After noting the social-prophetic phase of Barth's theology inspired by Kutter and Ragaz, Line pointed to Barth's conception of God and God's relation to the world as his fundamental concern. Line also reminded his readers that Barth was not a fundamentalist who intended to rehabilitate a pristine form of orthodoxy. Rejecting the notions of verbal inspiration and dogmatic inerrancy, Barth, Line noted, demanded freedom for criticism and scientific investigation. "But aside from and exceeding all this," Line cited Barth as saying, "is the fact that one is confronted in the Bible by a World, a Reality, a sovereign will that stands without or above the ordinary current of our life and thought."[81] Barth produced a powerful picture of God's revelation which portrayed not our movement to God, but what is always first and foremost, God's movement toward us. We do not search or think God out; we think after God (*Nachdenken*). All of this made Barth, Line concluded, a fascinating and disturbing writer, whose "paradoxes fell like sledge-hammers on our conventional and complacent habits of thought."

Line's review of Barth's work was followed six months later by D. L. Ritchie's assessment of Barth and Barthianism. Ritchie, a professor at Montreal's United Theological College who was then studying in Europe, gave an overview of Barth's life and work, the themes of his theology, and the thought of Barth's colleagues Thurneysen, Brunner, Gogarten, Heim, Bultmann, Merz, and Schmidt. Noting the response Barth's insights received among liberal Protestants and Roman Catholics, Ritchie argued that Barth's theology was characterized by an emphasis on the transcendence of God, the dialectical method of theology, the Protestant position on sin and grace, the resurrection of the crucified Jesus, and the relation between Word and Spirit.[82]

The reception of Barth and Barthianism in Canada was undoubtedly complicated by church union. In the same way that the events before and after 1925 mitigated the polarity of the fundamentalist-modernist controversy in Canada, "denominational conflict," as one Scottish theologian observed, "impeded the growth of an original reception of the theology of Barth."[83] Despite the initial interest in Barth and Barthianism among some United

---

[81] John Line, "Barth and Barthianism," *Canadian Journal of Religious Thought* 6.2 (1929) 100.

[82] D. L. Ritchie, "Barth and Barthianism," *Canadian Journal of Religious Thought* 6.5 (1929) 317–25.

[83] Richard H. Roberts, *A Theology On Its Way? Essays on Karl Barth* (Edinburgh: T. & T. Clark, 1991) 136.

Church theologians, there was no concerted effort to marshal the resources of the theology of crisis to deal with the realities of the 1920s and the 1930s or to shore up the identity of the new United Church of Canada. In fact, E.H. Oliver's assertion was more typical of the United Church response.[84] Oliver maintained that neither the liberal "God of Humanism" nor Barth's "God of Pessimism" could meet the challenges facing the churches. This was precisely the point at which Bryden begged to differ. Having been somewhat marginalized by choosing to remain a Presbyterian, Bryden suggested from the sidelines that the United Church was avoiding the challenges posed by Barth's trenchant critique of church and society. The confidence in the coming of an earthly Kingdom of God could no longer be sustained in the face of the social, economic, political, and intellectual crises of the 1930s. Unquestioning faith in the ideal of progress appeared obscurantist when set against the realistic situation of the day. As one might expect, Bryden did not get much of a hearing in the United Church, but he set the same challenge before theological students and ministers of the continuing Presbyterian Church. Among them he was received enthusiastically. While the rest of Canadian Protestants set Barthianism aside until after World War Two, Walter Bryden was busily engaged in mining its resources for Canadian Presbyterians during a period of ecclesial crisis. Bryden was therefore not only one of the earliest interpreters of Barth on the Canadian scene, he was the first to see the significance of the theology of crisis for the Canadian churches.

Although Bryden did not write an article on Barth for the *Canadian Journal of Religious Thought*, he contributed no fewer than seventeen book reviews in the years 1930–32 in which his Barthian instincts were at work. The books reviewed represented works in church history, New Testament, and philosophical theology, and in them Bryden continued to explore the meaning of the Christian experience of God, often with the theologies of Calvin, Barth, and Brunner in the background. In a review of M.S. Enslin's *The Ethics of Paul*, Bryden criticized the separation of faith-union and mystical-union in Enslin's interpretation of Paul. There was no such division in Paul, Bryden argued, as he reflected Calvin's emphasis on union with Christ. The experience of God's revelation in Paul, if it is to be described in mystical terms, Bryden contended, was an experience of Christ-mysticism based on a spiritual union with Christ through faith. Mysticism in any other form, whether it was found in Schleiermacher's mystical God-consciousness or Radhakrishnan's mystical monism could simply not be reconciled with Paul's Christ-centered emphasis. In a review of J.E. Turner's *The Revelation of Deity* Bryden criticized the author's failure to address what he considered to be the most vital of issues: how do the powers of Supreme Reality operate in

---

[84]   Marshall, *Secularizing the Faith*, 235–36.

individual experience through the work of Christ? The existential meaning of God's revelation in the life of the individual was the note that Bryden now sounded with greater intensity and consistency. The grand schemes of idealism no longer carried any weight whatsoever in his thinking except to provide the foil against which a renewed Reformation understanding of the gospel was to be developed.[85]

John Dickie's *The Organism of Christian Truth* pointed Protestants in just this direction. Bryden was not interested in a recovery of Reformation ideals or a repristination of Reformation doctrine. He longed for a profound renewal of Reformation faith in the modern era:

> Dr. Dickie's insight into and profound understanding of the religion underlying the Reformation experience, before that experience was pauperized by the ensuing Protestant scholastics, is a noteworthy characteristic of his writing; and is refreshing, in view of the studied misunderstanding to which that experience is repeatedly subjected. His recognition everywhere of the deep paradoxical element in the Christian apprehension of truth, and his contention that the poles of such antinomies must be held fast, even though they cannot be synthesized, will appeal to the most thoughtful of readers . . . this is a book of fine discrimination and truly Christian exposition, conserving the great essentials of our faith without violating our modern ethical and religious sensibilities . . . .[86]

No phrase captures Bryden's reception of Barth's theology better than this one: "conserving the great essentials of our faith without violating our modern ethical and religious sensibilities." Bryden believed that Barth was a prophet of the Reformed faith in the modern world, whose theology, as the years went by, became ever more pregnant with meaning. Barth was a truly modern theologian in the Reformation tradition who was not intimidated by the modern world and used it to go through modernism, recovering the great essentials of New Testament Christianity for the modern world in the process. Dickie's book was an expression of this same sentiment.

This concern for both tradition and modernity was precisely why Bryden did not think that the confessional Calvinists could negotiate an appropriate and adequate way through the contemporary challenge. They were stuck in the post-Reformation ideals of the seventeenth and eighteenth centuries, between the dynamics of sixteenth-century Reformation faith on the one hand,

---

[85]   Bryden, Review of M. S. Enslin, *The Ethics of Paul* in *Canadian Journal of Religious Thought* 7.4 (1930) 244–46; review of J. E. Turner, *The Revelation of Deity* in *Canadian Journal of Religious Thought* 8.4 (1931) 339–40.

[86]   Bryden, Review of John Dickie, *The Organism of Christian Truth* in *Canadian Journal of Religious Thought* 9.1 (1932) 79–81.

and the idealism of the Enlightenment on the other. Lorraine Boettner's *The Reformed Doctrine of Predestination* was a good example of this problem. In his review Bryden wondered whether Boettner had truly apprehended the heart of the Reformed faith. The theologies of Barth and Brunner, Bryden suggested, were distinct signs pointing to a rejuvenation of Protestant theology. Their method was much more promising because it insisted on getting behind the thought formulations of the sixteenth and seventeenth centuries to that experience of God which impelled such formulations. In short, Calvin was far more significant for the challenges of the contemporary church than Calvinism, and Luther than Lutheranism.[87]

Shortly after the articles by Line and Ritchie were published, and as Bryden continued his work as one of their major reviewers, the *Canadian Journal of Religious Thought* printed two more articles on Barth, one by Jenkin H. Davies and another by the Dutch theologian W. A. Visser T'Hooft. Davies identified three main ideas in Barth's theology: paradox, crisis, and the Word. Barth had identified the altar-piece, painted by Matthias Grünewald at Isenheim, as an illustration of his theology. Commenting on this, Davies pointed to the startlingly strong and stark language Barth used to proclaim the paradox of faith:

> The message of the Bible is the Easter message. It is resurrection. Death is a door. There is no way from man to God. This is man's doom. But God makes his way to man. Eternity comes into time. The Creator enters into his creation. *But only through death.* Death is Life. Mortality is Resurrection. Despair is Hope. Abandonment is Salvation. Rejection is Election. Man can only find God this way by God's finding him. The Door of death is the perception of God's remoteness from man, his condemnation by Him, his powerlessness before Him. Death is the great question mark. And death is the Divine answer. The terrible No is the Divine Yes.[88]

As Bryden adapted the insights of Barth to the Canadian scene, he not only embraced such paradoxes, he reveled in them. He could also testify, with Visser T'Hooft, to the significance of Barth's theology:

> Barth opens up for us the wonderful objectivity of God's world. He delivers from the anxious seeking for religious treasures. His is the theology of spiritual poverty. Many of us who have spent fruitless hours in building up our inner experiences and always found them wanting when we needed them most—have been saved from our-

---

[87] Bryden, Review of Loraine Boettner, *The Reformed Doctrine of Predestination* in *Canadian Journal of Religious Thought* 9.2 (1932) 142–43.

[88] Jenkin H. Davies, "The Ideas of Karl Barth," *Canadian Journal of Religious Thought* 7.4 (1930) 329.

selves, from our old Adam by accepting this great truth, that the only thing which matters is God's Holy Spirit and that that Spirit is with those who are hungry and thirsty, not with those who are spiritually well-fed. And others who have tried to keep their ideals of human achievement and progress alive in a world where these ideals are constantly submerged by the floods of this abundantly realistic life, have been saved from both their ideals and their disillusionments by accepting the truth that God's kingdom comes at His appointed time and that God relates their efforts to it in His own way, of which we do not and need not know.[89]

No one made a more decisive and deliberate turn away from the ideals of human achievement and progress in Canadian Protestantism than did Walter Bryden in the late 1920s when those ideals began to be submerged in the floods of realism.

Christian Realism

The neo-orthodoxy embraced and espoused by Walter Bryden reflected not only the movement known as the theology of crisis and dialectical theology, it was also shaped by the theology of Reinhold Niebuhr, who together with his brother H. Richard Niebuhr, Walter Marshall Horton, and John Bennett created a post-liberal approach to theology in America that came to be known as Christian realism. As Robert Wright has noted, Barth held an indirect but profound influence in some quarters of Canadian Protestantism during the depression. And the critical conduit of European ideas in Canada, as in the United States, was Reinhold Niebuhr of Union Seminary in New York.[90] Behind this development lay Emil Brunner's argument that the theology of crisis was able to provide the basis for a Christian ethic which could transcend the apparent contradiction between concrete reality and abstract ideals. Natural ethics, Brunner contended, drifted between the pole of an easy-going naturalism, a tendency to adjust oneself to the world without much conflict, and the pole of a radical and abstract idealism that proclaimed high-sounding programs and postulates too far removed from the real world to be practical. This idealism was manifested in Christian faith, for example, when the Sermon on the Mount was set forth as a moral code or social program apart from the reality of God and the call of the gospel. The ethics of faith, Brunner maintained, were absolutely radical but also thoroughly concrete and practical since human beings were confronted by the call of God in the midst of

---

[89] W. A. Visser T'Hooft, "An Introduction to the Theology of Karl Barth," *Canadian Journal of Religious Thought* 8.1 (1931) 50–51.

[90] Robert Wright, "The Canadian Protestant Tradition 1914–1945," in *The Canadian Protestant Experience,* edited by George A. Rawlyk (Burlington: Welch, 1990) 179.

real historical and psychological situations. The will of God was the will of the creator and redeemer, and in eschatological fashion, it revealed the difference between what was and what was yet to come. The ethics of realism, therefore, were rooted in a desire to imitate God the creator and God the savior in the midst of real life.[91]

Similarly, Wilhelm Pauck described the outstanding feature of Barth's theology as a return to religious realism. Just as the subjectivism of impressionist art and early twentieth-century architecture in Germany had been giving way to a new objectivism, so philosophy was moving beyond idealism, and theology was becoming concerned with objectivism, factualism, and *Sachlichkiet*.[92] The radical and revolutionary consequence of modern theology was the loss of the realism of faith. By this the neo-orthodox theologians meant the certainty of the existence of God, which in the pre-rationalistic era was held without serious difficulty, since it accorded with, and was foundational to, many worldviews and philosophies. Since modern philosophy and science allowed only a concept of God, theology was faced with the challenge of explaining the reality of God on which religion depended in a manner different from the orthodox faith which had been marginalized and, in the minds of many, disqualified. Liberal Protestant theology since Kant and Schleiermacher appealed to the subjectivism of religious experience as the basis for explaining the reality of God, religious experience brought to expression in historical, cultural and moral ideals. It was precisely against this form of idealism that Barth, Brunner, and Niebuhr launched their vehement protest. Walter Bryden joined them. Theology had to be grounded in the reality and objectivity of God. Christian realism, therefore, was fundamentally a protest against the idealism of liberal Protestantism and the secularization of the human spirit. At the same time, however, the Christian realists wished to speak of the reality of God and the realism of faith without lapsing back into what they perceived as a rationalist and Biblicist orthodoxy. Theology which did not account for the critical judgments of modern thought, they argued, could not be counted as realistic. It was, rather, obscurantist. At the beginning of Barth's theology, Pauck believed, stood the message of the reality of God, with the Bible as a collection of documents which pointed to this fact: that God could be considered real, absolute, and sovereign. It is this critical realism which Bruce McCormack has recently identified as the key to the epistemological framework within which the genesis and development of Barth's theology is to be set.[93]

---

[91]   Brunner, *The Theology of Crisis*, 81–82.

[92]   Wilhelm Pauck, *Karl Barth: Prophet of a New Christianity?* (New York: Harper, 1931) 20.

[93]   Ibid. 97–99, 62; see also McCormack, *Karl Barth's Critically Realistic Dialectical Theology.*

Walter Marshall Horton's 1934 book *Realistic Theology* sought to address the question raised by John Bennett in a 1933 *Christian Century* article "After Liberalism—What?" Like Bryden, Horton and Bennett were convinced that liberalism as a system of theology had collapsed and had to be replaced, although its insights must not be allowed to die. Sensing a great ground-swell of new life in the general "realistic tendency" of the times in which they were living, Horton believed that it was possible to find in their era the guiding principles for the formulations of a new "realistic theology." Furthermore, he was convinced that such a new statement of Christian belief would show former conservatives and former liberals that they had much more in common than they supposed. Like Reinhold Niebuhr, Horton found that the exigencies of the time were driving him politically to the left, theologically to the right, an experience with which Walter Bryden could resolutely identify. Horton argued that unlike theology in Europe, liberal Protestantism in America had emerged from World War One relatively unscathed. Self-confident and aggressive, liberal theology exercised increasing dominance on church life. That was until the 1930s when it became clear that the most important fact about contemporary American theology was the disintegration of liberalism. Harried by fundamentalism on the right and routed by humanism on the left, liberalism was dying. This meant, Horton argued, that multitudes of sincere Christians were being plunged into a crisis of uncertainty.[94] Sensing the same crisis in Canada, Walter Bryden was looking for what might come after modernism.

The announcement of the death of liberalism was, of course, quite premature, but its decline for a season created an occasion for the rise of a new religious realism with Reinhold Niebuhr as one of its chief exponents. Niebuhr dismissed as unrealistic and romantic the social and political views which had been given birth by liberal Protestant theology. A revolt fuelled by American pragmatism was raging in the culture against anything which smacked of the romanticism, idealism, and optimism of the nineteenth century. In continental Europe this note of realism was being trumpeted loudly by the theologians of crisis who stood against all forms of subjectivism and monistic idealism. The American theologians sounded a note of caution, however, concerning what they perceived as the over-reaction of a theology which negated the nineteenth century so vehemently that it practically drove God out of recent history, and opposed liberal theology so antithetically that it managed to be wrong wherever liberal theology was wrong—except in the opposite sense. The American Christian realists did not wish to identify too closely with what they perceived as an excessive response to liberalism. They were comfort-

---

94 Walter Marshall Horton, *Realistic Theology* (New York: Harper, 1934) ix, 2, 8; John Bennett, "After Liberalism—What?" *Christian Century* 50.45 (November 8, 1933) 1403–6.

able standing between the older liberalism and the newer forms of European dialectical theology. Echoing American pragmatic concerns, they concluded that "Negatively, as a criticism of the liberal theology, we shall do well to lay it to heart; but positively, it cannot help us to a new statement of the Gospel, and that for a simple reason: we have just recently abandoned Calvinism, and cannot be expected to enter with any sense of joy and emancipation into a movement whose slogan is 'Back to Calvin.'" In short, Barthianism represented an "unstable combination of crude realism with respect to man and a wistful idealism with respect to ultimate reality, just as humanism is an unstable combination of crude realism with respect to ultimate reality and a wistful idealism with respect to man."[95]

Horton's assessment shows just how indebted Bryden was to the American realist appropriation of Barth by Horton, Bennett and Niebuhr. Bryden clearly shared their critical analysis of modernism, idealism, and liberalism. At the same time, when it came to answering the question "After Modernism, What?" Bryden was much more optimistic about Barth's theology and a re-appropriation of Calvinism. Less driven by pragmatic concerns, Bryden advocated a greater discontinuity with the insights of liberal Protestantism than did Niebuhr. Bryden, following Barth, was willing to accept the paradoxical disjunction between time and eternity, while Niebuhr was convinced that this made speech about God meaningless. Like Niebuhr, however, Bryden found the crucial point of intersection between God's transcendence and immanence in the realm of personality. And in this sense, like Niebuhr, Bryden could at one and the same time speak polemically against liberalism and admit basic liberal insights into his thinking. The Word of the transcendent God became immanent, Bryden argued, in the life process of the human being. It was, to be sure, an act of God which always had its origin in the reality of the incarnate Christ, mediated by the Holy Spirit, but at the same time no discontinuity could be admitted which precluded the possibility, indeed the necessity, that this revelation was a radical experience of authentic faith.

Far more significant for Bryden, however, was Niebuhr's account of theology and social criticism. The transition from an agriculturally-based rural economy to an industrialized urban economy in Canada had already begun by the early twentieth century, as we noted earlier. The theological response of the Social Gospel, initially attractive to Walter Bryden's generation, was in deep trouble by the 1930s. The Great Depression, soon to be followed by World War II, created a backlash against the optimistic outlook of Social Gospel progressivism. Disillusioned by what he perceived as a naïve, unwarranted and superficial theology, Niebuhr attempted to rehabilitate its critical

---

[95]   Horton, *Realistic Theology,* 10–12, 14–15, 36–38.

social insights without its ethical idealism. He sought to marshal classical theological themes such as the sovereignty of God, the sinfulness of humanity, and the apocalyptic dimensions of the Kingdom of God, in the service of a new theological ethic. Sydney Ahlstrom has described Niebuhr's *Moral Man and Immoral Society* as "probably the most disruptive religio-ethical bombshell of domestic construction to be dropped during the entire interwar period" in America. It became the major document in the "Protestant search for political realism" and established Niebuhr's dominance in American neo-orthodoxy. It also pointed to the fact that one of the primary purposes of the movement in America was a revision of the Social Gospel. Neo-orthodoxy in Niebuhr's hands, it could in fact be argued, was a self-critical moment in the theology of the Social Gospel. No American did more to transform the old liberal Social Gospel movement and to demonstrate the relevance of biblical insights and Christian affirmations for social criticism than did Reinhold Niebuhr. With a message that often appeared to be more prophetic than evangelical, Niebuhr's tone appealed to Bryden in the Canadian context.[96]

By the 1940 publication of *The Christian's Knowledge of God*, Bryden had developed an approach to theology, indebted to Barth and Denney (and Kierkegaard), that bore all the marks of what came to be recognized as neo-orthodoxy. He spoke of crisis, used dialectical method, emphasized paradox, focused on the encounter with God that created authentic existence, and developed a prophetic social criticism that paralleled the work of Reinhold Niebuhr. Persistent in his appeal to Calvin and Luther, he pointed toward a theology of the Word to address the epistemological aspects of unbelief in the twentieth century. He employed all this to redeploy the theology of Presbyterianism at a critical moment in the history of Canadian Protestantism, and by the 1940s, from his platform as principal of Knox College, Walter Bryden's neo-orthodox voice dominated the theological discourse of his denomination.

College Principal, 1945–1952

Walter Bryden became principal of Knox College in 1945, in the words of Brian Fraser, after "the controversies over administration, teaching, and doctrine in the 1920s and 1930s drained a tremendous amount of energy from the task of educating clergy for the continuing church."[97] Despite vigorous opposition on the floor of the General Assembly by those who were opposed to Bryden's theological and political views, by now well known across the

---

[96] Sydney Ahlstrom, *A Religious History of the American People* (New Haven: Yale University Press, 1972) 942.

[97] Fraser, *Church, College, and Clergy*, 161.

church, the appointment was approved and Bryden was inducted in October 1945.

Just months after the end of World War Two, Bryden used his inaugural lecture as an opportunity to cement the neo-orthodox worldview that had already come to dominate the ethos of Knox College primarily through his influence. Echoing Barth's emphasis on relying wholly on a wholly-other God, Bryden reminded the church that, in a time of grave and urgent responsibility, not the least important qualification for those who are called to serve "is the realization that they have actually *nothing* to meet what is demanded of them." This was not, Bryden argued, "to put a premium on ignorance, weakness, inefficiency, or to disqualify human virtues, but simply to recognize the foundation-axiom of our faith that human qualities as such are totally inadequate to the tasks of God."[98] Sensitive to the criticism launched against Barth's theology that its low evaluation of human beings "demeans the human personality and ignores man's undoubted accomplishments," Bryden reminded his hearers that the great servants of God, including Luther and Calvin, were "so little concerned about such things" as their human dignity and human personality.

This protest against progressive idealism, accompanied by a call to return to the spirit of theological renewal and ecclesiastical reform of the sixteenth century, continued to mark Bryden's tenure as principal. An increasing number of Canadian Presbyterians became convinced that the neo-Reformation theological orientation, shaped by Walter Bryden's appropriation of Barth, provided a unique and necessary approach to the Gospel that could sustain and nourish the witness of the continuing Presbyterian Church within Canadian Protestantism. That church, as James Smart noted, was confronted by the challenge of "the true nature, function, and destiny of the Church." Writing in the 1950s, Smart pointed to Bryden and the Trinitarian Theological Society where Smart and his classmates "began in the early thirties to see their Church's destiny as that of being an instrument through which Canadian Protestantism might be recalled to its heritage as a Church reformed and ever anew reforming according to the Word of God in Scripture."[99] Walter Bryden's appointment as principal ensured that this legacy would be enshrined at Knox College for a generation to come.

As Brian Fraser has noted, Bryden put his stamp on Knox College and its graduates in the seven years from 1945 until 1952 when he served as principal:

---

[98]   Bryden, "The Church of God and the World," in *Separated Unto the Gospel*, 46.

[99]   James D. Smart, "Canadian Presbyterianism Since 1925," *Presbyterian Record* (February 1954) 17; cited in Fraser, *Church, College, and Clergy*, 165.

All but one of the new generation of faculty who came to Knox between 1944 and 1952 were former students who acknowledged Bryden's formative influence. They were rooted in and committed to the core affirmations of the neo-orthodox culture that had come to be the dominant perspective among the leadership of Canadian Presbyterians. The next two successors to Bryden as principal, J. Stanley Glen from 1952 to 1975 and Allan Farris from 1976 to 1977, were drawn from this group of faculty. To add to the strength of this position at the college, all but one of the new appointments and replacements made in the 1960s were Knox graduates influenced by Bryden as well. All built on the theological foundations of their mentor, though they interpreted and applied Bryden's neo-orthodoxy in their own unique ways. The dominance of Bryden's students on the faculty and the fact that Knox continued to provide the majority of the clergy for the church ensured that his legacy in theology and his agenda for the reconstruction of the denomination continued to shape the church's understanding of itself, its clergy and their theological education.[100]

In fact, no less than seven of Bryden's students were appointed to the Knox faculty between 1945 and 1975. Numbers of his students were called to influential Presbyterian pulpits across Canada and at least two of his students, Arthur Cochrane and James Smart, were appointed to teach in American seminaries (Cochrane at Dubuque, Iowa, and Smart at Union, New York). So it was that Bryden's theological voice was multiplied in the ministries of others.

It has to be said that when Walter Bryden was appointed to the principalship his most creative theological work was behind him. He had written what was clearly one of the most articulate critiques not only of church union but of Canadian Protestantism in *Why I Am A Presbyterian* (1934). His 1935 article "The Presbyterian Conception of God" sketched his neo-orthodox conception of revelation against the background of fundamentalism and modernism. His major work, *The Christian's Knowledge of God,* had been published in 1940, and what it lacked in clarity of style it more than made up for in prophetic passion and insight. This was the book in which Bryden's central theme emerged: any knowledge of God about which human beings may speak does not belong to them in and of themselves, nor may they attain it themselves. It is given as sheer gift, but it is really given. It is received as sheer gift; but it is really received. It is revealed in the God who speaks in the person of Jesus Christ. It is a participation in the self-revelation of God, God's sharing of God's self-knowledge with human beings; and it always comes as a word of judgment and a word of salvation: the yes contained

---

100 Fraser, *Church, College and Clergy,* 166.

within the no, and the no within the yes. Bryden's indebtedness to Calvin, Luther, Kierkegaard, Barth and Brunner was everywhere evident.

To be sure, Bryden continued to teach and write as principal. Moreover, he exercised his leadership as a theological vocation. But the writings became more occasional and ad hoc in nature. In 1945 and 1950 he wrote articles for the *Presbyterian Record* on the nature of theological education and the role of Knox College within the denomination.[101] Three of his articles were published in the journal *Crisis Christology* which had been started by some of his students: "The Holy Spirit and the Church," his inaugural address as principal, and a sermon preached on the radio, "St. Paul, the Preacher, as Separated Unto the Gospel." In the late 1940s he waded into the debate surrounding a new course of religious study for Protestants that was introduced by the Ontario provincial government. Disheartened by the liberal Protestant slant of the material, Bryden wrote the foreword to a critical assessment of the proposed curriculum written by some of his former students.[102] In 1949 he contributed an article on John Calvin to the *Presbyterian Record* and in 1950 he delivered the opening address to a pre-Assembly congress of The Presbyterian Church in Canada.[103]

The ascendancy of Bryden's Barthian influence within the Presbyterian Church was also evident in places besides Knox College, particularly with the creation of the General Assembly's Articles of Faith Committee in 1944, the year after Bryden addressed the Assembly on "The Significance of the Westminster Confession of Faith." The committee was created in response to the stirring of theological inquiry that took place at the 1942 General Assembly, in Knox Crescent Church in downtown Montreal, because of two overtures having to do with the Westminster Confession of Faith and the question of the Civil Magistrate. The Basis of Union in 1875 had declared that the Westminster Confession of Faith's chapter on the civil magistrate was not binding, and the church had permitted full freedom of conscience on the matter. The result was, the overtures argued, that church members, elders, and ministers "were left without definite guidance in the important matter of how to affirm their loyalty to the State; and the State on its part left without assured knowledge of its powers and duties, under the Lord Jesus Christ toward the Church." As a member of the committee charged with the

---

[101]   Bryden, "The Church and the College," *Presbyterian Record* 70.8 (September 1945) 232–34; "Knox College, To Be Or Not To Be," *Presbyterian Record* (June 1950) 182.

[102]   Bryden, "Foreword," in Frederick Bronkema et al. *The Christian Faith and Religion in Ontario Schools.*

[103]   Bryden, "John Calvin: Apostle of God's Sovereign Power," *Presbyterian Record* (December 1949) 324–25; "Introduction to the Congress," *Addresses From The Pre-Assembly Congress of 1950 and the 76th General Assembly* (Toronto: The Presbyterian Church in Canada, 1950) 6–11.

responsibility of drafting a new statement of faith which was to clarify the confusion surrounding the Canadian Presbyterian understanding of church and state, Bryden found himself in the midst of the very same confessional issues that had plagued Presbyterians throughout their history. In response, he prepared a brief essay called "The Church and the Economic Order" in which he argued that questions of church and state could not be addressed outside questions concerning social and economic justice. In October 1946 he wrote a piece for the *Presbyterian Record* called "Shall We Adopt the Statement of Faith?" in which he argued the affirmative position.[104] Battling with confessional Calvinists on the right, and liberal Protestants on the left, Bryden spoke strongly in favor of a new confession for the Presbyterian Church in Canada. In the years that followed Bryden was instrumental in putting forward statements on "The Doctrine of the Word of God" and "Calvin's Doctrine of Predestination" which reflected the influence of Barth's retrieval of the Reformed tradition. In the end, and after some controversy, The Presbyterian Church in Canada overwhelmingly adopted "A Declaration Concerning Church and Nation," in 1955, three years after Bryden's death. It would take another generation before a complete new statement of faith was adopted (*Living Faith*, 1998) as a subordinate standard in addition to the Westminster Confession of Faith. Nevertheless, Bryden's Barthian voice, by then long in the grave, echoed throughout that document as well.[105]

Bryden's steadily deteriorating health in the late 1940s and early 1950s curtailed his academic and ecclesial activities. Invited by Dr. George Pidgeon to participate in the founding assembly of the World Council of Churches in Amsterdam in 1948, he did not attend due to illness. He was to have retired at the end of the 1951–52 academic year but suffered a heart attack at the college board meeting which was deciding his successor, and died five days later on March 23, 1952 at the age of sixty-eight. The obituary notices described him as "one of Canada's leading theologians" and an "international figure in the theological field."[106]

Conclusion

As a Presbyterian minister Bryden's theological voice had been tested and tried by Marxist social criticism, philosophical idealism, and ecclesiastical ecumenism. For almost seventeen years he preached weekly. As a parish minis-

---

[104] Bryden, "The Church and The Economic Order," in *Separated Unto the Gospel*, 71–76; "Shall We Adopt the Statement of Faith?," *Presbyterian Record* (October 1946) 269–70.

[105] A. Donald MacLeod, "The Formation of the Articles of Faith Committee: Ascendant Barthianism in the 1940s in the PCC," Canadian Society of Presbyterian History, September 25, 2004.

[106] The University of Toronto Archives, Walter Williamson Bryden Box.

ter he had experienced the influence of World War One on his congregation's faith. Among the theologians he read was John Oman. More importantly, he immersed himself in a study of Paul's letters to the Corinthians in the New Testament. When called to a professorial position at Knox College in the post-union church, he threw himself into the task of teaching church history and the history and philosophy of religion as he began to rethink the progressive and liberal Calvinism that had become so dominant. P. T. Forsyth helped him regain some theological perspective. But it was Bryden's encounter with the theology of Karl Barth that was decisive. Barth provided the categories with which to articulate the themes that Bryden had been striving to set forth. Barth pointed Bryden back to the Bible, Calvin and Luther, and the theology of James Denney. While it may be argued that Bryden came through to his basic theological position on his own, in parallel to Karl Barth, it has to be said that Bryden's theological contribution is incomprehensible apart from the neo-Reformation theological movement associated with Karl Barth. The roots of Bryden's theology are certainly to be found in late nineteenth and early twentieth-century Scottish liberal evangelical Calvinism. The ground had been watered for Bryden by Denney, Oman, Forsyth and others. But the fruit of Bryden's theological contribution flourished through the influence of Barth's work. And as an early interpreter of Barth and Barthianism in Canada, Walter Bryden provided a theological critique of Canadian Protestantism that made sense to many Canadian Presbyterians at a critical moment in their history.

Having sketched the intellectual background and genetic development of Bryden's theological contribution, we turn now to an exposition and exploration of its substance. The remainder of this book, therefore, is primarily theological in character and focuses specifically on the understanding of revelation which Bryden put before the Canadian church in the second quarter of the twentieth century. The next chapter examines Bryden's dialectical christocentric conception of the Word of God in its objective dimension as it was developed against modern idealism and rational fundamentalism. Bryden's neo-orthodox conception of revelation—developed in the shadow of Barth's critically realistic dialectical theology—incorporated the insights of existentialism and realism in an effort to re-appropriate Calvin's doctrine of the knowledge of God for Canadian Presbyterians after church union. Bryden's essay "The Presbyterian Conception of the Word of God" provides the clearest expression of this theological protest in outline, and forms the structure of our analysis. The substance of the argument is developed largely in terms of Bryden's book *The Christian's Knowledge of God* and the unpublished manuscript "After Modernism, What?"

One final comment is in order before moving on. Before, behind, and beyond any formal analysis of Bryden's thought stands the following crucial point: in all his theological work—whether it was preaching, teaching, or writing—Bryden was conscious of his plight as a Reformed pastor and theological teacher. In the words of Barth, Bryden knew that as a minister he ought to speak of God. He was human, however, and knew that he could not speak of God. He knew that he had to recognize both his obligation and his inability and by that very recognition give God the glory. This was his perplexity. Bryden's neo-orthodox voice fades into insignificance apart from this realization. Without it, all talk of God becomes mere child's play. Theology on the written page cannot capture it. When reading the theology of Walter Bryden, therefore, one must bear in mind that as a dialectical theologian he regarded "this Kafka-esque plight as paradoxically healthy."[107]

---

[107]   Karl Barth, "The Word of God and the Task of Ministry," in *The Word of God and the Word of Man*, 186. James M. Robinson, *The Beginnings of Dialectical Theology* (Richmond: John Knox, 1968) 1:15.

3

The Judging–Saving Word of God

And so, finally, the Word of God is Jesus Christ, and Him crucified, with nothing to be added or subtracted from simply that.
—Walter Bryden

THE neo-orthodox protest was characterized by a concern to recover the reality of revelation. The theologians who engaged in the protest, whatever else they may have said and done, understood themselves as church theologians of God's free and sovereign Word. What then, Walter Bryden asked, should Presbyterians mean by the Word of God? What was the inwardness of that sixteenth-century understanding of the Word which would justify the Protestant church in contending that it was a truly living apprehension of the Word of God? What actually revolutionized religious thought at that time, and thereby gave new direction to European civilization and culture?[1] What was the dynamic at work in the thought of Calvin and Luther which, if rightly appropriated by Canadian Protestants, could overturn the domestication of revelation that had come to dominate the church of the twentieth century? Why had the church succumbed to the temptation to equate the Word of God, always living, with human ideals and doctrinal propositions? Why were Christians satisfied to speak about God in general terms or seek traces of divine life in the world rather than experience the radically transforming power of God's Judging–Saving Word?

These were among the central questions that motivated Walter Bryden's theological work through the 1930s and 1940s as he pointed Canadian Presbyterians to a theology of the Word. While the neo-orthodox emphases of crisis, dialectics, paradox, and realism resonated with Bryden, the central feature of the insight to which he bore witness, and the designation which undoubtedly best conforms to his intention, is a theology of the Word. Bryden

---

[1] Bryden, *Separated Unto the Gospel*, 179.

130

consistently conceived of revelation in terms of the Reformation rediscovery of the witness to Jesus Christ in the Bible. He leveraged this rediscovery to overturn the concepts of revelation at work in liberal Protestantism and confessional Calvinism. In their stead, he proposed a positive reconstruction of the religious problem through a recovery of Calvin's Reformation theology of the Word. The purpose of this chapter is to examine Bryden's neo-Reformation dialectical christocentric conception of the Judging–Saving Word of God and the manner in which it functioned as both a prophetic protest and constructive proposal in Canadian Protestantism.

The "Conception" of the Word: Recovering the Reformation

In his introduction to "The Presbyterian Conception of the Word of God," Walter Bryden argued that the church's authentic existence lay in a rediscovery of its identity in the Reformation conception of faith and life. He had already argued, in *Why I Am A Presbyterian*, that the Reformed faith was constituted not by its doctrine of ministry and ecclesiastical orders but by its conception of the gospel of grace and its insistence on the centrality of the Word of God. Now, just a few years later, he argued that the distinctive nature of the church held by Presbyterianism rested in its conception of the Word of God, which, the church believed, created and sustained its faith and life:

> What will be said in this article will be based strictly on the understanding that the true significance of the Presbyterian Church has to do primarily with its view of Faith, that is to say, with the conception it holds in regard to what it conceives to be its particular witness to Christ. In other words, this is to claim that the 'originating constitutive principle' of the Church of God is fundamentally 'spiritual,' and not 'institutional.' The Church of God is, in final analysis, the creation of the Word of God.[2]

Bryden did not argue that Presbyterianism justified its existence only through an appeal to the New Testament. He did, however, contend that the emphasis placed upon the Word of God, as that which constituted the basis of the church in the New Testament, owed its origins to the Reformation rediscovery of this principle. This particular perspective on revelation and its implications for faith and the church, representative of the view originally held by the Reformed churches, constituted any distinctiveness claimed by the Reformed churches. When asking what Presbyterianism stood for, or (and this amounted to the same thing for Bryden) what is the Presbyterian conception of the Word of God, "it is impossible to leave these considerations

---

[2] Ibid., 176.

aside. In fact, they must receive first attention."[3] Bryden believed that the church in the modern era had to recover the great themes of the Reformation, namely *sola gratia, sola fide, Deo soli gloria, sola Christus,* and *sola Scriptura,* but he also believed that these great Protestant distinctives had been stripped of their prophetic power by the rationalizing tendency of post-Reformation Calvinism. He was determined, therefore, in the face of the idealist challenge, to get back to what had been taught by Calvin and mediated through Geneva to the church in Scotland, and through Scotland, to Canada. Acutely aware that idealism could not be answered adequately by simply throwing Calvinist doctrine at it, Bryden pointed to the dynamic experience of faith which stood at the center of the original Reformation movement and longed to see a living faith in the church of his day. In short, "It is not too much to hold that it was a completely fresh and living apprehension of the Word of God which constituted the primal inspiration of the Reformation movement as a whole; and it is not an injustice to other Churches to claim that no one among the great Reformers was so keenly conscious of the significance of this great discovery, for Christian thought and for the life and practice of Christian believers, as was John Calvin."[4]

Bryden's choice of the word "conception" in describing the Word of God was deliberate and signaled his concern as a modern Reformed theologian. It reflected his insistence on a fresh and living experience of faith as the basis for Christian life in the modern world. The Word of God was no mere concept to be understood, doctrine to be affirmed, or ideal to be emulated. The Word of God, rightly apprehended, Bryden argued, was not rationalized, objectified, idealized, historicized, or moralized. In short, the Word of God resisted all human attempts to control and domesticate the revelation of God. The revelation of God, accessible to faith alone, was "a relationship or an experience which may exist" between the soul of a human being and God, "through Christ, and without any other form of mediation."[5] Christian theology proceeded as critical thought on speech about "the Christian conception of a holy God" and God's relation to sinful men and women. Theology served the proclamation of the gospel in the church, which consisted of those "who have heard the Word of God in the solitary privacy of their own souls, and because of that fact, find themselves in a peculiar unity with others similarly apprehended."[6] Walter Bryden was not a restorationist who wished to reproduce Calvinist concepts of revelation. He was a modern theologian who believed that the experience of faith which created the Reformation could

---

3   Ibid., 177.
4   Ibid., 177–78.
5   Ibid., 175.
6   Ibid., 176–77.

be experienced in his day. He longed for the church of his day to recover the authentic conception of the Word of God which constituted its true life and witness. A concept was an abstract and general notion for Bryden while a conception was an act in which something was born or created. A concept was rationalized, objectified, and synthesized beyond what was conceived in the soul of a human being by God's Spirit. A conception, however, more accurately reflected God's primordial activity before such rationalization occurred.

In this sense, Bryden followed Barth in understanding revelation as an act of God. Moreover, revelation was an act of God in which God shared divine self-knowledge with human beings, i.e., the Word of God was an expression of the self-revelation of God. The idea that revelation was a set of propositional truths set forth once for all time, or a series of insights gleaned from history and culture, was neither appropriate nor adequate for Christian faith in the modern world. The datum of revelation, Bryden contended, was not the sum of a set of ideas about God, but rather a radically transforming knowledge of God which occurred when human beings had been quickened into new life by God's own Spirit and Word.[7]

It has to be said that, inspired by Barth, Bryden's neo-Reformation conception of the Word of God, notwithstanding the new respect for the Reformation tradition of the churches it demanded, was not a throwback to any pre-modern tradition. Throughout his lectures, sermons, and books Bryden made traditional-sounding appeals to the Word of God and the authority of the Bible. Like Barth, Bryden replaced the liberal Protestant emphasis on natural reason with an orthodox-sounding appeal to revelation, but the conception of revelation he borrowed from Barth was derived from the distinctly modern tradition of Hegelian idealism. As Gary Dorrien and Bruce McCormack have argued, "It was from G.W.F. Hegel, the nineteenth-century tradition of right-wing Hegelian theology, and more directly," the neo-Kantianism of Wilhelm Herrmann, "that Barth adopted the idea of revelation as non-propositional divine *self*-revelation."[8] Like Barth and Herrmann, Bryden believed that the experience of God was self-authenticating and did not arise with necessity from a longing for God. If anything was normative for Herrmann, it was the experience of faith itself prior to being conceptualized. So too it was for Bryden. Barth's later departure from Herrmann, and Bryden assumed this, entailed an emphatic insistence that God was really and truly known—that *Gottes erkenntnis* was possible. Where Herrmann had reduced God to an idea of the believing subject, Barth had insisted that

---

[7] Bryden, Unpublished Lecture Notes on Augustine, 10.

[8] Gary Dorrien, *The Barthian Revolt in Modern Theology*, 7. Bruce McCormack, *Karl Barth's Critically Realistic Dialectical Theology*, 29–77.

God was real, whole, and complete as divine being in and of Godself apart from the knowing activity of the human subject. The reality of God preceded all human knowing. Theology, as speech about God, was made possible by the objectively real, self-presupposing, divine subjectivity of God in revelation. In other words, theology started with God. It is not clear that Bryden fully understood or consistently applied this insight because at points he appeared to stand closer to Herrmann's view than Barth's reconstruction of it. Nevertheless, for Bryden, Christ was not made present to human beings by an authoritative teaching about him. It was the case, rather, that a doctrine brought to human beings from without was simply an expression of someone else's faith, which at best provided an occasion for a personal encounter with revelation, an encounter which took place not in the conceptual realm of ideas but in the depths of the soul.[9]

In *The Christian's Knowledge of God* Bryden found that even the word "conception" had to be handled carefully when used to describe the experiential knowledge of God. A Christian, he argued, may possess conceptions of God which approximate outwardly very nearly the truth about God. But no one should confuse this with knowing God because "No system of truth, even though employed as representing the necessary symbols in the constitution of the Christian Creed, can mediate to man the Truth as it is in Jesus Christ."[10] Bryden employed the language of personal relationship to describe the experience of God and believed that this relational experience, framed by the revelation of the righteousness of God in the cross of Jesus Christ, constituted a Christian distinctive. "There seems to be lacking in all pagan religious experience," he contended, "that personal relationship with God in which the Righteousness of God—representing, as it does in Christianity, Jesus Christ crucified, God's absolute judgment upon man—is the primary and all important determinant."[11] It is important to note Bryden's insistence on the particular shape and content of this personal relationship. It was not a general experience of God arising from human religious consciousness. It was the particular experience of knowing the judgment of God upon one's life which created the possibility of the relationship. The experience of knowing, therefore, presupposed the revelation of God which, as Barth noted in his commentary on Romans, demands participation, comprehension, and co-operation, because it is a communication which presumes faith in the living God, and which creates the faith which it presumes. Bryden's conception of the Judging-Saving Word, therefore, sought to preserve the objectivity of the divine subject in revelation. Like Barth, Bryden insisted that the Word of

---

9   McCormack, *Karl Barth's Critically Realistic Dialectical Theology*, 65–67.
10   Bryden, *The Christian's Knowledge of God*, 220.
11   Ibid.

God was the primary and all-important determinant. The knowledge of God, framed by this personal relationship with God, conformed to the revelation of God's righteousness in Jesus Christ crucified, not the other way around. Liberal Protestantism rightly emphasized experience, Bryden believed. The problem was that it made the divine subject conform to human consciousness.

Bryden employed the category of "existential thinking" in an effort to describe the kind of thought which arose from a personal relationship with God. So long as God remained an idea or a synthesis of ideas, revelation had not actually come to human beings. During the nineteenth century, revelation became identified with the ideas and ideals which emerged from human consciousness. Historical, philosophical, cultural, and ethical ideals had been substituted for the reality of revelation. Idealism and rationalism bred what Bryden described as "spectator thinking" in which a human being might stand and judge among the objects of his/her religious affections. The revelation of God creates "existential thinking" in which a human being believes him or herself to be under the constraint of the judgment of God. This was the "constraint" which distinguished the theology of the Reformers from all other theologies and philosophies. "It is a difference of this kind," Bryden argued, "which appears most clearly to differentiate between Medieval theology and that of the early Reformers. It is not that these respective theologies were dealing with an essentially different subject-matter. The Reformers, in what they described as the 'true gospel' and 'true doctrine,' introduced nothing that was really new to Medievalism. What distinguishes them is the fact that they seem to be under different kinds of restraint."[12] Echoing Martin Luther, Bryden understood revelation and faith as a matter of life and death. During the sixteenth century Luther had declared that "Living, or rather dying and being damned make a theologian, not understanding, reading or speculating." The revolutionary effect of the Reformation, Bryden therefore argued, rather than resulting from the introduction of new subject-matter to the church, rested on the attitude and action created by a renewed apprehension of the Christian message. The critical issue confronting the sixteenth-century church was epistemological and existential. The enduring witness of the early Reformers at this crucial point, Bryden believed, had been obscured by Protestant scholasticism and liberal Protestantism.

It is important to note that Bryden's interpretation of the Reformation on this point reflected the "Luther and Calvin renaissance" that accompanied the emergence of neo-orthodoxy in the second quarter of the twentieth century. In an important study of Calvin's doctrine of the knowledge of God, E. A. Dowey gathered up the discussion that had been taking place during this

---

12   Ibid., 221.

time. Dowey argued that for Calvin the knowledge of God had an existential character and could never be separated from the answer that human beings gave through worship and obedience. The language of the knowledge of God in Calvin's theology was inextricably bound up with the ideas of encounter and response. It was a practical knowledge of God that was always to be distinguished from something that was purely theoretical. Non-speculative in nature, it engaged the whole personality, and as Lobstein argued, "it solicits all the energies of the conscience and heart, putting in motion all the spiritual faculties."[13] Having affirmed the non-speculative and experiential character of the knowledge of God in Calvin's theology, Dowey interestingly interpreted Calvin's theological epistemology in terms of twentieth-century philosophical existentialism. Here we find an important clue to Bryden's reading of Calvin. Dowey believed that a more adequate term to describe the practical and experiential nature of Calvin's conception of the knowledge of God was that to be found in the thought of Kierkegaard and its expression in the theologies of Barth, Brunner and their theological collaborators. The word "existential" connoted for Dowey "the knowledge that determines the existence of the knower." He cited H. R. Mackintosh, Paul Tillich, and F. W. Camfield, all of whom described existential thinking as something that is personal, decisive, passionate, determinative, and related to one's ultimate concern. On this basis, Dowey concluded that "One needs scarcely to prove that Calvin's concept of religious knowledge belongs to those that can be classified as existential."[14]

Walter Bryden's interpretation reflected precisely this approach to Calvin's theology. As neo-Reformation theologians, the neo-orthodox interpreters of Calvin utilized modern categories to express Reformation insights. Ellen Charry has recently pointed out the limitations of this strategy specifically with respect to Calvin's theology. Arguing that modern scholars lack a vocabulary for the aretegenic (virtue-shaping and character forming) nature of Calvin's theology, many identify it in terms that come from the commentator's own time. Edward Dowey's classic work on the duplex knowledge of God in Calvin's theology, "written at the height of the influence of religious existentialism," Charry argues, is a good example. Dowey emphasized that Calvin, who eschewed the use of speculative philosophy in theology, was interested primarily in the existential effects of revelation. "While existentialism may have been an understandable vocabulary for describing Calvin's project in the early 1950s," Charry notes, "it neglects the moral and ethical

---

[13]   P. Lobstein, "La Connaissance religieuse d'après Calvin," *Revue de théologie et de philosophie* (Lausanne) 42 (1909) 53–110; cited in E. A. Dowey, *The Knowledge of God in Calvin's Theology,* rev. ed. (Grand Rapids: Eerdmans, 1994) 25.

[14]   E. A. Dowey, *The Knowledge of God in Calvin's Theology,* 26.

dimensions of godliness."[15] Charry's own proposal to read Calvin as a spiritual or pastoral theologian whose primary concern was godliness in Christian living need not concern us here. Her observation that Dowey (a student of Brunner) used a twentieth-century category to interpret a sixteenth-century thinker is critical to understanding the neo-orthodox reading of Calvin and the neo-Reformation impulse at work in their project. This was the impulse at work in Walter Bryden's theological witness in the 1930s and 1940s.

The existential thinking represented by Reformation theologians, the theologians of crisis argued, embodied the rule that ought to govern the church's faith and life. Echoing Tillich's "Protestant Principle," Bryden referred to it as the law of constant critical recurrence to the Word of God. The Reformation was the classical instance of the application of this law since it represented the de-hellenization of the Christian faith where hellenization was the name of a tendency to seek a comprehensive view of reality and to bring the Christian notion of God into conformity with this view. Hellenization, in other words, represented idealism. Without naming him, Bryden clearly had in view the idealism represented by John Watson in Canadian Protestantism. Watson, as we noted earlier, had argued that the Christian ideal stood in continuity with the Greek and Jewish ideals. That ideal, embodied in the teaching of Jesus, was replaced during the medieval era by "a hard and almost mechanical idea of the external world, by a stern denunciation of the utter perversity and evil of society, and by the postponement of the kingdom of heaven to the future life."[16] A remarkable change came over the Christian consciousness during the Middle Ages, Watson argued, dominated by three main characteristics. Firstly, a universal belief predominated that the kingdom of heaven could not be realized in this life, but was entirely a thing of the future life. Secondly, a belief was universally accepted in the absolute authority of the Church in all matters of faith and worship, and in the consequent distinction between the clergy and the laity. The third characteristic of the Middle Ages was the opposition of faith and reason. Late medieval scholasticism, however, dug its own grave and prepared "the way for the great modern movement which began with the Renaissance and the Reformation and is still going on." Watson was sure of one thing: "that nothing short of a perfect harmony of science, art, and religion can permanently satisfy the liberated human spirit." The Renaissance and Reformation in Watson's eyes, therefore, represented the recovery of Christian idealism that was lost during the medieval period.[17]

---

[15]   Ellen Charry, *By The Renewing of Your Minds: The Pastoral Function of Christian Doctrine* (New York: Oxford University Press, 1997) 199–200.

[16]   John Watson, *Christianity and Idealism* (New York: Macmillan, 1897) 111.

[17]   Ibid., 110–18.

Walter Bryden agreed with Watson that medieval Christianity represented a departure from the teaching of Jesus and Paul in the New Testament, and that the Reformation represented a recovery of original Christianity. Bryden's reasons, however, were precisely the opposite of those put forward by Watson. For Bryden, medieval Christianity represented a Hellenizing (read idealizing) tendency in Christianity. Thomas Aquinas' magisterial theology represented the best example of this tendency because it assumed a synthesis between reason and revelation by way of analogy. Even though Thomas conceived of revealed knowledge as unique and exclusive in character, he made it possible to have a knowledge of God prior to and apart from the revelation of God in the Word of God. Luther's theology, on the other hand, arose out of an encounter with God's living Word "in which as a broken and contrite man he seems to know more immediately and profoundly the joy of God's salvation."[18] The reality of revelation which created the Reformation movement was living, contemporaneous, personal, and immediate in contrast to idealism's speculative, universal, and abstract notion of the knowledge of God. For Bryden, idealism represented the enemy from which the Reformation had delivered Christianity; in Watson's mind idealism expressed the essence of Christianity which the Reformation had recovered. In the same way that Watson, as a modern thinker, appealed to idealism, Walter Bryden appealed to existentialism. In Bryden's case, however, he utilized a modern thought form, not to reconstruct traditional Christianity, but to overturn the idealist form of modern Christianity. The neo-Reformation conception of the Word to which Bryden bore witness was, in fact, a highly creative and sophisticated blend of modern insights with traditional Reformation thought.

This governed Bryden's approach to the Reformation. While he often invoked Luther and Calvin, he believed that it was impossible and undesirable to go back to them in any literal way. Not all of their theological positions were to be accepted, certainly not some of the implications of their thought. Nor would it be advisable to emulate their lives. Nothing would have horrified Calvin more, Bryden noted, as the thought that future generations might attempt to imitate him. Calvin struggled against such idolatry all his life. What Calvin meant primarily by the "Sovereignty of God," Bryden noted, was "to be found in a true understanding of his attitude in this regard, namely, that no Father of the Church, however revered, no Church, however sacred, no Council, however ecumenical, no priesthood, no saint, no good man, nor the good lives, the pieties, and the true thoughts of the same, dare ever come between the soul of man and the living Word of God."[19] Nevertheless, the Reformers had something profound to teach the Protestant

---

[18]   Bryden, *The Christian's Knowledge of God*, 223.
[19]   Bryden, *Separated Unto the Gospel*, 178.

churches in the twentieth century. If the Presbyterian church was to possess any convictions worthy of a truly Christian faith, Bryden believed, it had to get back to something of that understanding of the Word of God which created both Calvin and the Reformed faith. Convinced that the future of the church in Canada depended on such a conception of revelation, Walter Bryden was prepared to use whatever theological tools were required in order to point Canadian Protestantism to the enduring witness of the Reformation, and away from the idealism and rationalism of modern faith.

The Reality of Revelation: Against Modern Idealism

Convinced that theology was becoming concerned with the concreteness of the real situation within which the church found itself in the second quarter of the twentieth century, Walter Bryden trumpeted a decisive "No!" against the idealism which had dominated Canadian Protestantism. Bryden used the critical realism of the neo-orthodox movement, as articulated by Barth and Brunner, and especially their America collaborators Reinhold Niebuhr, Walter Marshall Horton, and John Bennett, to challenge the liberal or modern view. Unlike his American counterparts who responded to pragmatism, however, Bryden was battling a powerful form of British idealism deeply embedded in Canadian religious thought. This was the idealist worldview within which he had been educated as a university student. It was the idealism that had elicited highly sophisticated theological responses to which Bryden had been introduced as a theological student. And as a Presbyterian minister he had seen firsthand the problems that this idealism created for people in the pew who were afraid that the personality of God was not being preserved, that the experience of grace was being replaced by ethical imperatives, and that the divine significance of Jesus Christ was being relativized.[20] By the 1920s he was no longer simply suspicious of idealism, he was convinced that the liberal or modern view which had been built upon it neither reflected the Reformation conception of revelation nor resonated with the changing cultural climate of the churches. In Europe a revolt was raging against anything that smacked of romanticism, optimism, and idealism. On the Canadian front, Walter Bryden had become one of the leading neo-orthodox protagonists. The idealist concept of the Word of God, he believed, had to be defeated once and for all.

The liberal, modern, or modernistic views of the Word of God, Bryden argued, were based on common, distinctive, religious principles "which can-

---

[20] Bryden, "After Modernism, What?" Unpublished manuscript, chapter 1, Introductory.

not correctly be said to have emanated from the Protestant Reformation."[21] These principles revolved around three fallacious assumptions. First, liberal Protestantism had assumed that a certain identity existed between idealism and the Christian faith. The norms of this idealism were acquired empirically and were shared by all advanced religions and philosophies. Liberalism, Bryden believed, had substituted a code of conduct to be achieved for what was always a matter of the unmerited grace of God. Religion had been reduced to a matter of ethics alone. Second, liberalism had assumed that the Christian faith could find its authentication in history and in empirically verifiable historical evidence. And third, modern theology had assumed that a purely objective position could be attained by human beings as such, by which truth could be discerned and evaluated. In its own way, Bryden argued, modernism had invested the autonomous rational individual with supreme authority. In short, modern theology had subordinated the Word of God to ethical, rational, and historical ideals in an effort to secure a place for religion in the optimistic, progressive and harmonious world envisaged by idealism. These were the assumptions Bryden sought to overturn for Canadian Protestants.

Religious-Ethical Idealism

First, Bryden attacked the ethical idealism that dominated the religious understanding of the Word of God for liberal Protestants. According to Bryden, liberalism meant "primarily by the Word of God those supreme moral and religious values which find expression in the Old Testament and especially in the New Testament—but which exist preeminently in the teachings of Jesus as these are embraced and find vital expression in the unique perfection of Jesus' life and personality."[22] The challenge posed by the Word of God for modern people, in this view, appeared to lie in the ethical imperatives which confront individuals and society. The basis for this view of the Word of God is the historical Jesus, whose life is to be emulated as the ideal man, the great exemplar, the first Christian, and the supreme religious subject. The revelation to be found in Jesus consists primarily of profound ideas and deep insights about the meaning of life, the nature of God, and the nature of humanity which find expression in Jesus' life, teaching, and death. The ideas and ideals to be found in Jesus constitute the Word of God for modern men and women. When confronted by this Word, they should be able to understand the ultimate truth about life, and should be able to govern themselves accordingly. Salvation, in the hands of liberal Protestants, refers to possessing the mind of Christ, the "mind" signifying the qualities of heart and mind,

---

[21]   Bryden, *Separated Unto the Gospel*, 188.
[22]   Ibid.

motives and spirit which Jesus exhibited while on the earth. In short, the Word of God provided the pattern for Christian men and women to identify the footsteps of Jesus and in them plant their own.[23]

The power of this idealist understanding of the Word of God ought not to be underestimated. For many Canadians struggling to come to terms with the meaning of Christian faith—given the influence of, among other things, Darwinian evolution, Marxist socio-economic analysis, and Freudian psychology—the ethical vision of the Christian religion set out by idealism provided an attractive alternative to a seemingly obscurantist orthodoxy and outright secular atheism. It appeared to offer Canadians the option of maintaining Christian faith while making peace with the modern world. The price of this compromise between Christianity and modern culture was, however, in Walter Bryden's view, far too high. Furthermore, he didn't believe that liberal Protestantism delivered what it promised.

The critical issue for Christian faith, Bryden believed, is always Jesus Christ and him crucified, the one foundation upon which Christianity is built. The Christology of liberal Protestantism, and the concept of salvation built upon it, produced a ghastly impoverishment of the person and work of Jesus "to those who have been nurtured in the thought of St. Paul and in the atmosphere of John Calvin."[24] Rather than reformulating the faith for a new day, idealism had eroded the foundation upon which the Christian faith was built. The idealist vision of the Word of God was not, Bryden argued, a recent invention, and therefore could not easily be overturned. It was the culmination of a long process that began with the Renaissance, an era in which the predominant influence of Aristotelian Greek thought reintroduced concepts of reason, nature, and humanity that were antithetical to the Christian worldview. The inductive method of securing truth, Bryden believed, was particularly influential. "Indeed," he said, "if it were imperative to choose just one thing as an explanation of Modernism, surely the inductive method should find first consideration." The inductive method "meant eventually that truth was to be sought and found through interrogation of nature, man and history, entirely without prejudice of any given postulates of thought, or of a Revelation of an a priori character."[25] Unlike the Canadian Calvinists of the nineteenth century who had appealed to Common Sense philosophy and the inductive method to shore up orthodox faith, Bryden believed such philosophical systems and methods were irredeemable. The damage done by the inductive method to theological epistemology was evident in the thought of three influential philosophers.

---

[23]   Ibid., 188–89.

[24]   Ibid., 189.

[25]   Ibid., 191.

First, Descartes applied the method to religion in a thorough-going manner and maintained that any true knowledge of human beings or of God must begin from a basic doubt, or perhaps better, from a basis in those things which cannot be doubted. According to Descartes, the only reliable starting point in the pursuit of truth, including religious truth, is self-consciousness. *Cogito ergo sum*, "I think, therefore, I am." This was the first time in Christian history, Bryden argued, that it was implied that religion required no given, transcendent element. By the nineteenth century, in Schleiermacher, religion was grounded in the human consciousness. Following Barth, Bryden believed that the logic of the Christian faith differed from this Cartesian logic in fundamental respects. The starting point for Christian thought is not self-consciousness but awareness of the reality of God. God precedes not only our thought about God but also our thought about ourselves. Not "I think, therefore I am," but "God is, therefore we are." Revelation was rooted in the reality of God, not in human consciousness. The Word of God preceded all human thoughts and words about God.

The second philosopher, Baruch Spinoza, introduced the monistic conception of life and the universe in his quest for religious and intellectual coherency and unity. The problem here, as Bryden saw it, was that a consistent monism required a view of God that was strictly immanental. God is the soul of the universe, its creative principle, or the power which drives history progressively forward. This view held no place for a God who transcends the universe. Spinoza's identification of nature with the primal substance lying behind both phenomenal nature and ordinary human thought, led to the idea that nature was the ultimate reality, i.e., God, and that this ultimate reality could only be apprehended by pure reason. In the hands of Hegel, this synthesis provided the basis for identifying God with thought. Thought was to be interpreted as the rational, particularly in its idealistic aspect. The irony, Bryden pointed out, was that idealism did not represent anything truly transcendent. It simply signified that important aspects of human moral and rational life had been transcendentalized. That which is truly transcendent, Bryden argued in words that echoed Kierkegaard, is that which is above and qualitatively different from human thought. Where no infinite qualitative difference exists, God is nothing more than human history writ large. Modernism, Bryden concluded, had created God in the image of humanity.[26] Barth's criticism of Schleiermacher, Bryden believed, was well-placed: "One can *not* speak of God simply by speaking of man in a loud voice."[27]

---

[26] Ibid., 192–93.
[27] Karl Barth, *The Word of God and the Word of Man*, trans. Douglas Horton (Boston: Pilgrim, 1928) 196.

In this critique of modern theology and Hegelian idealism, it has to be said that Bryden borrowed heavily not only from Kierkegaard, but also from Marx, Freud, Nietzsche, and Durkheim, and their acceptance and negation of liberal modernity. Like the European dialectical theologians of the 1920s, Bryden was able to utilize the critique of modernity that had emerged from within the modern worldview itself. Marx and Durkheim had convinced many that religion was a sociological phenomenon, Freud that it was a neurosis, and Nietzsche that God was dead. They offered up a trenchant critique of domesticated religion which Bryden used against the dominance of idealism in the culture Protestantism of Canada. David Tracy is right: the neo-orthodox theologians were compelled to challenge their liberal forbears not out of a lack of regard for the theological relevance of culture analysis but out of a different post-modern cultural analysis.[28] In short, Bryden believed the church could use the modern critique of modernity to clear away idealism and make room for true faith.

The third key idea which had a determining influence in modern thought, as Bryden understood it, was that of development and progress, first introduced by Francis Bacon of England and Jean Bodin of France. According to Bacon, the advance of knowledge was the hope of the future. Although Bacon had no fully developed theory of development, his contention that knowledge may advance, and that it had in fact advanced since the earliest times, gave rise to such a theory, in an idealistic and theoretic form in Germany, and a practical, sociological form in France. Eventually the principle of progress came to be used to explain almost every aspect of life. It was central, for example, in the positivist philosophy of Auguste Comte. It was employed in science, especially in the biological interpretation of the universe. The scientific method in turn was applied to the study of human beings with the result that the idea of progress and development became central in the social sciences. Herbert Spencer's optimism was built on the assumption that progress was inevitable. Lessing's book *The Education of the Human Race* interpreted the religious development of Jews and Christians within this paradigm.

All this prepared the ground for the emergence of the concept of progressive revelation in Christian thought. Bacon's emphasis on "utility" as the supreme worth of knowledge created the tendency to estimate culture and religion in terms of the worth of ideas. The value of a religion, therefore, was not to be found in particular historical facts, but in the ideas to which they gave expression. Idealism, in short, delivered up a form of practical Christianity that appeared serviceable in the modern world.[29] For Walter

---

[28]   David Tracy, *Blessed Rage For Order* (New York: Seabury, 1979) 27–28.

[29]   Bryden, *Separated Unto the Gospel,* 193–94.

Bryden, however, idealism had failed at two fundamental theological points. First, as noted above, it had failed to deliver a version of the Christian faith that truly resonated with the contemporary cultural transition. Given the challenges and changes of a culture in crisis, the optimistic world envisaged by idealism appeared increasingly quaint. All talk of progress seemed shallow in light of the international political and economic situation of the 1920s and 1930s. A different philosophical and theological analysis of culture was required. Secondly, idealism failed to deliver a version of Christianity that was recognizably consistent with the Protestant faith of the Reformation. The origins of the liberal or modern worldview were entirely understandable, but the theological implications of the modern view were, Bryden believed, devastating for the church's faith and life.

In the first place, the Christian doctrine of God had been reformulated to accommodate the idealist worldview. As a result, God was conceived in modern thought almost entirely from the perspective of immanence. Moreover, the tendency of modernism, under the influence of this concept, was to depersonalize God. The Holy Spirit was understood as some impersonal creative principle operating in the world as the source of higher cultures, including religion. The Reformers, on the other hand, had borne witness to a personal transcendent God whose Spirit "has proved always to be the stumbling block to all rationalizing or naturalizing of the Word of God."[30]

Secondly, liberal Protestantism tended to dissolve the traditional view of revelation by setting aside the assumption that an absolute barrier exists between sinful human beings and a holy God. Revelation and redemption were viewed in terms of a process of religious education or enlightenment in which the symbols of the Christian faith represented profoundly challenging ideas acquired by human beings. The Reformation view of revelation, in distinction, emphasized revelation as a supernatural event in which God achieved for human beings that of which they themselves were absolutely incapable. Furthermore, it emphasized the reality of sin and evil for which rational monism had no explanation at all.[31]

The dividing line for Bryden was clear: modernism and Reformation thought were two mutually exclusive alternatives. They worked with qualitatively different conceptions of God and revelation. Bryden acknowledged that the anthropology of the modern view was impressive, in which human beings were conceived in the beginning as very imperfect, though always potentially good, and therefore requiring only the necessary discipline, education, and enlightenment to progress towards the achievable goal of human flourishing and fulfillment. The traditional view, as he saw it, regarded human beings as

---

[30]   Ibid., 196–97.
[31]   Ibid., 197–98.

so disaffected by sin, that they could not, of themselves, ever achieve the life for which they were created. For a time, Bryden believed that these two views were not so disparate as they appeared, and that it was the task of modern theology to reconcile them. By the late 1920s, however, he had reached the conclusion that the two views were incompatible and irreconcilable. Neo-orthodoxy was not, therefore, as he saw it, an attempt to synthesize the modern and traditional views. That task belonged properly to liberal Protestantism. At the same time, neo-orthodoxy was not simply an attempt to reassert the traditional view, as if one could establish the truth and relevance of Christian faith by spouting the same old orthodoxies more loudly in the face of its challengers. It was, in the hands of Walter Bryden and the Canadian church, an attempt to recover the dynamics of Reformation theology while remaining fully cognizant of modern sensibilities. Rather than seeking to integrate Christian thought with the modern worldview, however, it emphasized the paradoxical and dialectical character of Christian revelation, creating a kind of dualism in which either/or choices were appropriate, required, and indeed celebrated.

Bryden could not, of course, go through modern theology without acknowledging the important influence of Schleiermacher and Ritschl. Schleiermacher's emphasis on an original a priori God-consciousness which formed the basis of his appeal to religion's cultured despisers resulted in two tendencies in subsequent theology. First, as a theology of religion it placed Christianity and Christian revelation in a category with the revelations of others cultures. Bryden contended that this relativized the universal and absolute nature of the claim traditionally made by Christian faith. Secondly, it led to a subjectivism in the interpretation of God which allowed Freud and Jung to speak of God as a "wish-belief," a shadow of human beings flung upon the clouds.

Even though Ritschl, for his part, pointed theology back to the facts of the New Testament and the Christian experience of redemption, he substituted moral-rational value-judgments for what properly belonged to the Spirit of God—the Reformed *testimonium spiritus sancti internum*. By giving too much over to the ethical dimension of human life, the criterion for revelation in Ritschl was determined from the side of human beings, while in the Reformation it was determined emphatically from the side of God alone. Ritschl's ethical idealism papered over the vast modernist impulse of his theological system with a very thin veneer of traditional Christian language. Ritschl assumed that humanity's highest moral values and ideals constituted the truest revelation which human beings could possess. Indeed, Bryden argued, Ritschl's faith in the power and influence of ideas and ideals to effectuate the work of Christ was unbounded. No one should make the mistake of thinking that Ritschl was anything less than a Christian idealist par excellence. If he had not completely secularized the whole conception of the Kingdom of God, he had certainly rationalized and ethicized the concept. Ritschl failed to see, Bryden contended, that the whole outlook of the New Testament is eschatological rather than evolutionary.[32]

Bryden's critique of Schleiermacher and Ritschl, written before he had completely worked out the conception of the Judging–Saving Word that was to appear in *The Christian's Knowledge of God*, shows a theological mind struggling to come to terms with a Reformation conception of revelation in the light of the modern worldview. Like Barth, Bryden affirmed that there was nothing in the being or knowing of the human subject which brought about the event of revelation. There was no moral or rational capacity which provided a necessary pre-condition for its occurrence. The only capacity for revelation was that which God graciously provided anew in the event of faith itself as a gift. In the event of revelation, then, human knowledge was made to conform to its divine object. Bryden recognized that the position he had adopted was vulnerable to the charge it demeaned human personality and ignored human accomplishments.[33] But it was a position he believed to be essential to the proclamation of the Christian gospel. Without it, modern preaching had become a façade of Christian teaching interpreted purely from the standpoint of idealism. Canadian Protestant ministers preached sermons, Bryden complained, about the hope of immortality rather than the resurrection from the dead, the ideal of human community rather than the radical call to be the church, the progressive unfolding of human history rather than the apocalyptic character of the reign of God.

As might be expected, not all Canadian and American Protestant theologians agreed with Bryden's assessment of modern theology and church life. In a review of Bryden's posthumously published book, *Separated Unto the Gospel*, the United Church theologian John Line complained that

> in tracing the course of Liberalism our author is hardly just either to its causes or to its objectives. If it is true that the Gnostics in the early church lost out in the record through our reports of them being mostly from their enemies; when we note how Liberals and Barthians currently portray each other we may hope the future is not storing up a similar fate for them.[34]

Similarly, S. Vernon McCasland questioned Bryden's insistence upon the absolute character of the revelation of God. He wondered how such a revela-

---

[32] Ibid., 199–200.

[33] Ibid., 46; McCormack, *Karl Barth's Critically Realistic Dialectical Theology*, 17.

[34] John Line, Review of *Separated Unto the Gospel* in *The Canadian Journal of Theology* 3.3 (1957) 189–90.

tion could ever be authenticated as genuine, and its reception assured in the mind of the Christian believer.[35] To be sure, Bryden painted with a broad brush intellectually. But it must be remembered that he was arguing against philosophers and theologians whose genius was their ability to gather up and harmonize every sphere of human life in a compelling idealist meta-narrative. In the face of such a challenge, Bryden protested against monism's tendency to naturalize revelation. He also rejected any dualism which sought a synthe-sizing rational principle. Christian revelation rightly understood, he argued, precluded the possibility of such syntheses. Revelation, rightly understood, was self-authenticating. Synthesizing systems which sought to authenticate truth by rational arguments appealed to modern people, Bryden concluded, precisely because the intellectual offence created by the scandal of the cross had been set aside. For Bryden, however, the scandal of particularity created the crisis which created real faith. The Christian message was, as the Apostle Paul described it, "foolishness to those who are perishing" but the power of God to those who are being saved (1 Corinthians 1:18). The only correlation between God and humanity is Jesus Christ and him crucified. The reality for Bryden was that the Word of God alone creates a relationship between God and human beings.

Philosophical Rationalism

The synthesis between reason and revelation to which Bryden so strenuously objected deserves further consideration. Modernism, according to Bryden, had assumed the authority of the autonomous rational individual as the ob-jective basis for the discernment and critical analysis of truth. Bryden was willing to admit that such an assumption was entirely appropriate for philos-ophy and science. Philosophy and science, after all, were understandings of life acquired from an appreciation of the general needs of human experience. They were to be accounted as abstract evaluations of life based on an under-standing of principles observed to inhere in and govern nature and history. They were systems of thought built upon results achieved from an objective examination of life's facts, on the one hand, and its values on the other, with a view to some sort of coalescence of these. Reason as the independent arbiter of truth within the realm of philosophy and science, therefore, made abun-dant sense to Bryden.

But that's where Bryden drew the line. Theology did not derive from the results of human discovery, whatever character those discoveries might take. The paramount concern of Christian theology, Bryden argued, was always

---

[35] S. Vernon McCasland, Review of *The Christian's Knowledge of God* in *The Journal of Bible and Religion* (August 1941) 179–80.

that which the church has been, and is under compulsion to think and say under the constraint of what it has been pleased to call God's Word, always recognizing itself to be strictly a creature of that Word. Theology was concerned with thinking that arose out of the most radical of all self-negating experience: repentance and confession. When the church throughout its history attempted to make the Word of God conform to the particular commanding thought-conceptions which happened at the time to prevail, this understanding of theology was often lost. In earlier times the church utilized the conceptual language of Greek philosophy to articulate Christian faith. In the modern world the church appealed to the insights of the empirical sciences and philosophical idealism. Both appeals, Bryden believed, had undermined rather than enhanced faith's claim for the reality of revelation. The attempt to justify faith by reason in the modern world resulted in three quite distinct but equally problematic issues for the Christian conception of revelation: religious subjectivism, progressive revelation, and secularization.[36]

Schleiermacher's subjectivism arose from his desire to strengthen the claim of religion in general by revealing its primal and universal place in human experience. By appealing to an a priori God-consciousness Schleiermacher believed he was able to vindicate the Christian religion in particular by exhibiting it as the concrete realization of this more general religious experience. While pietism and romanticism undoubtedly figured in the concept of religious experience developed by Schleiermacher, the driving force behind his theological project was the desire to justify and commend Christian faith to its cultured despisers in Europe. As noble as this might have appeared at the time, it led, Bryden argued, to disastrous consequences for the Christian conception of revelation. God, conceived mainly as humanity's ideal consciousness, served as the instrument by which human beings were to be brought to a higher self-realization. The object of theology was no longer God, as God had been understood in historic Christianity, an absolutely radical challenge for human beings as such, but the human experience of God. The universal consciousness of God about which Schleiermacher spoke was not simply the capacity or pre-understanding which might be seen as a necessary precondition for revelation—it was the revelation itself. The symbols of the Christian faith were subsequently re-interpreted in the wake of this revolutionary understanding of revelation. Jesus became the ideal man with the ideal God-consciousness. Redemption became the experience of religious illumination through participation in this ideal. The genius of Schleiermacher's approach, Bryden believed, was its rationally justified subjectivism. The problem, as Bryden saw it, was that it never conceived of God in any sense as One truly

---

[36]   Bryden, *The Christian's Knowledge of God*, 30–31.

objective to human beings. In short, rationalism and subjectivism were cut from the same philosophical cloth.[37]

Secondly, the liberal Protestant doctrine of progressive revelation embodied the ideal of inevitable evolutionary progress. The idea that revelation was a matter of gradual education and enlightenment in which moral and religious truths were received by human beings could be justified, it was argued by liberals, not simply by an appeal to the modern worldview, but also by an appeal to the progressive self-disclosure of God in the Bible. Bryden countered that the Scriptures presented revelation as something which belonged strictly to the apocalyptic, eschatological category of thought, and represented a view of life that was incompatible with the ideas of inevitable progress and evolution. Furthermore, a progression in mere moral and religious ideas as the criterion of revelation had resulted in relativizing the revelation of God among the many revelations in the religions of the world. Bryden recognized that many liberal Protestants maintained that the Christian revelation represented the most perfect revelation and fulfillment of all other revelations. Nevertheless, the uniqueness and absolute character of the claim had been lost in modern theology. The notion of fulfillment at work in the idea of progressive revelation was also troubling to Bryden. In liberal Protestantism the true significance of Christian revelation was thought to consist in the consummation of a long moral and religious achievement in human history prior to the coming of Christ. Revelation, in this view, formed the apex of a religious pyramid, the base of which was to be found in the diverse religious intuitions of human beings. In the New Testament, Bryden argued, fulfillment was not the completion of a long process. It was the bringing to an end, in a very real sense, of the order which had previously existed, and the inauguration of a completely new beginning in Jesus Christ.

Bryden was aware that the doctrine of progressive revelation had a long and noble history in Christian theology long before liberal Protestantism. In Roman Catholicism the idea of religious development had been extended to the time subsequent to Christ, and applied to the church as the extension of the incarnation. In this sense, revelation progressed through the doctrinal development of the church, through its dogmas, orders, and traditions. The apostolic tradition was fulfilled by the ongoing authority of the church's teaching office. As a Protestant, Bryden believed that this notion of progressive revelation failed to do justice to the unique revelatory authority of the Bible. But there was another problem. Both liberal Protestantism and Roman Catholicism, it seemed to Bryden, sought to rationalize the Word of God in terms of progressive revelation and doctrinal development. The concept of revelation in modernism was subordinated to the idea of inevitable evolu-

---

[37] Ibid., 32–36.

tionary progress. In Roman Catholicism, the concept of revelation was sub-ject to the traditions and dogmas of the institutional church. In words that echoed those of Barth, Bryden argued that if forced to choose between the two, he would most certainly choose the Roman Catholic because it had shown itself to be genuinely concerned to maintain the supernatural charac-ter of revelation.[38]

The irony of the subjective and progressive reconstructions of revelation in modern theology was that they had not stemmed the tide of seculariza-tion that seemed to be sweeping over the western world. In fact, and this was Bryden's third point, they hastened secularism's ascendancy. The naturaliza-tion of the Christian faith did not Christianize the world, it secularized the church. The justification of Christianity through the use of rational ideals left the church wholly without the power of revelation and the knowledge of God in the world. What was the point of now defending a gospel, as liberal Protestants wished to do, which had already been gutted in order to defend the gospel? Like madmen on a rampage, liberal Protestant theologians had destroyed revelation in order to save it. The Christian faith had lost its mean-ing through secularization since only "that which belongs to an order other than this world can be truly provocative, and thus provide the necessary cor-rective for this world." Unlike modernist theologians, Friedrich Nietzsche at least was honest. Nietzsche's rejection of the Christian faith was based on a clear understanding of the essential claims of Jesus Christ. He understood "far more clearly than the Christian theologians of his day the radical nature of the claim essential Christianity had made for Christ." Rationalism in religion, Bryden argued, obfuscated the daring paradoxes with which modern men and women were truly confronted. Either God was who God was revealed to be in Jesus Christ, or God was dead. There was no middle ground. The modern church's attempt to stake out just such a ground only made matters worse. It gave people just enough rational religion to inoculate them against the real and radical claims of Christian revelation.[39]

Given the polemical and prophetic character of Bryden's rant against rationalism, it did not take long for Canadian philosophers and theologians to train their sights on him. The most trenchant critique was mounted by F.H. Anderson of the University of Toronto's philosophy department who described Bryden as "an irrational enthusiast." In his review of *The Christian's Knowledge of God*, Anderson argued that Walter Bryden was very good at tell-ing people what revelation was not, while making few constructive propos-als about what revelation might be, especially in relation to human reason. Did Bryden really believe, Anderson presumed to ask, that revelation was

---

[38] Ibid., 36–49. Compare Karl Barth, *Church Dogmatics*, I.1,xiii.

[39] Bryden, *The Christian's Knowledge of God*, 57–70.

too personal and too immediate for any theological description whatsoever? Was it truly the case that the Christian knowledge of God was not a species of natural knowing at all? If so, then how was it achieved, if not through the natural powers of reason?[40] Theological shots were also fired from within the Presbyterian Church. Frank Beare, at the time a lecturer in Church History at The Presbyterian College, Montreal, fulminated against what he felt was the noxious influence of Bryden's neo-orthodox irrationalism. "Barthianism," he wrote in *The Presbyterian Student* in 1937, is not synonymous with Christian theology. . . . I warn our Barthian friends that neither the Presbyterian Church in Canada nor any church which is truly catholic will ever allow itself to be chained in such a fashion."[41]

It has to be said that through Barth's early influence Bryden decided to cast his lot with the tradition of theology that went back to Tertullian rather than the one that was traced to Justin Martyr. The heresies themselves, Tertullian had argued, receive their weapons from philosophy. What is there in common, he asked, between Athens and Jerusalem? between the academy and the church? Justin Martyr, on the other hand, was quite willing to affirm that all writers were able to see the truth darkly, on account of the implanted seed of the Logos which was grafted into them. Bryden's rhetoric clearly belonged to the school of Tertullian. Like Luther, Bryden was quite willing to call reason a whore. Like a prophet with a single burden, Walter Bryden maintained his protest against rationalism and "his witness to the judgment of God on every human pretension, especially in ecclesiastical and theological dress" until the very end of his life.[42] Some of his students, notably Joseph C. McLelland, questioned whether Bryden's constant harping on the note of judgment did not become tiresome. Bryden's protest presupposed the positive "Yes!" of the gospel, McLelland argued, but because Bryden could not discern clearly the signs of its acceptance, he continued to sound his "No!" Unlike the later Barth, Bryden never seemed able to articulate a positive role for reason in Christian theology. While he was more than willing to affirm that true faith should seek understanding, he seemed more than a little nervous about exploring the rational and intelligible sense of what was believed. Bryden tended to see God's Word to humanity in a bare encounter between human beings and the divine Subject who stood over against them as Lord. Unlike Barth, who came to see that this encounter was also rational with the

---

[40] F. H. Anderson, "On A Certain Revival of Enthusiasm," *The University of Toronto Quarterly* 10.2 (1941) 194.

[41] Frank Beare, "Against the Barthian Theology," *The Presbyterian Student* (March 1937) 9–10. See also A. Donald MacLeod, "The Formation of the Articles of Faith Committee: Ascendant Barthianism in the 1940s in the PCC," in *Papers of the Canadian Society of Presbyterian History* (September 2004) 3.

[42] Joseph C. McLelland, "Walter Bryden: 'By Circumstance and God,'" 125.

rationality of God, Bryden seemed to assume that reason was irredeemable. Through his study of Anselm and his engagement with Protestant orthodoxy, Barth had come to understand that God's Word was not only a personal address, but also God's own divine intelligibility. In the words of Alasdair Heron, this did not mean that intelligibility could be wholly captured in the formulations or in the mind of the theologian; it did, however, mean that the divine intelligibility really came across to humanity, that God gave the divine Subject to be truly known and truly understood. Bryden never quite got this. To a church that needed a prophetic protest against the magisterial authority of autonomous human reason in religious faith in the second quarter of the twentieth century, Bryden appeared as a gift from God. To other Canadian Protestants, who looked for guidance to solve intricate problems of historical theology, or modern questions of methodology and epistemology, Bryden's diatribes against philosophical rationalism were less than compelling.[43]

Historical Criticism

Many of the issues identified in the challenges of religious idealism and philosophical rationalism came to a focus in liberal Protestantism's reconstruction of the authority and interpretation of the Bible. According to Bryden, modernism presupposed that the Christian revelation could be authenticated in history by empirically verifiable evidence. Indeed, he argued, modernism represented "a deliberate and sustained tendency to discover the revelation contained in the New Testament upon the purely historic plane and by purely empirical method."[44] The result was catastrophic for a Christian conception of the Bible because the eschatological, apocalyptic, and transcendent dimensions of Scripture were dismissed out of hand. Since the publication of David Strauss' *Leben Jesu*, revelation in the New Testament had been subsumed under the category of the 'historic Jesus' alone, in which the unique personality of Jesus, the incidents of his human life and his moral religious teachings constituted the matters of prime consideration.[45] More concerned with ideas that could be derived from the life and teachings of Jesus than with the facts themselves, revelation, in the hands of liberal Protestants, became the disclosure of ideals useful for modern living. Ironically, the quest for the historical Jesus behind the texts of the New Testament sought to give 'historical ground' to these ideals. As far as Bryden was concerned, Albert Schweitzer had discredited the historical justification for an idealist interpretation of the New Testament once and for all. Deeply impressed by Schweitzer's claim in

---

[43]   Joseph C. McLelland, "Walter Bryden: 'By Circumstance and God,'" 125–26. See also Alasdair I. C. Heron, *A Century of Protestant Theology* (London: Lutterworth, 1980) 84.

[44]   Bryden, *The Christian's Knowledge of God,* 17.

[45]   Ibid.; and idem, *Separated Unto the Gospel,* 202–3.

The Quest for the Historical Jesus (1906) that the "eschatological formed not only an integral part of the New Testament outlook, but was of the very essence of Jesus' own thought,"[46] Bryden employed Schweitzer's insight when interpreting the New Testament long before Bryden had encountered Barth's theology. The belief in progress Bryden argued, was irreconcilable with the biblical conception of time. The Jesus of nineteenth-century scholarship, he concluded, never actually existed except as a cipher for modern ideals.

Bryden's sharp critique of the historical critical method rested upon the belief that 'the historic critics' were not true to their own methods; that is, they were not critical enough. By dismissing the New Testament worldview out of hand they had, in fact, set aside critical historical insights that were essential to biblical interpretation. The Christology of liberal Protestantism was a case in point. The significance of Jesus for the church rested on the impression made upon the disciples by the spirit and words of the historical Jesus. Insofar as the ideals of the historical Jesus, portrayed in the existent records, still made an impression today, men and women could hope to gain insight for modern life. But this view, Bryden argued, dismissed the place of the witness of the Holy Spirit as absolutely necessary for believing in Christ at all. It constructed a Christianity devoid of the transcendent, supernatural, and apocalyptic worldview that dominated the texts of the New Testament. The impressive historical feature of the New Testament, as Bryden understood it, was its claim that God somehow makes the divine Self known to us, and who thereby makes us known truly, for the first time to ourselves. And that God does this in Jesus Christ alone, but only as witnessed to by the Holy Spirit. Modernism forgot or deliberately ignored this historical fact: the early church believed that the Holy Spirit witnessed to the Word.[47] Revelation for modernists, rather than being the act of God's self-disclosure, was the reception of empirically verifiable historical ideals intended for human edification and enlightenment. The personal qualities of Jesus were identified with the higher qualities of human life, especially as these were understood in terms of the moral and religious values of nineteenth-century European culture Protestantism. In short, in the hands of the historic critics Jesus became the justification of a particular form of western civilization.

In making his case against the modernist theological results of the historical critical method, Bryden also appealed to the "impressive and penetrating works of the so-called Form-Geschichtliche school in general, and Rudolf Bultmann's *Jesus* in particular."[48] Bultmann demonstrated, Bryden believed, that what we know about the life and personality of Jesus is as good as noth-

---

[46] Bryden, *The Christian's Knowledge of God*, 19.

[47] Ibid., 19–20.

[48] Ibid., 8.

ing and that most of what was written during the late nineteenth and early twentieth centuries about Jesus was purely fantastic and romantic. The interesting thing about Bultmann's position, Bryden contended, as ridiculous, challenging, or depressing as it might appear to some, was that Bultmann arrived at it himself as a product of the historical critical method of investigation. Bultmann had overturned the search for the historical Jesus behind the biblical texts by reminding historians that the only Jesus presented in the texts of the New Testament was the early church's Christ of faith. The only knowledge of Jesus available to the church today, therefore, was that mediated through the forms of the faith which men and women had in Jesus. Bultmann, rather than bemoaning this fact as an insurmountable challenge to faith in the modern era, celebrated it as the church's liberation from historicism. Walter Bryden, with certain qualifications of the claim made by Bultmann, found himself in agreement with Bultmann's basic insight. For Bryden, this confirmed the New Testament understanding that the revelation of God in Jesus Christ, and the deep things of God pertaining to it, were not observed or discovered directly from Jesus' historic appearance alone.[49]

Bryden's attempt to turn the historic critics back upon themselves met with measured success for a time. An attempt to unmask the bankruptcy of liberal Protestant Christianity, Bryden's analysis threw down the gauntlet before the Canadian church establishment. Given the climate of crisis which emerged in the 1930s, some church leaders, especially ministers and students within the Presbyterian Church in Canada, were prepared to raise questions concerning both the image of Jesus that emerged in nineteenth-century liberal Protestantism and the effect that such a view had made upon the church's understanding of itself and its role in Canadian society. It was folly to equate, as modernism had, the Jesus of history with the ideals of modernity, and to assume that this equation could be justified through the use of historical criticism. But in the long run, there were problems with the neo-orthodox conception of revelation and history that could not be avoided. If the 'Christ of faith' could never be discerned through historical investigation alone, as Bryden argued, what role, then, if any, did historical investigation play in coming to understand the claims of Christianity? If, as Bryden believed, the supreme obligation of the church was not to rediscover Jesus historically, but rather to rediscover him spiritually, was there, then, any need for historical inquiry as a basis for Christian faith?

It has to be understood that for Walter Bryden, as for most of the neo-orthodox theologians, the relationship between revelation and history was rather complex and ambiguous. They believed that Christianity was an historical faith and that God worked in and through history. At the same time,

---

[49]   Ibid., 84–85.

and this is crucial, they rejected the notion that revelation could simply be identified with historical events. Historical events, to be sure, were the means through which and in which human beings encountered God. But revelation itself was supra-historical. The revelation of God revealed "history beyond history" and, as such, was not available for historical investigation and verification. Revelation was a spiritual reality in which an individual was encountered by the living Word of God. Revelation belonged to the sovereign God alone who, in love and freedom, graciously elected to share divine self-knowledge with human subjects in and through the history of Jesus Christ.

The problems inherent in this understanding of revelation and history in Canadian Protestantism have been noted by Michael Gauvreau who argues that neo-orthodoxy shared the general modern revulsion against history that characterized the intellectual climate of Europe and America in the 1920s and 1930s. The failure of the churches during World War I, as Barth and his theological collaborators saw it, led them to seek a "disengagement" of theology and history. They appeared to deny the validity of human reason in the interpretation of religion, and they posited an acute contradiction between revelation, which they termed as "super-history," and human history. They appeared to proclaim the irrelevance of historical research and the historical personality of Jesus to the believer's faith. These tenets of the emerging "theology of crisis," Gauvreau argues, were characterized by a modernist and existentialist sense of absolute contradiction between the uncertain, constantly changing record of human history, and the eternal, unchanging, incomprehensible revelation of God. The term neo-orthodoxy, therefore, is a misnomer, because these theologians broke decisively with the theology of history that had informed and sustained the evangelical tradition in Canada.[50] The Scottish approach to theology, strongly represented in the Canadian colleges, avoided the extremes of Barthian modernism "founded on despair concerning the historical process and the aggressive Baconianism of the American fundamentalists, which verged on an outright denial of the knowledge of the Bible provided by historical criticism since 1860."[51] Thus, Gauvreau concludes, "neo-orthodoxy had no widespread currency within the church until the 1930s brought a fresh mood of crisis to colleges and pulpits."[52]

Gauvreau correctly notes that the neo-orthodox theologians introduced a rather novel conception of the relation between faith and history, but he neglects to show how this was worked out in the thought of North American Protestant theologians and church leaders. Furthermore, the neo-orthodox approach to history could not ultimately be sustained for reasons that are

---

[50] Gauvreau, *The Evangelical Century*, 267–68.
[51] Ibid., 270.
[52] Ibid., 271.

far more compelling than those he sets out. The so-called disengagement from history he describes may have been indebted to modernism, but it was a modern existentialist move against modern idealism. That is, it was also a protest against modernism. In particular, it was intended to forestall the new morality implicit in historical knowledge since the Enlightenment. Prior to the eighteenth century, historical inquiry had been viewed as an ally of faith. The Enlightenment had not simply introduced new and more reliable methods of historical study, but an ethic which required the suspension of belief as its fundamental presupposition. The epistemological significance of faith, therefore, was marginalized. Rather than providing the basis from which historical inquiry might proceed, faith was now viewed as an obstacle to be overcome, and doubt (i.e., methodological skepticism) was celebrated as a cardinal virtue. The problem of faith and history, therefore, as Van Harvey has argued, was not simply a problem of two different forms of logic or two methodologies; it was a problem of two ethics of judgment.[53] Both conservative and liberal Protestant theologians proceeded to fashion understandings of revelation and history in response to this new ethic of judgment. Conservative Protestants attempted to shore up the old pre-modern ethic through various strategies (e.g., Common Sense philosophy, Paleyite natural theology, and Baconian inductive reasoning) while liberal Protestants attempted to reconstruct the old orthodoxies in ways that accommodated the new ethic. Through the nineteenth century and the first part of the twentieth century these two strategies appeared to have some merit and success. In Canadian Protestantism, largely through the influence of Scottish theology, the two options not only lived in harmony side by side, but often resulted in a blended form of evangelical piety and historical criticism of the sort in which Walter Bryden was educated.

As early as the 1920s in Canada, however, Bryden had come to the conclusion that such a blended option was no longer credible. In response, therefore, he participated in the neo-orthodox attempt to relativize historical inquiry by radicalizing the concept of justification by faith. Faith, in this view, was not to be conceived in terms of assent to historically derived doctrinal propositions or historically generated religious ideals. Faith was, in contrast, the realization that an abysmal gulf existed between God and human beings which made Lessing's "ugly ditch of history" appear miniscule by comparison. Historical inquiry had to be set within the framework of the infinite qualitative difference between time and eternity. Faith was a recognition that life was ambiguous and that history was questionable. Genuine faith was a void, a not-knowing, a questioning, the utter dissolution of certainty. So

---

[53] Van Harvey, *The Historian and the Believer: The Morality of Historical Knowledge and Christian Belief* (New York: Macmillan, 1966) 102–4.

conceived, faith now had a structure analogous to the skepticism of the new morality of knowledge. Radical faith and Enlightenment knowledge were not opposites but correlates. The new morality of knowledge was not the antithesis to faith but its expression. The hermeneutic of suspicion with which the dialectical theologians approached history was, in their minds, the logical and consistent application of the historical method rather than a disengagement from history altogether. Historical inquiry and biblical criticism could proceed without restraint because Christian faith rested upon a wholly other basis. In short, the neo-orthodox theologians understood themselves as truly modern Christian theologians in a way that they believed neither conservative nor liberal Protestants could claim.

As a strategy to overturn the dominance of idealism in Christian theology, the existentialist move made by Walter Bryden and others worked for a time. But, as Van Harvey has so ably pointed out, dialectical theology contained within itself the seeds of its own demise. The radical interpretation of justification by faith which permitted them to accept the new morality of knowledge also appeared to permit the conclusion that faith had no essential relationship to a past historical event, even the life, death, and resurrection of Jesus which the neo-orthodox theologians so loudly trumpeted. As Heinz Zahrnt bluntly stated the case in 1961: "It is clear . . . that the fundamental problem of all theological work is history. The impact of 'dialectical theology' (neo-orthodoxy) succeeded in repressing it for a time, but it could not be dismissed completely. The attempt to use dogma as it were to overrun history has proved a failure."[54] Nevertheless, in the hands of Walter Bryden, the neo-orthodox conception of revelation and history became a powerful tool in the theological reconstruction of The Presbyterian Church in Canada by the late 1920s, and it dominated the denomination from the 1940s on.

Natural Theology

One final point is worth noting briefly in relation to Bryden's rejection of liberal Protestantism, especially in terms of its significance for Bryden's re-appropriation of Calvin's Reformation theology. On the question of general revelation, Bryden stood against the possibility of any universal or natural revelation through general religious experience which might supplant the knowledge of God in Jesus Christ. Like Barth, he believed that liberal Protestant thought was an idealist form of natural theology which assumed that knowledge of God was possible prior to and apart from special revela-

---

[54] Heinz Zahrnt, cited in Sydney E. Ahlstrom, *Theology in America: The Major Protestant Voices from Puritanism to Neo-Orthodoxy,* 87. See also Harvey, *The Historian and the Believer,* 131ff.

tion. The modern conception of revelation, he argued, tended "to merge the traditional claim for a "special" Christian revelation in that of a general or universal revelation."[55] Liberal Protestantism, Bryden argued, had synthesized the fundamental distinction between the knowledge of God the creator and the knowledge of God the redeemer upon which Calvin had structured his *Institutes of the Christian Religion*. The Reformers had protested against the late medieval synthesis which posited a basic continuity leading upwards from a rational to a revealed knowledge of God. They emphasized, rather, the incapacity of human beings to come to God apart from grace. Calvin in particular denied that general revelation provided any preparation for the gospel.

This was the fundamental point of difference, Bryden noted, between liberal Protestantism and the theology of the Reformation. Modernism accepted a principle of continuity between God and humanity similar to that of late medieval scholastic theology, while the theology of the Reformation posited a knowledge of God which came only by the judging and saving activity of God's Word and Spirit. Bryden acknowledged that Calvin never denied that the "natural man" had a certain "so-called knowledge of God." Calvin, Bryden recognized, saw that God bears witness to God's being in creation and providence. But Bryden was quick to point out that for Calvin the *sensus divinitatis,* although real and indestructible within humanity, always leads fallen humanity away from both a genuine knowledge of God and a proper relationship of worship and obedience to God. By eradicating the distinction between general revelation and special revelation, Bryden concluded, liberal Protestantism asserted what Calvin denied—that human beings can have a saving knowledge of God apart from the revelation of God's Word. Modernism interpreted Romans 1 and Acts 17 to mean that all humanity shared a common sense of God upon which Christian faith could be built, while Calvin, Bryden contended, understood such passages as bearing a negative witness to the knowledge of God that human beings *should have had.*[56]

Two important features of Walter Bryden's rejection of liberal Protestantism are to be noted. First, Bryden stood somewhat aloof from the debate that was raging in the 1930s between Barth and Brunner over natural theology. Brunner had affirmed that there are, indeed, two kinds of revelation. Scripture testifies to the revelation of God in Jesus Christ and also to the revelation of God given in creation. The Bible assumes that God's action in the world as creator leaves an imprint of the divine nature in creation and history and that genuine knowledge of God is accessible through the law. God is, Brunner believed, objectively revealed in creation, but true natural

---

55 Bryden, "After Modernism, What?" chapter 1, Introductory.
56 Bryden, Lectures on Augustine, 32.

knowledge of God is given to those who receive the knowledge of God in Jesus Christ. This was, Brunner argued, consistent with Calvin's Reformation position. Barth, on the other hand, sounded an angry "No!" against Brunner's interpretation of Scripture and Calvin. For reasons that had to do with the political situation in Germany in the 1930s, Barth denied that God was revealed objectively in creation. In the background was the same concern that had fuelled Bryden's rejection of liberal Protestantism: natural theology undermined the special saving revelation of God in Jesus Christ. In the foreground, however, was Barth's insistence that Brunner's position created the possibility of support for the Nazi regime in Germany. For reasons that are not altogether clear, Bryden believed that he stood with Barth while he affirmed an interpretation of Calvin that looked more like that of Brunner. In any event, Bryden believed strongly that the Calvinist doctrine of sin had noetic implications. And in response to the modernist subordination of special revelation to general revelation, Bryden appealed to Calvin's doctrine of the twofold knowledge of God that effectively subordinated general revelation to special revelation.

Second, if, as Joseph C. McLelland has argued, the natural theology of Canada is a "natural theology, the study of religious truths through reason rather than divine revelation,"[57] then Walter Bryden's neo-orthodox conception of revelation sounded a note of protest against the natural theology of establishment Protestantism in the Canadian context. It has to be said, however, that the tradition of liberal Protestant theology, which developed the type of natural theology rejected by Bryden, had been mediated and moderated in Canada via Scottish theology. Bryden's rejection of the modernist concept of revelation, therefore, was not simply a protest against liberal Protestantism as such. It was a stand against the idealist tendency in the Canadian Protestant churches. In short, Bryden interpreted the development of Protestantism in Canada in terms of its naturalizing, rationalizing, idealizing, and historicizing tendencies.

The Authority of Scripture: Against Rational Orthodoxy

As polemical as his critique of modernism may have been, Walter Bryden believed that a simple reaffirmation of the old orthodox Reformed doctrine of revelation would not suffice. In the second section of his 1935 essay "The Presbyterian Conception of the Word of God," he set out a critical exposi-

---

[57] Joseph C. McLelland, "The Natural Theology of Canada: Philosophy of Religion in Canadian Theological Education," in *Theological Education in Canada,* edited by Graham Brown (Toronto: United Church Publishing, 1988) 1.

tion of the view of revelation held by the fundamentalists. In *Why I Am A Presbyterian* he had described as "rationally orthodox" that section of the pre-union Presbyterian Church which was obscurantist in theology, ultra-conservative, and even fundamentalist in its views concerning religion and the Bible. Now he defined them as those who held to a view in which "the Word of God is to be identified simply with the written Holy Scripture, in its wholeness, this Scripture to be literally interpreted because it is verbally inerrant and plenarily inspired."[58] Bryden contended that this view of the Word of God did not originate with Calvin and the early Reformed churches but rather in the scholastic aftermath of the Reformation. Adopting one of the characteristic features of the neo-Reformation theologies of Barth and Brunner, Bryden argued that a theological shift took place during the seventeenth century in which the Reformation emphasis on the Bible's saving function was replaced by a concern to define the divine form of Scripture. A new doctrine of inspiration and infallibility emerged to shore up the new emphasis on form, and the post-Reformation theologians adopted Aristotelian categories to explicate Reformed doctrines. As the Reformation churches became the religious establishment in many parts of Europe, their theologies lost the dynamic life of the original Reformation impulse for theological renewal so that, to quote Emil Brunner's powerful image, "the age of Orthodoxy appears like a frozen waterfall—mighty shapes of movement, but no movement."[59] The contemporary church, Bryden believed, had to reach back behind this frozen waterfall to drink anew from the wellspring of Reformation faith and life.

The fundamentalist doctrine of the Word of God, Bryden argued, ignored Calvin's identification of God's Spirit with God's Word. Calvin's doctrine of the internal testimony of the Holy Spirit (*testimonium Spiritus sancti internum*) had been replaced by a scholastic doctrine of inspiration in which rational arguments were used to justify the authority of the Bible. Arguing for the self-authenticating authority of the Bible, Bryden pointed out that for Calvin the testimony of the Holy Spirit was superior to all human reason. "God alone," Calvin declared, "is sufficient witness of Himself in His Word, so also the Word will never gain credit in the hearts of men, till it be confirmed by the internal testimony of the Spirit. It is necessary, therefore, that the same Spirit who spake by the mouths of the Prophets, should penetrate into our hearts to convince us that they faithfully delivered the oracles which were divinely entrusted to them."[60] This was, Bryden argued, no chance text from Calvin's writings. It represented a principle fundamental to the aim and

---

[58]   *Separated Unto the Gospel,* 181. See also *Why I Am A Presbyterian,* 42.

[59]   Emil Brunner, *The Divine Human Encounter,* 22.

[60]   John Calvin, *Institutes of the Christian Religion,* I.7.4; see Bryden, *Separated Unto the Gospel,* 182.

the motive of Calvin's *Institutes* as a whole. If the fundamentalists wished to justify the authority of the Bible as God's Word through an appeal to rational arguments, they should not seek support for this procedure in Calvin's theology. The sovereign and free Word of God, Bryden contended, resists all attempts to be rationalized and objectified in human thought, speech, and writing. Revelation is not the reception of propositional truths; it is an encounter with God's Word by God's Spirit. "Only by becoming flesh in His Word and by the Holy Spirit's work in the heart, does God expose the sin of man and of the world. That God is not rationally cognized but spiritually discerned is fundamental to reformation theology."[61] Bryden did not believe that the theory of verbal inspiration, when seriously employed as an authoritative basis for Christian faith, was intellectually defensible in view of the critical work of modern scholarship. But the overwhelming reason for rejecting this view of the Word of God was that it tended to falsify completely the true nature of Christian faith. When such a great emphasis was placed upon the capacity of human beings to know the Word of God in the Bible, revelation was objectified. This rationalization and objectification of the Christian faith, Bryden argued, was more akin to the later medieval Roman Catholic conception of natural theology than Calvin's conception of faith. And ironically, it shared the same rationalizing tendency as modern idealism. The Holy Spirit was identified with universal ideals in liberal Protestantism and, in rational orthodoxy, with propositional truths.

Bryden sought to defend himself against the charge of mysticism and enthusiasm by noting that Calvin argued against fanatics who wrongly appealed to the Holy Spirit in revelation. Calvin did not believe, according to Bryden, that the internal testimony of the Holy Spirit meant a self-sufficient, impersonal "inner light" which might speak to the souls of human beings at random, apart from the Word of God. Calvin conceived of the Holy Spirit, as Bryden saw it, as a witness "to that which was in the Bible alone, to the Word of God there, as found in the whole Bible."[62] But Bryden pointed out that Calvin's use of term "whole" in relation to the Bible was quite different from the meaning attributed to it by the fundamentalists. First, Calvin was concerned that the Bible be permitted to speak for itself, free from the interpretations of particular ecclesiastical interests and second, Calvin conceived of the Word of God christologically. The Word of God was actually represented in the Old Testament, just as in the New, in the law and the prophets proleptically, but finally and supremely in the person of Jesus Christ, who died humanity's death and was raised by the power of the Spirit of God to new

---

[61] Bryden, Unpublished Lecture Notes on the "Post-Reformation History of the Church," 4.
[62] *Separated Unto the Gospel,* 184.

life. It was this total manifestation of God, according to Bryden, which ultimately constituted the Word of God for Calvin. According to Calvin, Bryden
argued, faith was "that knowing of Christ in His saving efficacy which comes
alone by the revealing of the Spirit."[63] Despite appearances to the contrary,
this did not mean that faith was a matter of private subjective judgment.
Bryden believed that while Calvin conceived of faith as a solitary relationship between the soul and God which could not be mediated by any church
or priest, Calvin also affirmed that the Word of God which encounters human beings in the supreme relationship of faith was objective in a sense that
nothing on earth, not even the church of Christ, was objective. This was the
Word, Bryden argued, which stood over against men and women, which
judged them and yet uplifted them, which in times past had spoken, once
and for all, in the Event of history, and now continued to speak directly to
the souls of women and men. It is this, Bryden declared, which is objective.
"The Word of God itself, in this profound sense, is the cause of man's faith,
and determines its nature."[64]

It is not unimportant that the earliest and perhaps clearest expression
of Bryden's conception of the Judging–Saving Word is to be found in the
context of this attempt to retrieve Calvin's doctrine of revelation from the
clutches of what he perceived to be a rationally orthodox Calvinism. The appeal to the testimony of the Holy Spirit, and the distinction to be made between the Bible and the Word of God did not, as the fundamentalists feared,
Bryden argued, transform faith in the revelation of God into a purely subjective experience. The Word of God was a wholly other word which stood over
against human beings. It was precisely the character of the Word as judge that
created the knowledge of God which was made to conform to its divine object. In the event of revelation, men and women encountered a divine Word
that questioned their existence, demanded their attention, and required their
participation, comprehension, and cooperation. It was a word, to paraphrase
Barth, which presumed faith in the living God, and which created the faith
which it presumed. Revelation occurred precisely in the awareness that there
was nothing in the human subject which helped to bring this event about.

As he followed Barth's interpretation of Calvin, Bryden distanced himself not only from the liberal axiom of revelation as "God in us," but also
from the fundamentalist axiom of revelation as "God in Scripture." Instead,
he turned towards a conception of the Word of God which acknowledged
the sovereign freedom of the divine subject in the process of revelation. A
sharp distinction was to be drawn between an objectively self-revealing God
and the subjective human consciousness. At the same time, the objectivity of

---

63   Ibid., 184–85.
64   Ibid., 185.

the Word of God did not rest on the doctrine of verbal inspiration. It rested in God as God. In the wake of Barth's theology, then, Bryden adopted what was intended to be a truly modern Reformational approach to the Word of God in Scipture. Not only did he assume the usefulness and appropriateness of the historical critical method, but he also adopted a critical appropriation of Reformation epistemology. The somewhat naïve, metaphysically grounded realism of classical medieval and post-Reformation scholastic theologies assumed the existence of an objectively real empirical world which presented itself to the human knower to be known. The approach of Common Sense by Reformed theologians, for example, assumed that principles necessary to account for the world could be based on the observations made by the human knower, and that these principles could be extended to derive a knowledge of God. Such a procedure, which dominated Calvinism in Canada during the first seventy years of the nineteenth century, was uncritical because it did not take seriously the Enlightenment turn to the human subject as an active participant in constructing knowledge. At the same time, Bryden rejected the idealist assumption that the revelation of God was embedded in human history and experience. In short, Bryden sought to recover the objectivity of Calvin's doctrine of the Word by attempting to cut a post-critical swath through both fundamentalism and modernism.[65]

In order to accomplish this, Bryden recognized that a critical reading of Calvin was required. Convinced by Calvin's insistence on the significance of the Holy Spirit in the economy of God's revelation, Bryden admitted that Calvin was not always true to this essential insight into the Word of God. Since the Protestant Reformers found it necessary to assert the authority for the basis of their faith, Calvin sometimes appealed to Scripture as a textbook for doctrine and ethics, using proof-texts to buttress arguments, and contributing to the legacy of rationalistic exegesis which emerged in the post-Reformation era. But even on this point Bryden defended Calvin. It was certainly true that in his exegesis, commentaries and polemical writings Calvin used words, phrases and texts as if they possessed the authority of God in themselves. But it has to be remembered, Bryden argued, that Calvin waited upon the words of the Scriptural text in order that their hidden meaning might be revealed to his struggling spirit by the Spirit of God. The Word of God for Calvin, Bryden asserted, was "something quite different from the mere text." The Word of God cannot be

> merely rationally perceived, nor can the truth which it represents be vindicated or demonstrated by reason or be objectified in any system

---

[65] I am indebted to Bruce McCormack, *Karl Barth's Critically Realistic Dialectical Theology* (17, 107, 129) for the structure and language of this analysis.

of (human) thinking whatever. Its truth must be brought home to (the human) heart by the effectual working of God's Spirit. It therefore seems apparent to me that the Fundamentalist position, in its craving for proofs, historical and logical, in its corresponding endeavor to demonstrate to (the human) mind the truth of the Christian Gospel, and in the intellectual character of belief which it encourages, places itself precisely in the rationalistic category of interpretation which John Calvin, above all things, was anxious to avoid.[66]

The application of these insights to the reading and interpretation of the Bible meant that Bryden sought to move beyond the mere blend of evangelical piety and historical criticism which had dominated the Calvinist approach to the Bible in the first quarter of twentieth-century Canadian Presbyterianism. Although deeply rooted in both traditions, he recognized that it was no longer a matter of balancing two disparate approaches to the faith through the use of "a disciplined intelligence." A wholly other theological exegesis was required which, to be sure, admitted the insights of evangelical piety and historical criticism, but which was grounded in a profoundly theological understanding of the Word of God. The Word of God is prior to Scripture, creates Scripture, and emerges from Scripture. Historical criticism, without a doubt, saved Protestantism from sheer bibliolatry and supplied a method to better understand the history and language of the Bible. But "no amount of fearless facing of critical questions and courageous acceptance of their implication, no prodigies of learning, no scrupulous or painstaking industry in the letter of scriptural records, will disclose . . . what is the Word of God by which this very Scripture itself came into existence at all."[67] What was needed in the church, Bryden argued, was a completely new type of biblical commentary which was concerned primarily with discovering the theological meaning of Scripture. In a comment that was perhaps as self-reflective as it was prophetic, Bryden noted that scholars, when they cease to be prophetic, and thus fail to be theologians, possess a significance little more than that of scribes. Biblical interpretation proceeds properly when theologians and preachers acknowledge that "both the Old and New Testaments witness pre-eminently to one thing, namely to what we are pleased to call the Judging-Saving Word of God, which in a different form in each is the Christ of God. The Old Testament is Scripture, indeed, just because and only because it, in this sense, witnesses to Christ."[68] Revelation takes place when the faith that is created by the Word of God wholeheartedly embraces its basis.

---

66   *Separated Unto the Gospel,* 187.
67   *The Christian's Knowledge of God,* 23–24.
68   Ibid., 131.

Revelation, therefore, is not Scriptural revelation except when faith is coincident with it, and faith is not New Testament faith except when men and women perceive themselves judged as sinners (not just sinful), yet sinners saved by God's grace. God's judgment itself is (to the one who belongs to God) God's mercy, God's grace. Revelation moreover, is always personal, personal in a sense that no other relationship in life is personal—personal, because, being an encounter between God and the soul alone, it is utterly exclusive and unique.[69]

In sum, it was always correct, Bryden believed, "to say that the Scripture is the Word, because Scripture is the only place in all literature, religious or secular, in which there appears faith's witness to God's self-revelation in Jesus Christ through the Holy Spirit, but it is scarcely legitimate to say that the Word of God is Scripture. Jesus Christ and He alone is God's Word to a sinful world."[70]

As one might expect, Bryden's approach to the Bible created more than a little controversy in Canadian Presbyterianism and beyond. In a blistering review of *The Christian's Knowledge of God* which appeared in *The Christian Beacon*, the theological paper published by Carl McIntire and the Bible Presbyterians, the Rev. R. Allan Killen berated Bryden for teaching Canadian ministerial students that the Bible had discrepancies, contradictions, doubtful morality, and religious myths. Clearly at issue was the distinction Bryden made between Scripture and the Word of God, and his emphasis on the testimony of the Holy Spirit rather than the doctrine of inspiration. Bryden's position, Killen maintained, departed from the teaching of the New Testament and the Westminster Confession of Faith, and represented a wholesale capitulation to the new Barthian theology.[71]

Confessional Calvinists within the Presbyterian Church in Canada who sought to be more ecumenical and catholic in their ecclesiology distanced themselves from Killen's polemics and yet registered their own concerns about Bryden's neo-orthodox theological influence. Since Bryden had painted the fundamentalists with a rather broad brush, it would have been naïve to think that they would not respond from various quarters. The strict confessional Calvinists whom Bryden labeled as rationally orthodox represented a not inconsiderable influence within the continuing Presbyterian Church. They had supported the anti-unionist side by insisting that the doctrine, polity, and worship set out in the Westminster Standards was the only true interpretation

[69] Ibid., 106.

[70] *The Significance of the Westminster Confession of Faith*, 32.

[71] R. Allan Killen, "Canadian Ministerial Students Are Taught The Bible Has Discrepancies, Contradictions, Doubtful Morality and Religious Myths," *The Christian Beacon* (April 3, 1947) 2.

of the Scriptures. Their champion, Ephraim Scott, the octogenarian editor of the *Presbyterian Record* was elected moderator of the continuing Church meeting just before midnight in Knox Church, Toronto (Spadina) on June 10, 1925. More than that, the position Bryden rejected had had a long and noble history within Canadian Presbyterianism prior to 1925. As noted earlier, Bryden had been introduced to the Princeton theology of Charles Hodge by William MacLaren at Knox College. "The Protestant Rule of Faith," Hodge had insisted, taught that the Christian faith, in whole and in part, rested upon the authority of an infallible Bible created by the supernatural inspiration of God. The prophets and apostles, Hodge wrote, were representatives of God whose word they delivered. Inspiration extended equally to all parts of Scripture and made the Bible an inerrant record of divine speech.[72]

By the 1920s, however, the ecclesiastical landscape of Presbyterianism in North America had been dramatically altered, not simply by church union in Canada, but also by the fundamentalist-modernist controversy in the United States. While it has to be said that Canadian Presbyterians did not take their bearings entirely from what occurred south of the border, it was inevitable that the developments at Princeton Seminary in 1929 would spill over into Canada. One of Princeton Seminary's instructors, J. Gresham Machen, left to found Westminster Seminary in Philadelphia because of the so-called modernist takeover of the New Jersey seminary. In his book *Christianity and Liberalism*, which was read by numbers of Canadian Presbyterian ministers and students, Machen argued that Christian experience, if it was truly Christian, depended upon the life, death, and resurrection of Jesus as narrated in the Bible. The content of Scripture, Machen insisted, was unique, and the authority of the Bible was established upon the revelation of that content as mediated by an inspired text. "The latter doctrine means that the Bible not only is an account of important things, but that the account is true, the writers having been so preserved from error . . . that the resulting Book is the 'infallible rule of faith and practice.'" This was the view of biblical authority, Machen concluded, that lay at the heart of the Protestant Reformation. Christianity was founded on the Bible. Liberalism, on the other hand, was founded upon the shifting emotions of sinful men and women.[73] Hodge's doctrine of Scripture in the hands of Machen became the "cri de coeur" of conservative Calvinists during the theological battles waged between fundamentalists and modernists. The old Princeton doctrine of Scripture which Bryden rejected, therefore, had become a symbol of the larger debate and division. A number of Westminster graduates, along with conservative Calvinist graduates of Knox and Presbyterian College, championed the cause

---

[72]   Charles Hodge, *Systematic Theology*, 3 vols. (New York: Scribners, 1871) 1:153.

[73]   J. Gresham Machen, *Christianity and Liberalism*. (New York: Macmillan, 1923) 72–73.

of Reformed orthodoxy within the continuing Church and perceived the ascendant Barthianism centered in the leadership of Walter Bryden as a new and alternate form of modernism.

The debate between the confessionalists and the so-called Barthians reached a climax in the work of the Articles of Faith Committee during the 1940s. The Reformed orthodox position was ably articulated by W. Stanford Reid, a Westminster Seminary graduate who expressed deep appreciation for Bryden's theology. In addressing issues about revelation, Scripture, and theological epistemology within the committee, Reid tried to orchestrate a coalition between those who maintained strict adherence to the Westminster Confession of Faith and the advocates of the neo-orthodox conception of the Word of God. As A. Donald MacLeod has noted, "it was risky for someone in his camp to do so: in 1946 Westminster Seminary professor Cornelius van Til had labeled Barthianism (in a book with that title) *The New Modernism*."[74] Reid was far more generous and conciliatory than Killen had been in assessing Bryden's theology:

> While one may feel that Bryden and his supporters do not go as far as a thoroughgoing Calvinist might wish, nevertheless it must be recognized that their influence upon the church has been healthy. They have emphasized a return to the Scriptures, a return to doctrine, and also have stressed the doctrine of salvation by grace alone. True, they do not always place quite the same content in these terms as we might wish. Nevertheless, they have exercised a good influence on the church in calling people back to examine the church's standards, to see if the church is loyal to that which it professes.[75]

In the end, however, no rapprochement on the critical issue of the authority and interpretation of the Bible was possible within the committee. Bryden's conception of revelation, however it may have been characterized, was clearly unacceptable to both fundamentalists and modernists.

The Centrality of Christ: Revelation after Modernism

The witness of Karl Barth and his theological collaborators demanded, Bryden believed, that modernism and fundamentalism alike reconsider the whole question of Christian revelation. If revelation was to possess any specifically

---

74 A. Donald MacLeod, "The Formation of the Articles of Faith Committee: Ascendant Barthianism in the 1940s in the PCC," Paper delivered at The Canadian Society of Presbyterian History, September 25, 2004, 6.

75 W. Stanford Reid, "The Presbyterian Church in Canada 1. Historical Background." *The Presbyterian Guardian* (10 May 1946) 141–42.

religious significance worthy of attention in the twentieth century, it must, Bryden argued, in the words of Wilhelm Pauck, pertain to that "something in life which does not seem to originate from facts or inherently belong to them as their own product."[76] If Christian revelation is essentially what the church's confession, from the very beginning has consistently made it out to be, then it is a revelation, based upon extraordinary facts, the true significance of which, however, will not be perceived in the mere facts themselves, but only through the witness of the Holy Spirit. Theology after modernism, therefore, must consist solely of an exposition of that revelation, as it has been presented to human beings in its historical factual form, and as it continues to present itself in the present day. Revelation in the Christian tradition presupposes that God has spoken and that God speaks. The Word of God, therefore, cannot be conditioned by philosophies any more than it can be sustained or vindicated by apologetics. Bryden believed that the move beyond modernism and fundamentalism, as Barth contended for it, was an attempt to recover a first principle of Christian thought for a post-Enlightenment world. The recovery of that principle, for Bryden, was fueled not only by Barth and Barthianism, but by the entire reorientation of thought that had been taking place in different realms of thinking during the first quarter of the twentieth century. Kierkegaard, Nietzsche, Schweitzer, Bultmann, and others stood against the idealizing, rationalizing, historicizing, and naturalizing tendencies of modern thought.[77] The meaning of faith, the nature God's kingdom, the importance of creeds, and the practice of Christian ethics, all required radical revision in light of what was now known to have been the peculiar religious outlook of the New Testament.

Throughout his writings Bryden often only hinted at the direction that theology and the church might move in the wake of what he considered to be revolutionary theological developments. But he was forthright in his belief that the conception of revelation was central to whatever the church was to be and become, if it was to do what it was, and to become what it did. The Word of God was an event in which God had acted decisively in the crucified Jesus. In the humanity of Jesus Christ God shared God's self-knowledge as God with human beings. Revelation was the self-disclosure of the divine subject in a human subject, the unveiling of the divine word in words veiled by human flesh. The Word of God in Christ was a word of judgment and salvation, a word of death and life, and a word that touched both time and eternity as it encountered men and women in the infinite contradictions of their lives. The Word which God spoke and continues to speak required no justification other than that which occurred by the witness of the Holy Spirit.

---

[76]   Wilhelm Pauck, *Karl Barth*, 25; cited in Bryden, "After Modernism, What?" Conclusion.

[77]   Bryden, "After Modernism, What?" Conclusion.

In short, and not to overstate the case, Bryden bore witness to revelation as an objectively self-authenticating realistic dialectical christocentric self-disclosing act of God in Word and Spirit. The unpacking of this rather thick theological description provides the conclusion to this chapter and the transition to the next.

It has to be emphasized that the conception of the Word of God operated magisterially as the framework within which Bryden read the Bible and interpreted the Christian tradition. The Word of God was the raison d'etre of the world, Scripture, and the church. The conception of the Word of God to which the Bible bore witness, he believed, owed its origins not to Greek philosophical ideals concerning the nature of the *logos* but rather to the more dynamic Hebrew conception of *dabar*. In this understanding, God's word and God's work are confluent. God speaks and it is done. Divine speech and divine act are not separated. The Word of God, therefore, rather than being the communication of rational conceptual thought, is the power and action of God in which God discloses the divine identity and will to a covenant people. That Word came to Israel in creation, covenant, law, and wisdom, but it was the prophetic word which struck Bryden as particularly significant in the Old Testament. In the prophets are to be found individuals who, having heard and received the Word of God, understood that this Word had created and called them. The Word demanded more than notice or understanding or sympathy. It demanded participation and comprehension because it was a Word which presumed their faith, and which created the faith it presumed. The prophets, in turn, became witnesses to the Word through whom they had been created, namely Jesus Christ. The term Word of God, Bryden argued, along with the terms revelation, God-come, Christ-sent, God-become, or apprehended by the Holy Spirit, were all designed, in reference to Jesus Christ, to convey the same essential idea about the knowledge of God, namely that creation, revelation, and salvation are uniquely the acts of God in the person of Jesus Christ.[78] The knowledge of God created by the Word of God was not a fuller knowledge in continuum with that already possessed by human beings, but "something so radically new that it served to negate in a sense all preceding religious beliefs and traditions."[79]

The emphasis on revelation as act, and the sharp distinction between Greek and Hebrew thought, was a characteristic feature of the biblical theology movement which developed in the wake of the dialectical theologians. And like other significant features of the neo-orthodox conception of revelation, it was a creative blend of biblical, Reformation and modern insights. The idea that revelation was an event in which divine truth was disclosed—

---

[78] *The Christian's Knowledge of God*, 16.
[79] Ibid., 13.

rather than the communication of divine truth in propositional form—owed as much to nineteenth-century philosophical theology as it did to Jeremiah, Paul, or Calvin. The semantic distinctions between *logos* and *dabar* upon which an entire theology was built, were the fruit of historical critical scholarship (although it was later dismantled by James Barr in his seminal *Semantics of Biblical Language* in 1961). Taken as a whole, the neo-orthodox view provided an impressive account of the knowledge of God which utilized language that appeared to be both appropriate to the Christian tradition and adequate to the challenges of modern sensibilities that had now become disillusioned with idealism.

Revelation was not only an act of God, it was an act of self-disclosure. This is what made revelation personal and existential and gave it the character of encounter. In the language of Emil Brunner, Bryden believed that "the self-revelation of God is no object, but wholly the doing and self-giving of a subject—or, better expressed, a Person." God is a Person, or rather "the Person," who reveals himself and demands and offers Lordship and fellowship. This is the most radical antithesis to everything that could be called object or objective. God is not object but subject. Faith, the personal act of trust, is the antithesis of everything that could be called subjective, if by subjectivity we mean that which can become actual only when it is over against an object, that subjectivity which appropriates what is outside of it. Truth in the biblical sense is truth as personal encounter, and "This Biblical truth is as different from what otherwise is called truth as this personal encounter and the double-sided self-giving and its resulting fellowship are different from the comprehension of facts by means of reasoning." Bryden was aware that this conception of revelation as espoused by Brunner was influenced by Kierkegaardian existentialism and the personalist philosophy of the Jewish writer Martin Buber. In his major work *I And Thou* (1927), Buber had drawn a basic distinction between personal ("I–Thou") and impersonal ("I–It") relationships. Personal relationships entail an encounter between two active subjects who meet as persons in mutuality and reciprocity. The person of each is disclosed to the other. Brunner applied Buber's relational analysis to the doctrine of revelation in order to overcome the idea that a choice had to be made between revelation as the communication of objective information (rational orthodoxy) and revelation as the universal subjective experience of the divine (liberal Protestantism). Bryden fashioned Brunner's approach to meet the challenges of Canadian Protestantism.[80]

Behind this emphasis on self-revelation set out by Barth and Brunner, and adopted by Bryden, lay the dialogue between Hegelian idealism and Kierkegaardian existentialism. Hegel introduced the idea of revelation as the

---

[80]   Emil Brunner, *The Divine-Human Encounter*, trans. A. W. Loos (London: SCM, 1944).

unveiling of Absolute Spirit in history which, in the hands of a neo-Kantian like Wilhelm Herrmann, one of Barth's teachers at Marburg, became a tool to dismantle the concept of propositional revelation. Hegel also emphasized, along with the idealists before him, the importance of self-critical reflection which transcended the object-subject dichotomy. The non-propositional character of revelation and the importance of critical reflection now assumed, Walter Bryden adopted Kierkegaard's emphasis on the reality of the reflective individual self in opposition to Hegel's comprehensive individual-absorbing dialectic of Absolute Spirit. Bryden's refutation of idealism presupposed the non-propositional form of revelation which idealism had established and, at the same time, emphasized the existential character of revelation. The divine-human encounter was now interpreted dialectically from the standpoint of the reflective self in the midst of crisis.[81]

The self-revelatory act of God which constituted revelation for Bryden was thoroughly christocentric. That is, it was centered in Jesus Christ. While it was undoubtedly the case that Bryden picked up a good deal of his chris-tocentrism from Karl Barth, the influence of James Denney was decisive, especially in framing Bryden's understanding of the importance of faith and revelation. For Denney, the central reality of Christianity was faith in Jesus Christ: "Christianity may exist without any speculative Christology, but it never has existed and can never exist without faith in a living Saviour."[82] Jesus "stands over against the world," Denney argued, "and He knows that He has what all men need, and has it in such fullness that all men can obtain it from him." Jesus can do for human beings, what human beings need to have done, and he can give to all human beings, what all human beings need to receive. In the company of Jesus, Denney wrote, "misgivings die, for He is the Author of perfection, of eternal life, to those who receive Him." Denney viewed every aspect of the Christian faith and life from the vantage-point of God's revela-tion in Christ, and had confidence that this was a firm foundation upon which to base a coherent worldview. He expressed confidence in the historical Christ witnessed to in Scripture but rejected the traditional Calvinist apolo-getic reasoning used by Paleyite natural theology and Common Sense phi-losophy to shore up that history. At the same time, Denney was adamant that a worldview centered in Christ looked very different from the post-Kantian and neo-Hegelian idealism that dominated Protestantism in the late nine-teenth century. Most importantly, Denney emphasized the cross of Christ as the moment in time when the sin and suffering of the world was borne by God. The self-disclosure of God is the revelation of the redeemer. For Bryden, this connection between revelation and redemption in Christ was

---

[81] I am indebted to Gary Dorrien, *The Barthian Impulse in Modern Theology*, 7, 69.

[82] James Denney, *Jesus and the Gospel*, 30.

central for it meant that the eternal God, "hitherto unknown, unrevealed in the ultimate significance of His nature and His purposes, or, if and when revealed in a certain sense, only in an entirely unique but indirect and enigmatic way: to Whom, nevertheless, the preceding Israel of God had been born to witness and of Whom the prophets one and all spoke as the true and living God—One always recognized as far remote from men, yet at most times disturbingly, sometimes blessedly, near to them—had now become actually manifest among them in this man Jesus Christ; indeed, necessarily manifest for their salvation."[83] In Christ, Bryden argued, a knowledge of God had come to humanity which could not be categorized with any knowledge hitherto possessed by human beings. Moreover, the condition of humanity had been such through sin that a specific act of God was a necessity for the salvation of men and women. This act, he affirmed, had been effectuated in Jesus Christ alone.[84]

The christocentric act of God which defined the Word of God for Bryden was thoroughly dialectical. Although he did not often explicitly use the term, Bryden's theology was rife with what might be described as a dialectic of the Word. Dialectics operated in two distinct but related ways in his thought. First, Bryden's thought was dialectical in the sense that he privileged the concept of paradox. As a way of structuring human thinking and speaking in theology, Bryden reveled in the approach that called for every "theological statement to be placed over against a counter statement without allowing the dialectical tension between the two to be resolved in a higher synthesis."[85] Of all the paradoxes with which one was confronted in the Christian faith, none was more compelling and central than the Judging-Saving Word of God in Jesus Christ. The Bible witnesses preeminently to one thing, Bryden believed, namely to what he was pleased to call the Judging-Saving Word of God. This Word, Bryden noted with reference to Hebrews 4:12, was living and active, sharper than any double-edged sword, and penetrated even to dividing soul and spirit, joint and marrow. It judged the thoughts and attitudes of the heart. It was a completely-judging, completely-saving Word; it was death-dealing, and for that reason alone it was a life-giving Word. Just because it negated it affirmed. It was this two-fold character which constituted the uniqueness claimed for it. It was the paradoxical finality of the Word, for Bryden, which always qualified the conception of revelation presented in the Christian Bible. The prophets heard and spoke this Judging-Saving Word; Jesus Christ was this Word.[86]

---

83   *The Christian's Knowledge of God*, 3–4.

84   Ibid., 6.

85   McCormack, *Karl Barth's Critically Realistic Dialectical Theology*, 11.

86   *The Christian's Knowledge of God*, 136.

Second, the dialectical character of Bryden's thought related to his emphasis on existence and encounter in the life of the Christian believer. Bryden believed that revelation was an act of God (what God had done and what God was doing) which created an act on the part of the human subject in correspondence to the act of God. The act of divine self-revelation, and the human act of faith which was created by the divine act, constituted the event of revelation in which God shared divine self-knowledge and in which that knowledge was really received, comprehended, embraced, participated in, and responded to. The divine-human encounter was existential because, from the standpoint of the individual, it emphasized the self-critical awareness of the absolute need for divine authentication of human existence. The closed, coherent, intelligible universe of idealism in which God and the world were synthesized was replaced by the real world of God in which a person found him or herself in crisis and under judgment. Rather than being thrown back on oneself and the illusion of freedom, one was thrown by faith back into the freedom of God. The dialectical tension between the act of God and the act of the divine subject could never be justified, rationalized, synthesized, naturalized, historicized, or idealized. It was precisely the attempt to do so in most Protestant theology, conservative and liberal, that Bryden found not only distasteful, but astonishingly destructive of authentic Christian faith.

Furthermore, revelation for Bryden was objectively real in the sense that he shared in the theological realism which characterized the neo-orthodox impulse of post-liberal Protestantism. The problem with idealism, as Bryden understood it, was that it reduced God to an idea which synthesized the divine reality with the world. Barth's theology resonated with Bryden precisely because Barth had been able to construct a realistic account of God which acknowledged the idealist critique. Barth believed that God was real, whole, and complete as divine being apart from the thought patterns, idealist or otherwise, of human beings. As Bruce McCormack has shown, God, for Barth, was the reality which preceded all human knowing, including the individual knowing of the self. In his second commentary on Romans, Barth had emphasized that God and the world were in "diastasis," a relation in which the two members stood over against each other without any possibility of a synthesis.[87] Barth was engaged in the attempt to find a realistic starting point for theology, the seemingly impossible task of thinking from a standpoint from within the divine being itself. As noted earlier, however, this attempt did not represent a return to the metaphysically grounded assumptions of medieval and post-Reformational theology. Thomist theology and Reformed orthodoxy both began with the uncritical assumption that an objectively real, empirical world not only existed but also that it presented

---

[87] McCormack, *Karl Barth's Critically Realistic Dialectical Theology*, 129.

itself to the human knower to be known in a way that the human knower did not play a significant role in receiving and constructing the objects of knowledge. Such a procedure was also naïve in that it simply identified the first principles of knowledge with the God described in the Bible. Barth was after a realism which acknowledged the reality of God and the reality of the world (as affirmed by Thomism and Reformed orthodoxy). But it had to be a critical realism which acknowledged the epistemology of the Enlightenment. (In this sense "neo-orthodoxy" may in fact be an apt term for a theology that seeks to retrieve the contents of Christian orthodoxy in ways that acknowledge and appropriate the critical insights of modern thought.) In seeking to establish a form of theological realism, Karl Barth everywhere assumed the validity of Kant's epistemology (as applied to knowledge of empirical reality) and the success of Kant's critique of metaphysics. The truly "real" world, for Barth, was the world of God. The world of the wholly other God stood in sharp contrast to the empirical world, and there was no epistemological way which led from the empirical world to its divine source in the world of the wholly other God. The way of metaphysics taken by classical orthodox realism, therefore, was forever closed to the modern critical mind. The only road left open to travel was the road taken by the self-revealing God in Jesus Christ. Barth's attempt to develop a realistic account of God, therefore, assumed the success of the critical element in idealism. Indeed, as McCormack notes, "without idealism, it would have been unthinkable."[88] Walter Bryden's attempt to retrieve Calvin's conception of revelation everywhere assumed the success of Barth's post-idealist account of theological realism.

Finally, Walter Bryden appealed to the self-authenticating character of revelation. The term (*autopistos* in Greek) literally means "trustworthy in and of itself." The Protestant scholastics had used the term to denote the self-authenticating character of scriptural authority. If the Bible was trustworthy in and of itself, no external authority was required in order to justify Scripture as the norm of faith and practice. The Bible was a self-norming norm. The use of the term as an attribute of Scripture figured prominently in the Protestant orthodox debate with Rome over the role of church and tradition in biblical authority. The Protestant scholastics had developed the term, however, on the basis of their exposition of Calvin. In arguing that the church was itself grounded upon Scripture, Calvin asserted that the Bible exhibited its own self-asserted and self-authenticating authority: "Indeed, Scripture exhibits fully as clear evidence its own truth, as white and black things do their color, or sweet and bitter things do of their taste."[89] Scripture was by definition, Calvin argued, authoritative, and the witness of the Holy Spirit

88   Ibid., 130.
89   Calvin, *Institutes*, I.7.2, 76.

was the means through which God alone acted as a fit witness of himself in his Word.[90] Scripture bears its own witness, Calvin declared: "Let this point therefore stand: that those whom the Holy Spirit has inwardly taught truly rest upon Scripture, and that Scripture indeed is self-authenticated." It was not necessary, therefore, to subject the Bible to proof and reasoning.

This was the view Bryden wished to retrieve from Calvin in his battle against idealism. However, rather than aligning it with the doctrine of the inspiration of the Bible as the post-Reformation scholastics had done, Bryden emphasized the self-authenticating character of the Word of God in Jesus Christ to which the Bible bore witness. Furthermore, he emphasized, as Calvin had done, the importance of the Spirit's witness in the souls of men and women to whom this Word came. Bryden was not always careful to point out what he assumed, namely, that this appeal to experience was radically different from the understanding of experience in liberal Protestantism. There, religious experience was grounded in a pre-existing moral religious consciousness and authenticated by human reason. For Bryden, religious experience was self-authenticating. The self-authenticating character of revelation, therefore, rested in this twofold understanding: the Word of God in Jesus Christ and the witness of the Spirit in the soul of the person whose faith had been created by that Word. It has to be emphasized again that this reconstruction of Calvin's conception of revelation by Walter Bryden would be unimaginable without the idealism to which it was crafted as a response. Under the influence of Denney and Barth, Walter Bryden sought to use all the theological tools at his disposal to retrieve the Calvinist tradition that stood behind Protestant scholasticism and reassert it by going through rather than around modernism. The way in which Bryden conceived of this self-authenticating experience of revelation after modernism is the subject of the next chapter.

---

[90] Ibid., I.7.4, 79.

4

A Theology of the Spirit

When we speak of spirituality, therefore, we should be concerned primarily with that direct apprehension of God, in which faith perceives God as judgment and mercy, in Jesus Christ . . . . It is anchored in love, the love alone, however, which is God's, and which is shed abroad in the hearts of believers by the Holy Spirit.[1]
—Walter Bryden

WALTER Bryden stood in a tradition which has often been accused of ignoring the work and reality of the Holy Spirit. American Presbyterian theologian Lewis Mudge, for example, has argued that Reformed creeds and confessions do not do justice to the work of the Holy Spirit, with the result that "in reading what the Bible says about the Spirit we are blind and deaf."[2] Of all the criticisms that might be leveled appropriately against the theological thought of Walter Williamson Bryden, the charge that he was "blind and deaf" when it came to what the Bible taught about the Holy Spirit would not be among them. Beginning with *The Spirit of Jesus in St. Paul,* and continuing through to his final articles on Reformed theology, Walter Bryden wrestled with the meaning of pneumatology for the church of his day. He resisted the attempts of idealism to merge divine spirit with human spirit, and argued vehemently against the tendency of rational orthodoxy to ignore the testimony of the Holy Spirit in the authentication of Holy Scripture.

The Spirit was essential to Bryden's understanding of the knowledge of God. He insisted that Calvin had been right in the opening lines of *The Institutes of the Christian Religion*: "Nearly all the wisdom we possess, that is to say true and sound wisdom, consists of two parts: the knowledge of

---

[1] Bryden, *Why I Am A Presbyterian*, 112.
[2] Lewis Mudge, *One Church: Catholic and Reformed* (Philadelphia: Westminster, 1963) 63.

God and of ourselves."[3] The knowledge of God and the knowledge of self about which Calvin spoke, though distinct, were intimately and intricately related in important respects: both were created by an act of God in Word and Spirit. True knowledge of self followed in the wake of true knowledge of God. At the same time, Bryden was adamant that the knowledge of God and the knowledge of ourselves should not be confused. The Spirit of God was not to be confused with the human spirit or the human word. When God was disclosed to human beings in revelation, God made the divine reality known, and God made human beings known to themselves for the first time. Enabling us to know God, and to know ourselves as creatures before God, was the epistemological work of the Spirit.

Throughout his theological labors, Bryden appealed again and again to Calvin's emphasis on the Holy Spirit, not only in relation to Scripture, but in relation to the Spirit's role in uniting the believer with Christ, and Christ with the believer, by grace through faith. The Spirit who indwells the Christian man and woman of today, Bryden emphasized, is the same Spirit who indwelt Jesus; it is, in fact, the Spirit of Jesus. The purpose of this chapter is to examine this understanding of the experience of revelation in the Christian life, or what Bryden referred to as the Christian's knowledge of God. The chapter focuses on two issues: the conception of the Holy Spirit as the Spirit of God's Judging–Saving Word; and the nature of the experience of faith created by Word and Spirit in the midst of crisis and encounter. The basic argument continues: Walter Bryden sought to recover Reformation pneumatology in reaction to idealism and rationalism in Canada, and in concert with the theology of Karl Barth and the dialectical theologians.

The Spirit of Revelation

Bryden's conception of revelation, christocentrically and dialectically reconstructed, rested upon the identification of the Holy Spirit as the personal agency of God's Judging–Saving Word. He was impressed by the fact that the Reformers always conceived of the Holy Spirit as personal. Their view contrasted with what he considered the apparently vague and impersonal apprehension of God which seemed to pervade the modern thinking of his era. Ever vigilant for the wholly other character of the divine, however, Bryden reminded his students that they should not draw erroneous conclusions as to how Calvin conceived of a personal God. "Calvin had too great a reverence for the majesty, the glory, and the altogether incomprehensible nature of God" to ascribe to God any such human characteristic as was implied in words such as "personal" or "personality." Indeed, Bryden argued, "it was the Socinians,

---

[3] John Calvin, *Institutes of the Christian Religion*, I.1.1, 35.

the first Unitarians, who were responsible for causing Christians to speak of the 'personality of God.'" From Bryden's perspective, the Christian church did not acquire such familiarity with God from Calvinism. Nevertheless, it was Calvin's impressive conviction that God did speak to human beings in a personal way. This was the arresting fact about Calvin's faith which should be heeded above all else.[4]

From Bryden's perspective, Calvin believed that God spoke to human beings in such a way that they could no longer stand in a position in which, so to speak, they might weigh, or choose between, the respective ideas about God which they happened to possess. When God really speaks to a person, he or she can no longer permit the church, a priest, or friends, to assume the responsibilities which, by virtue of such personal speaking, now become his or hers alone. God's speaking creates a moment in which that person must come to a decision about life itself. God addresses a person as if that person were the only person in the world. It is a radical confrontation in which every aspect of existence is questioned. According to Bryden, this was what Calvin implied when he thought of God as speaking personally to human beings. When God thus speaks, we have, Bryden argued, what Calvin meant by the Holy Spirit. When the speech of God becomes so great a reality that it brings about a personal encounter between God and a human being, as subject with subject, then we experience what God the Holy Spirit is. It was the fresh discovery of this truth in early Protestantism, Bryden noted, that Emil Brunner never wearied from reiterating: when God speaks personally, and consequently calls for decision, a human being for the first time becomes truly a person. Authentic personhood is created in an authentic encounter with God's Judging–Saving Word by the Holy Spirit. In the words of Bryden, when the Holy Spirit challenges us we become real for the first time. That is, we are enabled to accept ourselves as we really are in the sight of God; and bravely face the world in this newborn utter humility, but also in this newly acquired personal worth.[5]

The Spirit of Jesus in St. Paul

Bryden arrived at this understanding of the Spirit after a long and arduous theological journey that began with his study of Pauline theology in the midst of pastoral ministry. In *The Spirit of Jesus in St. Paul* he contended that, in modern use, the terms "the Spirit of Jesus" or "the Spirit of Christ" meant something quite different than what Paul and the early church had intended. Modernism had repackaged the Holy Spirit as qualities of heart and mind.

---

[4]   Bryden, *Separated Unto the Gospel,* 211–12.
[5]   Ibid., 212–13.

Paul, however, thought of the Spirit as a power or presence in the world, and in the hearts of believers, which effected or created ethical and spiritual realities. The Spirit, according to Bryden's reading of the New Testament, was the source of Christian faith and life rather than an ethical ideal to be emulated. The identification of the Spirit with Jesus was fundamental to Bryden's understanding and, in his mind, the only viable historical explanation for the emergence of the Christian community. The conviction that the risen and ascended Jesus was truly present through the mediating power of the Holy Spirit was the conviction chiefly responsible for the church's creation, continuance and permanence. The origin and development of the Christian church could not be justified historically in the teachings of Jesus alone, not in the personal devotion, admiration and attachment of the disciples to the person and example of Jesus alone (no matter how inspiring), and not even in the resurrection appearances of Jesus alone. There had to be something more at work to explain the impulse of the first Christians to risk all for the sake of a message they barely understood. That something more, Bryden argued, "lay in an experience, a new life which" the early Christians were "beginning to be able to live, and which though difficult" they "felt impelled to pursue. These people believed that they were still being taught and led by the Spirit of the Living Christ."[6] It appeared to Bryden that there was at work in the earliest days of the Christian community a power of God which could not be made to coalesce with any or all of the combined agencies so readily given as explanations of the church's origin. This, the earliest Christians attributed to the Spirit or the presence of the Living Lord in their midst.[7]

It has to be emphasized, as Joseph McLelland has noted, that Bryden's earliest book "presents an aspect of Bryden's thought necessary to recall the mighty positive from which he uttered his prophetic theology. This is a book about experience, about presence, about mysticism." "It seems strange," McLelland pointed out, "to hear Walter Bryden speak so positively about 'the mystical,' knowing his worry over Schleiermacher's experiential theology, or his rejection of Radhakrishnan's mystical monism. Indeed, he sees (as few besides Karl Barth have) the inner connection between mysticism and rationalism." "But in St. Paul" (and here McLelland put his finger on the crucial point) Walter Bryden found "a Christ-mysticism, a case of Christ's being formed in man by the energy of the Holy Spirit, and he reckons that this is authentic mysticism, and the proper mystery."[8] The Christ-mysticism at the center of Pauline theology which so impressed Bryden was to be found

---

[6]   Bryden, *The Spirit of Jesus in St. Paul*, 20.

[7]   Ibid., 20–21.

[8]   J. C. McLelland, "Walter Bryden: 'By Circumstance' and God," 125.

in the little phrase "in Christ." Paul spoke of "being in Christ" and "Christ being in him."

The experience about which Paul spoke, however, was no mere enthusiasm. The church had no more hope of maintaining itself on long relays of enthusiasm—even though that enthusiasm be Christian—than on the strength of its image as an effectively organized humanitarian and educational enterprise. No, if the church was to live it had to be permeated with nothing less than the knowledge and experience of God. The true knowledge and authentic experience of God was precisely what both modernism and rational orthodoxy had obfuscated. Modern idealism tended toward a monism in which the spiritual and the material were organically united. Rational orthodoxy tended to perpetuate a dualism in which spirituality focused solely on otherworldly concerns. Bryden believed that for the Reformed faith, based on Pauline theology, spiritual life referred to all or any aspect of life—physical, mental, moral, and religious—as touched and transformed by the Spirit of God. This stood in contrast to the life of the flesh, which referred to all or any aspect of life not so touched and transformed. The kind of mysticism which Bryden was after, therefore, represented an experience of God which was created by an encounter with a wholly other God, but wholly within this world.

The irony of modernism, Bryden contended, was that it had not only undermined the Christian conception of God, it had also undercut the basis for authentic existence and human flourishing in God's world, and it had done so in the name of making Christianity more relevant to modern culture. In other words, it had the destroyed the foundation of the very thing it was intended to promote. The Christians of the early church made an impact on the culture of their day, Bryden argued, precisely because "they impressed their hearers with possessing a certain knowledge of God." God's work in the souls of men and women was the result, not, as was so often suggested, of their limited intellectual and scientific outlook, but of a thorough-going, honest, and unreserved personal consecration to the things which they believed to be true. They knew God, and by a surer method than that which was purely intellectual or inferential.[9] Analogical thinking, especially as it was harnessed by Roman Catholicism, Protestant scholasticism, and liberal Protestantism, was "proving nothing less," Bryden believed, "than paralysis to our whole religious life." To infer a conception of God from even the highest traits to be discovered in human character tended inevitably to anthropomorphism on the one hand, or, if scientific, to a kind of pantheism on the other. The spiritual life was not, Bryden emphasized, based upon a merely intellectual or inferential search after God. There had to be an understanding

---

[9]   Bryden, *The Spirit of Jesus in St. Paul*, 54–55.

of revelation that acknowledged the real participation, comprehension, and correspondence of the human soul in the knowledge of God. Bryden already appeared sensitive to a complaint that was to characterize the later criticism of the neo-orthodox theology he espoused, namely that it tended to devalue and demean human personality as well as ignore humanity's undoubted accomplishments. But he was clear. "There must be possible," he argued, "a spiritual achievement of the soul of man over and independent of, its purely psychical self, by which it wins direct access to the very Spirit of God and thereby knows Him."[10] There had to be, he believed, a real knowledge of God, which, on the one hand did not originate in human experience and understanding, but on the other hand was authentically and genuinely human.

The reality of revelation thus understood constituted the center of the Christian gospel not only for Paul, but also for Martin Luther, Wycliffe, John Knox, John Wesley, Robert Murray McCheyne, and Andrew Bonar. Their gospel, Bryden argued, "was the fact of Christ, His living presence in the world in their day and generation. His power to change and transform completely the characters of men who believed in Him."[11] The peculiar work of the ministry, as Bryden had experienced it in Lethbridge, Woodville, and Melfort, was that of communicating this living knowledge of God—the very spirit and nature of God—to other human souls. The church of his day needed, above all else, Bryden argued, "a message born of the knowledge of God." The real center of religious faith, as he saw it, was "a real experience of God's presence and helpfulness," of God's grace and mercy. Bryden seemed still to be expunging the influence of idealism from his thought, when he noted that the experience of the knowledge of God was a consciousness that unfolded "in a new morality and ethic which are themselves the results of this new knowledge, and which become the creative potencies of our new and higher beings." But about the importance of revelation he was clear: revelation and the knowledge of God that results from the exercise of the rational faculty upon it, "together with the modes of imparting these to others, prophesying and teaching, constituted for Paul the supreme content of Christianity as these also have done for the historic church."[12]

It was noteworthy, Bryden believed, that Paul appealed to the Spirit to authenticate and authorize his preaching. The knowledge of God revealed to Paul by the Spirit constituted the basis of his apostolic witness. This was not, as many modern scholars contended, merely the work of a man trying to imitate and re-create the ministry of Jesus in his own time and place. This was, rather, the ministry of someone who lived his life with the conviction that

---

[10] Ibid., 55.
[11] Ibid., 58.
[12] Ibid., 66, 84, 88–89, 131.

he lived and moved and had his being in communion with the living Christ. Bryden was aware of the dangers such language posed:

> The terms which Paul so lavishly uses to describe his experience are not mere imitation phraseology; they are, indeed, living attempts to convey the impression which he so strongly feels, that Christ's life is in him, or that he finds himself in it. We may run the danger of a vague pantheism, of an unhealthy mysticism, by dwelling too much on the fact that God in Christ does dwell in the Christian man. Even so, we can never know Christ unless we find and interpret His life in our own. In truth, explain it how we will, there seems to be no possibility of real knowledge except by some form of interpenetration or communion of personalities.[13]

During the 1920s already, Bryden was striving for relational language to transcend the dichotomy between subject and object in revelation without reverting to pantheism or mysticism. The language he adopted anticipated the renewal of Trinitarianism in Reformed theology that occurred in the second half of the twentieth century, largely through Barth's influence, and especially in conversation with Eastern Orthodox theology. God not only makes the divine reality known in qualities of personality as we commonly understand that term, but God is the Person whose triune personhood constitutes the human person in relationship. The self-knowledge of God is an eternal knowledge of the three persons of the Triune God who, by some form of interpenetration or communion of persons, share divine self-knowledge with one another in unending procession. The knowledge of God in which human beings participate is a sharing in this divine self-knowledge, in and through the Word of God in Jesus Christ, by the power and presence of the Holy Spirit.

Standing in the wake of Hegelian idealism Bryden was more than willing to acknowledge that Christianity was the religion of the Spirit. But the conception of the Spirit that Bryden had in mind, at least as the Spirit was described by Paul in the Corinthian letters, was radically different than what the idealists had in mind. The Holy Spirit in the New Testament was not to be identified simply with inner conscience, religious consciousness, and the natural evolution of the laws of moral progress, as it had been by liberal Protestant theologians. At the same time, idealism had forever closed the way back to the rationally orthodox Calvinist conception of the Spirit as a supernatural phenomenon imposed upon women and men which overrode their humanity. The essential thing in religion, Bryden believed, was "a real apprehension of God which is neither a purely intellectual or moral, nor yet an

---

13   Ibid., 154.

emotional experience of life. . . . It is the spirit of man apprehending the Spirit of God in a peculiar consciousness of and sensitiveness to wrong, in love and mercy, and in a higher leading than this world grants us."[14] It was a paradox, to be sure, but the identity and work of the Holy Spirit was to be understood in relation to divine and human agency in Jesus Christ. "Paul's conception of the Holy Spirit, although he never attempts to define it in essential character, is, at least, in perfect accord with his view of Christ, in that both are transcendent manifestations."[15] Paul's view of a Spirit-filled person consisted of a new person on a different plane of living altogether—as over against a "psychical soul" whose religious consciousness had been realized. Revelation in the individual's life was that light, Bryden concluded, that broke upon personal labor and patience, and courageous and obstinate adventure in the sphere of the Spirit, and which revealed itself in a knowledge earmarked of God.[16]

The Spirit of Presbyterianism

This was the theology of the Spirit Bryden had worked out before he encountered Barth's theology in the late 1920s, and it remained, except for a clearer Christological focus, essentially unchanged. The significant thing, as the story unfolded, was the way in which Bryden leveraged this conception of the Spirit against the church union movement in Canada in the years immediately after 1925. Given the prominence of the Spirit in idealism it was not surprising that church union was seen by many as the inevitable outworking of historical progress, and that any and all attempts to oppose it were often interpreted as going against the will of God. This annoyed Bryden to no end. *Why I Am A Presbyterian* was written with such arguments in the forefront. "I have in mind especially, however," Bryden wrote, "the efforts by reputable ministers to frighten people by the assertion that, by opposing church union, they were resisting the Holy Spirit. How often in the history of the Church has the Holy Spirit been made to bear the burden of man's own ill-advised, though well-intentioned, schemes, his ambitions, and even the resulting tragedies."[17] There was, to be sure, a genuine unity in the Spirit which characterized the early church, Bryden agreed, but it was a "fellowship of the Spirit" which was neither forced nor manufactured. It was rooted, rather, in the very realities of faith upon which the advocates of church union put little stress, namely "the character of belief or theology, or the necessity for spiritual oneness in Christ and the Holy Spirit."[18]

---

14   Ibid., 237.
15   Ibid., 241.
16   Ibid., 253.
17   Bryden, *Why I Am A Presbyterian*, 15–16.
18   Ibid., 17.

Sensitive to the charge that the continuing Presbyterians were stuck in history and opposed to theological progress, Bryden argued that a truly confessional and confessing church acknowledged the leading of the Holy Spirit in the church's ongoing task of reformulating the faith. This was undoubtedly the view of the Westminster divines themselves who never imagined for a moment that they were setting down eternal truths once for all time. They acknowledged what had gone before them and they anticipated what might come after them:

> They acknowledge also that these earlier framers of the articles of Faith had been obviously led by God's Holy Spirit, but humbly recognize at the same time that, through new untoward circumstances which had eventuated, it was now necessary to amplify the previous work, and make necessary emendations. They believed that they were impelled to do so by the same Holy Spirit. Let me point out that, if it is a true estimate of the attitude assumed to such matters by these early Presbyterian fathers, it is very unlikely that they would deny the possibility that the Holy Spirit might lead Christian people three centuries afterwards to execute, if necessary, a similar work in regard to the same matters. Any other suggestion would be one which would lead Presbyterians into spiritual insolvency.[19]

Bryden was more than willing to concede that the Holy Spirit might well lead the churches of his own day into some form of organic church union but he was convinced that such a movement would be characterized by a profound confessional integrity, a deep spiritual unity, and a generous Christian charity. He felt, and regrettably so, that the movement for church union in Canada was based on entirely different motives and fueled by a quite different understanding of the Holy Spirit.

Bryden was also less than optimistic that church union would cultivate the kind of spirituality which he believed was characteristic of the Reformed tradition at its best. Spirituality, rightly understood, Bryden argued, could not be reduced to a certain kind of piety, a right mode of believing, or a particular pattern of behaviour. The precocious pieties of conservative and liberal forms of Protestantism had bankrupted the spiritual life of the church. What was needed, he believed, was a spirituality which moved beyond modernism by retrieving the provocative piety of the Reformation, not because Reformation spirituality was to be emulated in and of itself, but because the Reformers had recovered a sense of the peculiar spiritual life that had animated the New Testament church. Spiritual discernment, for them, meant a unique understanding, "not so much of the truths about Christianity, as about the Truth apprehended alone by Christian faith." The spiritual life,

---

19   Bryden, *Why I Am A Presbyterian*, 90.

then, was "that creative life which is the outcome of just such revelation and apprehension." As the following lengthy quotation shows, Bryden wrote eloquently and incisively about the nature of the Holy Spirit in the life of the Christian, in light of his conception of the Judging–Saving Word of God:

> It is that peculiar informing of the spirit-life of man which is the consequence of the judgment, witness and comfort of the Holy Spirit. Such life always centres in Christ and His redeeming work. Apart from the recognition of both the judgment and the mercy which are manifest in the revelation of Christ, and as witnessed to by the Holy Ghost, spiritual life has neither meaning nor existence in a Christian sense. When we speak of spirituality, therefore, we should be concerned primarily with that direct apprehension of God, in which faith perceives God as judgment and mercy, in Jesus Christ. It means for the believer condemnation and acquittal, humiliation and exaltation, a penetrating and permanent sorrow for sin, and yet the profoundest gratitude and freedom, in which the man that was has been slain forevermore, and yet is alive forevermore. This is the deepest, the most central and determining element in the Christian life, and the basic creative principle upon which alone the union of Christian peoples, when rightly conceived, is far more sensitive, more personal, more fundamental, and more radical than any based upon conventional, naturalistic, or even idealistic bases. It is anchored in love, the love alone, however, which is God's and which is shed abroad in the hearts of believing men by the Holy Ghost.[20]

Bryden's dialectics were everywhere evident in the pneumatology he set out in this post-union rationale for continuing Presbyterianism in Canada. First, the Spirit acts as both judge and comfort in bearing witness to God's Judging–Saving Word in Jesus Christ. Unlike idealists, Bryden did not use his understanding of the Spirit to resolve this paradox in a higher synthesis. Second, the Spirit creates the authentic existence which is centered in Christ. The Spirit is the bond between the act of divine self-revelation and the act of human faith in which that revelation is apprehended. In short, the Holy Spirit's dialectical work bears witness to the dialectical Word. "True spiritual life," therefore, Bryden argued, "issues from personal perception and individual choice, which are free and responsible, and yet which, at the same time, are under constraint of the Holy Spirit."[21] Those who had experienced this constraint discovered, according to Bryden, their oneness in Jesus Christ, and this constituted the true unity and catholicity of the church. Authentic Christian spirituality and true Christian unity, therefore, were different sides

---

[20] Ibid., 112.
[21] Ibid., 132.

of the same coin. The economy of revelation implied in each constituted the doctrine of the Trinity. Bryden then made explicit what had been only hinted at in his earlier book:

> The Bible makes plain the incomprehensible God can only be known through the Son, witnessed to, by the Holy Ghost. This is the profoundest significance to be attached to the Trinitarian doctrine. That is to say, God is unknown to man except through the revelation of Jesus Christ; and Jesus Christ is unknown except through the witness of the Spirit, and the Spirit is unknown except through Jesus Christ.[22]

In this account of pneumatology, then, Walter Bryden insisted upon a fundamental unity between God's Spirit and God's Word as the sum of God's relations with human beings. This theological unity, he believed, constituted the distinguishing originality of Calvin's teaching on revelation and the knowledge of God. Bryden argued that, for Calvin, the Holy Spirit was not an impersonal light which might illumine the souls of men and women in an indeterminate manner. It was, rather, the act of God as personal divine witness which bore testimony to the Word of God as found in Holy Scripture. It was precisely this connection between the Holy Spirit and a personal God who speaks that had been set aside by liberal Protestantism's identification of the Spirit as some creative principle operating in the world, as the source of higher culture. Modern theology, Bryden believed, had failed to recognize the importance of the Holy Spirit in the economy of God's revelation. In "The Presbyterian Conception of the Word of God" he reiterated the theme originally enunciated in *The Spirit of Jesus in St. Paul.* "I believe," Bryden wrote, "that modern Liberalism constitutes a distinct rationalization of what the Christian revelation and faith essentially claim to be. It is as true today as it was in Paul's time." Quoting Paul, Bryden pointed out that "No one can say Jesus is Lord except by the Holy Spirit" and "If a person does not have the Spirit of Christ, that person does not belong to Christ." "Spirit here," Bryden concluded, "signifies the source, and not just the temper or quality of Jesus' life."[23]

The Spirit and Knowledge of the Triune God

In *The Christian's Knowledge of God* Walter Bryden continued to appropriate Calvin's interpretation of Pauline pneumatology and use it in his attempt to overthrow modern conceptions of the Spirit. The transcendent witness of the Spirit, he argued, was absolutely essential to faith because without it faith could not exist. The Spirit was a gift of God which the early church under-

---

[22]   Ibid., 165.
[23]   Bryden, *Separated Unto the Gospel*, 209.

stood as descending from above without which all other gifts were nothing. "The early Christians attributed their faith in God and their hope for and joy in the things of this world," Bryden emphasized again and again, "to the unique work of the Holy Spirit in their hearts."[24] The creedal affirmation of faith in the Holy Spirit stood centrally between belief in God in Jesus Christ and belief in the church. The Holy Spirit thus understood, Bryden contended, was an essential article of faith, not because Christian faith required rational assent to propositional truths about the Holy Spirit, but because Christian faith itself could not exist apart from the Spirit's witness. Simply put, the Christian's knowledge of God was the fruit of the Spirit's work. This was the point that had been lost on modern Protestant theology. Rather than understanding that God was known in God's utter transcendence, not by rational cognition, liberal Protestantism sought to get at the essence of the Christian faith through historic surveys of the life of Jesus. The point of the New Testament, Bryden argued, was that God is known by God's own revealing of Godself in God's Son. The Son is known as Lord by one known as the Holy Spirit. The transcendent and all-determining place given to the Holy Spirit in the New Testament "constitutes the abiding stumbling block to every attempt to naturalize faith." In fact, Bryden maintained that the Holy Spirit exposes the emptiness of the human virtues that liberal Protestantism affirmed as the center of faith. The Holy Spirit unveils the unreality of the human soul in and for itself and, at the same time, furnishes that soul with every good and true gift. The Spirit who judges the bankruptcy of the soul without God also creates the new life which the soul may experience in relationship with God. On this point Walter Bryden followed the logic and the lead of two fourth-century theologians: Athanasius, who affirmed that only God can reveal God and save humankind; and Basil, who affirmed that the Holy Spirit is God. It was God, and God alone, who made God known, and God did so as God through the Holy Spirit.

> The Holy Spirit is God, in his essential Self-hood and in His utter uniqueness, *acting* personally and immediately upon the soul. Here, as someone has recently said, 'God's action and His essence are one,' although the latter is never known in and for itself by man. We know God always because He first *knows* us. This represents God's characteristic *action* in His purpose to save; and *action*, as thus applied to God must always be understood in the sense that man knows God, because of having been 'known of Him.'[25]

---

24 Bryden, *The Christian's Knowledge of God*, 94.
25 Ibid., 214.

Bryden summarized his thinking about the Spirit, revelation and the church in a 1944 article published in *Crisis Christology*. He employed the now-familiar arguments against idealism and rationalism and added a third against enthusiasm. In each case Bryden focused on what he saw as the reductionist conception of the Holy Spirit at work and its implications for the life of the church. In the first instance, he noted that, too often, the Holy Spirit was treated in a merely scholastic fashion, as nothing more than a Christian doctrine to be fitted into an accepted system of Christian theology. Bryden contended that mere academic interest, motivated by spectator thinking, however sincere, yielded no genuine experience of God's Spirit.

Secondly, Bryden noted that the history of the church was filled with a whole series of what might be called "spiritual" reactions representing various understandable protests against ecclesiastical formalisms, spiritual apathies and orthodox rationalizations of the faith. Such movements of enthusiasm pointed to the spontaneous life of the Spirit as providing the one mark of a true and living church. Citing a range of movements from the New Testament era to the twentieth century, including the radical Anabaptists, the Pietists, and numerous Protestant sects of his own day, Bryden contended that all could be explained as reactionary movements inspired by an apparent spiritual vacuum in the church. As one might expect from a Reformed analysis of such movements, Bryden concluded that this "particular emphasis on the Spirit has too often been at the expense of any intelligent understanding of Jesus Christ and His true work, and has therefore, resulted in sheer individualisms, immoral excesses on the one hand, meticulous moralisms on the other, or has degenerated into mere enthusiasms of a purely subjective nature, devoid of any reliable means of evaluating Christian life at all."[26] Painting with a rather broad brush, Bryden made his point more than clear: reactions to rationalism, formalism, and nominalism in the church, which emphasized experience at the expense of reason, were to be repudiated. Whenever the Holy Spirit was identified exclusively with religious feelings or extraordinary experiences, a reductionist pneumatology was at work.

But what was Bryden really concerned about in Canadian Protestantism on this point? Who and where were the enthusiasts of his own day? While Bryden may have had a passing acquaintance with evangelical pietist groups, Anabaptist churches, and the emerging Pentecostal movement in Canada, as a mainline church leader he did not appear to be much concerned about their enthusiasms. Rather, his critique of enthusiasm, it seems clear, was motivated by a theological concern. As noted earlier, Bryden saw the inner connection between mysticism and rationalism, and he was concerned about any and all forms of mysticism that made their way into Canadian Protestantism un-

---

[26]   Bryden, *Separated Unto the Gospel*, 39–40.

der the guise of rationalism and idealism. Furthermore, he no doubt wished to defend himself against the charge of "irrational enthusiasm" which had been leveled against him by F.H. Anderson's 1941 review of *The Christian's Knowledge of God*. In Germany, Harnack had savaged Barth's early theology by suggesting that it would come to nothing more than the founding of a sect. Having borne the brunt of similar charges in Canada, Bryden was fully sensitive to the need to draw a sharp distinction between neo-orthodox existentialism and religious enthusiasm.

As significant as the challenges of rationalism and enthusiasm were to the church's pneumatology, they did not constitute, separately or together, the most serious threat to the spiritual life of Canadian Protestantism. That threat consisted in idealism. As a teacher in a theological college, Bryden wrote, he had the impression that many students, "though assuming a knowledge of, and belief in God and Jesus Christ, acknowledge at the same time that the Holy Spirit conveys little, if any, meaning to them."[27] This perplexity among students, he argued, reflected a condition prevalent in the church as a whole, due at least in part to the theological vagaries of modern Protestantism. More precisely, it was due to the dominance of idealism in modern Christian thought and practice. Idealism produced a religious atmosphere in which people were encouraged to think of their Christian responsibility as merely accepting Christ's life and teachings as so many ideals to be achieved, or as representing approved principles to be applied by good men and women to the existing conditions of life and society.[28] Idealism, accompanied by a new legalism, reduced the Holy Spirit to a general principle of life. Devoid of spiritual life, the church turned to elaborate organizations, splendid efficiencies of one kind or another, programs for unity and renewal, but somehow it lacked the power to do those things for which God had called the church into existence. It remained unable to actually change its self-conceits, self-deceptions and misguided intrigues. With few exceptions the churches of the early twentieth century in Canada were not persecuted, Bryden argued, because they posed no threat, real or imagined, no danger, clear or present, to the civil authorities or the culture, in whole or in part. In fact, the idealism of the church, Bryden averred, muted the voice of the Spirit speaking to the churches, and allowed the churches to be used to prop up a social structure that was the very antithesis of life in the Spirit. The rich and the powerful patronized the church, political leaders praised the church for its loyalty to the state, but they never feared the church. The Spirit had been secularized and civilized to the point that the church had become a religious expression of the *Zeitgeist*. The spirit of the churches, Bryden protested, had become the spirit of culture

---

27   Ibid., 32.
28   Ibid., 32–33.

Protestantism. The church served to help society advance material welfare, pursue intellectual and cultural ideals, and promote national interest.[29]

Bryden's judgment of the modern church was rooted in his understanding of Enlightenment idealism, especially the philosophy of Hegel as it had been transmitted to Canadian Protestantism through John Watson. Bryden recognized that in idealism, as in classical theology, the Spirit proceeded from the *logos* or the Word. In idealism, however, the *logos* was conceived as the higher rational principle immanent in human beings and in the world, presumed to be the sole creative agency of all that was of worth in civilization, culture and religion. Modern Protestants had been taught to think of the Spirit in relation to the Word in this way, creating an antithesis between the inner, moral, rational, and disciplined life and the external, sensual, unregulated, passionate life. The Spirit was now conceived as that which ordered life and created a culture within which men and women could flourish as civilized human beings. Bryden did not quarrel with the need to create a culture of human flourishing by the Spirit. But he contended that when this was the first and only way in which the Holy Spirit was understood, the practical consequence was disastrous for Christianity. The Holy Spirit was used to engender self-sufficiency and independence at the personal and national levels. The "fruits of the Holy Spirit" were transformed into civic and political virtues and cultural appreciations, reducing the term "Christian" to the status of the good citizen. More seriously, it promoted among Anglo-Saxons a sense of racial, ethnic and cultural superiority. Rather than calling men and women to repentance and confession before God, the Spirit was identified as that which precluded dependence upon God. In short, by marrying the language of the Christian message to the aspirations of western culture, the idealization of the Holy Spirit transformed Christianity into the very antithesis of what it was intended to be. While in American Christianity the philosophical tool that had facilitated this marriage was pragmatism, the modern Protestant churches in Canada had been shaped by idealism.[30]

Walter Bryden concluded that modern Protestantism was plagued by a constant tendency to domesticate the Spirit of God. Rational orthodoxy had reduced the person and work of the Spirit, he argued, by identifying the Spirit almost exclusively with the words of a verbally inspired Bible. Movements of enthusiasm had reduced the identity of the Spirit through their insistence upon extraordinary religious experiences as the mark of the Spirit's presence. Idealism had eradicated any real distinction between the Holy Spirit and the human spirit in its monistic conception of God and the world. Against all this Bryden pointed to Calvin's insistence on the work of the Spirit in bear-

---

[29]   Ibid., 37–41.
[30]   Ibid., 40–44.

ing testimony to the revelation of God in Scripture and uniting the person of faith to Jesus Christ. It was Calvin, he argued, who emphasized that the Holy Spirit dealt with men and women personally and concretely, and made them to know, for the first time, their true selves, as those, indeed, who had been living in unbelief and rebellion against God. It was Calvin's theology of Word and Spirit which was capable of putting into words, insofar as this was possible, the great verities and mysteries of what actually happened when faith was created in the soul of a person.

On this point, Walter Bryden found Karl Barth disappointing initially. When it came to pneumatology, Bryden did not find Barth's early offerings clear or helpful. In the early 1930s Bryden questioned why Barth had not placed the constitutive principle of the Ecclesia, the Church, or Fellowship of the Saints in the Holy Spirit, and especially in the creative aspect of the Spirit's work. To read what Barth said on the Holy Spirit, Bryden noted, was most interesting and rewarding. But the emphasis in Barth's theology, he felt, was not on the creative positive aspect of the Spirit's work in the individual's heart, as it seemed to be in the New Testament. Barth seemed to have substituted something more negative, paradoxical, and indirect. Bryden expressed some sympathy for what he surmised may have been Barth's reason for doing so. Barth wished to avoid the Roman Catholic or Pietist presumption of a claim for a human possession of the Holy Spirit. In this, Bryden conceded, Barth was like Calvin and the originators of the Reformed churches. They emphasized the free and sovereign work of the Spirit, especially in the emphasis placed upon the necessity of the testimony of the Holy Spirit for authentic Christian faith. But at the same time Calvin and the Reformers, Bryden pointed out, always gave the impression that the subject of the Holy Spirit, particularly the work of the Holy Spirit in the life of the believer, properly belonged to theological investigation. Bryden therefore had some sympathy for those who complained that Barth had neglected the doctrine of the Holy Spirit. Bryden was grateful for Barth's emphasis on the fact that the Word of God addresses us. The speech of God is God's action alone, even if it was veiled in the humanity of Jesus. Bryden agreed with Barth's insistence that neither the human nature of Christ, nor spirit and letter of the first witnesses, nor word and sacrament of the church, were God's Word in and of themselves. Barth was right: they were these things insofar as they had received God's Word for this service, so far as God spoke through them. The problem was that Barth did not attach the truth of this claim as definitely as was necessary to the work of the Holy Spirit. In this respect, Bryden felt Barth was unnecessarily ambiguous. Bryden found Barth's references to the work of God in the soul of the individual too negative and too complex. Barth had helped Bryden to see that faith was primarily a matter of being apprehended by God in crisis. But Bryden looked back to Calvin to understand the nature of this experience. One questions whether, judged from the standpoint of Barth's theology, Bryden was sufficiently sensitive to the importance placed upon the Holy Spirit in Schleiermacher's theology, and Barth's attempt to distance himself from it. In the 1920s Barth had not yet found a way of speaking about the Holy Spirit that did not immediately conjure up resonances of Schleiermacher and Hegel. Later Barth spoke about the gathering, upbuilding, and sending of the church by the Holy Spirit. During the earlier period in his theology, however, Barth tended to remain silent when it came to the Spirit. It was precisely this silence that Bryden found perplexing.[31]

In time Bryden came to see Barth's understanding of the Holy Spirit somewhat differently. In his lectures on Augustine, Bryden took time to review Barth's *The Holy Spirit and the Christian Life,* which had been written in answer to questions of the sort raised by Bryden concerning the place of the Holy Spirit in Barth's theology. Bryden noted Barth's rejection of any theology that failed to draw a sharp distinction between the Spirit of God and human spirit, notably the Roman Catholic understanding of the *analogia entis,* and the liberal Protestant view, which assumed an essential unity between the two. In a lengthy exposition of Barth's critique of Augustine, Bryden explained Barth's reasons for insisting upon the radical discontinuity between divine spirit and human spirit that characterized his pneumatology. According to Bryden, Barth had rightly understood the parallel between the work of the Holy Spirit in creation and in redemption. In the same way that the Holy Spirit originally created human beings out of nothing and made them in the image of God, so too the Spirit of God re-created human beings by compelling them to see the utter and absolute nothingness of their situation in alienation from God, convicting them of sin, judgment, and death, and at the same time graciously offering forgiveness, comfort, hope and new life in Christ. Bryden came to understand Barth's emphasis on the eschatological dimension of faith on this point. The Spirit is different from the human spirit, for while it is present in the believer's soul in revelation, it is always present eschatologically as a promise to be fulfilled, and not immanently as a reality to be possessed. "The Holy Spirit," Bryden noted, "makes an end of all man's attempts to justify himself, to establish in himself some potential likeness to or claim upon God, or to presume to think that by his own good works, he may merit favor with God. Barth, although sympathetic always with sincere attempts to interpret the faith, whether modern or medieval, stands in judgment of both, on the ground of the Scriptural witness as well as Christian experience itself."[32] Bryden had already been convinced, by Albert

---

[31]   W. W. Bryden, "After Modernism, What?" Unpublished manuscript.

[32]   Bryden, Lectures on Augustine, 47.

Schweitzer and others, of the importance of the eschatological interpretation of the New Testament. Now Karl Barth had provided an eschatological explanation for what Bryden considered to be one of the most important issues in revelation, namely what happened in the soul of a person who was encountered by God's Judging–Saving Word. The Spirit's witness, Bryden came to realize, was provisional. The Spirit's work, Bryden concluded, created faith, hope, and love in the midst of negation and nothingness. The Spirit was not a symbol of continuity with what was, but a sign of what was to come.

In sum, Bryden worked out an approach to the Holy Spirit against rationalism, idealism, and enthusiasm which was shaped by (1) Barth's radical distinction between the Holy Spirit and human spirit, (2) Barth's emphasis on the eschatological character of the Spirit's work in the life of the believer, (3) Calvin's conception of the interrelatedness of the knowledge of God and the knowledge of self, (4) Calvin's doctrine of the testimony of the Holy Spirit, and (5) Calvin's teaching on union with Christ. Throughout Bryden assumed the centrality of God's Judging–Saving Word in Jesus Christ as the Word to which the Spirit bore witness in the souls of men and women. But what did that experience look like? Was it possible to describe this encounter with God's gospel, which demanded participation, comprehension, and cooperation? What was the nature of the faith that was both presumed and created by revelation? What was the future reality to which the Spirit pointed? Here Bryden turned for help, not only to Calvin, but also to Luther.

The Spirit of Faith

The Nature of Faith in Protestant Theology

"This is what Calvin means by faith, the knowing of Christ in His saving efficacy which comes alone by the revealing of the Spirit."[33] When it came to understanding the nature of faith, Walter Bryden clearly understood himself as standing in the tradition of John Calvin, who defined faith as the "firm and certain knowledge of God's benevolence toward us, founded upon the truth of the freely given promise in Christ, both revealed to our minds and sealed upon our hearts by the Holy Spirit."[34] But Bryden was faced with the question of how to appropriate Calvin's conception of faith within the context of the divided mind of modern theology.

In the history of Christian thought, two general tendencies concerning the concept of faith had dominated the thinking of the church. First, faith was regarded as belief based on cognition, or as mental assent (*assensus*)

---

[33] Bryden, *Separated Unto the Gospel*, 184.
[34] Calvin, *Institutes*, III.2.7, 551.

to some truth or truths, whether about the nature, being and work of God (supernatural truth) or about the decisive events of the past (historical truth). Second, faith was understood as the basic disposition of the total person that included belief but was best described as trust (*fiducia*), confidence, or loyalty. Many of the disagreements between Protestants and Roman Catholics in the sixteenth century, as well as among Protestants themselves, may be understood in terms of these two distinct, but not mutually exclusive, conceptions of faith. In general, the theologians of the early church tended to regard faith as the apprehension of eternal and divine truth embodied in the Christian tradition, although they did not conceive of the entire Christian life in these terms. Faith was supplemented, in their understanding, with mystical experience, the cultivation of virtue, charitable works, and sometimes with a higher mode of intellectual intuition or *gnosis*. During the late medieval period Thomas Aquinas developed a highly sophisticated system in which faith was regarded, as Van Harvey has noted, "as an intellectual act of approving assent to certain supernatural truths or dogmas because of their divine authority."[35] Thomas and his theological heirs also argued, however, that the will moved the intellect and that faith therefore included an element of trust as well as assent. While it would be wrong to say that Thomas regarded faith as merely an intellectual act, Protestant theologians noted that the element of trust in Thomas "is directed to the divine authority, and, therefore, is not said to constitute the act of faith itself but, rather, is a motive anterior to it."[36]

At the Reformation, Martin Luther rejected the limitation of faith to assent, which characterized late medieval Roman Catholic theology, and regarded faith as the response of trust by the total person to the faithfulness, graciousness, and righteousness of God as these were revealed in Jesus Christ. Faith for Luther, therefore, since it was the basic inclination of the heart or will, included hope in God and love for God. The object of faith, in Luther's understanding, was not supernatural truth about God but God himself. To make his point, Luther often contrasted belief in the doctrine of the incarnation with trusting in the benefits of Christ's life, death, and resurrection. The Christ in whom faith was to be placed was the "Christ for us." To be sure, Luther himself accepted orthodox doctrine, and affirmed the importance of cognition and assent, but the logic of his position led to the view that doctrine was an attempt to express faith in words, and not the object of faith itself. This provided some basis for the conclusions drawn by Protestants in the nineteenth century concerning the relative and historically conditioned nature of doctrine. Doctrinal formulations, it was argued, were relative to the

---

[35]   Van Harvey, *A Handbook of Theological Terms* (New York: Macmillan, 1964) 96.
[36]   Ibid., 96–97. I am indebted to Harvey's summary of the development of the concept of faith throughout this section.

historical situation in which they were articulated. It was the church's ongoing task to "get at" the "real faith" behind these symbols. Calvin's view of faith was similar to that of Luther, except that Calvin placed greater stress on the intellect by defining faith as knowledge (*cognitio*). But when Calvin referred to faith as a "a firm and certain knowledge" it seems clear that he did not simply mean a knowledge about God's essence or existence but a knowledge of God's goodwill toward the elect. Faith is based on the assurance that the promise of God freely given in Jesus Christ is true. The truth of that promise is revealed to the mind rather than arrived at through human reason, and it is sealed upon the heart by the Holy Spirit.[37]

The post-Reformation Protestant scholastic theologians tended to emphasize the intellectual model of faith, although they also added that it was necessary for the person affirming the truths to have confidence that the truths affirmed applied to them. Nevertheless, the emphasis on right belief prevailed, and in reaction to what was perceived as a cold, rationalistic, and often dead orthodoxy, pietism emerged to emphasize the priority of the "heart" over the "head." During the eighteenth century the American theologian Jonathan Edwards provided a robust account of faith which blended Calvinist orthodoxy, pietism, and John Locke's faculty psychology in order to transcend the identification of faith with the mind, will, and heart alone.

The nineteenth-century Protestant theologians were faced with the challenge of reformulating the concept of faith in light of the impact of science, biblical criticism, idealism, and the social criticism of religion. Since it was generally conceded that faith could no longer be based on metaphysical speculation or historical certainty, Friedrich Schleiermacher, who had been influenced by both pietism and Romanticism, emphasized the importance of religious experience over belief in orthodox Christian doctrine. The doctrines of the Christian faith, Schleiermacher argued, were neither the objects of faith nor the speculative inferences of supernatural revelation. Doctrines, he contended, were simply the expressions of religious experience set forth in speech and symbols. Ritschl, who sought to emphasize Luther's notion of faith, argued that any and all notions of faith that identified the priority of assent were expressions of the essence of Roman Catholicism. The neo-Kantian Wilhelm Hermann, who was, as already noted, one of Barth's most revered teachers, stood in Ritschl's tradition, and emphasized that Protestant orthodoxy and Roman Catholicism shared a similar approach to faith, the only difference being that Roman Catholics were required to believe the Bible *and* tradition, while Protestants were required to believe in the Bible *alone*. In Canada, John Watson argued that faith, rightly understood, stood in har-

---

[37] Ibid., 96–97.

mony with the rational apprehension of the real universe being revealed in the realization of "absolute spirit."

By the time Walter Bryden was confronted by questions concerning the nature of faith, therefore, a number of different theological strategies had been employed to address the challenges of modern thought. He found all of them wanting. Bryden was supremely conscious of the tendency in various forms of post-Reformation and modern theologies to justify faith by grounding it in some other reality, including Common Sense (Reid), religious feeling (Schleiermacher), speculative reason (Hegel), moral values (Ritschl), and scientific religious history (Troeltsch). The response of Barth and the other neo-Reformation theologians to the problem of faith appealed to Bryden for at least two reasons. First, they not only rejected the liberal Protestant strategies outright but did so on the basis of what Bryden considered to be a devastating and irrefutable critique. Second, they did not return to a pre-modern intellectualistic model of faith. They regarded faith's object as the wholly-other God, who, by grace shares divine self-knowledge in Jesus Christ. Instead of forcing a choice between faith as intellectual assent to objective truth or faith as the subjective experience of trust, they emphasized that faith was born in the midst of encounter, disclosure, and crisis. It was not long, however, before different conceptions of faith arose among the dialectical theologians who stood together during the 1920s. Some regarded doctrines as relative attempts to make intelligible what was implied in the encounter with God in Christ. Karl Barth, however, argued that there was an objective reality to revelation itself, and that faith contained a real and objective knowledge of God, although he rejected both the Roman Catholic and Protestant orthodox accounts of the matter. While Walter Bryden tended to side with Barth on the issue, he worked out a conception of faith in the midst of these differences among the neo-orthodox theologians, and in continuing conversation with Luther and Calvin.

Faith as the Correlate of Revelation

Faith, for Bryden, was an experience of radical negation and affirmation. Faith was created by, and conformed to, the revelation of the Word of God in Jesus Christ, made real in the midst of encounter and crisis, by the power and presence of the Holy Spirit. In true Reformed fashion, Bryden insisted that faith was the work of God graciously given as the means of apprehending, comprehending, participating in, and cooperating with, the Judging–Saving Word of God. Faith was part of the act of God which constituted revelation. "Accordingly," he wrote, "faith is always understood, somehow as that which comes from the side of God. There is no faith where revelation—a self-disclosure of God to the soul of man—has not taken place." Where such revelation and faith have occurred, Bryden noted, "that in the New Testament is described as salvation." This was an experience, moreover, which called for absolute obedience. Faith in the New Testament was accurately described as the knowing, or rather being known of, God who called to a decision and an obedience which was of an absolute character. "It will be observed," Bryden concluded, "that faith is therefore always conceived as a 'miracle,' whether in the Gospels, in St. Paul or in St. John."[38]

The conception of faith set out in the New Testament was radically different from that at work in idealism. Idealism, as Bryden interpreted it, emphasized faith as an adventuring upon life with Jesus as a model, or the adopting of an ideal or ideals furnished from Jesus' teachings. The Bible, on the other hand, he argued, never descended to the superficial, sentimental level of faith in which it was possible to speak of the Christian life as merely following in the steps of Jesus. Holy Scripture speaks of faith as the gift of God, which is received by those who have been truly encountered by the Judging–Saving Word. The new life bestowed by God is not mere human existence refined and extended *ad infinitum*, but a wondrous new life that comes about by God's grace. Indeed, it becomes the criterion by which human life and human existence as such are judged. The Holy Spirit, through which this faith and new life were created, is also denominated as the gift of God in the New Testament, rather than being the extension and exaltation of human spirit, as idealism seemed to suggest. "*Believing*, as the Church has spoken of it," Bryden noted, "is not just possessing this or that conviction which may grow out of man's ordinary natural experience." It was, rather, that "soul-constraint which is of the Grace of God."[39]

Bryden insisted on the inclusion of faith as basic to revelation's biblical character. "Revelation, therefore," he wrote, "is not Scriptural revelation except when faith is coincident with it, and faith is not New Testament faith except when man perceives himself judged as *sinner* (not just sinful), yet sinner saved by God's grace. God's judgment itself is (to him who belongs to God) His mercy, His grace."[40] For Bryden, faith might be described as the divinely-created interior structure of revelation within men and women who had been truly encountered by the Word of God. Revelation, in this sense, was always personal, personal in a way that no other relationship in life was personal, because, being an encounter between God and the soul alone, it was utterly exclusive and unique. Revelation was that which eventuated when God as Godself encountered an individual concretely and personally. Faith

---

[38]   Bryden, *The Christian's Knowledge of God*, 89.
[39]   Ibid., 96–97.
[40]   Ibid., 106.

was always the correlate of the revelation. Straining for language to describe what took place, Bryden could only describe it as paradoxical, enigmatic, and ambiguous, but took comfort in the fact that this was precisely how the first Christians described their encounter with Jesus. Faith, whatever it was and however it was to be described, was conformed to the paradoxical nature of the revelation of God in Jesus Christ. If the revelation of God in Christ was paradoxical, it stood to reason that the act of God in creating the faith by which the Word of God was apprehended would also be paradoxical. The New Testament bears witness to the fundamental conviction that Jesus is truly man and truly God. But not all who encountered Jesus during his life and ministry believed this. Jesus was one thing to his disciples and quite another to those who chose not to follow him. Why did some believe that Jesus was truly man and God, while others neither saw nor believed this about him? This, Bryden argued, was the paradox of faith implied in revelation, and it was just as true in the twentieth century as it was in the first century. "Jesus is one thing to men within the faith, quite another to those outside the faith, but more important, as we shall see, is the fact that to the former He is truly man but He is also God."[41]

As Bryden saw it, this conception of revelation framed the way in which the historic facts of the incarnation, atoning death, and resurrection of Jesus were to be understood. The mere historic significance of these events alone did not deliver the revelation of God. This was the reason that Bryden distanced himself from all dogmatic rational orthodoxies which he felt failed to indicate clearly the nature of the revelation of God in Jesus Christ and the faith it engendered. Traditional orthodoxies, for the most part, required the acceptance of these historic facts simply as historic facts, "and in this way presume to express the essence of the revelation of God in Jesus Christ."[42] There were two problems with this approach. Firstly, it presumed that men and women could be compelled to believe on the basis of some authority, whether within or outside of themselves. Secondly, and more importantly, traditional orthodoxies presumed that the historical facts themselves revealed God. Bryden, however, argued that those facts must be perceived by faith. That faith, he maintained, must be created by the work of God's transcendent Spirit in the hearts of men and women who knew themselves as being drawn into the judgment and death of the cross (as the old self died), and who were beginning to know themselves, in light of the resurrection of Jesus, as new creatures in Christ. Both traditional orthodoxies and modern liberalisms, Bryden argued, had stressed the mere external facts, as if revelation might be accessed by reason alone. The paradox of faith in the New Testament,

---

41   Ibid., 109.
42   Ibid., 110.

however, was "that there is no revelation . . . apart from the historic facts of Christ's incarnation, death, and resurrection, and yet in these, of themselves, the revelation of which the New Testament speaks is really never made."[43] Bryden's insistence on the paradox of faith, however, was seized-upon by his critics, who argued that it permitted a conclusion that Bryden seemed especially anxious to avoid, namely: that faith had no essential relationship to past historical events. This was an important criticism, which we will explore further. For the moment, however, the point to be emphasized is the correlate nature of faith which lay at the heart of Bryden's thought.

Despite the ambiguities concerning history, Bryden emphasized that biblical revelation, if it were to be understood in its radical nature, was never to be interpreted merely in terms of human activity and human power. The knowledge of God which faith generated was not, in the first instance, human knowledge, but rather God's knowledge which stood in peculiar contrast to human knowledge. The creative and saving activity of God belonged to God alone. The failure to recognize the sovereignty of God in faith and revelation had resulted in attempts to rationalize and idealize the Christian faith. The operations of faith and revelation, Bryden argued, when thought of in terms of natural force, compulsions, impingements, infusions, coercions of one kind or another, or again, in terms of that influence engendered by ideas or by human personality, substituted what belonged to human beings, belonging to the space-time world, for what was God's.[44] Revelation, in this unique sense, Bryden contended, represented an action of God for which there was no human analogy. Rightly understood, revelation did not enlighten human beings, it dealt with them.

In sum, for Walter Bryden, faith was the act of an individual in response to the revelation of God. But faith was the act of a human subject in the sense that it was a genuine human reality created by the act of God. It was created in response to God's act in the life, death, and resurrection of Jesus Christ, God's Judging–Saving Word, and it was created by the witness of the Spirit in a person's life. Without that witness, no revelation may be said to have eventuated. There is a theological unity between these two aspects of revelation grounded in a Christological reality. In the incarnation God has by miracle become what humanity, in its essential nature, is, thereby uniting the divine will with a human will, without confusion or change or division or separation (to quote Chalcedon), in one acting subject (person). The same paradox, Bryden accepted, was at work in binding fallen human beings to Christ, enabling them to participate in the saving revelation of God. The Holy Spirit by miracle creates faith which is, in its essential nature, a genuinely human

---

43 Ibid., 111.
44 Ibid., 126.

act of the mind, will, and heart. In short, revelation has occurred when the Word of God in Jesus Christ has not only been manifested, but when the manifestation of the Word has been met with the participation, comprehension, and cooperation it demands and presumes. The revelation of the gospel by the Spirit presumes faith in the living God, and the Spirit creates that which is presumed.

As noted in the discussion concerning Bryden's theology of the Word, this is an inherently dialectical concept which refers to a relation of correspondence between an act of God and an act of a human subject. For Bryden, the act of the human subject is not simply the occasion in which an individual acknowledges the revelation of God; it is a real participation in the revelation itself. Put even more sharply, it constitutes revelation, for without it no revelation has eventuated. There is nothing, however, in the being or knowing of the human subject which contributes to the event of revelation. There is no capacity or pre-understanding which acts as a necessary precondition of the faith which is essential to revelation. The only capacity required is one which God graciously provides in the encounter itself as a gift, namely faith. The Christian's knowledge of God is a gift of grace and the relation of correspondence which establishes faith as a correlate does not become a predicate of the human subject. The "being" of the human subject is not altered through the experience of faith's knowledge of revelation. Rather, the individual who has been encountered by God's Judging–Saving Word participates in the new life which is and which will be an eschatological reality. Throughout Bryden sought to hold up Calvin's insistence upon the sovereignty of grace in faith while negotiating through the difficulties posed by modernity's confidence in the human will, and he did so with the assistance of Barth and the dialectical theologians.

Faith as the Existential Experience of Utter Negation

The kind of faith described by Walter Bryden as the correlate of revelation, was experienced, in the first instance, as a profound sense of disillusionment. If the Word of God in Jesus Christ was a truly Judging–Saving word, the leading edge of revelation was a word of judgment, and the initial experience of being encountered by God was one in which any and all self-estimates were destroyed. The person who met God as subject-to-subject was deprived of any feeling of pride and assurance he or she may have had in this world and its achievements, as these existed in and for themselves.[45]

Bryden recognized that he was making a rather extravagant and extreme claim, but he defended himself, pointing to the witness of the Bible, and

---

[45]   Ibid., 132.

insisting that this was precisely what was meant by God as Absolute: "In some essential sense an Absolute must negate, if it is to prove itself as such, i.e., if it is to authenticate itself." [46] God, in other words, is God precisely because God stands over against humanity. God is the wholly-other Absolute against whom the lives of men and women are measured. Only God is able to do this. "The truth is," Bryden wrote, "man in his entire life's experience, is never encountered by that which truly negates him except in that event when God comes personally and establishes a relationship with him . . . ."[47] Paradoxically, therefore, the Absolute known to the Christian faith is not the Absolute Spirit of idealism which stands in continuity with the progress of human development, but a personal-Absolute, "who proves Himself indeed to be such by His power to challenge *man* himself, rather than challenge merely certain aspects of his life."[48] The experience of being encountered by such a personal Absolute is akin to the experience of death. It creates the most fundamental crisis for a human being—the crisis of existence itself. It forces a human being to deal with that which is final and ultimate. Contrary to the tenets of modernism, God is not apprehended in rational reflection on the development of history, the moral progress of humanity, or the religious consciousness. God is encountered as an antagonist who threatens everything that a human being clings to for security and authenticity. Revelation forces human beings to know that God is God and they're not. "The very pith of revelation, therefore, according to the biblical representation of it, is that it *places* man: in other words, it makes him know that 'God is God and man is man,' makes him know that as fallen man he is 'sinner,' enemy of God and alienated from God."[49] In short, God negates before God affirms, God excludes before God embraces. Revelation negates and excludes what human beings imagine themselves to be without God. Faith begins in brokenness, with the acknowledgement that things are not the way they're supposed to be, nor are they the way human beings pretend them to be.

It is to be emphasized, and strongly so, that Bryden drew heavily from Luther's theology in this understanding of faith. Luther's emphasis on the Bible as the cradle of God's Word had already been instrumental in the development of Bryden's understanding of revelation. Bryden adopted Luther's notion that Jesus Christ was not proved by Scripture but Scripture by Jesus Christ. Subsequently, Bryden emphasized the Bible's unique role in bearing witness to what he called the Judging–Saving Word—God in God's unique redemptive activity—even Jesus Christ. Even more, Luther represented a way

---

[46] Ibid.
[47] Ibid., 133.
[48] Ibid.
[49] Ibid., 134.

of faith that was to be distinguished from all forms of rationalism, idealism, and scholasticism. Luther understood that revelation "places no sort of imprimatur upon man's inherent qualities or capacities, nor upon his past experience in religious achievement, but constitutes not only a breaking in, but a breaking diagonally across, and a breaking completely away" from all forms of moral, religious, or rational imperatives. When confronted by God, Luther was an utterly broken man, but he rejoiced to be thus broken by God. Luther's theology arose not from speculation, Bryden argued, but from an encounter with God's living Word, "in which as a broken and contrite man he seems to know more immediately and profoundly the joy of God's salvation." To Luther, scholastic rationalism presumed to provide some sort of preparation for a saving knowledge of God. He believed it actually produced a 'security' against the judgment of God's living Word. Thus, Luther's profound hostility to scholasticism. And thus, we might add, Bryden's profound hostility to idealism.[50]

In this sense, Bryden understood himself as a true Protestant who stood in Luther's tradition. Indeed, Walter Bryden was one of the few Canadian Protestant theologians at the time to see the significance of Luther's *theologia crucis* for the experience of faith. Luther emphasized that "the humiliation and suffering of Christ , in which God hid his revelation, corresponded to the humiliation and suffering of the sinner, for whom God concealed his real work (*opus proprium*) of salvation behind his strange work (*opus alienum*) of alienation, which furthered it. Only the humbled sinner, struck down by the experience of what Luther called *Anfechtung* ("spiritual conflict") can know the God who for his/her justification underwent the humiliation and condemnation of the cross."[51] Following Luther, Bryden insisted on an experiential basis for theology and could affirm Luther's experience: "Living, or rather dying and being damned make a theologian, not understanding, reading or speculating." Theologies of glory, i.e., Protestant Scholasticism and liberal Protestantism, Bryden argued, looked for the power, wisdom and goodness of God in history, morality, and religion. Theologies of the cross, on the other hand, looked on the visible rearward parts of God, as Luther put it, as seen in the suffering of God's crucified Messiah. The Judging–Saving Word of God, for Bryden, was Christ crucified, with nothing to be added or subtracted from that. The faith demanded and created by that Word was born in the midst of suffering, crisis, disillusionment, and negation. The mystery of the gospel was that in the midst of the God-forsakenness of the cross, God was at

---

[50]   Ibid., 215, 223.

[51]   Richard Bauckham, "Cross, Theology of the," in *New Dictionary of Theology*, edited by Sinclair B. Ferguson et al. (Downers Grove, Ill.: InterVarsity, 1988) 181–83.

work, and the paradox of faith is that in the midst of absolute negation, the Holy Spirit is at work creating faith, hope, and love.

Judged from the perspective of the emergence of dialectical theology in the 1920s and 1930s, Walter Bryden took full advantage of biblical criticism and existentialism in developing this conception of faith. In the case of historical criticism, biblical scholars had concluded that the Gospels could not be used as sources for reconstructing the personality of the historical Jesus as had been done throughout the nineteenth century. The Jesus of the Gospels, they argued, was the resurrected Jesus proclaimed by the early church. On this basis, the dialectical theologians insisted that the kerygma, which constituted the object of faith in the New Testament, was not about the inner life of Jesus but about God's act of judgment and renewal which was revealed in his life and death. A distinction could be drawn, therefore, between the Jesus of history and the Christ of faith, between the man Jesus and the hidden Word of God. Faith then depended neither upon assent to historical facts nor emulation of historical ideals. In an important book dealing with the confrontation between modern historical principles of judgment and the Christian faith, as noted earlier, the theologian Van Harvey argues that, by adopting this approach to faith, the dialectical theologians radicalized the Protestant doctrine of justification by faith. Rather than seeing modern historical inquiry and Christian faith in opposition to one another, they now saw the critical principles of judgment employed by modern historians as a secularized version of faith.[52]

Karl Barth's second edition of his commentary on the *Epistle to the Romans*, Harvey argues, provided the earliest and clearest exploration of the significance of this radical principle of justification by faith for all aspects of life. Barth argued that faith was not to be identified with belief, religious feeling, morality, religion, or any other aspect of human experience. Faith, rightly understood, was the realization of the abysmal gulf that separated human beings from God. Faith was the recognition of the "qualitative distinction between time and eternity." Faith was closely identified with a recognition of the ambiguity and questionable nature of life. It emerged only when this all-embracing contrast between an individual and God was acknowledged. Genuine faith, therefore, was a void, a not-knowing, the utter dissolution of human beings and all of the possibilities in which they took pride. Grace, in Barth's view, rather than bridging the massive gulf between God and human beings, exposed it, and exposed it in such a way that men and women were able to accept God as the one they do not know. Only in the awareness of the total ambiguity of the human situation before God could men and women experience the gift of God's acceptance and so love the one who has judged

---

[52] Harvey, *The Historian and the Believer*, 131–34.

them. Revelation, therefore, was not the communication of truths otherwise inaccessible to reason, but the precipitation of the crisis in which the negation of all human aspirations was exposed. The Christian perceived this crisis in Jesus of Nazareth, not in the example of his superior piety or morality, but in his ignominious death. Jesus' greatest achievement was a negative achievement because he bade farewell to all those achievements by which men and women obscured the fact of death. God's crucified Messiah sacrificed every human possibility and put an end to a humanity alienated from God. His death therefore is the clue to the meaning of life.[53]

Harvey points out that the dialectical theologians interpreted revelation to refer to the manifestation of the ambiguity of human righteousness. Faith, then, was a rejection of all that was distinctly human. The way to a genuine and non-idolatrous affirmation of humanity was through the way of negation, i.e., through the crucifixion of the self. Although this might strike one as unrelieved negativism (and that charge was certainly laid against Walter Bryden by some of his critics) it allowed the dialectical theologians to argue that faith was not only compatible with the radical intellectual doubt which characterized modern epistemology, but it also implied a recognition of the partial and ambiguous character of any claim to truth, including, and especially, any religious claim. In the hands of theologians like Walter Bryden, faith became the primary tool for the critique of religion. This is why, as Van Harvey rightly notes, so many of the dialectical theologians (Bryden among them) were impressed by existentialism. Existentialism, especially of the Kierkegaardian type, exhibited a certain contrariety, and constituted a criticism of all attempts to speak about God based on reason, history, religion, or morality alone. The existential problem which confronted human beings was not simply what they believed, but more fundamentally how they believed what they believed. For Walter Bryden, the problem of Protestant orthodoxy was not that it taught the wrong thing, but that it provided no way for modern men and women to believe authentically. Liberal Protestantism, on the other hand, appeared to provide an account of how people might believe, but radically revised Christian faith and doctrine in the process. Bryden saw the dialectical theology of Karl Barth as a revived form of Protestantism and a radical appropriation of Luther's doctrine of justification by faith, which provided an understanding of Christian belief after modernism.

Faith as the Existential Experience of Absolute Affirmation

The radical faith created by the Word of God did not, however, leave human beings broken, contrite and in despair before God. "The Word of God,"

---

[53] Ibid.

Bryden wrote, "also affirms man's life."[54] As a saving Word, the revelation of God in Jesus Christ created authentic existence through which human beings might not only flourish, but find their true selves before God. Here Bryden seemed to revel in the dialectics and the paradoxes which he believed were to be found at the heart of Christian faith. The Word of God alone affirmed an individual's life precisely because it negated it. It was the absolute nature of the negation that forced men and women to cry out to God. Anything less than this absolute negation created the possibility that human beings might continue to be thrown back on themselves, on their world, on their ideals. But when a human being had been confronted by God and utterly disillusioned in the encounter, that human being for the first time knew that this was very God with whom she or he had to do. Here, and only here, and then, and only then, could a person be assured that this God was truly concerned about her or him. This was precisely the point, Bryden argued, at which the Word of God was an objectively realistic revelation. The objectivity of God might be spoken of, Bryden contended, in distinction from other forms of objectivity with which we might be familiar, because God alone truly negates. By standing over and against human beings in judgment and negation, God for the first time is revealed as God apart from any and all human images, pre-understandings, or capacities. There is nothing on the side of the sinner which contributes to the manifestation of God as the Absolute who negates. And when God is unveiled in this manner, the sinner experiences him- or herself for the first time as someone in whom God's interest is affirmed, as someone loved by God, as someone for whom the God-forsakenness of the cross was intended. The Christian faith, Bryden argued, affirmed human life precisely because it first negated it; it denied the world before affirming the world God intended: "We do well to observe that the Christian faith is a world-denying faith and yet a world affirming faith. It denies man and this world . . . and yet affirms the reality of and significance of man in a fashion of which ancient and modern idealisms have not even a first acquaintance. The Christian is an optimist, not from any particular evidence that the world itself can supply as testimony of God's concern for man, but because he believes God has come and does come into this world. The Christian's faith and hope lie in the fact that the Word is made flesh."[55] The Word of God, therefore, Bryden emphasized, was a double-edged sword; it was a completely-Judging, completely-Saving Word; it was death-dealing and for that reason alone it was a life-giving Word. Just because it negated it affirmed. For Bryden, the two-fold character of the Word of God and the two-fold character of faith as the Word's correlate constituted the uniqueness of the Christian revelation.

---

[54] Bryden, *The Christian's Knowledge of God*, 135.
[55] Ibid., 136.

It was precisely this paradoxical finality of the Word which qualified the conception of revelation presented in the Christian Bible.[56] And, Bryden added, this was the claim made by the early Reformers concerning the conception of revelation they had rediscovered in the pages of the Old and New Testaments, which brought a completely fresh apprehension of God to the churches of their day.

At this point, of course, Bryden was left with the question as to why it was the case that the revelation of God created faith out of nothing in the lives of some and not others. The answer, not surprisingly, threw him back upon the doctrine of election. To begin, Bryden emphasized again that the Word of God did not merely challenge the evil that was in an individual, but the individual's life itself. The Christ of the New Testament, he argued, was not a Christ who appealed to people with a view of producing a cultivated, ideal personality, but a Christ who condemned the whole person in order to create what the Bible called a new creature in Christ. This absolute view of revelation, Bryden fully recognized, implied a view of divine *apprehension* or *election* of individuals to salvation. The doctrine of election, Bryden argued, was the church's attempt to spell out theologically the absolute, unique and exclusive character of God's Judging–Saving Word and its correlate of faith. The two primary modern objections with which the doctrine of election met had to be confronted honestly. If saving faith was created by a sovereign God, it was argued, did it not in the first instance undermine any sense of moral responsibility? And secondly, did it not prohibit any real significance from being attached to life itself.[57] Bryden was more than willing to deal with the difficulties presented by the doctrine of election. But he added the proviso that no rational solution was possible, since one was left, in the end, with the paradox of faith. From Bryden's perspective, this did not constitute special pleading. It was, rather, a recognition of the fact that all attempts to provide rational explanations had tended to synthesize, naturalize, and idealize the raw material of faith. And these were precisely the tendencies in rational orthodoxy and modernism against which Bryden fought tooth and claw.

Bryden began by drawing upon the philosophical discussions concerning free will and determinism. The force of the claim being made for Christian faith did not seem quite so absurd when set beside the naturalistic, materialistic and biological interpretations of life which always presupposed some sort of determinism. Modern psychology had identified the importance of the sub-conscious as constituting an important factor in determining the actions of an individual. In view of such interpretations, therefore, it was exceedingly difficult, Bryden argued, to provide any clear definition as to

---

[56]   Ibid.
[57]   Ibid., 149.

what was meant by free will or free choice or human responsibility. The old Faculty psychology, which had separated out the human will as the locus of human actions, and with which Reformed theology had sought to find a compromise in the eighteenth and nineteenth centuries, had been completely discredited. In his own unique manner, therefore, Bryden questioned the so-called triumph of the human will in the modern world. It seemed clear to him that there was not now, nor had there ever been, something which might be denominated as a free will. "On any view of free will, promulgated at any time, we might ask: does this *free* will represent some sort of entity, unsubjected to any influence beyond itself (i.e., of God, of man, or of environment) which condition might constitute a deciding factor in any decisions it might take? A *free* will, as thus understood, would exist as some sort of 'wild thing,' utterly independent."[58] Nicolas Berdyaev, Bryden noted, entertained precisely this conception of free will in his concern to explain the origin of evil. Free will belonged to an utterly irrational category, because Berdyaev perceived, as humanistic philosophies and liberal idealisms did not, that evil was utterly irrational, and therefore could not be rationalized. The ease with which modern Protestantism spoke about free will, therefore, betrayed a lack of understanding, not only of Christian faith, but of the profound ambiguity underlying modern conceptions of personality and existence.

This brings us to the very core of Bryden's concern in faith and revelation. Was it possible to reconcile God's uniquely active saving grace with responsibility and free choice on the part of human beings? Bryden freely admitted that most of the attempts made by theologians to answer this question had yielded little more than sophistry. Modern Liberal theologians tended simply to synthesize without exposing the difficulty involved. Rational orthodoxy continued to uphold the essential insights of the biblical understanding of revelation and faith, but tended to do so in a mechanistic manner that was now wholly unsatisfactory. Of all the theologians writing on this question in his day, Bryden had perhaps the most respect for John Oman's attempt, in *Grace and Personality*, to reconcile the utter "religious dependence" of human beings upon God with their necessary moral independence. Both, Bryden recognized, seemed necessary to the integrity and reality of the human soul. Yet Bryden also felt that Oman's chain of argument was only as strong as its weakest link, "the link in this case being the failure to explain what actually happens at that crucial point in which, what God the creator essentially is, meets what creature and sinful man essentially is, in order to *create* what is known as Christian faith." [59] Bryden undoubtedly put his finger not only on the critical issue in revelation and faith, but also on the weaknesses of both

[58]   Ibid., 151.
[59]   Ibid., 152.

traditional and modern solutions. But was Bryden able to provide an adequate and appropriate answer to his own perplexing question?

If, Bryden argued, there was something creatively new in the event by which a person became a Christian, then it surely followed, that there could neither be a preparation in the individual for this new factor, nor could it be the case that the individual her- or himself might choose this new factor. Despite the fact that not all of his critics saw that this necessarily followed, Bryden insisted that when the Christian tradition spoke of God's unique activity in creation it referred to *creatio ex nihilo*, meaning, to bring existence out of non-existence. The fact that Bryden spoke of becoming a Christian at all was, of course, alarming to a Canadian Protestant establishment that assumed being a Canadian citizen was co-terminus with being a member of the Christian church. It was precisely this understanding of the Christian faith that Bryden wished to overthrow, and the way to do so, he believed, was to emphasize the radical discontinuity between faith and everything that might be considered as the basis for faith, other than God's free and sovereign action. Modern people, he argued, used the term "create" to signify the reorientation and transformation of that which already exists into something of beauty, meaningfulness, order and harmony. The Christian faith, on the other hand, when using the term in reference to God means to signify the bringing of existence out of non-existence, something new out from a void of nothingness, life from death. This is the language, although limited, which best accords with the experience of faith. It has to be said that, for Bryden, this was an existential reality, if by existential is meant the way in which the relationship between God and human beings defies all rational and idealist systems of thought. So, he argued, "What actually happens when God engages the soul of man . . . is nevertheless of a nature to defy human rational explanation."[60] The dilemma posed by the antinomies inherent in faith and revelation, and here we come to Bryden's central point, was to be accepted as a paradoxical reality, and celebrated as such, rather than understood as a problem to be solved. The fundamental flaw of Protestant scholasticism and liberal Protestantism was that both assumed they were dealing with a philosophical problem to which rational and ideal solutions might be provided. Quite the contrary, Bryden argued: this was a theological reality to be embraced by faith. The influence of James Denney continued to loom large in Bryden's thinking.

But what was the basis for this appeal to paradox, mystery, and miracle? How did Bryden defend himself against charges of fideism, mysticism, subjectivism, and irrational enthusiasm? Like Denney and Barth, and the Reformers before them, and Athanasius before them, Walter Bryden turned

---

[60]   Ibid., 154.

to the doctrine of the Incarnation. In Jesus Christ, God became a human being and thereby God made Godself "apprehensible" to and capable of being appropriated by human beings. The Christian church can say something about the 'why' and the 'what' of this reality, but nothing really significant about the 'how' of it. How it was that God became human eludes the grasp of human control. Whenever and wherever the church assumed that it had penetrated this paradox, a theology of glory was at work. Whenever and wherever Christian theologians and philosophers (e.g., John Watson) boasted about finding the underlying unity which resolved the antinomy, one could be sure that the very reality they intended to affirm was being denied. The fact that the Christian church has had to content itself with speaking about the doctrine of the incarnation in symbols and paradox was testimony to the theological power of the reality to which the Christian movement bore witness.[61] In short, Bryden was convinced that the church as the church had no choice but to throw itself upon the reality of faith which was grounded in the objectively real revelation of God in Jesus Christ.

This contention, he believed, was borne out in the practical work of ministers. No doubt reflecting upon his own experience as a Canadian Presbyterian pastor for some seventeen years, Bryden noted that "the utter importance of what God does" in a person's "salvation is repeatedly brought to the minister's attention." He went on:

> An enquirer, for instance, asks what precisely it is to be saved and the minister is baffled. He can tell him about it, even point out the way; indeed he is obligated by the presence of God and the Holy Spirit in his own soul to do so. Nevertheless, he only speaks in signs and symbols; he cannot give to him an intimate knowledge of what salvation is. Until God works creatively in the enquirer's heart, as He has done in the minister's heart, the latter cannot make the former know that about which he asks information. It is this creative thing, this "increase of God" which is all important, which is unique, which as a matter of fact is not ever chosen by man; and for this he has never antecedent preparation.[62]

Strangely enough, Bryden noted, it was precisely in the event of revelation, understood as the free act of a sovereign God, that men and women recognized and accepted full responsibility for their lives. In the act of revelation a person became for the first time an authentic human being who genuinely acted on his/her own behalf. The sovereign grace of God did not contradict human freedom; human freedom was created by it. The person of faith made no excuses and did not blame others. Rather than offering a low evaluation of

---

61 Ibid., 154.
62 Ibid.

humanity that demeaned the human personality and negated human responsibility, Bryden argued that Protestant faith, rightly understood, affirmed human dignity and required human responsibility.

The abandoning of human responsibility would be, Bryden believed, to lapse into an unhealthy mysticism. After *The Spirit of Jesus in St. Paul* Bryden never employed the term mysticism positively because he had come to see an inner connection between rationalism and mysticism. Mysticism, he argued, represented "merely an extension of the rationalizing process, although into regions not supposed to be strictly rational, with a view to satisfying the human, rational, as well as the religious instinct for unity." The distinction between all types of mystical experience and "that experience which is known as the Christian evangelical" is mediation. "Mysticism, in its desire and claim for immediate union with the divine, actually does not require mediatorship of any kind." The New Testament, on the other hand, insists upon the centrality of the one mediator, Jesus Christ. Bryden saw a connection between mysticism and immanence whereas the biblical conception of revelation emphasized the mediation of the wholly-other and transcendent God in Jesus Christ, with whom the believer is united by faith.[63]

The symbol that tied all this together for Walter Bryden was, again, the doctrine of election. Acutely alert to the fact that this doctrine had been the cause of interminable controversy during the history of Christian thought, Bryden nevertheless observed that all the truly great theologians had been obliged to render an account of this doctrine because, what it signified, was the way God dealt with human beings as embedded ineradicably in the Old and New Testaments. But Bryden's approach here was important. The doctrine of election was important, not because it was an eternal propositional truth to be affirmed as necessary for faith, but because it rendered an account of the nature of faith itself. Election, if it was to be understood correctly, emerged "as a necessary consideration in the experience of Christian faith, i.e. of faith-revelation." God elects, Bryden argued, "*in the very revealing of Himself.*" Election was the language used by the person who had to speak about faith because of the character of his or her experience in Christ. And in an important theological move, Bryden turned away from the speculative nature of the doctrine that he saw in a good deal of the Reformed tradition. He followed Barth's lead in reconstructing the doctrine christocentrically. Due to its importance, Bryden's indebtedness to Barth is quoted at length:

> Moreover, as Karl Barth has recently pointed out in an important work—and this is a truly significant consideration in regard to this doctrine—the whole question of election, for its primary meaning,

---

[63]   Ibid., 216–18.

should be approached from the point of view of God's saving action on behalf of man, rather than from any thought of a determinism in regard to man's fates. Fundamentally, therefore, it is a doctrine arising out of a consideration of God and His saving work. It has to do with the fact of God's sovereign freedom in His will to save sinful man, in which there is the attempt to show that this saving decree of God has nothing arbitrary in it, nothing which would do less than justice to God's absolute righteousness. In other words, God freely decreed to save sinful man, but in order to conserve His own righteousness He bears sin's penalty in Himself, i.e. in the Eternal Son, the elect Man. When, however, this more fundamental view of the doctrine of election has in turn been applied to individuals—and we believe it will of necessity be so applied—it has frequently been thought and said that God decreed salvation to certain men and apparently not to others. This constitutes the error into which theologians have often fallen; it seems to imply that there was a time before Christ, or rather, in some sense apart from Christ—i.e., apart from the Judging–Saving Word of God—in which God arbitrarily decided men's fates. The idea, however, which this doctrine was meant to convey was that God, freely of His infinite Love, and yet never arbitrarily nor whimsically, but in strict regard to His own Righteousness, decreed salvation to men in His Word, Jesus Christ, alone.[64]

The doctrine of election, rightly understood in Christ, Bryden argued, did not constitute a denial of freedom. To the contrary, it was required to explain the real meaning of Christian freedom. The doctrine of election for Bryden, it might be argued, provided the grammar of grace to speak about a God who willed to disclose self-knowledge in Jesus Christ. Without the will of God exercised in this manner, it was impossible to conceive of a knowledge of God which was truly true or really real. It was the only way in which, as Bryden saw it, one could speak about a knowing of God which did not originate within the human subject. The doctrine of election reminded the church that no capacity or pre-understanding provided the precondition for the creation of faith. The will of God, Bryden emphasized, is "not just the human will absolutized, nor is God's knowledge man's knowledge *ad infinitum*." The Christian's understanding of God's will, God's power, and God's knowledge, as a matter of fact, did not derive from human cognition at all, but from God's own self-revelation.[65]

Here we bump up against the kinds of statements that caused Daniel Day Williams of Union Theological Seminary to characterize *The Christian's Knowledge of God* as a classic statement of neo-orthodox theology. When all

---

[64]   Ibid., 158–59.
[65]   Ibid., 159–60.

was said and done, the doctrine of election was re-appropriated to emphasize the self-authenticating self-revelation of God which created the faith it presumed. "Revelation brings about its own category of interpretation," Bryden argued, "as the co-respondent or co-relative faith possesses its own axiom of understanding itself."[66] Revelation and faith were not first to be correlated rationally with the forms and categories of human reason. To do so, Bryden believed, would be to make human reason the judge of God, God's revelation, and faith. The doctrine of election was intended to guard against precisely this philosophical instinct, despite the fact that in the history of the Reformed tradition the doctrine had been co-opted on more than one occasion to fulfill exactly such an agenda. In place of a rationally explicable causality for faith, Bryden proposed a divine transcendent causality for which no entirely satisfactory rational explanation could be given. Rational arguments, when employed as the means to explain divine causality, inevitably tended towards determinism. The doctrine of election, centered in the dialectics of God's paradoxical Judging–Saving Word, i.e., Jesus Christ, reminded the believer that God's will occasioned responses which were truly human, although one cannot say 'how.' The fact that revelation occurred as an event in relationship, as subject-to-subject, however, pointed to the fact that something other than the antithesis of abstract wills was in view. The truth was, Bryden concluded, "if we synthesize at this point, we lapse definitely into that manner of thinking which has caused our trouble in the past. That is to say, we have succeeded in resolving 'transcendence' again, as applied to God, into some sort of impersonal, relative immanence."[67] In short, without a healthy respect for the mystery of revelation and faith implied in the doctrine of election, Bryden believed that rationalism reigned unfettered in Protestant theology.

It is beyond the scope of this book to enter into a comprehensive assessment of Bryden's doctrine of election, especially in relation to Calvin, The Westminster Confession of Faith, Schleiermacher, and Barth, although such an examination would undoubtedly prove fruitful. It is worth noting that Bryden and some of his colleagues on the Articles of Faith Committee proposed a statement on election and predestination to the Presbyterian Church in Canada in the 1940s which reflected the influence of Barth as described above. In this they were opposed strenuously by W. Stanford Reid and other confessional Calvinists who saw the Barthian impulse in theology as a threat to the church's subordinate standards. The point throughout this exposition, however, has been to emphasize the way in which Bryden grounded his conception of revelation and faith in an appeal to the doctrine of election, rather than to focus on the doctrine of election itself. Bryden's concern was theologi-

---

[66] Ibid., 160.
[67] Ibid., 162.

cal epistemology, and he was thrown back on the doctrine of election to shore up his paradoxical conception of faith. But, with the help of Barth, Bryden retrieved a version of Calvin's doctrine of election that sought to avoid the pitfalls of rational Calvinism while addressing the epistemological concerns of modernity. This was typical of the manner in which Bryden worked out the meaning of most Christian doctrines in light of the importance he attached the sovereign self-authenticating self-revelation of God in the Judging–Saving Word. The Trinity, for example, Bryden wrote, "represents the fact of very God manifesting Himself to man, of making Himself known, not in terms of man's needs as he himself conceives these, but in terms of man's needs as God reveals the same to him; consequently, the resultant experience is one which comes directly from the divine rather than from the human side."[68] In sum, for Walter Bryden the Christian experience of faith, as utter negation, and absolute affirmation, could not in any way be said to be an extension of religious experience. It was, for him, actually a complete break from it, and it was precisely in the discontinuity that the Christian's knowledge of God was born.

Faith and Revelation in Critical Perspective

It remains for us now simply and briefly to summarize the critical concerns that are raised by the theology of revelation and faith espoused by Walter Bryden during the 1930s and 1940s in Canadian Protestantism. Three problems are isolated: (1) faith and history, (2) faith and religion, and (3) faith and reason.

First, the problem of history. As noted above, Bryden's approach to faith and history was a double-edged sword. On the one side, he appealed to critical biblical scholarship to undermine the historical Jesus of liberal Protestantism. Historical criticism, rightly employed, he believed, demonstrated that the revelation of God could not simply be deduced or "read off" from the events of Jesus' life, death, and resurrection. The Bible pointed, rather, to the faith which was created by God's Word and Spirit in the proclamation of the early church. The preaching of the first Christians, in fact, emphasized God's act of judgment and salvation which was revealed in the life and death of Jesus. In short, Bryden employed biblical criticism to demonstrate the limits of historical knowledge rather that to secure revelation by historical knowledge. That is to say, he employed modern historical methods to tunnel through modern historical conclusions. On the other side, the same radical interpretation of faith and revelation which permitted Bryden to employ historical knowledge seems to permit the conclusion that faith has no essential rela-

---

[68] Ibid., 209.

tionship to a past historical event. The conception of faith and revelation with which Bryden worked, his critics argued, implied that revelation, and its correlate faith, was a possibility in the present, as an act of God, without any necessary connection to past historical events. Yet, this was precisely the conclusion that Bryden rejected, because he refused to cut the cord between faith and Jesus of Nazareth. But how, then, is this conception of faith to be reconciled with the church's traditional insistence upon the centrality of a historical event in the first century?

This is the basis of Michael Gauvreau's assertion that the neo-orthodox theologians in Canada broke decisively with the evangelical tradition's theology of history in their attempt to divorce revelation from history. Gauvreau fails to note, however, that the neo-orthodox theologians did this through the use of historical-critical methodologies. In his own defense against such criticisms, Bryden insisted upon the uniqueness of the historical character of revelation. Biblical revelation, he argued, refers to "that which is supra-human, supra-historical, and yet which invades the human and historical as a concrete occurrence" with definite unique effects.[69] Revelation, while never subject to history, must eventuate in history and in the human being. Revelation was not a category interpreted by history; history was a category to be interpreted by revelation. "In revelation God particularizes Himself in an event which is exclusive and unique, that is to say, God reveals Himself, not in general history, but in concrete events in history."[70] The paradox implied in all this seemed, to Bryden, to stand at the center of the Reformed faith: "The true Reformed Churchman finds, however, that he must never transcend the incarnation-miracle from the human rational side. For him, neither flesh nor blood, nor any human nor material thing, can reveal the Christ known to faith alone. The human itself cannot objectify what is truly God—not even the human history of Jesus."[71]

Such statements, of course, made many of Bryden's critics more than a little nervous. Did Bryden really mean to imply that the human history of Jesus was not an objectively real revelation of God? Or was he simply pointing out that the revelation of God could not be reduced to human history alone, not even the human history of Jesus? The lack of clarity with which Bryden seemed to approach the question of faith and history caused D.M. MacKinnon to ask the following question in a review of *The Christian's Knowledge of God*: ". . . but I would ask him how far he is justified on his

---

[69]   Ibid., 49.
[70]   Ibid., 67.
[71]   Ibid., 116.

own view of the historical Christ in his unexpected bouquet to Bultmann's strange work?"[72]

Second, Bryden's insistence on the sharp distinction between Christian faith and religious experience tended to promote a theology of religions which focused on the uniqueness of the Christian faith-revelatory encounter. Religions, Bryden argued, could rightly be described as the manifestation of the human longing for God. In the end, however, religion, even Christian religion, produced nothing more than mere ideas about God. Bryden argued that the unique thing about the Christian encounter with God was that it was a personal relationship, created and established by God alone. The decisive fact within it was that men and women were completely overcome and subdued by God. The neo-orthodox critique of religion, which Bryden embraced, emphasized that religion represented a human movement towards God. The Christian gospel, as he understood it, in contradistinction, bore witness to the movement of God toward humanity in Jesus Christ alone. Karl Barth leveraged this insight to distinguish the radical nature of the Christian faith from the domesticated form of culture Protestantism which dominated western Christendom. As a critical principle, this insight worked exceedingly well. As the basis for constructive engagement between Christianity and other religious traditions it appeared to offer little because it denied any point of contact between Christian faith and the phenomenon of religion.

It has to be said, however, that Bryden sought to apply this theology of revelation to an understanding of religion in what was at the time a responsible and creative manner. Rather than speak in generalities, he examined the history of many of the world's religions in great detail with his students. In his lectures and writings Bryden paid particular attention to the significance of religious ideas for the development of Christianity. He also believed that non-Christian scholars often offered important insights for Christian self-understanding. Radhakrishnan, for example, a Hindu thinker for whom Bryden had a great deal of respect, pointed to the sense in which both Hinduism and Christianity were world-denying faiths in ways that even notable western scholars such as Rudolf Otto failed to grasp. Bryden also found it useful to explore the parallels between the teachings of other religions and the doctrines of the Christian faith, as well as the nature of religious experience in the world's religions. At the end of the day, however, neither a defense of Christian doctrine nor an explication of Christian religious experience, as Bryden saw it, constituted an adequate apologetic for Christianity. In fact, comparative studies confirmed that Christianity did not offer a superior doctrine or a more profound experience; it pointed to "Jesus Christ crucified,

---

[72]   D. M. MacKinnon, *Scottish Journal of Theology* 2 (1949) 210.

God's absolute judgment upon man" as the primary determinant of an encounter with God.[73]

In the hands of religious pluralists like John Hick and Canadian Wilfrid
Cantwell Smith, the neo-orthodox position implied that the divine self-revelation was effected in such a way that only a small portion of humanity, those
with a saving knowledge of Jesus Christ, could be saved. Bryden would have
rejected such a narrow interpretation of what he was trying to say. But his
position, to be sure, left no room for the views espoused by Hick and Smith:
that all religions bespeak the same spiritual reality and lead to the same God.
At the same time, the position espoused by Barth, Kraemer, and Bryden was
continued in the legacy of Lesslie Newbigin, a seasoned interpreter of both
Christian faith and religions of the Indian subcontinent, who affirmed the
reality of religious plurality within the world while rejecting the notion that
all religions could be treated as equally valid aspects of some greater whole.
In short, despite the problems associated with the implications of the neo-
orthodox theology of revelation for religious dialogue, Walter Bryden stood
at the forefront of the conversation between theology and religious studies in
Canada on this important matter.[74]

Third, Bryden's insistence upon the limits of reason and the power of
paradox continued to create an offence to many Canadian Protestants. The
problem for the critics, however, was that neo-orthodoxy was not an obvious retreat into obscurantism and anti-intellectualism in the face of the
Enlightenment. The concept of faith espoused by the neo-orthodox theologians, as Van Harvey sets out clearly, had a structure that was almost analogous to the critical and scientific thinking of the Enlightenment.[75] In fact,
Gogarten argued that the Protestant doctrine of justification by faith made
the autonomy and responsibility of the sciences possible. Luther's message
had challenged the closed world of the middle ages and allowed the Protestant
Reformation to shatter the *Weltanschauung* of the medieval world. On this
basis, the dialectical theologians believed that the virtues of autonomy and
intellectual responsibility were integrally related to faith. Walter Bryden
noted that this was a position to be distinguished from rational orthodoxy
and liberal Protestantism, both which tended to view critical thought as the
anti-thesis of faith. Fundamentalism was characterized by a rejection of criti-

---

[73] *The Christian's Knowledge of God*, 142–43, 170–71, 207, 220. See also Bryden's unpublished
"Lecture Notes on Religion"; idem, *The Significance of the Westminster Confession of Faith*,
13–14; and idem, *Why I Am A Presbyterian*, 142.

[74] See Hendrik Kraemer, *The Christian Message in a Non-Christian World* (London: Harper,
1938); John Hick, *An Interpretation of Religion* (London: Macmillan, 1989); Wilfrid Cantwell
Smith, *Towards A World Theology* (London: Macmillan, 1991); and Lesslie Newbigin, *The
Gospel in a Pluralist Society* (Grand Rapids: Eerdmans, 1989).

[75] Harvey, *The Historian and the Believer*, 135–39.

cal thought altogether; liberal Protestantism was committed to finding the required synthesis. When faith was construed by the dialectical theologians as radical questioning of all that humanity has and is without God, it functioned as a correlate to the Enlightenment principle of critical thought. From one side, therefore, it looked as if the dialectical theologians had provided an approach to faith which neither rejected nor capitulated to modern structures of thought. But there was also a problem. The neo-orthodox theologians turned the tool of reason in upon itself. They employed the critical principle to deconstruct that upon which it was based, namely the indubitable, autonomous, rational thinking subject. As existentialists, they turned away from the idealist confidence in reason and towards despair. They shared this negation of liberal modernity with Marx, Freud, and Nietzsche. And they insisted upon the radical model of authentic faith rather than autonomous reason as the basis for human existence. As in the case of history, they used the critical principle of the Enlightenment to find their way through its rationalism. To its critics, however, the neo-orthodox theology represented nothing short of an all-out retreat from the reasonableness of the Enlightenment thinking which was demanded of modern Christianity. F.H. Anderson, in writing about the problem in relation to Bryden, summed it up this way:

> Thus does Professor Bryden land with consistency and candour in the predicament of the irrational enthusiast. He does not, moreover, seem to regret his predicament; his plight, he believes, might be infinitely worse: he might, for example, be in the position of those who believe that finite man, with his relativities and "anthropomorphizations," can fathom the Eternal! In any case, he portrays the theologian as a prophet without an apologetic, a dogmatic, a Christian ethic, or a missionary message amenable to statement in the terms of rational truths and to apprehension through the natural powers of man. That unique experience which the theologian would witness proves too personal for intelligible communication, too transcendent to be brought within the confines of an epistemological object shared by cognitively perceptive agents.[76]

At the end of the day, however, what Anderson saw as an intractable philosophical problem, Walter Bryden celebrated as the theological liberation of the church to be the church. Revelation and faith required, Bryden believed, either/or choices to be made. And that, in short, represented the two roads that diverged in the wood of modern Canadian Protestant theology in the 1920s and 1930s: modern idealist liberalism and neo-Reformation 'neo-

---

76 F. H. Anderson, "On A Certain Revival of Enthusiasm," *The University of Toronto Quarterly* 10.2 (January 1941) 194–95.

orthodoxy.' Bryden made it his business to point the Canadian Protestant church of his day to the road less traveled.

As was noted earlier, Anderson maintained that Bryden was very good at explaining what the Word of God, faith, revelation, and Christian knowledge were *not*. About what they *were*, Bryden said very little.[77] For Walter Bryden, however, a Protestantism chastened by the lessons of modernism, and truly led by the Spirit, was a Protestantism of modesty, humility, and paradox. The negative pole, without a doubt, tended to dominate Bryden's writing. But it was a negativity driven by the desire to burrow through all forms of modernism without retreating into obscurantism. It was negativity, he would argue, that was shaped by the Protestant principle itself, namely Luther's theology of the cross. It was a negativity fuelled by the element of judgment in the Word of God. But it was also a negativity which pointed to the provisional nature of God's eschatological promise. This was the theology of revelation that sustained his work, shaped his person, and persuaded many of his students in the Presbyterian Church in Canada to follow him into neo-orthodoxy. He worked like a prophet with a single burden, to overturn the dominance of rationalism and idealism in Canadian Protestantism, so that the church might once again proclaim a gospel that could be heard and believed. It is to that vision of a confessional and confessing church that we now turn.

---

[77]   Ibid., 188.

5

A Church Reformed and Reforming

No one has put greater emphasis on the unique reality and divine significance of the Church than has John Calvin. He was the true High-Churchman in contrast with the high-ecclesiastic. And we are not yet true Presbyterians, let me affirm, if we do not profoundly understand what Calvin was striving for, and insisting upon, in this regard.[1]
—Walter Bryden

BRYDEN's entire theology should be seen, as Joseph McLelland has noted, "against the horizon of the people of God—that group visited and redeemed by God's Word and Spirit, called to witness to the 'Judging–Saving Word,' constrained to meditate on its behalf in the disciplined way called theology."[2] The neo-orthodox theology of revelation espoused by Walter Bryden did not simply shape his conception of the church as one doctrine among others. His understanding and experience of the church provided the framework for his entire theology. More importantly, Walter Bryden had not found his way into theology by way of academic pursuit; he felt called to a theological vocation through preaching; "he saw himself caught in the net of God's Word, no longer free to dabble in speculative philosophy, but appointed to serve the Gospel."[3] Revelation and the Word of God, the Holy Spirit, the knowledge of God, faith, and election—these were, for Bryden, matters of church doctrine.

Through his study of church history Bryden had aligned himself with the theological tradition represented by Athanasius, Augustine and especially Luther and Calvin, which resolutely required the acceptance of biblical revelation as the starting point for reasoning out the church's faith. The revela-

---

[1]   Bryden, *Why I Am A Presbyterian*, 142.
[2]   J. C. McLelland, "Walter Bryden: 'By Circumstance and God,'" 121.
[3]   Ibid.

tion of God was the reality which created, sustained, accosted and renewed the church. For Bryden, theology mattered to the church, and the church mattered to theology. Both were indebted to God's Judging–Saving Word for their very existence. It is in the context of a churchly theology, therefore, that his theology of the church should be placed. Bryden's understanding of the nature of the church, its confessional position, its unity, its ordained ministry, and its witness in the world arose from, and revolved around, this fundamental conviction.

In the aftermath of church union, Walter Bryden emerged as one of the most articulate and influential of a growing number of continuing Presbyterians who felt compelled to think more radically about what the church was and what it was called to be.[4] His historical studies and theological instincts had drawn him to the Genevan Reformation in which he found an understanding of the church's faith that was "far more profound and challenging because it is essentially theological rather than ecclesiastical." Bryden became convinced that what revolutionized Europe in the sixteenth century was not a new church, but a new vision of God, and that the church in Canada, pauperized theologically as it was by rationalism and idealism, "needed to be open to the same radically challenging vision if it was to recover its proper sense of mission."[5]

That conviction concerning the church, planted by Calvin and nurtured by Denney, was only strengthened when Bryden encountered the theology of Karl Barth and the dialectical theologians. They emphasized the radical authenticity of the new humanity in Jesus Christ. "To put it another way," he wrote in his 1945 inaugural lecture, "this world would not have the remotest idea of the radical nature of God's will concerning man, were it not that this very Word had become flesh in the Person of Jesus Christ; that he thus dwelt among us—yet without sin—and that, because of this event, there had arisen a community of believers, a "fellowship of the Spirit," a "Body of Christ," charged with *one* supreme responsibility, namely to *witness* to Him of Whom the world was ignorant."[6] This view of the church provided not only the basis for Bryden's *apologia* for remaining a Canadian Presbyterian, it also became embodied in the subordinate standards of the Presbyterian Church in Canada in the Declaration Concerning Church and Nation, adopted by the General Assembly in 1955. Looking back on the post-union situation of Canadian Presbyterianism from the perspective of the 1950s, James Smart noted that "through the leadership of Dr. Bryden in particular and influenced by European trends in Protestantism, younger men in the Presbyterian

---

4   Brian Fraser, *Church, College, and Clergy*, 148.
5   Ibid.
6   Bryden, *Separated Unto the Gospel*, 51.

Church began in the early thirties to see their church's destiny as that of being the instrument through which in Canada Protestantism might be recalled to its heritage as church reformed and ever anew reformed according to the Word of God in Scripture."[7] It is the substance and significance of that ecclesiology which forms the focus of this chapter.

The Nature of the Church

In the words of the creed, Walter Bryden believed in the holy, catholic and apostolic church. The church, he noted, was placed in the Apostles' Creed "among those things which are *to be believed in.*"[8] The point he wished to emphasize, however, was that the faith with which the church was embraced was created by the Holy Spirit and not simply by the natural faculties which were characteristic of humankind. The Christian's confidence in God has God as its source, and the effect of the Holy Spirit is God-ward. But the Holy Spirit's work is also directed towards human beings. It was only because of that effect, Bryden argued in a letter to a critic, that human beings can believe in the church.[9] God created, in men and women of faith, a vision of a new and authentic humanity and community in Jesus Christ. As a Protestant theologian, therefore, Bryden set himself against the tendency, especially in some trajectories of Reformed theology, to see the church as merely the external and human means through which God's redemptive purposes were accomplished in history. The church mattered theologically, and it was to be understood in relation to the revelatory acts of God. For this reason, he did not find Calvin's treatment of the creed's phrase "in the church" satisfactory. At the same time, Bryden recognized the need to distinguish between the self-revelation of God and the identity of the institutional church, and on this point, he argued, Calvin was immensely helpful. Unlike Calvin, however, Bryden considered it quite permissible to regard the church as the extension of the incarnation, if one distinguished between the head (i.e., Christ) and its members.

The church existed because of divine action in the world. That action, for Bryden, was centered in God's Judging–Saving Word. The church must strive, he argued, "to rediscover the Word of God—that Word, I mean, which in the beginning gave rise to Holy Scripture, and which alone gave existence to the Church of God, and apart from which that Church cannot stand."[10] There was, he argued, "a very definite and necessary relation between the New Testament conception of revelation and the New Testament conception of

---

7   James D. Smart, "Canadian Presbyterianism Since 1925," *Presbyterian Record* 79.2 (Feb 1954) 17–19.

8   Bryden, *The Christian's Knowledge of God*, 96.

9   Letter to Jamieson, The Presbyterian Church Archives, Bryden Fonds.

10   Bryden, *The Christian's Knowledge of God*, x.

the church."[11] Consistent with this fundamental insight, Bryden contended that "the Word of God is prior to and transcends both the Scripture and the Church and we may add it is prior to and transcends Creation as well. Briefly, the Word of God is the Source, the raison d'etre of all three."[12] In the same way that the revelation of God created the faith which was demanded and presumed for its reception, so too God's Judging–Saving Word created the church. The revelation of God demanded and presumed the participation, comprehension, and cooperation of a people named by God, a community within which faith in the living God was received as a gift of grace. As with faith, the Word of God created that which it presumed. It was incumbent, therefore, upon the church to listen for the "Word of God in relation to the kind of faith it inspires in man—a faith which indeed, has given existence to the Church of God itself."[13] "Revelation, therefore, and the Church are interdependent existences so to speak. The latter, at least, possesses no significant meaning except for the former."[14]

The Word of God which created the community within which faith was born was always, in the act of revelation, accompanied by the Spirit. In this sense, the constitutive principle of the church, Bryden argued, was spiritual and not institutional. "The church consists of those who in their hearts share the peculiar effects of the Word and of the Spirit of God—such as actually know themselves as sinners before God, yet as belonging to God by His grace."[15] The emergence, continuance, and permanence of the church was to be attributed, Bryden argued, to the belief by the early Christians that there was in their midst a presence and a power which they knew as the Spirit of Jesus. The constitutive principle of the church was not to be discovered in programs, forms, or orders but "in that experienced spiritual union or fellowship which exists between Christ and His people as a whole, and in which the Grace of God is evidently manifested."[16] The church was, in the final analysis, Bryden insisted, a creature of God's Word and Spirit. It was a fellowship in which men and women discovered themselves, rather than one which they themselves achieved. The membership of the church consisted of those who had heard the Word of God in the solitary privacy of their own souls, by the witness of the Spirit, and because of that fact, found themselves in a peculiar unity with others similarly apprehended. This was, in Bryden's judgment, the

---

[11]   Bryden, *The Christian's Knowledge of God*, 4.
[12]   Ibid., 14.
[13]   Ibid., 132.
[14]   Ibid., 180.
[15]   Ibid., 238.
[16]   Bryden, *Why I Am A Presbyterian*, 38; see also idem, *The Spirit of Jesus in St. Paul*, 15.

New Testament consciousness of the church, and the view he took to be fairly representative of that held by the Reformed churches.[17]

The problem, as Bryden saw it, was that the churches of his day had domesticated the radical claim of God's Word and Spirit upon the church. Rational orthodoxy had identified the essence of the church with doctrinal propositions to be affirmed, while modern idealism had substituted general religious principles for authentic faith. When those doctrinal propositions and general religious principles could no longer be sustained against the assault of modernity, the church turned to a thoroughly secular account of its own life. It was precisely within the context of such developments that Bryden pled for a theological account of the church's life. The church, in his view, was the God-ordained, Christ-established, and Spirit-animated community of salvation, and he despaired about attempts at organizational restructuring which failed to account for the reality demanded by God's revelation upon the community of faith. The insights of sociology, as important as they were to understanding significant dimensions of human relations which constituted the church's life, could never have described the church as it was before God. The church's knowledge of itself, rightly understood, was not a knowledge it gained through human insight alone. It was a knowledge of the church experienced in light of its knowledge of God. The church, as the church, knew itself truly *Coram Deo* (in the presence of God). This, Bryden argued, was the fundamental dynamic of the church which the Reformers had rediscovered in the midst of late medieval scholasticism, which Barth and the dialectical theologians had retrieved in the face of liberal Protestantism, and which Canadian Protestants desperately needed to recover in the twentieth century.

Bryden's development of the doctrine of the church in terms of a neo-orthodox conception of revelation, it might be argued, rested upon individualized and experiential, perhaps even privatized, conceptions of the Holy Spirit and faith. To be sure, Bryden conceived of the church as the union of individual Christians who had been united with Jesus Christ through an experience of crisis in their own souls. And in speaking about "the Christian's knowledge of God" Bryden appeared to give priority to the experience of the individual over the faith of the church. But that criticism is somewhat short-sighted when considered against two important factors. First, Bryden's conception of revelation was developed in the context of a church undergoing a crisis in Canada, and his writings were intended, at least in part, to respond to this crisis. The presenting crisis was church union, but the real crisis, as Bryden saw it, was a church that had lost its theological way, primarily through the influence of rationalism and idealism. The polemics against denominational

---

17   Bryden, *Separated Unto the Gospel*, 176–77.

bureaucracies, organizational structures, and sociological analyses, therefore, were intended to stress the priority of revelation and faith as theologically construed. It is within this attempt to correct an understanding of the church as institution that Bryden's emphasis on God's encounter with the individual is to be understood.

But there is a second and more important reason why this criticism of Bryden's ecclesiology is short-sighted, a theological reason which has to do with Bryden's understanding of the Reformed faith. Despite his emphasis on the priority of revelation and faith for the individual soul, Bryden never conceived of the church as a voluntary association, a gathering of individuals who, by the exercise of their autonomous rational wills, joined together to make common cause. On the contrary, for Bryden, the church was constituted by those who, in the privacy of their own souls, had been forced to confront the awful reality of God's judgment and the joyful promise of God's salvation. The reality of revelation about which Bryden spoke presupposed the electing grace of God. The church was a covenant community which, Bryden argued, existed because God had first chosen a people in Christ. The community of faith, therefore, preceded the individual in God's redemptive purposes in history. In short, if revelation and the church were interdependent realities in Bryden's thought, both were rooted in God's sovereign goodwill toward creation in Jesus Christ. Bryden's conception of the church, therefore, was a doubled-edged sword he wielded to cut through the theological tangle of twentieth-century Canadian Protestantism. On the one hand, he used it to cut through the idealism and rationalism which had dominated Protestantism in Canada from the late nineteenth century. On the other hand, he used it to attempt a defense against the challenges of privatism and individualism in an increasingly secular Canada.

Confessing the Faith

Walter Bryden stood in a tradition which affirmed that "the people of God," in the words of Jack Rogers, "have always paused at critical historical moments to summarize and declare who they are and what they most deeply believe. These high moments are remembered and passed on to succeeding generations to preserve the identity and vitality of the community."[18] Presbyterianism in Canada, therefore, was marked by confessionalism, by "the view that a church must have a confession of faith to be constituted as a church or denomination."[19] As a Reformed church, it inherited a confessional

---

[18]   Jack B. Rogers, "Creeds and Confessions," in *Encyclopedia of the Reformed Faith*, edited by Donald K. McKim (Louisville: Westminster John Knox, 1992) 89–90.

[19]   Donald K. McKim, *Westminster Dictionary of Theological Terms* (Louisville: Westminster John Knox, 1996) 57–58.

theology which used creeds and confessions as guides to biblical interpretation and as a basis for church beliefs. In particular, The Presbyterian Church in Canada had adopted the Westminster Confession of Faith as its confessional standard. An important theological statement written by Calvinists during the English Civil War, it was presented to the English Parliament in 1646, and ultimately became the primary subordinate standard for the Church of Scotland and its inheritors. The Westminster Standards include all the documents produced by the Westminster Assembly (1643-1649): the Westminster Confession of Faith (1646), the Larger and Shorter Catechisms (1647), Directory for the Public Worship of God (1644), and Forms of Presbyterial Church Government (1645).

Behind this confessionalism lay the conviction that Christians were called to affirm their faith (Lat. *confessio),* especially in the midst of persecution and heresy, as Bryden noted. In the twentieth century, the name "Confessing Church" was applied to the Protestant church movement that resisted the "German Christians," who had ascended to power in the Evangelical Church and supported, or at least accommodated, the Nazi ideology. Prominent among the leaders of the resistant "Confessing Church" was Karl Barth (who had been instrumental in writing the Barmen Declaration), Dietrich Bonhoeffer (1906–45), and Martin Niemoller (1892–1984). Bryden taught and wrote about confessionalism in Canada, therefore, at a critical moment in European Protestantism, and he leveraged these insights to question church union and the future of Canadian Protestantism.

It should be no surprise, then, that Bryden's earliest statements concerning the nature of confessionalism appeared in his *apologia* for the continuing Presbyterian Church (*Why I Am A Presbyterian*). As a creature of revelation, Bryden believed, the church was set apart as a community called to confess its faith in response to God's Judging–Saving Word. The revelation of God demanded not only comprehension and cooperation in faith, it also demanded confession. And like faith, it was a revelation that presumed confession of the Word of God, and which created the confession it presumed. Such confession, Bryden argued, emanated from a church living under the constraint of God's Word. The church and its theology, he contended, "have their rightful origin in a confessional witness to the Christ who was crucified and risen."[20] For Bryden, a confession was not simply a body of doctrine to be affirmed; it was the act of affirmation, witness, and proclamation to which a church was called. The act of confession entailed far more than the recitation of creeds. It was to be understood as an event created and empowered by God's Word and Spirit. In a 1941 article in *The United Church Observer* called "Continental Movements and The Theological Thought of Tomorrow" Bryden drew atten-

---

[20]   Unpublished lecture manuscript on Augustine, 10.

tion to the "Confessing Church" movement and distinguished between statements of faith and confessions: "It is easy to make statements of our faith, but
confessions are wrung from men who have been on their knees. A theology
which may be acquired objectively is not Christian theology; the latter appears only when men are under the power and constraint of God's Word."[21]

Bryden's view of confessions made him more than a little uneasy
about the tendency of confessional Calvinists to insist upon a rigorous doctrinal adherence to the confessional standards. The future of continuing
Presbyterianism could not, he argued, be sustained by the resolution passed
at the 1925 continuing General Assembly "reaffirming a very strict adherence to the recognized Standards of the Church."[22] Mere intellectual assent
to the doctrines of the Christian faith was not necessarily the same thing as
possessing faith in Jesus Christ, the Word of God. Confession implied faith,
and faith implied trust as well as assent. The creeds and confessions had an
important place in the church as expressions of knowledge *about* God, but a
confessing church proceeded in its life and witness in the belief that it had a
knowledge *of* God. Continuing to stress the dialectical character of Christian
faith, however, Bryden refused to relinquish an insistence upon the necessity
of creeds. Creeds and confessions, to be sure, did not guarantee the confessional life of the church. Furthermore, they always stood in strict subordination to Holy Scripture within which the witness to God's Judging–Saving
Word was contained. But faith also demanded that the creeds be seen as "the
necessary sign-posts on the Christian way to God. Without them there is
no Christianity. Like windows in a dark room they serve as those apertures
through which man must look, if he is to see at all the liberating spaces that
lie beyond."[23]

Bryden's continuing commitment to the necessity of creeds and confessions was fueled by his belief that they were made by people who had a genuine
knowledge of God in a particular time and place. The contemporary church
ignored and marginalized this witness, he contended, at its peril. "Creeds are
not made; they are always born," Bryden argued, "often born in blood."[24]
Creeds and confessions reflected the church's ongoing struggle to bear witness
to its faith in the revelation of God. The Westminster Confession of Faith,
without a doubt, reflected the peculiar conditions of its time and embodied a
tendency to intellectualize the Christian faith. Nevertheless, Bryden emphasized, it was "undeniable that the framers of that Confession, as was the case

---

[21] "Continental Movements and the Theological Thought of Tomorrow," *United Church Observer* (June 15, 1941).

[22] Bryden, *Why I Am A Presbyterian*, 43.

[23] Ibid., 52.

[24] Ibid., 80–81.

with all the other Reformed Confessions, had seen God anew."[25] Even with its defects and its limitations, the Westminster Confession of Faith symbolized what a confession can be: "However defective in some important respects we may consider our present Confession of Faith, we can do no other but await the necessary circumstances which can give birth again to that which, in our day, 'must be said concerning God' first, and then concerning 'man and this world.' Nothing less than this can hope, in any permanent way, to provide a Confession which will arouse men's interests, or produce a statement of belief to which they will be obliged to give eager obedience and true fidelity."[26]

In taking aim at both rational Calvinism and liberal Protestantism in his approach to the confessional identity of Presbyterianism, Bryden intended to defend the importance of doctrinal integrity. The Presbyterian Church in Canada, he argued, ought neither to reduce confession to mere intellectual assent nor to lay aside doctrinal considerations altogether. Both tendencies, he argued, were at work on both sides of the church union debate. "The Presbyterian Church in Canada," Bryden urged, if it was to be true to its heritage, and indeed to its present trust, "must remain steadfast by this characteristic doctrinal emphasis." This, in his judgment, constituted its "supreme spiritual mission in this country at the present time."[27] He had little confidence that the Basis of Union for the United Church of Canada provided the necessary grounds for either doctrinal integrity or confessional unity. As a basis of union it did not capture, Bryden believed, the confessional spirit of the Reformed churches. At the same time, he was certain that the attitudes represented by the confessional Calvinists and the liberal Presbyterians within the continuing Church would do little to advance the cause of a truly confessional spirit.

By the late 1930s Bryden had incorporated his understanding of creeds and confessions into the very nature of the theological enterprise. The church's language about God, upon which the church reflected critically in its theological work, was by its very nature not theoretical but confessional. And true confession could not be manufactured by the church. "The one great question before the Church of this time," Bryden argued, was that of how men and women "are to affirm, in terms which do not evade, confuse or camouflage the real issue, the absolute nature of God and His Christ." Neither mere theoretical reflection, however serious, nor schemes for the unification of the churches, however desirable, could produce an understanding of the gospel that would sustain the life and witness of the church in the world. Such an understanding, Bryden emphasized, will "arise out of confession—

---

25 Ibid., 82.
26 Ibid., 81.
27 Ibid., 95.

the Church confessing." Bryden was quick to point out, however, that "the present confusion derives from the fact that the Church of itself cannot create confession. Confession, as it is with repentance, faith, love, and hope, is of God; these must wait on the creative activity of God."[28] Confession of Jesus Christ as Lord was an act of God's Word and Spirit which demanded and presumed the participation, comprehension and cooperation of the people of God. It was not, therefore, a mere human act undertaken in response to divine initiative. It was, however, a genuine participation by the church in God's actions, made possible by God's actions.

In June 1943 Bryden was invited to address the General Assembly of the Presbyterian Church in Canada, meeting in Hamilton, Ontario, on the occasion of the tercentenary of the Westminster Confession of Faith. Stuart C. Parker, as noted earlier, the minister of St. Andrew's Church (Simcoe) in Toronto was so incensed by the positive attitude to the Confession displayed throughout the lecture that he had to be physically restrained from accosting Bryden afterwards. Parker represented the liberalism against which Bryden often fulminated; a position which, as Bryden later noted, regarded the Westminster Confession as "outmoded and a document which for practical purposes might well be forgotten." In the words of Bryden, Parker and others like him believed it was "ridiculous to assume that the Church has not advanced in Christian knowledge in the course of three centuries." "One wonders," Bryden mused, "how the Apostles' Creed would fare if this criterion of evaluation were applied to it." Pulling no punches, Bryden equated historic liberalism with heresy; it had always shunned specific definitions, and in times of testing it would fall because it would find that it had no definite principle for which to fight.[29]

What appeared to irk Parker most was that Bryden had argued throughout the lecture that the subordinate standard should be taken seriously by the Presbyterian Church as an essential part of its Reformed witness. Bryden reminded his readers in the version of the lecture revised and expanded for publication that confession presupposed saving faith, that is, a knowledge of ourselves and God through the Spirit's work, a faith which alone permitted belief in God and thus enabled Christians to do God's work.[30] As Bryden saw it, the Westminster Confession of Faith was worthy of continuing study for at least three reasons. Firstly, it constituted the essential part of the ministerial vows for ordained pastoral leadership within the Presbyterian Church in Canada. Secondly, it was questionable, Bryden argued, "whether faith is

---

[28]   Bryden, *The Christian's Knowledge of God*, 75.

[29]   Bryden, "Shall We Adopt the Statement of Faith?" *Presbyterian Record* (October 1946) 270.

[30]   Bryden, *The Significance of the Westminster Confession of Faith*, 8.

ever truly revived except through the church's traditional witness." On this point Bryden emphasized the doctrine of the church over against a purely personalized and individualized interpretation of Christian faith. And thirdly, there was a great deal more "to be learned from the great affirmations of the faith which the church has made in the past than most of us suspect." The Westminster Confession of Faith was, to be sure, perplexing at points, but its overall achievement should, Bryden urged, elicit humility within the church.[31]

Having set out reasons for the continuing relevance of the Westminster Confession of Faith by way of introduction, Bryden developed his argument and analysis under three main points. First, he argued, the confession of Jesus as Lord constituted the church's very life. The early Christians were convinced that the church existed and was maintained only in those who had been constrained to make such confession. This basic confession in the course of time was formulated into creeds, which, as such, became the signposts of the church's faith. Such creeds, Bryden contended, were "of necessity a positive dogmatic utterance; the Church speaks by the authority of a faith which of itself it had not created and could never have anticipated." They arose out of the need to combat the heresies threatening the early church's fundamental confession of Jesus as Lord. Whatever importance was to be attached to the Westminster Confession of Faith could only be appreciated in light of the ultimate significance the church gave to confession itself.[32]

Second, the Reformation, Bryden argued, arose because an increasing number of church leaders in the sixteenth century perceived the need to recover the central tenets of New Testament confession, namely the sovereignty, grace, freedom, and transcendence of God as revealed in Jesus Christ as Lord. On this point, it was to be noted that the Westminster Confession of Faith, written some one hundred years after the events of the Reformation, tended to represent "not so much a true 'confession' as a rational explanation of what it deemed to be Reformed theology."[33] Pushing his criticism further, Bryden noted that the problem with the Westminster Confession of Faith was not that it had absorbed teachings altogether foreign to the Bible, but that, owing to the absence of a truly confessional spirit, it had failed to give its various truths proper Christian expression and had, moreover, drawn rational conclusions from them that were not strictly in accord with Scripture.[34] The text of the confession, therefore, should not be accepted by the church as the setting forth of eternal truths in rational forms once for all time. It invited the

---

[31] Bryden, *The Significance of the Westminster Confession of Faith,* 10–11.
[32] Ibid., 12–18.
[33] Ibid., 22.
[34] Ibid., 30.

church, rather, to the task of interpretation in terms of the historical, ecclesiastical, social and political context within which the Confession was written, and with a recognition that it possessed fundamental weaknesses. Under the authority of Scripture, and within the church's ongoing call to confess the faith, the Westminster Confession was an important and useful signpost.

Where did all this lead? In the third part of the lecture Bryden laid out four principles of Christian thinking which he discerned within the Reformed witness with which the Westminster Confession of Faith appeared to be in general agreement. First, the Reformed church had placed a great emphasis on the necessity for a doctrinal and theological understanding of the Christian way of life and must continue to do so if it was true to its calling. Of all the gifts which the Presbyterian Church might offer to Canadian Protestantism, its theological witness was paramount. Second the Reformed church had been signally loyal to the church's creeds and confessions, believing these to have come by the instigation of God and through God's guidance and providence. Third, the Reformed church, in Bryden's judgment, had a due respect for tradition and wholesome reverence for the early church theologians, a respect and reverence which Bryden believed ought to continue to characterize the witness of the Presbyterian Church. And fourth, the Reformed faith had emphasized that all true faith must be a living and personal faith: "Each individual must in a personal relationship to Christ be alive to God and individually responsible to Him."[35]

This was, in sum, the enduring witness of the Westminster Confession of Faith and the demand, Bryden argued, which it laid upon the continuing Presbyterian Church in Canada. The documents produced by the Westminster Assembly represented neither outmoded expressions of Christian faith without anything but historic significance, nor absolute norms for Christian faith today. They were not intended to be emotional symbols serving to rally continuing Presbyterians to their Scottish tradition. Rather, they reminded the continuing Church that it lived and moved and had its very being as a confessing community of faith under the constraint of God's Word and Spirit. The Westminster Confession provided a signpost which reminded the church of the faith it had inherited and the faith it was called to confess anew.

Had Bryden's writing on the nature of confession concluded with his 1943 address to the Assembly, his contribution to the continuing Church would have been considerable. But there was still more to come. During the last decade of his life he became embroiled in the Presbyterian Church's struggle to write a new statement of faith. In 1942 the General Assembly received two overtures asking for clarification concerning the statement in "the Basis of Union of 1875 [that] the Confession of the Church re 'The Civil

---

[35]   Ibid., 31–38.

Magistrate' was declared to be not binding, but rather that full freedom of conscience is permitted to everyone." The result was, the overtures argued, that "people, elders and clergy [were left] without definite guidance in the important matter of how to affirm their loyalty to the State; and the State on its part is left without assured knowledge of its powers and duties, under the Lord Jesus Christ toward the Church."[36] The committee struck to craft a response to these overtures included Walter Bryden.

The work of the committee expanded to a review of the Westminster Confession of Faith, the Doctrine of the Revelation and the Word of God, the Reformed Doctrine of Election, as well as the issues related to church and state. When a new statement of faith was proposed to the General Assembly for adoption, Bryden argued for the affirmative position in the *Presbyterian Record*. According to Reformed principles, the church's faith, Bryden reminded his readers, was always in subjection and subordination to Scripture. The new statement of faith, therefore, was to be set within the same theological framework in relation to the Bible. Furthermore, the committee did not intend to provide some sort of substitute for the *Westminster Confession*. The new statement of faith was to stand in continuity with the stream of Reformed confessional statements that had gone before. In short, Bryden had some sympathy for those who opposed the new statement of faith because it appeared to raise questions about Scripture and the Westminster Confession of Faith. He had little patience, however, for those who insisted that the development of a new statement of faith was somehow illegitimate. The church was a confessional and confessing community, and it was called by God to confess its faith anew amidst the changing circumstances of life. No confession was an absolute statement which set forth the truth of the gospel once for all time. At the same time, the church was not free to do and say whatever it wished. "Confessions of Faith," Bryden argued, "are not made to suit by the will of man, to suit his convenience to the passing situations of this life. Living and real confessions, it is true, are born in circumstances, but only as these are determined by God's will. And these are always essentially in harmony with the Church's peculiar faith from the beginning."[37] In Bryden's opinion, the movement in the Presbyterian Church in Canada to renew its Confession "can result in nothing but good. It will put iron into the blood, put real substance into the Church's teaching and preaching, engender true

---

36 Gordon Peddie, *The King of Kings: The Basis of Union of the Presbyterian Church in Canada, and its relationship to the present need of the Church for a Confession of Faith in Jesus Christ as Lord of Church and State, together with The Petition of a Memorial of the Presbytery of Paris to the General Assembly, 1942* (Toronto: Age Publications, 1942).

37 Bryden, "Shall We Adopt the Statement of Faith?" 269.

spiritual life among us, and give zest to all our activities."[38] As it happened, the new statement of faith never saw the light of day in the form it was presented. After Walter Bryden's death, however, the Presbyterian Church in Canada adopted the Declaration Concerning Church and Nation in 1955 as the answer to the original overtures.

Despite the many criticisms that might be leveled against Bryden's understanding of confession, this much can be said with certainty: it was consistent with his conception of revelation, faith, and the church. He employed an existential understanding of faith to rehabilitate a Reformed understanding of creeds and confessions, an understanding which he believed had been rationalized in Protestant scholasticism and idealized in liberal Protestantism. Bryden believed that the Reformed confessions, rightly understood, overcame the dichotomy between the subjective experience of faith and the objective content of faith which bedeviled modern Christianity. "The traditional confessions of Protestant theology," he argued, "so much disparaged today, are far more skillful in suggesting the deeper and richer aspects of the Christian experience and its objective source, than are many of the modern religio-philosophic disquisitions on the meaning of Christian faith and grace."[39] Confessing the faith was demanded by the gospel. It was one of the ways in which the people of God participated in the reality of revelation. The communication of the gospel presumed and created the faith out of which the confessions emerged. Confessions were living expressions of the radical and authentic encounter between God and the new humanity in Jesus Christ. In league with Karl Barth and the dialectical theologians, then, Walter Bryden used modern categories to tunnel through modern theologies and retrieve Reformation faith. Some of Bryden's students, notably Arthur C. Cochrane and James D. Smart, interpreted and applied the Confessing Church movement in Germany to the situation in Canada. The result, for better or worse, was that the confessional position of the Presbyterian Church in Canada was reoriented for a generation. In the words of James Smart, Walter Bryden "did two things that are not likely to have to be done again; he commanded an interest and respect for the faith which speaks in the Westminster Confession and he destroyed every pretext in our tradition for a literalistic confessionalism that would make the Westminster Confession of Faith not a guide but an iron-bound shackle upon the faith of the church."[40]

---

[38]   Ibid., 270.

[39]   "After Modernism, What?" Unpublished manuscript, chapter 1, Introductory.

[40]   James D. Smart, "The Evangelist as Theologian," in *Separated Unto the Gospel*, xi.

The Ministry of the Word

Walter Bryden's theology of ministry, shaped by the same conception of revelation that had formed his theology of the church, created a kind of theological nerve in the lives of those preparing for the ministry of Word and Sacraments within the continuing Presbyterian Church. Those called to exercise pastoral leadership in the aftermath of church union, Bryden believed, had to move beyond the sentimental and superficial ideals held about the clergy, to a renewed sense of faithful and prophetic ministry. Christian ministers were not employed to provide a professional service to cultural and civic ideals, but were called and compelled by God to serve the Judging–Saving Word. As someone who felt himself to be under constraint, Walter Bryden offered his students a credible model of the minister as confessing, prophetic theologian, one who strove to put faith into words. His students saw him as one who sought to embody the message he proclaimed.

That model was itself shaped by Bryden's understanding of Paul's ministry. As John McFadyen had noted in his foreword to *The Spirit of Jesus in St. Paul*, what interested Bryden most of all in the Corinthian letters was "the character of Paul, as that character was moulded and controlled by the spirit of Jesus." Bryden's discussion, McFadyen commented, was not conducted out of speculative interest: "Throughout it runs an undercurrent of appeal to the Christian minister today to search and try himself by the standards exhibited in that first and greatest of Christian ministers . . . ."[41] The perplexing problems which confronted the clergy in the 1920s, Bryden argued, were not dissimilar to the circumstances surrounding the Apostle's Corinthian experience and so it was natural that one should turn to Pauline theology and practice for help. Bryden fretted over the fact that the ministry of the Word was being marginalized in the modern church. "Executive and organizing ability," he commented, "rather than preaching power had gradually become the most necessary qualification of those who occupy our modern pulpits."[42] The peculiar work of the Christian ministry, he believed, was that of communicating a living knowledge of God. Ministers of the Word were, in Paul's terms, "stewards of the mysteries of grace." Paul was able to preach because he believed in the reality of God, that God was for him the most real factor in life through the power and presence of Jesus by the Spirit. As a result, Paul "preached Jesus Christ and Him crucified, not a philosophy but a Person, and at that, a crucified Person."[43] The effectiveness of Paul's preaching, it was to be noted, had little to do with its rhetorical style, its reasonable presenta-

---

41 J. E. McFadyen, "Foreword," in *The Spirit of Jesus in St. Paul*, 7–8.

42 Bryden, *The Spirit of Jesus in St. Paul*, 54.

43 Ibid., 74.

tion, not even its being delivered with passion and conviction. The condition which made Paul's preaching effective was a certain attitude of the soul to God which seemed to release the powers of God in the life of the preacher. The gospel, therefore, was not simply the message delivered in preaching; the revelation of the gospel created the reality of preaching; it demanded that it be preached. The preaching of the gospel demanded more than notice, or understanding, or sympathy. It demanded participation, comprehension, and cooperation. The revelation of the gospel presumed the reality of preaching as a communication, and created that which it presumed. While Karl Barth held that preaching was a form of the Word of God, Bryden maintained that preaching was a form of the Judging–Saving Word.

Walter Bryden had been called on early in the aftermath of church union to help stabilize, recruit, and educate the ministry of the continuing Presbyterian Church. In his 1927 tract *The Christian Ministry* he provided a theological rationale for ordained leadership at a time when the relationship between clergy and laity in the continuing Church was characterized by mistrust. In the eyes of the laity the clergy who had voted overwhelmingly in favor of church union had betrayed the cause of Presbyterianism in Canada. At the same time, those ministers who had opted to remain within the Presbyterian Church often did so at great personal cost and were respected for having done so.

In the midst of such confusion and uncertainty, the still relatively unknown Bryden sought to orient his church towards an understanding of ministry rooted in the reality of revelation. If the church was created by God's Word and Spirit, then so too was its ministry. Appealing to the Westminster Confession of Faith, Bryden argued that the ministry, oracles, and ordinances of God had been given to the catholic, visible church by Christ himself, who, by his own presence and Spirit, made them effectual according to his promise.[44] The gift of Christ to the church was created by the call of Christ in the lives of those to be set apart for such ministry. The validity of ministry rested upon the inner reality of Christian experience and the individual's sense of a divine call which, when recognized by the people, was regularized through ordination by the presbytery. The gift of ministry, however, was to be understood within the life of the whole people of God, an insight which the Protestant churches owed to the Reformers. "The Church, they felt, was a completely new and higher order which had emerged by the creative power of God Himself." "It was," as Bryden saw it, "a 'Fellowship of the spirit,' in which men and women found themselves in possession of new gifts, powers, and an entirely new attitude to and new outlook on life. The Church was the body of which Christ was the Head. He alone animated, sustained and

---

[44] Bryden, *Westminster Confession of Faith*, 25.3 cited in *Separated Unto the Gospel*, 120.

empowered it to fulfill its peculiar prerogative." It was from the consciousness of this fact, Bryden concluded, "that Protestants had derived their great and distinctive doctrine of the priesthood of all believers."[45] The doctrine of the priesthood of all believers did not, as its critics argued, negate the doctrine of ordained ministry. Quite the opposite: it provided the theological context within which ordination and ministry were to be understood. Among the gifts which the ascended Christ poured out on his church by the power of the Holy Spirit was the gift of pastoral leadership. Within the early church there were those specially gifted and sent by Christ to be leaders of the people. Ordination recognized and confirmed the call and appointment of those so gifted by Christ. Ordination, Bryden believed, symbolized the church's deepest conviction concerning ministry: it was created by the Word of God, it was a gift of the Word of God, and it participated in the revelation of the Word of God through the ministry of preaching. Without wanting to be polemical, Bryden sought to set out a high doctrine of the ministry of the clergy as Christ's supreme gift to the church, while refusing to ground this high doctrine in "meticulous ecclesiastical claims for Church government or ministerial orders."

Though he taught church history and the history and philosophy of religion rather than homiletics, Walter Bryden nevertheless inspired a new generation of preachers for the continuing Presbyterian Church. Indeed, he believed that a truly Reformed theology and practice of preaching might constitute one of the gifts of continuing Presbyterians to Canadian Protestantism. In order for this to happen, however, Presbyterian preachers would have to recover that which had been lost, not through church union, but through the long influence of idealism and liberalism on preaching in the years leading up to church union. The fact of the matter was, as Bryden had experienced it, Canadian Protestantism had been characterized by a dearth of biblical, doctrinal and experiential preaching for decades. The root of the problem, or so it appeared to Bryden, was the failure of ministers to wrestle with the reality of God in their own souls. "Everything in a Church," he wrote in *Why I Am A Presbyterian*, "on final analysis, depends upon the reality that exists in the souls of its ministers, especially in respect to those profound matters which concern their own personal attitudes to what is essentially Christian truth." The first task of every person who would serve in the Christian ministry, Bryden argued, was to come to terms with oneself before God. "A truth is worthless, either to yourself or to your people, except as it has become truth to you through personal insight and spiritual perception."[46]

---

45 Bryden, *Separated Unto the Gospel*, 122–23.
46 Bryden, *Why I Am A Presbyterian*, 97.

The Judging–Saving Word of God, if the gospel was to be preached prophetically, had to be encountered first by those commissioned to preach. Christian preaching proceeded from a living apprehension of God's Word, an existential encounter with Jesus Christ as Lord. Without the reality of revelation at work in the soul of the preacher, the ministry of the clergy became nothing more than a profession. Quoting from Kierkegaard, Bryden argued that the ministry was "not a mere making of sermons, visiting the sick, and directing Church functions. Nor is the genuine minister . . . one seeking promotion as his due reward, securing a living for himself and his family, supporting himself from the fact that Christ was crucified, deploring the fact that there are so few Christians in the community, certain enough however that he is one of them, for is not he himself convinced of it?" "It has been the presence of those so conceiving the ministry," Bryden continued, "which has been the undoing of the Church of God in modern times. Christian preaching is at one and the same time the most dangerous and the most satisfying responsibility—dangerous because its Gospel is always an offence to the natural man, no matter under what name he may go, and satisfying because it has to do with things eternal."[47]

Bryden emphasized that the Christian ministry in its larger sense was a kind of incarnation. He pointed to the example of Mary Slessor's missionary work among the Africans in Calabar. The real test of ministry was what a clergyperson would do and inwardly be "in the face of deepest disappointment and baffling frustration, in the face of those people you are sure to meet who never seem to get the real and greater meaning of the thing you believe and try to teach." Ideas and ideals in themselves, Bryden argued, did not move people. They had to be incarnated in the lives of those who bore them. More importantly, when the gospel was truly preached and incarnated it elicited a response of reverence and awe in the face of mystery and majesty. "To see in the life around us, in the men and women we have known and in whose presence we have stood, humbled, and to see in this Christian religion, and in that unsearchable and indefinable person, Jesus Christ himself, *something* which eludes our grasp altogether and yet which haunts us as the ultimately real, which we cannot ever give up, to see this is to possess the soul of a preacher who will be able to help his fellow men." Preaching, Bryden concluded, had to be characterized by "*the* authentic note of that something 'Other' in the soul" of the preacher, who had in "some true and full sense surrendered himself to God, as God is revealing himself in this day and generation."[48] On more than one occasion Bryden quoted some verses from "an

---

47   Bryden, *The Christian's Knowledge of God*, xi.
48   Bryden, *Separated Unto the Gospel*, 141–45. See also Fraser, *Church, College, and Clergy*, 155–56.

obscure pastor of Hessen to his fellow-ministers" who had discerned the need of the church:

> God needs men, not creatures
> Full of noisy, catchy phrases.
> Dogs He asks for, who their noses
> Deeply thrust into—Eternity,
> And there scent eternity.
> Should it lie too deeply buried,
> Then go on, and fiercely burrow,
> Excavate until—Tomorrow.[49]

In short, the ministry of the Word was hard but fulfilling work. More than that, it was a participation in the reality of God's revelatory and redemptive purposes in the world.

Bryden's doctrine of the ministry, as Brian Fraser noted, "challenged too many people at too many levels to make it truly popular. Bryden himself would have been suspicious if it had been."[50] In the years following church union, however, Bryden's critique of the church and its ministry rang true for an increasing number of Presbyterian theological students and clergy who perceived the crises confronting both church and society. The idealism which had been used to create a national church aligned with cultural aspirations, they argued, was incapable of addressing the issues confronting modern men and women in the 1930s: economic depression, nationalist rivalries, and world war. Bryden had sounded a note that resonated with a generation of emerging church leaders. It could no longer be business as usual. The church was more than a national fraternity and its ministers had to be more than chaplains to the culture. At the same time, Bryden knew that this was no time for ministers to recycle rational Calvinist doctrine. In pointing ministers to Calvin and the Reformation, Bryden was insisting that the experience of God's Judging–Saving Word, which had created the ministry of the Reformed churches, could create the reality of ministry in his day. Without such a divine Word, the church was left with ministers, however noble their intentions, who amounted to little more than purveyors of religious rituals.

Church and Society

It is true that Walter Bryden's doctrine of the church and its ministry may not have been initially popular among Canadian Protestants. But it was his views concerning church and society, rife with radical *obiter dicta*, and delivered

---

49 Bryden, *The Christian's Knowledge of God*, xi.
50 Fraser, *Church, College, and Clergy*, 156.

with the passion of a prophet, which, more often than not, created the real offence. If the church was a creature of the Word of God, Bryden believed, so too was the world in which the church found itself. And if God's Word was a word of judgment, then both church and society stood beneath revelation's glorious gaze and critical glare. The whole point of modern theology, Bryden argued, appeared to be to get out from under the scandal created by this judgment. As Bryden saw it, nothing less than the principle of critical theological thought in the life of the church was at stake.

Supremely conscious of the criticism that the neo-orthodox emphasis on the transcendence of God tended to make Christianity something that was not practical, Bryden refused to give an inch to idealism. Protestantism in its modern form, he argued, had domesticated the Christian gospel and aligned it with the culture. In the process, it had undermined the power of the church to offer a trenchant social critique. Instead of making Christianity more practical for the modern world, as it had intended, idealism had in fact robbed the church of that which made it profoundly practical. "If anything in this world becomes practical," Bryden argued, "it is that absolute Judging–Saving Word, descending from above, which by its very nature puts everything else in the world on the defensive." The church, even when oppressed and persecuted, "just because it is loyal to a Word which completely transcends this world, is serving the State, indeed saving it, and it is having practical effects on life which cannot be estimated." No one, if they thought about it carefully, was genuinely interested in a church which was so much like the world and its ideals that it never actually challenged them.[51] The Word of God, as a word of critical judgment in the life of the church, challenged every aspect of the Christian's faith and life including, and especially, the church's relationship to the social, economic, and political structures of the day.

The question of church and state in Canada, Bryden believed, was a case in point. It constituted one of the essential reasons for critical theological thought and ongoing confessional renewal. The Westminster Confession of Faith, despite its profound significance for Canadian Presbyterians, did not provide much help in guiding the church's relationship with the civil state in the Canadian context. "Even our own Canadian Presbyterian Church," Bryden noted, "many years ago recognized that certain injunctions embodied in the Westminster Confession and concerned with the relation of State to Church could have no possible pertinence to the conditions existing in a country like Canada."[52] Seventeenth-century revolutionary England was not twentieth-century Canada. Nevertheless, it was incumbent upon the Canadian church to be clear about its commitments and priorities, especially

---

[51]   Bryden, *The Christian's Knowledge of God*, 260.
[52]   Bryden, *Why I Am A Presbyterian*, 47.

in light of the lessons being learned in the German church struggle. The new national United Church of Canada did not appear to have a clear confessional position concerning its relation to the state, which only confirmed Bryden's decision to continue as a Presbyterian.

For these reasons, among others, he worked for the adoption of the new statement of faith which emphasized the Lordship of Jesus Christ over both church and state, and outlined the responsibilities of each toward the other. Here again, he reached back behind the seventeenth-century confessional standards to the early Reformers' view of the state as an ordinance of God, "with a function only less significant in the purposes of God than was that of the Church itself."[53] In the Reformers' minds the church had a saving function, while the state had a protective or preservative function. The state did not have the authority to compel faith. It did, however, as Bryden saw it in the Reformed tradition, have the authority to ensure that conditions were such that the Word of God was freely proclaimed. Any and all attempts by state and its culture to determine and condition that Word were to be resisted. The church and society together, as Bryden saw it, stood under the critical judgment of the Word. Judged from the perspective of Canadian society in the twenty-first century, Bryden's arguments, it might be argued, appear quaint at best. Religious pluralism and social secularism have forced the churches to rethink their role in a post-Christendom culture. Like the Reformers of the sixteenth century, Bryden never questioned the Christendom paradigm itself. Nevertheless, his prophetic critique continues to have theological relevance if for no other reason than that it relativizes both church and state in relation to the Word of God, and speaks to the issue of religious freedom. It would be doubtful, from Bryden's perspective, that a just society could emerge within a state which had granted itself supreme authority over all areas of life.

Writing during the 1930s, Bryden was conscious that nationalism posed a grave danger not only to the churches, but to western civilization as a whole. Like idealism, nationalism tended to undermine the distinctive witness of the church and, in the end, could only lead to violence and war. Bryden was not naïve, however, and recognized that the church ignored its context at its own peril. But the Word of God to which Bryden bore witness transcended ecclesial and cultural contexts. "Local or national conditions, it is true," Bryden noted, "must inevitably leave their distinctive marks upon any Church. The respective outlooks of this or that particular people will condition the atmosphere, even the ecclesiastical structures, of those Churches to which these people happen to belong. It has been so in the past; it is good that it is so; and it will continue." But all this was accidental to the real life of the church. The local difficulties, regional necessities, or national predilections were not to

---

53   Bryden, *The Christian's Knowledge of God*, 259.

take precedence over the Christian community's particular witness to Christ. "The Church is and shall remain the Church of God in so far as she is not indigenous with the soil of any country, or determined by the habits, thoughts and customs of any people." Bryden continued: "A Church which tends to become purely nationalistic in its instincts and in its outlook is rapidly becoming a hybrid Church. The true Church belongs to no age and no country, is conditioned by no climate, and, in the hearts of believing men, is supreme over all patriotisms or loyalties of any kind which receive the attention of men."[54] Bryden has been quoted at length here because these comments provide the foundation and the framework for his critique of church and society. He assumed the legitimacy of the social critique of religion and applied it to Canadian Protestantism with a result that looked stunningly different from the social gospel. Instead of ideals to be emulated, Bryden emphasized crises to be confronted.

In the first instance, Bryden trained his theological guns on the economic order and took direct aim at capitalism. His experience with the miners of Lethbridge had left a deep imprint. The church and the capitalist economic system were not necessary correlates in theory, Bryden argued, and he despaired at the way in which the Canadian churches had been infected by a materialist spirit and co-opted by a capitalist agenda. "The argument that the Church is dependent upon, and linked up with, the Capitalist system is not essentially true, if we are to think of the Church as consisting of a great host of humble people who are endeavoring, as best they can, to trust and serve God." Bryden went on, however: "But if we are to think of the Church in terms of its financial supports, in terms of those who would, and often do, guide its policies, there is not a little to be said in support of such an argument."[55] The fact that none of this was questioned during the church union movement made Bryden more than a little suspicious. The ecumenical movement in Canada, as important as it was, did not appear, at this stage of its life, to be concerned about issues of fundamental social justice. Worse, it created an atmosphere which militated against the self-criticism of the churches.

Contrary to what might have been the case, Bryden's critique of the convergence between capitalism and Christianity did not push him into the camp of the Social Gospel. Why? Simply put, Bryden saw the Social Gospel movement as an expression of idealism. In their eagerness to address the real social conditions of the twentieth century the advocates of the Social Gospel appeared somehow willing to jettison too much of what Bryden considered essential. To equate essential Christianity "with what is known today as Christian Socialism—as is often done—is to be guilty of the most insidious

---

[54] Bryden, *Why I Am A Presbyterian*, 74–75.
[55] Ibid., 114–15.

teaching; a teaching more dangerous to the Christian faith, because . . . it is presuming to measure both God and man's needs by man's purely humanitarian, oftentimes sentimental, needs as conditioned by the transient world, and as emphasized at the expense of his one supreme eternal need."[56] This is another example, it might be argued, where Bryden painted with a broad brush. He failed to interact carefully with the work of people like Salem Bland and Walter Rauschenbusch. It is to be noted, however, that by the early 1930s Bryden was taking his cue on this issue from Karl Barth and especially Reinhold Niebuhr. The optimism of the Social Gospel movement had been shattered by the mood of crisis created by economic depression and world war. Along with others, Bryden assumed the failure of the Social Gospel, but never recanted his commitment to the urgency of a social critique of religion and a theological critique of society.

A prophetic critique of church and society, Bryden never tired of reminding Canadian Protestants, had to be grounded in the theological realism of a robust doctrine of God. The Judging–Saving Word was the revelation of a God who was wholly other, transcendent, sovereign, and free. In Jesus Christ the righteousness of God had been revealed as that which stood *over* human beings in judgment, and *with* human beings in saving solidarity. Since the Word of God wished to redeem all things, nothing escaped the judgment of God. "There is a Righteousness of God," Bryden declared, "which brings into judgment all the varied righteousnesses of men, yea, all their loyalties, their patriotisms, their nationalisms, and totalitarianisms, and even their exclusive brotherhoods and boasted classisms. Such a God does not belong to any particular race or nation or to any particular class."[57] This was the vision of God which inhabited the faith and life of the earliest Reformers, who bowed in the dust before this transcendent God. When such a God was known and worshipped the church inevitably found itself in tension with the civil authorities.

A grand and glorious vision of God, Bryden believed, provided clarity concerning the nature of God's reign in the world. In the Social Gospel, according to Bryden, the Kingdom of God had been equated with social readjustment. It had become something which men and women could advance by their labors and by their thoughts alone. The ideals of optimism and progress seemed to constitute that which was essential to a Christian analysis of society. For Bryden, however, the Kingdom of God belonged to God and to God alone. The reign of God was something that could only be given by God and received by faith: faith which God alone created in the

---

[56] Ibid., 164.
[57] Bryden, "The Presbyterian Conception of the Word of God," Unpublished portion of manuscript, Presbyterian Church Archives, Bryden Fonds.

souls of men and women. If New Testament scholarship in the early twentieth century had taught the church anything, Bryden argued, it was that the Kingdom of God was to be understood in strictly eschatological and apocalyptic fashion. Writing during the Great Depression, Bryden reiterated the need for the church to remain steadfast to this understanding of God's reign: "The Church, however, knows that if the present economic distress were to pass—and, sooner or later, the present strain will doubtless become easier through some cause or other—the deeper needs of men are the same in the twentieth century as they were in the first . . . This, however, at no time means that Christians need not be interested in political matters. They, of all people, should press for social justice and economic reformations, where the conditions obviously demand such. But a mere social gospel is never the Christian Gospel, and the Kingdom of God is not to be equated with advances in social readjustment."[58]

Given Bryden's view of God's righteousness and reign, one might be tempted to think that he continued to toe a traditional Protestant line when it came to issues of social and economic justice. Nothing was further from the truth. He not only opposed the systems that seemed to enslave modern men and women, but he worked tirelessly to ferret out the theological ideas which were used to prop them up in the modern Canadian churches. The fundamental problem with capitalism, for example, was that it tended to dehumanize human beings and despoil democracy. As if that were not enough, it insinuated itself into the churches and domesticated the divine reality: "The sober fact is that nothing has ever appeared among men which has been more cynically regardless of any ethic worth the name than the ruthless, competitive economic system which is known as Capitalism, a system which economists tell us is by the very force of circumstances, i.e., to save itself from its own inherent weakness, taking the form of a strictly "monopolistic" Capitalism to-day. Nothing, moreover, has so succeeded in despoiling democracy of any beneficial significance it might originally have envisioned for mankind, and nothing has so tended to secularize the Christian faith, owing to the fact that the Church has become so dependent on its goodwill."[59]

The modern Canadian church was so indebted to capitalism, Bryden believed, that it had compromised its ability to provide a prophetic word. As a result, large segments of the population, especially the poor and the working classes, had been alienated from the churches. The church could not ignore the fact that men and women were in revolt "against a condition in which human beings are being made impersonal means to an impersonal economic end, and are, moreover, forced into a situation in which their very

---

[58] Bryden, "The Presbyterian Conception of the Word of God."
[59] Bryden, The Christian's Knowledge of God, 244.

subsistence is at the mercy of economic lords, and is dependent upon the ebb and flow of profitable markets, which markets the lords themselves manage to manipulate . . . to serve their own purposes, and with callous disregard to the effects of the general public."[60] In offering this prophetic critique, Bryden denied that he was either a socialist or a communist in any orthodox sense; he understood himself as someone under constraint to the Word of God.

The capitalist character of the Christian churches in Canada was controlled by what Bryden called "the banker mentality" which seemed to pervade every aspect of the church's life. Decisions in the spiritual realm that should have been shaped by critical theological reflection were made for purely economic and materialist reasons. The most prominent counselors of the churches, "especially those of the laity, are too frequently men with the mentality of the banker, the outlook upon life of the Rotarian, and a conception of the Church as an agency among others with a purpose to train and discipline people in the things which belong to the 'respectabilities,' and to insure [sic] for those who observe these "amenities" a favourable balance for the life to come."[61] The real threat to Christian faith, as Bryden understood it, "lies not in science, even though it may appear to have slain the gods, *but in the domestication of the radical faith of Jesus Christ in the middle-class society.*"[62] Bryden found it deplorable that the church could contemplate with complacency conditions in which subtle and selfish intrigue, pure ecclesiastical politics and secular ambitions could not only prevail but triumph in the church. Conventional moralisms and spiritual platitudes were propped up by the possession of wealth and so-called social prestige. The church, in short, had substituted the veneer of Christianity for the insight and knowledge of God.[63]

It has to be said that Bryden offered no social program based on his theological insights. But he didn't intend to. The neo-orthodox social ethic tended to be episodic, occasional, and ad hoc, in which the Word of God made its own point of contact with the conditions of the world. "The Christian's judgment," Bryden argued, "in regard to economic change must never be one of rigid rule, governed by abstract principles which may be in his possession by tradition or by prejudice. It must be a judgment prayerfully taken in light of circumstances which immediately confront him and with a concern for human welfare in general; with the belief, moreover, that He Who is the Lord of all that takes place in life will be his guide."[64] From this perspec-

---

60 Ibid., 246.
61 Ibid., 248.
62 Donald V. Wade, "The Theological Achievement of Walter W. Bryden."
63 Bryden, *Why I Am A Presbyterian.*
64 Bryden, *Separated Unto the Gospel,* 76.

tive, Walter Bryden saw his role as one called to witness to the Word of God within the life of the church. "Only the Judging–Saving Word which judges men as such, rich and poor, civilized alike," he argued, "ever succeeds in truly mellowing the hearts of men in such wise that they will be truly concerned about one another." The church, it was true, could not busy itself "in creating programs, political or social, which must pass with the passage of time." But in the transcendent Word which has been revealed the church must be the judge of everything that adversely affects the lives of men and women. It was only with this kind of profound consciousness in regard to the world's various needs that the Christian could maintain with sincerity that it was the church's responsibility to "preach the Gospel only."[65] The failure of idealism had taught Bryden that all power "to change in any essential way the individual or corporate life of man depends entirely on the Word and Spirit of God." "Apart from God's utterly judging, utterly saving Word, Jesus Christ," he wrote, "all human culture and achievements become corrupt."[66] In sum, the social critique of the church and the theological critique of society which Bryden envisioned began and ended with God's Judging–Saving Word.

In the aftermath of church union Bryden's prophetic critique of church and society did two things that shaped the direction of Canadian Presbyterianism for a generation to come. In the first place, it injected a note of theological self-criticism into the post-union debates of the continuing Church. The judgment of God's Word should begin, Bryden believed, with the household of Presbyterian faith. Secondly, Bryden destroyed every pretext of a foundation in Canadian Presbyterianism for a spiritualized gospel which failed to acknowledge the social, economic and political dimensions of life. And he did so without leading the continuing Presbyterian church in Canada into the Social Gospel. It is true that he painted with a broad brush and that, like a prophet with a single burden, his harping on the negative tended to become tiresome. But as a prophet, he bore the burden which had been placed upon him in a way that not only inspired a new generation of students and clergy, but instilled within them a deep, theologically informed, social conscience.

Church Union and Christian Unity

One of the arguments made throughout this book has been that Walter Bryden was one of the most able and articulate critics of church union in Canada. He provided a theological rationale for the continuing Church in

---

65   Bryden, *The Christian's Knowledge of God*, 259.

66   Bryden, "Continental Movements and the Theological Thought of Tomorrow," *United Church Observer* (June 1941).

his post-union apologetic for Presbyterianism. He marshaled the theology of Karl Barth and the dialectical theologians, especially their theology of revelation, and leveraged it to dislodge the rational idealism which had dominated Canadian Protestant theology since at least 1870. Bryden argued that church union was the culmination of a theological development that went back to the nineteenth century. In the debates leading up to church union, he contended, the Canadian Protestant churches had failed to account adequately for the new theological movements of the twentieth century. The result, he concluded, was a conception of ecumenicity that could not sustain true Christian unity and witness. The final section of this chapter examines these arguments briefly.

From Bryden's perspective the impetus for church union had come primarily from a desire to establish a larger, more efficient and better organized church in Canada. Concern for external organization, however, in his judgment, did not constitute a sufficient basis for the unity of any church. Absent from the debate, Bryden argued, was any discussion about what was meant by the unity of the Spirit. The debate appeared to be dominated by considerations that were practical and bureaucratic rather than theological and spiritual. This was true, he believed, on both sides of the controversy.

Among the reasons proposed for rejecting church union, Bryden found two sets of arguments insufficient. Firstly, opposition to church union that was motivated by a desire to maintain a Presbyterian denomination or a Presbyterian ecclesiastical system for its own sake was short-sighted. Presbyterianism was an expression of Christianity which traced its roots to the Reformation of the sixteenth century and as such, it had a beginning, and it might well have an end. It was not eternal in the sense that Christian revelation was eternal. Modern New Testament scholarship combined with contemporary ecumenical sensitivities disabled any and all attempts to identify Presbyterianism as the only true form of the church. Furthermore, essential Presbyterianism, as Bryden understood it, consisted of much more than what might be embodied in a particular national church or form of church government. Bryden knew full well that some of his own colleagues had been motivated to oppose church union by their desire to maintain a Scottish Presbyterian church for purely sentimental reasons. To Bryden, it all smacked of the same idealism that had fueled the church union movement in the first place. A commitment to Scottish and Presbyterian ideals, no matter how noble, was simply an insufficient reason to oppose church union.

Secondly, Bryden also found unpersuasive the arguments against church union given by the confessional Calvinist wing of the Presbyterian Church. It was true, he argued, that church union was a manifestation of ideals set forth clearly in the liberal Protestant tradition. But the opposition to church union could not be justified by an appeal to Calvinist orthodoxy. Simply reasserting Reformed doctrine and the ecclesial divisions that had accompanied it for three hundred years was a wholly inadequate response to the call for ecumenical cooperation.

What, then, did Bryden offer as "reasons sufficient for refusing to enter the proposed union"? Here, again, he emphasized two things. First, Bryden pointed out that actually one-half of Presbyterians in Canada opposed church union in the votes leading up to the creation of the United Church. The debate about the actual percentages for and against, to be sure, was quite rancorous in 1925 and afterwards. At one level Bryden recognized that it was futile to make the debate about numbers. Nevertheless, he argued, it was a challenging fact that so many Presbyterians said "no" to church union despite more than twenty years of pressure to acquiesce. Furthermore, it reflected, he believed, a fundamental mistrust by church members of their leaders. For whatever reasons, a considerable percentage of Presbyterians were unwilling to follow their leadership into the United Church on the basis of the arguments put forward. The promise of a new, more efficient national church simply did not capture the imagination of as many Presbyterians as the unionists had hoped.

That being said, Bryden came to the heart of his concern. The church union movement, he complained, had failed to address critical theological issues. There seemed to be little awareness among the proponents of church union of the manner in which their theological framework was being challenged, not in superficial, but in fundamental ways. Canadian Protestantism during the 1920s seemed strangely unaware of the theological and cultural developments that were shaking the foundations in other parts of the western world. The advocates of church union, for example, had not thought carefully about what constituted a confessing church in a rapidly changing culture. Church union was born out of expedience rather than faith and doctrine. It was the product of a modern ideal rather than a theological vision. It was manufactured by human effort rather than the will of God. The unionists had failed to grasp the meaning of true spiritual unity. They were right in emphasizing the importance of church unity. It was demanded by the gospel. It was not an option, and those who opposed church union on superficial grounds, Bryden believed, were rightly chastised. The Word of God demanded participation in the one body of Christ. The revelation of God required co-operation within the church. And here we arrive at the crucial connection between Bryden's conception of revelation and his understanding of church unity. The unity for which the church rightly longed was not only demanded by the gospel, it was presumed by the gospel. And the Word of God alone created that which it presumed. The unity of the church was created by God's

Judging–Saving Word and Spirit. When measured against this understanding, Bryden argued, the movement for institutional church union in Canada was far less than what a true movement for the unity of the church ought to be. Walter Bryden rose to prominence in the continuing Church because he was one of its few leaders who was theologically able and articulate enough to make this point with clarity and passion.

Bryden took the opposition to church union, upon which the continuing Church was initially based, and tried to transform it into a new vision for the unity and mission of the Protestant churches in Canada. It has to be said, of course, that he had little success in doing so outside his own Church. Nevertheless, he explored the prospects for unity and reunion among the churches in Canada. Unity among the Protestant churches, between the Protestant churches and the Roman Catholic Church, and even among the religions of the world, constituted a noble ideal from a humanitarian perspective. Christian unity, however, was the work of God in which human beings fully participated.

> True spiritual life issues from personal perception and individual choice, which are free and responsible, and yet which, at the same time, are under constraint of the Holy Spirit. Those people so constrained discover, so to speak, their oneness in Jesus Christ, and this constitutes true unity, the true catholicity, of the Church in Jesus Christ. It is a unity independent of all forms and expressions, but it always presupposes a faith, which at once implies a theology and is apprehended and sustained by such . . . . This is what I conceive to be central to the whole problem of unity among the Churches.[67]

Finally, Bryden set out three characteristic features of the church which he believed ought to provide the basis for unity. First, a church, if it was to justify itself as a true church of God, "must be conscious of possessing the Gospel." It must, in the words of Karl Barth, participate in, comprehend, and co-operate with the revelation of the gospel in Jesus Christ. Second, a true church must "be essentially and radically missionary in attitude and spirit." It must, in the words of Karl Barth, participate in, comprehend, and co-operate with the mission of God in the world. Third, a true church must be catholic. It must be a participation of the whole church in the whole gospel for the whole world.[68] To be true to the Reformed tradition at its best meant, Bryden believed, that the continuing Presbyterian Church in Canada could not respond to church union by withdrawing from the wider work of God in the church and the world. In short, he provided a way for Presbyterians to

---

67   Bryden, *Why I Am A Presbyterian*, 132.
68   Ibid., 162, 166, 169.

remain Presbyterians while affirming, in the words of the creed, the one, holy, catholic and apostolic church in Canada.

Throughout his lectures, books, and articles Walter Bryden endeavored to show that the supreme vocation of the church was consistently that of a witness. The church, above everything else, was called upon to point to what was above all mundane interests, namely that ultimate reality, God's Judging–Saving Word.[69] This was, in sum, the understanding of revelation and the church which Bryden believed was central to the faith and life of Luther and Calvin in the sixteenth century. This was the theology which Karl Barth and the dialectical theologians helped Bryden understand afresh. And this was the conception of faith which Bryden offered as a post-union theological rationale for the continuing Presbyterian Church after 1925, especially to theological students at Knox College, for whom Bryden became a model and mentor. In word and deed Walter Bryden was a prophetic witness who led the continuing Presbyterian Church beyond modernism and fundamentalism to neo-orthodoxy. He pointed to the Divine Word on which he believed the church might journey, if not more surely and securely, then at least more faithfully and prophetically. This was, at its heart, the neo-orthodox theological protest which constituted the theological contribution of Walter Williamson Bryden to Protestantism in North America, especially in Canada, in the second quarter of the twentieth century.

---

[69]   Bryden, "After Modernism, What?" Conclusion.

6

The Witness of W. W. Bryden and the Neo-Orthodox Legacy

Walter Bryden is truly a remarkable theologian. I can't help but think that he is more like John Calvin than anyone I've ever known.[1]
—Thomas F. Torrance

It is impossible to understand Dr. Bryden's theology except as the fulfillment in a special sphere of this task of evangelist. His concern even in the most involved intellectual consideration was that the Gospel might be heard and believed.[2]
—James D. Smart

WALTER Williamson Bryden, as the foregoing pages have endeavored to demonstrate, lived an authentically theological existence during a critical period in Canadian Protestantism. For a generation or so following his death the verdict of history within the Presbyterian Church in Canada was more than kind. He was described as an evangelist for the church, a preacher's theologian, a servant of the Word, a prophet and apostle. James D. Smart attributed the renewed interest in theology which occurred within Canadian Presbyterianism during the 1930s and 1940s largely to Bryden's influence. Donald V. Wade noted that upwards of twenty of Bryden's students became professors around the world. Despite the fact that he had opposed church union, Bryden became known increasingly as someone whose thought had deep ecumenical significance. Although his theology gained no widespread hearing outside Canada, his books were read with critical inter-

---

[1] This was a comment made by Thomas F. Torrance to Donald V. Wade and cited in Wade's paper "The Theological Achievement of Walter Bryden," March, 1974.
[2] James D. Smart, "The Theologian as Evangelist," *Separated Unto the Gospel*, viii.

est in England, Scotland, and the United States. Daniel Day Williams of Union Seminary in New York, as noted earlier, asked his students to read *The Christian's Knowledge of God* as a classical example of neo-orthodoxy.[3]

Nevertheless, the long term prospects for the neo-orthodox theology of revelation espoused by Walter Bryden turned out to be less than stellar. By the early 1960s the daring paradoxes that had so impressed an earlier generation of theological students now sounded like stale platitudes. The turbulent culture within which the church found itself made it clear that the center would not likely hold and that it would be increasingly difficult for any theological consensus to prevail. Neo-orthodoxies, to quote Brian Fraser, were being replaced by diverging orthodoxies.[4] Perhaps Bryden, who insisted that each generation had to confess the Christian faith anew for itself, as its own faith, would not have been unsettled by these developments. At the same time, one suspects that he would have been more than a little suspicious of the renewed idealism and rationalism that seemed to emerge from a chastened liberal Protestantism.

The concluding chapter briefly examines the Bryden legacy from three different perspectives. They are: (1) Bryden's influence on a subsequent generation of Presbyterian ministers and theologians during the 1930s, 1940s, and 1950s, (2) the eventual decline and fall of neo-orthodoxy during the 1960s and 1970s, and (3) the continuing significance of Bryden's theological contribution for Canadian Protestantism at the beginning the twenty-first century.

Bryden: The Next Generation

The Bryden legacy was firmly in place at Knox College and in the Presbyterian Church in Canada well before Walter Bryden died in March 1952. An increasing number of theological students and clergy were convinced that the continuing Church had an important and valuable contribution to make to the Canadian church and nation through the neo-Reformation theology that Bryden taught. By the mid 1930s many of them had already picked up the torch he had lit. At times Bryden stood strangely aloof from the debates and allowed his students to lead. On other occasions he found himself in the midst of theological controversy. If the influence of a theological position can be measured by the amount of opposition it generates, then it has to be said that Bryden's neo-orthodox theology of revelation gained considerable ecclesial ground in a few short years.

---

[3]   Donald V. Wade, "The Theological Achievement of Walter Bryden," 3.

[4]   Brian J. Fraser, *Church, College, and Clergy*, 14.

The debate about the influence of the so-called Barthian theology in the Presbyterian Church emerged in a heated exchange that took place in the pages of *The Presbyterian Student*. Published by the students of the Presbyterian College (Montreal), Knox College (Toronto), and the Missionary and Deaconess Training Home (Toronto), the journal's policy was "to provide a medium for the free expression of ideas, believing that the discussion they provoke leads to the mental and spiritual development necessary for intelligent Christianity." In 1937 the journal had run a series of articles dealing with the church situation in Germany. The February issue carried a piece by James D. Smart, one of Bryden's earliest students, who wrote on the significance, for the Canadian church, of the conflict within the German church. He reminded Canadian Presbyterians that they faced the same questions and temptations as did the Christians of Germany. The same issue carried a strongly worded, even pugnacious, call by Arthur Cochrane, to heed the voice of Karl Barth and the confessional church. Cochrane, one of Bryden's students, had gone to study with Barth in Germany and Switzerland, and later went on to become professor of theology at Dubuque Theological Seminary in Iowa.[5]

All of this was too much for Frank Beare who taught at the Presbyterian College, Montreal. In an article called "Against the Barthian Theology," Beare declared war on those Canadian Presbyterians who had developed, in his judgment, "an unquestioning adherence to the theology of Karl Barth, and in some cases a kind of terrifying dogmatic intolerance to which this theology appears to give birth." Beare challenged them at every key point. He had the impression that Barth suffered at the hands of his followers and interpreters, almost as seriously as "the wide and generous mind of Calvin suffered at the hands of Barth himself." In addition to questioning the legitimacy of their appeal to the Reformers, Beare rejected their view of revelation. "Christian thought has never looked upon the revelation of God in Christ," he argued, "as the annihilation of non-Christian knowledge, but as its consummation and crown." The Word of God, far from being absolute and unique, comes to human beings, at least in seminal form, through other religions, philosophies, and cultures. The reality of God, far from being wholly other, was to be found and experienced by human beings, who bear the image of God. The Barthians, Beare lamented, paid only lip service to the historical-critical study of the Bible. In conclusion, Beare declared, Canadian Presbyterians should not be ready "to adopt the semi-Mohammedan creed that 'There is one God,

---

[5] James D. Smart, "The Conflict Within The Church," *The Presbyterian Student* 2.3 (Feb. 1937) 2–4; Arthur C. Cochrane, "Karl Barth and the Confessional Church," *The Presbyterian Student* 2.3 (Feb. 1937) 8–9.

and Karl Barth is his prophet.'" Judging from the rhetoric, Beare had been annoyed and offended most by Cochrane's polemical and provocative tone.[6]

The December 1937 issue of *The Presbyterian Student* carried a response by Smart who took issue with Beare's characterization of the debate as between "broad-minded tolerance and narrow bigotry." The issue, as Smart saw it, was between two irreconcilable views of the nature of Christianity. At its core, the difference revolved around the meaning of revelation. Was revelation to be understood as the sum total of all the best thoughts of the world's wisest teachers, or was a particular revelation marked off definitely from the general wisdom and spirituality of men and women? The former view, held by Schleiermacher and the liberal Protestant tradition, and espoused by Beare in Canada, was precisely the view to which Barth was responding. Beare had misled himself into thinking that he was sounding the first blast of the trumpet when in fact, Smart concluded, the battle was already far advanced.[7]

This particular phase of the debate came to a conclusion with an article by Smart in March 1938 called "Is Karl Barth's Theology Extremist?" Responding to charges in Canada and Britain that Barth's theology was beyond the pale of moderate Presbyterian theology, Smart argued that Barth represented the Reformed tradition at its best. Canadian Presbyterians could learn a great deal from the Swiss theologian who had directed theology back to the church and the church back to theology. Barth's critical recovery of the Scripture principle and the Reformed confessions, Smart contended, made it possible for modern men and women to be Presbyterians in the fullest sense of the word "and to be neither shamed nor embarrassed by the historic doctrinal standards" of the church.[8]

Walter Bryden neither participated directly in this exchange nor was his name mentioned in any of the articles. His influence, however, was everywhere evident. As Bryden's students, Smart and Cochrane had been introduced to Bryden's emerging neo-Reformation emphasis and had gone on to discover and study Barth's theology for themselves. As they sought to introduce Barth's theology to Canadian Presbyterians, they emphasized many of the neo-orthodox themes that were central in Bryden's teaching and writing, especially the rejection of idealism and rationalism. For Beare's part, he knew full well that in taking up arms against the Barthians in Canada he was battling the influence of Walter Bryden through whom Barth's theology had

---

[6] Frank Beare, "Against the Barthian Theology," *The Presbyterian Student* 2.4 (March 1937) 9–10.

[7] James D. Smart, "Defence and Counter Attack," *The Presbyterian Student* 3.1 (December 1937) 5–9, 27.

[8] James D. Smart, "Is Karl Barth's Theology Extremist?," *The Presbyterian Student* 3.3 (March 1938) 8–14.

found its way into the Canadian church. In the midst of it all Bryden appeared to stand back, content to let the next generation carry the torch.

By the early 1940s many of the students and clergy who had been influenced by Bryden organized themselves. In June 1941 a group began to meet informally under Bryden's leadership to discuss the future of the Westminster Confession of Faith in light of Barth's theology. In fact, Bryden had been instrumental in setting up such discussion groups for over a decade in order to pursue theological conversation. In December 1944, however, the group organized itself more formally as the Canadian Trinitarian Theological Society. The purpose of the society was "to meet regularly for the study, discussion, and dissemination of the Trinitarian theology," and its membership was "open to all Church-men in Canada who share the conviction that all the problems facing the Church are fundamentally theological in nature." The group consisted mainly of ministers from the Presbyterian Church and the United Church who continued to meet together until the late 1950s. Many of the Presbyterians who participated in the early years, including Bryden, also participated in the work of the Articles of Faith Committee and the movement to draft a new confession.[9]

Some of the ministers associated with the Trinitarian Theological Society were instrumental in the publication of a quarterly journal called *Crisis Christology*. Published between 1943 and 1948 in Dubuque, Iowa under the sub-title "With Christ in the Crisis," the journal carried no fewer than thirty-three articles by Canadian Presbyterians. Prominent among the contributors were Walter Bryden, J. Stanley Glen, Louis Sheen, Arthur C. Cochrane, Donald V. Wade, Charles Cochrane, Stuart Coles, Gordon Peddie, and Scarth MacDonnell. Glen, who succeeded Bryden as principal of Knox College in 1952, wrote about the practical aspects of the crisis of power, religious collectivism and Christian denominationalism, and contributed a study of the First Epistle of John. Louis Sheen, who became professor of philosophy at McMaster University, wrote articles on the relation of the church to the state, the Christian ministry as a spiritual power in modern society, and Kierkegaard's view of sin and despair. Arthur Cochrane wrote a series on Karl Barth's doctrine of God, the problem of revelation in church proclamation, and the knowledge of God in Reformed confessions. Donald Wade, who succeeded Bryden in the chair of the history and philosophy of religion at Knox College in 1947, contributed a series of articles on Kierkegaard's philosophy. Bryden himself contributed three articles. Without exception, the journal printed articles which were intended to advance the cause of the renewed Protestantism that had emerged through the influence of Karl Barth's theology. It not only sounded the note of crisis; it also represented the increasing

---

[9] Minutes of the Trinitarian Theological Society, The Presbyterian Church Archives.

influence of European theology mediated to Canada directly by Canadian theologians.[10]

By the 1950s the neo-orthodox impulse in Canadian Protestantism had aligned itself with the biblical theology movement, largely through the influence of James Smart. The movement, strongest between 1945 and 1965 in the United States and Canada, sought to recover the theological message of the Bible by emphasizing the unity of the Old and New Testaments, revelation as the acts of God in history, and the distinctive character of the biblical worldview. After graduation from Knox College in 1929, Smart completed a doctorate in Near Eastern Studies at the University of Toronto, studied in Germany, and served in three successive Presbyterian pastorates in Ontario. During the 1940s he served in Philadelphia as editor of "The Christian Faith and Life" curriculum of the Presbyterian Church U.S.A.. Smart rose to prominence in Canada and the United States initially through two long seminal articles published in 1944 in the *Journal of Religion* under the title "The

---

10   Louis Sheen, "The Relation of the Church to the State," *Crisis Christology* 1.3, 22–29; "The Christian Ministry as a Spiritual Power in Modern Society," *Crisis Christology* 1.4, 13–21; "An Analysis of Kierkegaard's View of Sin and Despair," *Crisis Christology* 2.1, 19–30. J. Stanley Glen, "Some Practical Aspects of the Crisis of Power," *Crisis Christology* 1.4, 7–12; "Religious Collectivism or Christian Denominationalism," *Crisis Christology* 2.3, 10–15; "A Brief Introduction to the First Epistle of John," *Crisis Christology* 4.3, 3–7. Arthur C. Cochrane, "The Triune God, A Study in the Theology of Karl Barth," *Crisis Christology* 1.4, 30–39; "The Grace and Holiness of God," *Crisis Christology* 2.2, 31–36; "The Mercy and Righteousness of God," *Crisis Christology* 2.3, 16–24; "The Patience and Wisdom of God," *Crisis Christology* 2.4, 46–53; "The Oneness and Omnipresence of God," *Crisis Christology* 3.1, 22–35; "The Immutability and Omnipotence of God," *Crisis Christology* 3.2, 11–20; "The Eternity and Glory of God," *Crisis Christology* 3.3, 20–27; "The Problem of Revelation in Church Proclamation," *Crisis Christology* 3.4, 23–40; "Review of *The Two-Edged Sword*, Sermons by Norman Langford," *Crisis Christology* 3.4, 43–44; "The Knowledge of God in the Church of England and Reformed Church Standards," *Crisis Christology* 4.4, 8–21. Donald V. Wade, "Kierkegaard's Concept of Individuality Compared and Contrasted With the Philosophical View," *Crisis Christology* 2.2, 16–30; "A Voice in the Wilderness (God in Kierkegaard)," *Crisis Christology* 3.3, 11–19; "God in Kierkegaard (Worms in Adam)," *Crisis Christology* 3.4, 14–22; "Decision, the Golden Key of the Soul (God in Kierkegaard)," *Crisis Christology* 4.1, 22–35; "The Boundless Grace of God—God in Kierkegaard," *Crisis Christology* 4.2, 8–21; "They That Worship Him—God in Kierkegaard," *Crisis Christology* 4.3, 27–45. Charles C. Cochrane, "An Exposition of Matthew 10:28-33," *Crisis Christology* 2.3, 29–33; "The Centurion's Case and Ours," *Crisis Christology* 4.2, 3–7. Gordon Peddie, "The Lord Hath Triumphed—Excerpts from a V-E Day Sermon," *Crisis Christology* 2. 4, 6–8. Stuart Coles, "Holy Church and Holy Scripture—The Question of Authority," *Crisis Christology* 4.2, 22–38; "After the Order of Melchizedec," *Crisis Christology* 5.1, 29–33; "Activities of the Canadian Trinitarian Theological Society," *Crisis Christology* 5.1, 34–35; "A Theological Discussion," *Crisis Christology* 5.3, 20–35. Scarth MacDonnell, "The Doctrine of Confirmation—Roman Catholic and Protestant," *Crisis Christology* 4.4, 22–40. Bryden, "The Holy Spirit and the Church," *Crisis Christology* 2.1, 5–18; "The Church of God and the World," *Crisis Christology* 4.1, 3–21; "St. Paul, the Preacher, as Separated Unto the Gospel," *Crisis Christology* 5.1, 3–9.

Death and Rebirth of Old Testament Theology." In 1957 he was appointed as Jessup Professor of Biblical Interpretation at Union Theological Seminary in New York.

Barth's 1922 commentary on Romans, Smart believed, set in motion a hermeneutical revolution which turned Protestant theology away from "a purely historical interpretation to a consciously and responsibly histori- cal-theological interpretation." As a pioneering work in theological exege- sis, Barth's commentary introduced changes to biblical interpretation which resulted in the disentangling of the historical-critical method from liberal Protestant theology. While Bryden and Smart both wholly embraced Barth's hermeneutics, it has to be said that they had been schooled in a tradition, dating back to the late nineteenth century in Canada, which did not force a choice between evangelical piety and historical criticism. In this sense, Barth confirmed and broadened the theological instincts that had already been at work for them. As a biblical scholar, Smart sought to advance the use of the historical critical method in the service of theological exegesis and biblical preaching. The biblical theology movement, therefore, as he understood it, had a much broader and richer agenda than that which might be identified with so-called neo-orthodox theology alone. Despite Smart's caveats, how- ever, it was quite clear that the biblical theology movement of the 1950s owed its life, as Brevard Childs noted, to the theological consensus identified with neo-orthodoxy.[11]

The significance of this consensus was not lost on Canadian Protestant theologians. In his presidential address to the Canadian Society of Biblical Studies in Toronto in May 1955, for example, Eugene Fairweather of Trinity College optimistically identified three promising features of the biblical the- ology movement. First, it sought to recover the authentically theological di- mension of the biblical text by rescuing it from its historical and archeological imprisonment as a manual of Near Eastern history or a source-book for the comparative study of religions. Second, biblical theology was eminently ecu- menical since it urged a return *ad fontes* bypassing much of ecclesial tradition and confessional theology. And third, it sought to avoid the imposition of an alien metaphysic and anthropology upon the Bible and theology.[12]

Also during the 1950s a new generation of theological students edu- cated by Principal Bryden found their way to Scotland for graduate study, often to work with the distinguished Church of Scotland theologian Thomas

---

[11] James D. Smart, *The Past, Present, and Future of Biblical Theology* (Philadelphia: Westminster, 1979) 61–80; Brevard S. Childs, *Biblical Theology in Crisis* (Philadelphia: Westminster, 1970) 9–50.

[12] Eugene Fairweather, "Christian Theology and the Bible," *Canadian Journal of Theology* 2.2, (1956) 65–75.

F. Torrance. Torrance, senior editor of the English translation of Karl Barth's *Church Dogmatics*, was at the time undoubtedly the most thorough English interpreter of Barth, and made an enduring contribution to theology based on the neo-orthodox emphasis on the objectivity of the divine Word. Torrance contended that Christian theology was a positive science and that its method, especially as practiced by Karl Barth, was analogous to the scientific method of modern physics. The Barthian theology of revelation, Torrance argued, emphasized that theological method is governed by its proper object. "In theology we have to do with a divine Object that demands and creates reciprocity so that our knowledge of God involves right from the start a union and not a disjunction between subject and object." As Torrance saw it, God is the divine object who makes human knowledge of the divine self possible through union with human subjects. But God reveals the divine self in a way that does not entangle God in human subjectivity. It is precisely because God distinguishes the divine self from us that we are enabled by God to know God.[13] Given the striking similarities with which Bryden and Torrance understood the modern religious situation and the importance of Barth's theology of revelation, it is not difficult to understand the enthusiasm with which Bryden introduced Torrance to Canadian Presbyterians at the 1950 pre-Assembly congress.

Nowhere was Bryden's influence during this period felt more strongly than at Knox College. As Brian Fraser has noted, in "the seven years from 1945 until 1952 when Bryden served as principal of Knox College, he put his stamp on the institution as well as its graduates."[14] Most of the new faculty who were appointed by the General Assembly to Knox between 1944 and 1952 were former students who acknowledged Bryden's formative influence. They were shaped by and committed to the core affirmations of the neo-orthodox theology of revelation that had become the dominant theological paradigm among Presbyterian church leaders. The next three principals of Knox, J. Stanley Glen from 1952 to 1976, Allan Farris from 1976 to 1977, and J. Charles Hay from 1978 to 1985, were students of Bryden's who worked hard to ensure that the theological and ecclesiastical culture Bryden had established continued to shape the college's graduates. Glen had become professor of New Testament in 1945 while Farris had succeeded Bryden in the chair of church history in 1952. Hay had been inducted into the new chair of homiletics, evangelism, and church administration after serving for eighteen years as a parish minister. The position in Old Testament was filled by D. Keith Andrews in 1945, and in 1947 Donald V. Wade was inducted

---

[13]   T. F. Torrance, *Theological Science*, 307–8. See Gary Dorrien, *The Barthian Revolt in Modern Theology*, 161.

[14]   Fraser, *Church, College, and Clergy*, 166.

into the newly created chair of the history and philosophy of religion and Christian ethics, in order to relieve Bryden's load of teaching two subjects in addition to being principal. All were indebted to Bryden's influence. They combined a commitment to historical critical scholarship with theological exegesis, and emphasized Bryden's evangelical catholicism, rooted in the tradition of Calvin and the Reformation. They saw the writing of creeds and confessions as the church's response to God's revelation. They pointed to a Reformed theology of Word and Spirit. They shared Bryden's suspicion of ecclesiasticism and continued to marshal the social critique of religion in the service of a theological critique of society. While each, in his own way, did far more than parrot what had been learned from Walter Bryden, there was never a doubt, from the late 1940s on, that the neo-orthodox theology of revelation had become the established position of Canadian Presbyterians.[15]

Neo-Orthodoxy in Crisis

By the 1960s it was quite clear that neo-orthodoxy had become a theology *in* crisis rather than a theology *of* crisis. In a 1965 article in *The Christian Century,* Langdon Gilkey sounded the alarm with respect to the neo-orthodox consensus that had prevailed in North American Protestantism since the end of World War Two. Until 1960, Gilkey argued, most North American theologians were comfortable with the basis of their task, fashioned by the great theologians of the 1920s, 1930s, and 1940s. The younger theologians often saw themselves as scholastics whose task was to work out in greater detail the firm theological principles already forged by their teachers. But during the 1960s, especially under the influence of the potent secularism of the day, there was a steady dissolution of many of the theological certainties of the previous three decades. Gilkey described it as "the washing away of the firm ground on which our generation believed we were safely standing." "What we thought was solid earth," he wrote, "has turned out to be shifting ice—and in recent years as the weather has grown steadily warmer some of us have in horror found ourselves staring down into rushing depths of dark water." This theological uncertainty was even more pronounced, Gilkey argued, among the younger ministers who were called upon to preach not only of doubt but of faith, not only of loss but also of finding, not only of despair but also hope.[16]

The growing lack of confidence in the neo-orthodox consensus, however, reflected more than a general sense of its inadequacy to address a changing

---

[15] Fraser, *Church, College, and Clergy,* 165–78.

[16] Langdon Gilkey, "Dissolution and Reconstruction in Theology," *Christian Century* 82.5 (Feb. 3, 1965) 135.

cultural situation. A new generation of theologians questioned the theological categories with which neo-orthodoxy had worked, especially the neo-orthodox conception of revelation. In a striking reinterpretation of the idea of revelation, German theologian Wolfhart Pannenberg and his colleagues led the way in proposing what they argued was "a more open, less authoritarian view of an important theological concept."[17]

Contemporary Protestant theology, by which Pannenberg meant primarily neo-orthodoxy, had been quick to characterize itself "as a pure theology of revelation." Barth's theology, Pannenberg charged, had been walled off against any mixture of "natural, non-theological, and non-Christian knowledge." Only that which could be established on the revelation of Christ was accepted as valid as a dogmatic statement.[18] Barth's antipathy against natural theology, which arose from a desire to emphasize the uniqueness of revelation in Christ, resulted in a reductionist conception of revelation.

In particular, Pannenberg and his colleagues took aim at the idea of revelation as self-revelation at the center of the neo-orthodox project. The revelation of God in neo-orthodoxy was not "God's making known a certain set of arcane truths, but—as Karl Barth puts it—the self-disclosure of God."[19] In one sense, Pannenberg argued, Barth simply carried forward an idea that Christian theology had always affirmed: that in every revelation God's prime disclosure was of the divine self. The new emphasis, however, was "the exclusive use of the concept "revelation" to mean the self-disclosure of God, without any imparting of supernatural truths." This innovation, Pannenberg argued, was the legacy of German idealism. The Enlightenment had destroyed the identification of revelation with the inspiration of the Bible, "the understanding of revelation as the transmission of supernatural and hidden truths." The assertion of such a revelation smacked of obscurantism that avoided the light of scientific reason. From the nineteenth century forward, therefore, the suspicion that supernaturalism was superstition required that the concept of revelation be rescued. The strategy employed by theologians, Pannenberg argued, was to reduce the content of revelation to God's *self*-revelation. Barth, therefore, was like Schleiermacher in one important respect: he chose to limit the concept of revelation to the religious sphere in the face of the Enlightenment critique.[20]

Pannenberg contended that the strictly-defined concept of revelation as the self-revelation of the absolute was introduced first by Hegel. With Hegel

---

[17]   Wolfhart Pannenberg, editor, *Revelation as History*, trans. David Granskou (London: Macmillan, 1968).

[18]   Wolfhart Pannenberg, "Introduction," in *Revelation as History*, 3.

[19]   Ibid., 4. See Karl Barth, *Church Dogmatics*, I/1 (1957) 340ff.

[20]   Pannenberg, *Revelation as History*, 4.

it became clear for the first time that the full self-revelation of God could only be a unique manifestation. "Hegel expressly reserved the designation 'a revealed and revealing religion' for Christianity," Pannenberg argued, "not because it contains truths that have been transmitted by supernatural means, but because, in distinction from all other religions, it rests on full disclosure of the nature of the absolute as spirit."[21] After Hegel, therefore, it was no longer permissible to think of a medium of revelation that was distinct from God himself.

The Hegelian Philipp Marheineke spelled out the implications of this for Christian faith clearly. As the medium of revelation, the man Jesus Christ was caught up to God in his distinctiveness and received in unity with God himself. A means of revelation that in itself, remained creaturely and held to its distinctiveness from God would, of course, imply a pollution of the divine light, presuppose an inadequate manifestation, and prevent the development of a full revelation. Marheineke argued that it was "not through the human spirit as such that God is revealed, but through [God] himself and then to the human spirit."[22] This understanding of revelation, Pannenberg noted, was echoed in Karl Barth's thesis that God's revelation to a human being cannot be apprehended by her or his own power, but only by means of God through the Holy Spirit. Barth, in fact, repeatedly cited this sentence from Marheineke and affirmed its truth.[23]

Pannenberg noted that Barth's understanding of revelation had other roots as well, and that to trace the origins of a theological idea to German idealism was not automatically to condemn it. Pannenberg's argument, however, demonstrates clearly, as was argued earlier, that Barth was an idealist of a higher order, and that the neo-orthodox theologians, including Walter Bryden, used distinctively modern ideas to overturn liberal Protestantism.[24] The idealist roots of this concept, however, did not constitute the problem, as Pannenberg saw it. The weakness of this position was that Barth's strict conception of God's self-disclosure issued in "a novel stress on the *uniqueness of revelation.*" In the hands of Barth revelation, by definition, became self-revelation. The exclusive locus of this self-revelation was Jesus Christ in whom the fullness of God was disclosed decisively. All other possibilities for revelation were ruled out of court.[25] On this basis, theologians had to do what

---

21 Ibid., 5.

22 Philipp Marheineke in ibid., 5.

23 Ibid.

24 Bruce McCormack cites the description of Barth as a "Hermannian of a higher order" favorably with reference to Barth's reformulation of the Marburg neo-Kantian emphasis on the self-authenticating character of self-revelation. See *Karl Barth's Critically Realistic Dialectical Theology*, 67.

25 Pannenberg, *Revelation as History*, 5–6.

Pannenberg could not accept: plead a special case. Theology, if it was to be truly scientific, Pannenberg contended, had to subject itself to rational scientific judgments which were universally acceptable and accessible.

Pannenberg was willing to concede that the neo-orthodox conception of revelation might have been justified if it could have been confirmed on the basis of the biblical witness. But it couldn't. At first glance, he contended, the biblical writings did not use the term revelation to refer to the self-revelation of God. Even the biblical term "the Word of God" did not have, or was only on the verge of having, the meaning that modern personalistic theology invested in it. "The modern personalistic theology of the Word (influenced by Ferdinand Ebner, Martin Buber, and others)," Pannenberg declared, "where Word is primarily the direct engagement of a person to a Thou, has its closest parallel not in the specifically biblical context, but rather in the Gnostic understanding of the Word."[26] It had to be concluded, then, that the theological assertion of a direct self-revelation of God as the only meaning of revelation could not be justified on the basis of the biblical conceptions of revelation.[27]

In place of the neo-orthodox theology of revelation Pannenberg and his colleagues proposed that revelation no longer be understood in terms of a supernatural disclosure or of a peculiarly religious experience and religious subjectivity, but in terms of the comprehensive whole of reality, which was a temporal process of a history that is not yet completed, but open to a future, and which was anticipated in the teaching and personal history of Jesus. To speak of revelation in this way, Pannenberg argued against fundamentalism, neo-orthodoxy and liberalism, did not involve any irreducible claims to authority, but was open to rational discussion and investigation.[28]

It is beyond the scope of this book to offer a critical analysis of Pannenberg's critique and the responses it generated. To do so would be to move into another chapter in the development of the conception of revelation in contemporary Protestant theology. Suffice it to say that Pannenberg's critique did not, as the work of McCormack, Hunsinger, Webster, and others has ably demonstrated, ultimately overturn the significance of Barth's theology for a new generation of scholars in North America and Britain. Indeed, one of the features of Barth's theology is that it continues to transcend the criticisms made against neo-orthodoxy. Nevertheless, in the 1960s, and in the context of this exposition of the theology of Walter Bryden and the neo-orthodox theology of revelation, Pannenberg's critique makes two things explicitly clear. First, the neo-orthodox theologians were truly modern theologians who employed modern categories to overturn liberal Protestantism.

---

[26]   Ibid., 12.

[27]   Ibid., 13.

[28]   Ibid., ix.

Second, the neo-orthodox definition of revelation as self-revelation did not initially withstand the scrutiny of a new generation of theologians because it appeared to lack biblical warrant and, equally serious, it seemed to wall off theology against any mixture of natural, non-theological and non-Christian knowledge. In sum, the neo-orthodox theology of revelation, its critics argued, created special categories that were not open to rational discussion and investigation.

As it happened, Wolfhart Pannenberg's attack against the neo-orthodox theology of revelation was only one of many that emerged in the 1960s. Langdon Gilkey uncovered the inconsistency of the neo-orthodox theologians when they spoke of divine activity using both orthodox and naturalistic language.[29] In *The Semantics of Biblical Language* (1961), James Barr dismantled the distinction between the Hebrew and Greek mentality of the Bible and showed how the biblical categories of "revelation" and "Word of God" had been inflated by the dialectical theologians.[30] As noted earlier, Van Harvey demonstrated that the neo-orthodox theologians employed a radical interpretation of justification by faith, which permitted them to accept the new morality of historical knowledge. That same radical view seemed to permit the conclusion that faith had no essential relationship to a past historical event. It seemed to suggest, therefore, the disengagement of theology and history.[31] John Hick and Wilfrid Cantwell Smith, among others, questioned the Barthian equation of religion with unbelief and argued that the neo-orthodox insistence on the uniqueness and absolute character of the revelation of God in Jesus Christ militated against genuine dialogue with other religions. The result of this barrage was that, in the words of Brevard S. Childs, "the breakdown of the theological consensus that had been held together with the amorphous category of 'Neo-orthodoxy' came more quickly than anyone could have imagined."[32]

The internal theological critiques were exacerbated by the added pressure of secularism which seemed, for many, to make the wholly-other God of neo-orthodoxy appear distant and displaced, far removed from the social

---

[29]   Langdon Gilkey, "Cosmology, Ontology, and the Travail of Biblical Language," *Journal of Religion* 61 (1961) 194–205. This was not, however, Gilkey's last word about the theology of Karl Barth. In a later essay he remarks how, to his surprise, graduate students at the University of Chicago in the 1980s continued to be interested in Barth's theology. Gilkey also noted that he was formed earlier in his career as a neo-orthodox theologian in America, without ever having read Karl Barth seriously. See Gilkey, "An Appreciation of Karl Barth," in *How Karl Barth Changed My Mind*, edited by Donald K. McKim (Grand Rapids: Eerdmans, 1986) 150–55.

[30]   James Barr, *The Semantics of Biblical Language* (Oxford: Oxford University Press, 1961).

[31]   Harvey, *The Historian and the Believer: The Morality of Historical Knowledge and Christian Belief* (New York: Macmillan, 1966) 131.

[32]   Childs, *Biblical Theology in Crisis*, 78.

and political experiences of people in church pews. The tensions, ambiguities, apparent uncertainties, and paradoxes, in which many of the neo-orthodox theologians delighted, no longer seemed relevant. In fact, Sydney Ahlstrom has argued that "probably no other aspect of neo-orthodoxy led to so much confusion in American churches with their long tradition of unambiguous, rationalistic moralism" and "their literal, propositional understanding of revelation."[33] Canadian Protestants, to be sure, seemed to possess a higher degree of tolerance for ambiguity. Nevertheless, even Canadian soil was not fertile enough to allow the neo-orthodox theology of revelation to take root long-term. Under Bryden's influence and Barth's enduring significance, however, The Presbyterian Church in Canada produced *The Declaration Concerning Church and Nation* and *Living Faith*, both of which show Barth's influence. They illustrate, contrary to the claims of many Canadian historians, that Barth's theology was heeded in the councils of some of the quarters of Canadian Protestantism.

The mark of Walter Bryden's influence on the Canadian Presbyterian church was so deep "that when in the 1960s the self-questioning and self-doubt began to ferment, it was Bryden's legacy around which, and often against which, the questions arose."[34] Diverging theologies became increasingly apparent among the faculty at Knox College and within the leadership of the Presbyterian Church as the neo-Reformation tradition espoused by Bryden was developed and applied in different ways. It was also challenged directly from within the church as being too parochial (by the ecumenically minded), too conservative (in light of new emerging secular theologies), and too liberal (by a confessional orthodoxy renewed through neo-evangelicalism).

Beneath all the criticisms were concerns about the neo-orthodox theology of the Word that had instilled new confidence in the continuing Presbyterian Church in the second quarter of the twentieth century. The pressing question now being asked by people inside and outside of the church was one of relevance. Did the ordinary means of grace, especially the preaching of God's Judging-Saving Word, provide an adequate basis for the faith and life of the church in Canada? Perhaps the emphasis on strategies, programs, and methods of church life, so disparaged by Bryden, deserved another look after all.[35] By the 1970s the neo-orthodox consensus, developed so forcefully by Walter Bryden, and upheld by a succeeding generation, had begun to dissipate. It was left to a new generation, in the midst of diverging orthodoxies, declining

---

[33]   Sydney E. Ahlstrom, *Theology in America: The Major Protestant Voices from Puritanism to Neo-orthodoxy* (New York: Bobbs-Merrill, 1967) 81.

[34]   Fraser, *Church, College, and Clergy,* 166.

[35]   Ibid., 170.

church attendance, religious pluralism, and secularism, to find for themselves some Divine Word on which they "might journey more surely and securely."

After Postmodernism, So What?

What, if anything, then, is the continuing relevance of Walter Bryden and the neo-orthodox theology of revelation for Canadian Protestantism and theology in North America in the twenty-first century? Bryden often preached and taught with prophetic passion and insight. For a new generation of students and clergy at a critical period in their church's life, Bryden embodied a model of Christian ministry centered in God's Judging-Saving Word. At the same time, his distinctive writing style, often powerful and persuasive, was also frequently characterized by what can only be described as a certain lack of clarity that did not always make his thought easily accessible. To some, he was also a prophet with a single burden whose harping on one note, usually polemical, often became tiresome. The prophetic and critical "No!" of judgment in Bryden's theology seemed to outweigh the positive and dogmatic "Yes!" of God's salvation. He often painted with a broad theological brush, especially when describing the theological and philosophical positions over against which he took his stand. And it is not always clear that he developed his theological themes—Christology, and the doctrines of salvation, Scripture, and election—adequately enough to sustain his theological critique.

Despite these obvious shortcomings, Walter Bryden did two things that were critically important for Canadian Protestantism. First, he was among the first Canadian theologians to point to the witness of Karl Barth, and most certainly the first theologian in Canada to work out the implications of neo-orthodoxy for the Canadian scene. He did this, not as an enthusiastic and recent convert to Barthianism whose only intention was to parrot the master, but as one who had been asking many of the same questions and struggling with similar issues. Second, he was undoubtedly the most articulate and able critic of church union, and one of the few, on either side of the debate, before or after 1925, who offered a truly theological argument informed by the traditions of Protestant thought and the developments of modern theology. That being said, do Walter Bryden and the neo-orthodox theology of revelation offer any enduring witness to the church today?

The times, of course, have changed for Canadian Protestants. Since the end of neo-orthodoxy in the 1960s and 1970s contemporary theology has experienced a remarkable period of fragmentation, diversity, and pluralism. The theology of hope, propounded by Jürgen Moltmann, emphasizes eschatology as the starting point for theology, so that Christian doctrines may be interpreted in terms of the promises of God and openness to the future.

Process theology, which emerged on the basis of the work of the philosophers Alfred North Whitehead and Charles Hartshorne, provides an account of Christian faith in terms of the new scientific worldview. Liberation theologies have forced the churches to confront the religious and theological sources of various forms of economic, political, and social oppression. Feminist theologies have sensitized the churches to the experiences, needs, and concerns of women. From the "Death of God" theology of the secular 1960s to the "Deconstructionist theologies" of the postmodern 1990s, an unprecedented array of theological options have been set before the Christian churches. And each, in its own way, has offered an account of the epistemological basis for belief and unbelief, and a theology of revelation quite distinct from neo-orthodoxy.

The plurality of Protestant theologies has been accompanied by the need to address changing ecclesial, religious, and cultural contexts. Ecumenical discussion and interreligious dialogue continue to press themselves upon the church. The explosive southward expansion of Christianity in Africa, Asia, and Latin America, and the enormous religious, political, and social consequences this portends, has, as Philip Jenkins notes, barely begun to register on the western consciousness.[36] Since September 11, 2001, the tensions between the Arab Islamic world and the Western Christian world have been heightened.

Two paradigms have been dominant in the discourse of the Christian community in North America during the past decade: post-Christendom and postmodernism. The disestablishment of the churches in the west, as Douglas John Hall has argued, is the fundamental fact of Christian existence with which the church must now come to terms.[37] Ironically, the post-Christendom paradigm for the church is being widely accepted at a time when American Christianity is experiencing a resurgence of evangelical belief aligned with national identity. At the same time, postcolonial theologies have emerged in other parts of the world, which challenge the theologies of empire operative in a good deal of North American Protestantism.

The postmodern paradigm points to the end of one worldview and the emergence of another. Speaking to the convocation at Carleton University in Ottawa in 1990, Canadian political scientist and former chair of the Canadian Radio-Television Commission (CRTC), John Meisel suggested that

> A major epoch is coming to an end, to be replaced by one whose contours are still only dimly understood. The world ushered in by the Industrial Revolution is giving way to one wrought by the infor-

---

[36]   Philip Jenkins, *The Next Christendom: The Coming of Global Christianity* (New York: Oxford University Press, 2002) 1–14.

[37]   Douglas John Hall, *Thinking the Faith*.

mation revolution. We confront nothing less than the fact that the ideologies that have dominated the modern world are wearing out . . . the ideological underpinnings of the contemporary world are collapsing and need to be replaced.[38]

Or, in the words of Vaclav Havel "We live in a postmodern world where everything is possible, and almost nothing is certain."[39]

In the midst of all this intellectual ferment and ecclesial confusion, does the thought of a man who wrote a book called *After Modernism, What?* in the early 1930s have anything at all to say to the church today? And what of his own little Christian community, The Presbyterian Church in Canada, which experienced a remarkable period of recovery, renewal, and growth in its first forty years after church union, only to be followed by forty years of decline, division, and, in some quarters, despair? Of all the things that might be said concerning Bryden's theological legacy, four aspects of his witness deserve ongoing consideration: the critical appropriation of the Reformed tradition; the continuing engagement with the theology of Karl Barth; the constructive emphasis on Word and Spirit as the basis for Reformed theology and spirituality; and the prophetic critique of church and society centered in the theology of the cross.

Firstly, Walter Bryden's theology stands as a constant reminder that the renewal of the church takes place in accordance with its own faith and life. The way forward for the church, Bryden believed, was to recover its roots in the Scriptures and in the Reformation. The Reformed churches, and the Presbyterian Church in Canada in particular, had to learn again and again what Calvin and the Reformers meant by God, God's Word, and God's gospel. Bryden knew that it was not possible in any literal way to go back to Calvin, nor did he think it would ever be desirable to do so. But he bore witness to the Christian's knowledge of God which shaped both Calvin's theology and the Reformed faith. He commanded an interest in the creeds and confessions of the church, especially the Westminster Confession of Faith, not in order to bind the church to a tradition of literalistic confessionalism, but in order to marshal creedal insights as a guide to confessing the faith anew. He pointed to the possibilities of critical biblical interpretation and theologically realistic exegesis when the historical-critical method was disentangled from liberal Protestant theology. He taught the church that its future always depended upon the critical appropriation of its past.

Secondly, Walter Bryden may not have been the best interpreter of Karl Barth in Canadian Protestantism, but he was undoubtedly one of the first, and the most daring. In light of what we now know about the development

---

[38] John Meisel, *Globe and Mail* (June 1990).

[39] Vaclav Havel, quoted by Richard Gwyn, *The Toronto Star* (July 24, 1994).

of dialectical theology and the influence of Barth's theology through contemporary Barth scholarship, Bryden's lectures and books can no longer be considered useful guides to Barth interpretation, except in a historical sense. Nevertheless, it is remarkable how clearly Bryden understood Barth and the dialectical theologians at the time, and how, at fundamental points, he got them quite right.

The long-term significance of Bryden's encounter with Barth, however, lies elsewhere. Bryden bore witness to the fact that Karl Barth was a theologian, a modern church father, whose thought deserved ongoing critical and comprehensive engagement. He thought carefully about the challenge Barth posed for Canadian Protestantism and began to work out those implications in his own books. The full impact of Barth's theology in Canada, however, has not yet been measured, nor can it be. Despite the challenges facing the church today, or precisely because of them, Bryden's thought offers this friendly provocation: Barth's theology provides an ongoing witness which Canadian Protestantism, in any age, ignores at its peril.

Thirdly, Walter Bryden's theology of Word and Spirit, in the tradition of Calvin and Barth, points to a heritage that emphasizes rigorous, theological thought combined with lively, evangelical piety. From a contemporary perspective, Bryden was a spiritual theologian, one who viewed the question of revelation from the perspective of the Christian spiritual life and the experience of God. He would have undoubtedly understood the contemporary interest in spirituality, but he also would have warned against all forms of mysticism grounded in human subjectivity.

When all was said and done, Bryden's ultimate concern was that the Christian gospel be heard and believed in the souls of men and women. Like Barth, he knew that the Christian message demanded participation, comprehension, and cooperation. He also knew that the revelation of the Word of God presumed faith in the living God, and that it created that which it presumed. The experience of God was possible from God's side, not humanity's. In revelation God shared divine self-knowledge with human beings, thereby creating the possibility of genuine human knowledge of God. This emphasis, perhaps more than any other, points to a rich resource for spirituality in the Reformed tradition. Thomas F. Torrance and James B. Torrance, among others, have developed this along Christological lines by emphasizing the mediation of Jesus Christ as prophet, priest, and king.[40]

The recent renewal of Trinitarian theology, especially in Reformed theology, stands in continuity with this aspect of Bryden's thought. In conver-

---

[40]   See Thomas F. Torrance, *The Mediation of Christ* (Grand Rapids: Eerdmans, 1983); and James B. Torrance, *Worship, Community and The Triune God of Grace* (Downers Grove, Ill.: InterVarsity, 1996).

sation with Eastern Orthodox theologians, Reformed theologians have discovered that there is significant convergence between the thought of Barth and someone like John Zizoulas who argues that "the Word of God does not dwell in humankind as rational knowledge or in the human soul as a mystical inner experience, but as a communion with a community . . . . So truth is not just something 'expressed' or 'heard,' a propositional or a logical truth; but something which is, i.e., an ontological truth: the community itself becoming the truth."[41] In short, the Trinitarian theology of Word and Spirit, to which Bryden bore witness, has continued to provide rich resources for a truly catholic theology and spirituality.

Fourthly, and finally, Bryden was a true Protestant who incorporated the principle of prophetic critique as the fundamental presupposition of all theological thought and action. Bryden made little reference to the thought of Paul Tillich but nevertheless shared Tillich's view that the Protestant Reformation embodied a principle that was implicit in Christian faith rightly understood. The Protestant Principle, negatively expressed, was the protest against any absolute claim for a finite reality, whether it was a church, a book, a symbol, a person, or an event. Expressed positively, it was the affirmation that the grace of God is not bound to any finite form. For Bryden, God was the ultimate and wholly-other. He argued that true faith began with an element of self-negation because it pointed beyond itself to this other and ultimate reality. The Protestant Principle was grounded in the centrality of the cross for Christian faith. Luther's theology of the cross expressed the conviction that the saving power of God could only be apprehended in the humility, weakness and death of Jesus.[42] The Judging-Saving Word of God to which Bryden bore witness was Jesus Christ, and him crucified. Bryden employed this principle, shaped by the masters of suspicion (Marx, Freud, and Durkheim), in a social critique of the Canadian church and a theological critique of Canadian society.

Bryden's theology, therefore, stands as a constant reminder to Canadian Protestantism and the North American churches that the Christian community is always in danger of co-opting the revelation of God to justify the church's existence and advance its own agenda. The threat to faith that Bryden saw in the domestication of the gospel and the trivialization of God in middle-class society is just as real today as it was in the second quarter of the twentieth century. Canadian churches, preoccupied with their own institutional survival, have borrowed wildly from the world of business in order to market the Christian message to a consumer society. "When the Big Three

---

[41] John Zizloulas, *Being as Communion: Studies in Personhood and the Church* (Crestwood, N.Y.: St. Vladimir's Seminary Press, 1985) 115.

[42] Van Harvey, *A Handbook of Theological Terms*, 197–98, 239.

supplant the Holy Three as the model of the church," writes Miroslav Volf, "prophetic rage is in order, not congratulation—sackcloth and ashes, not celebration."[43] Bryden would have agreed.

The bookshelves of clergy, once lined with biblical commentaries and theological tomes, are now filled with books on counseling and psychology to help ministers make the gospel palatable in a therapeutic culture. Canadian theologian Douglas John Hall, in many ways, stands in the tradition of Bryden when he speaks about the reality of the gospel and the unreality of the churches. The churches seem strangely unaware, perhaps blissfully so, that what happens on any given Sunday morning in the average Canadian parish bears little resemblance to what the church has done throughout most of twenty centuries. Visitors to a church will likely find a congregation comfortably relating, as Donald McCullough has noted, "to a deity who fits nicely within precise doctrinal positions, or who lends almighty support to social crusades, or who conforms to individual spiritual experiences." But there will not likely be much awe or sense of mystery. Reverence and awe have been replaced by a yawn of familiarity. The God described by the Bible as a consuming fire "has been domesticated into a candle flame, adding a bit of religious atmosphere, perhaps, but no heat, no blinding light, no power for purification."[44] The Canadian churches often appear to prefer the illusion of a safer, more manageable, congenial, serviceable God. The idealism against which Bryden railed, it seems, finds new life in every generation. This has always been *the* temptation and *the* failure of God's people.

The prophetic critique embodied in Bryden's witness also extended to Canadian society and the world order. Bryden was constantly aware that there was no place where men and women were so subject to self-deception as in their decisions in regard to their own ethical life and practice.[45] This fact so impressed Bryden that, apart from it, he could not conceive of social, political, and economic life in Canada and in the world situation. The dominance of unrestrained capitalism and American power at the beginning of the twenty-first century raises many of the same fundamental questions for Christians in Canada today. Bryden would no doubt also continue to argue that it would be difficult to justify, on moral grounds, that a meager population of thirty million people should have the right to monopolize three and a half million square miles, or one-fifteenth of the inhabitable portion of the

43   Miroslav Volf, *After Our Likeness: The Church as the Image of the Trinity* (Grand Rapids: Eerdmans, 1998) 6.
44   Donald McCullough, *The Trivialization of God: The Dangerous Illusion of a Manageable Deity* (Colorado Springs: NavPress, 1995) 13.
45   Bryden, *The Christian's Knowledge of God*, 243.

earth's surface.[46] Christians in Canada continue to be implicated in the materialism, consumerism, globalization, and nationalism of postmodern culture, and in the oppression that it produces for others. The state, for its part, continues to exercise more and more authority over every sphere of life, so that it now seems perilously close to making absolute claims for itself.

In such a context, and at such a time, it might be argued, the Protestant churches of North America still have something vital to learn from the witness of the past, from a theologian whose words pointed beyond the finite thoughts embedded in the best and most irrefragable of human doctrines, to a Divine Word which was heard in judgment and salvation alone. If the above estimate of Bryden's theological contribution to North American Protestantism in the twentieth century is the correct one, it would appear, "that we still await a truly saving, utterly cleansing Word from the One who is our God."[47]

---

[46] Ibid., 247.
[47] Ibid., 264.

Bibliography

I. Primary Literature

A. Books

Bryden, Walter Williamson. *The Spirit of Jesus in St. Paul: A Study in the Soul of St. Paul Based Upon the Corinthian Correspondence.* London: James Clarke, 1925. 256pp.

———. *Why I Am A Presbyterian.* Toronto: Presbyterian Publications, 1934. 176pp.

———. *After Modernism, What?* Unpublished manuscript. The Presbyterian Church in Canada Archives, The Bryden Files.

———. *The Christian's Knowledge of God.* Toronto: Thorn, 1940, 266pp. Reprinted, London: James Clarke, 1960. 266pp.

———. *The Significance of The Westminster Confession of Faith.* Toronto: University of Toronto Press, 1943. 43pp.

———. *Separated Unto the Gospel.* Edited by Donald V. Wade. Toronto: Burns and MacEachern, 1956. 218pp.

B. Articles and Pamphlets

Bryden, Walter Williamson. *The Christian Ministry.* The Presbyterian Church in Canada. Toronto: Upper Canada Tract Society, 1927. 21pp. Republished in *Separated Unto the Gospel,* 120–31.

———. "The Triumph of Reality." *Presbyterian Record* 54.7 (July 1929) 214–20. Republished in *Separated Unto the Gospel,* 131–45.

———. "Continental Movements and The Theological Thought of Tomorrow." *The United Church Observer* (June 15, 1941) 11, 28.

———. "The Holy Spirit and the Church." *Crisis Christology* 2.1 (1944–45) 5–18. Republished in *Separated Unto the Gospel,* 31–45.

———. "The Church of God and The World." *Crisis Christology* 4.1 (1946–47) 3–21. Republished in *Separated Unto the Gospel,* 46–70.

———. "St. Paul, The Preacher, As Separated Unto the Gospel." *Crisis Christology* 5.1 (1947–48) 3–9. Republished in *Separated Unto the Gospel,* 7–13.

———. "Foreword." In *The Christian Faith and Religion in Ontario Schools.* Essays by Frederick Bronkema, Arthur C. Cochrane, Charles C. Cochrane, J. Stanley Glen, A. Crawford Jamieson, Norman F. Langford, Gordon A. Peddie. Toronto: n.d., 3–4.

———. "The Church and the College." *Presbyterian Record* 70.8 (September 1945) 232–34.

———. "Shall We Adopt the Statement of Faith?" *Presbyterian Record* 71.9 (October 1946) 269–70.

———. "Message to the Graduates." *Presbyterian Record* 72.4 (April 1947) 166–67.

———. "To The Graduating Class." *Presbyterian Record* 73.5 (May 1948) 152. Republished in *Separated Unto the Gospel*, 167–68.

———. "John Calvin, Apostle of God's Sovereign Power." *Presbyterian Record* 74.11 (December 1949) 324–25.

———. "Introduction to the Congress." In *Addresses From The Pre-Assembly Congress of 1950 and the 76th General Assembly*, 6–11. Toronto: The Presbyterian Church in Canada, 1950.

———. "Knox College, To Be Or Not To Be." *Presbyterian Record* 75.6 (June 1950) 182.

C. Book Reviews

Bryden, Walter Williamson. Review of *English Religious Life in the Eighth Century*, by T. Allison. *Canadian Journal of Religious Thought* 7.3 (May–June 1930) 270–71.

———. Review of *The Life of Cardinal Newman*, by G. Glenn Atkins. *Canadian Journal of Religious Thought* 8.5 (November–December 1931) 414–15.

———. Review of *Why I Am and Why I Am Not a Catholic*, by H. Bellac and others. *Canadian Journal of Religious Thought* 8.1 (January–February 1931) 78–79.

———. Review of *The Reformed Doctrine of Predestination*, by Loraine Boettner. *Canadian Journal of Religious Thought* 9.2 (March–May 1932) 142–43.

———. Review of *The Kirk in Scotland*, by J. Buchan and G. A. Smith. *Canadian Journal of Religious Thought*, 8.1 (January–February 1931) 70–71.

———. Review of *The History of the Papacy in the Nineteenth Century*, by J. B. Bury. *Canadian Journal of Religious Thought* 8.1 (January–February 1931) 72–73.

———. Review of *The Church and the War, with a letter by Karl Barth*, by Arthur C. Cochrane. *Presbyterian Record* (1940s) 16.

———. Review of *The Organism of Christian Truth*, by John Dickie. *Canadian Journal of Religious Thought* 9.1 (January–February 1932) 79–81.

———. Review of *Science and the Unseen World*, by E. S. Eddington in *Canadian Journal of Religious Thought* 7.3 (May–June 1930) 273.

———. Review of *The Ethics of Paul*, by M. S. Enslin. *Canadian Journal of Religious Thought* 7.4 (September–October 1930) 344–46.

———. Review of *God and Ourselves*, by Edwin Lewis. *Canadian Journal of Religious Thought* 8.5 (November–December 1931) 409.

———. Review of *The Atonement and the Social Process*, by Shailer Matthews. *Canadian Journal of Religious Thought* 7.4 (September–October 1930) 354.

———. Review of *The Natural and the Supernatural*, by John Wood Oman. *Canadian Journal of Religious Thought* 9.1 (January–February 1932) 79–81.

———. Review of *The Church of England and the Church of Christ*, by A. J. Rawlinson, *Canadian Journal of Religious Thought* 8.1 (January–February 1931) 73–74.

———. Review of *Lectures in Hyde Park*, by C. F. Rogers. *Canadian Journal of Religious Thought* 7.3 (May–June 1930) 278.

———. Review of *The Spiritual Life and the Spiritual World*, by Sundar Singh. *Canadian Journal of Religious Thought* 8.4 (September–October 1931) 341.

———. Review of *Straight and Crooked Thinking*, by R. H. Thouless. *Canadian Journal of Religious Thought* 8.1 (January–February 1931) 81.

———. Review of *The Revelation of Deity*, by J. E. Turner. *Canadian Journal of Religious Thought* 8.4 (September–October 1931) 339–40.

D. Lectures and Theses

Bryden, Walter Williamson. "Church History: Introductory." The Presbyterian Church Archives, Bryden Fonds, 16pp, typed manuscript, n.d.

——. "Church History: The Period From the Great Creeds to the Reformation." The Presbyterian Church Archives, Bryden Fonds, 45pp, typed manuscript, n.d.

——. "Church History: Post-Reformation History of the Church (Up to 1648)." The Presbyterian Church Archives, Bryden Fonds, 32pp, typed manuscript, n.d.

——. "History of the Church in England." The Presbyterian Church Archives, Bryden Fonds, 57pp, typed manuscript, n.d.

——. "History of the Church in Scotland." The Presbyterian Church Archives, Bryden Fonds, 74pp, typed manuscript, 1943 and 1949. Compiled by Charles Henderson, Malcolm Mark, Willis Young, F. Norman Young, Allan L. Farris, Russell T. Self.

——. "St. Augustine: His Life, Times and Work." The Presbyterian Church Archives, Bryden Fonds, 53pp, typed manuscript, n.d.

——. "John Calvin and The Reformed Faith (Including Theological Differences Between Calvin and Luther)." The Presbyterian Church Archives, Bryden Fonds, 17pp, typed manuscript, n.d.

——. "Notes on the History of Religions." Edited by Donald V. Wade. The Presbyterian Church Archives, Bryden Fonds. Contains three series of lectures: (1) Introduction to the study of religions including general bibliography and notes on the religions of China and Japan, 57pp, typed manuscript, n.d.; (2) Persian and Indian Religions, 54pp, typed manuscript, n.d.; (3) The Greek Religion, 62pp, typed manuscript, n.d.

——. "Ludwig Feuerbach." The Presbyterian Church Archives, Bryden Fonds, 26pp, typed manuscript, n.d.

——. "The Reign of Naturalisms." The Presbyterian Church Archives, Bryden Fonds, 34pp, typed manuscript, n.d.

——. "Lectures on the Philosophy of Religion, Book II." The Presbyterian Church Archives, Bryden Fonds, typed manuscript, n.d. Four series of lectures dealing with (1) the nature of religion, (2) the relation of religion to the secular and to morality, science and art, (3) the development of religion and (4) the general problem of cognition.

——. "The Problem of God, Book I." The Presbyterian Church Archives, Bryden Fonds, 68pp, handwritten lecture notes, 1936.

——. "Lectures on Christianity and Other Faiths." The Presbyterian Church Archives, Bryden Fonds, n.d.

——. "Lecture on Optimistic Idealism and Pessimism." The Presbyterian Church Archives, Bryden Fonds, handwritten notes, n.d.

——. "The Theology of Karl Barth." The Presbyterian Church in Canada Archives, Bryden Fonds, handwritten notes dated in the early 1930s.

——. "Revelation." The Presbyterian Church Archives, Bryden Fonds, 55pp, typed manuscript, n.d.

——. "Authority in the Christian Faith." The Presbyterian Church Archives, Bryden Fonds, handwritten notes, n.d.

——. "Christianity." The Presbyterian Church Archives, Bryden Fonds, handwritten notes, n.d.

——. "Modern Significance of Paul." The Presbyterian Church Archives, Bryden Fonds, handwritten notes, n.d.

——. "The Life and Message of Jesus." The Presbyterian Church Archives, Bryden Fonds, handwritten notes, n.d.

————. St. Paul's Work in Detail." The Presbyterian Church Archives, Bryden Fonds, handwritten manuscript, n.d.

————. "A Verification of the Law of Weber, By The Method of Mean Gradations, With Reference To The Great Differences of Light Intensities." Unpublished Master of Arts Thesis, 1907, University of Toronto Archives.

E. Biographical Material

"Our Colleges." *Presbyterian Record* 52.10 (October 1927) 291–94.

"The Church and The College." *Presbyterian Record* 70.8 (September 1945) 232–34.

"Death of Principal of Knox College." *Presbyterian Record* 77 (May 1952) 9.

Walter Williamson Bryden, University of Toronto Archives. Clippings file includes book notices and reviews, notices of Bryden's academic and ecclesial appointments, and obituary notices. Information is also stored at the Alumni Affairs Office of the University of Toronto. Book reviews and notices of *The Spirit of Jesus in St. Paul* from *British Weekly, Belfast Witness, Edinburgh Scotsman, London Times Supplement, The Globe.*

Walter Williamson Bryden, University of Toronto Archives. Bryden's Faculty of Arts and Science Transcript Card.

"Rev. W. W. Bryden, M.A., D.D." In *The Acts and Proceedings of the Seventy-Eighth General Assembly of The Presbyterian Church in Canada.* Toronto, 1952, 358–59.

Bryden Files, The Presbyterian Church Archives. Bryden's Correspondence as Principal, 1945–1952; Lecture Notes; Examination Papers; Services of Induction and Remembrance; Assorted articles and papers.

II. Secondary Literature

Anderson, F. H. "On A Certain Revival of Enthusiasm." *The University of Toronto Quarterly* 10.2 (January 1941) 182–96.

Ahlstrom, Sydney E. *Theology in America: The Major Protestant Voices From Puritanism to Neo-Orthodoxy.* New York: Bobbs-Merrill, 1967.

————. *A Religious History of the American People.* New Haven: Yale University Press, 1972.

————. "The Scottish Philosophy and American Theology." *Church History* 24 (1955) 257–72.

Allen, Richard. *The Social Passion: Religion and Reform in Canada 1914–1928.* Toronto: University of Toronto Press, 1973.

Althaus, Paul. *The Theology of Martin Luther.* Translated by Robert Schultz. Philadelphia: Fortress, 1966.

Armour, Leslie and Trott, Elizabeth. *The Faces of Reason: An Essay on Philosophy and Culture in English Canada 1850–1950.* Waterloo: Wilfrid Laurier University Press, 1981.

Baillie, John. *The Place of Jesus Christ in Modern Theology.* Edinburgh: T. & T. Clark, 1929.

————. *Our Knowledge of God.* London: Oxford University Press, 1939.

————. *The Idea of Revelation in Recent Thought.* New York: Columbia University Press, 1956.

————, and Hugh Martin, editors. *Revelation.* London: Faber and Faber, 1937.

Balke, William. *Calvin and the Anabaptist Radicals.* Translated by William J. Heynen. Grand Rapids: Eerdmans, 1981. Reprinted Eugene, Ore.: Wipf and Stock, 1999.

Barr, James. *The Semantics of Biblical Language.* New York: Oxford University Press, 1961. Reprinted Eugene, Ore.: Wipf and Stock, 2004.

Barth, Karl. *Church Dogmatics.* Vol. I.1, I.2, and II.1. Edited by T. F. Torrance and G. W. Bromiley. Edinburgh: T. & T. Clark, 1956 and 1975.

———. *The Epistle to the Romans*. Translated by E. C. Hoskyns. London: Oxford University Press, 1933.

———. *The Knowledge of God and the Service of God*. Translated by J. L. M. Haire and I. Henderson. London: Hodder and Stoughton, 1938.

———. *The Word of God and the Word of Man*. Translated by Douglas Horton. Pilgrim, 1928.

———. *The Theology of the Reformed Confessions, 1923*. Translated by Darrell L. Guder and Judith J. Guder. Louisville: Westminster John Knox, 2002.

———. *The Theology of John Calvin*. Translated by Geoffrey W. Bromily. Grand Rapids: Eerdmans, 1995.

———, and Emil Brunner. *Natural Theology: Comprising "Nature and Grace" by Professor Dr. Emil Brunner and the reply "No!" by Dr. Karl Barth*. Translated by Peter Fraenkel. Introduction by John Baillie. London: Centenary, 1946.

Battles, F.L. "God Was Accommodating Himself to Human Capacity." *Interpretation* 31 (1977) 19–38.

Bauckham, Richard. "Cross, Theology of the." In *New Dictionary of Theology*, edited by Sinclair B. Ferguson et al. Downers Grove, Ill.: InterVarsity, 1988.

Bavinck, Herman. *The Philosophy of Revelation*. Grand Rapids: Baker, Reprinted 1979.

———. *Our Reasonable Faith*. Grand Rapids: Baker, Reprinted 1977.

Beare, Frank. "Against the Barthian Theology." *The Presbyterian Student* (March 1937) 9–10.

Bebbington, David. *Evangelicalism in Modern Britain: A History from the 1730s to the 1980s*. London: Unwin Hyman, 1989.

Bennett, John. "After Liberalism—What?" *Christian Century* 50.45 (November 8, 1933) 1403–6.

Berkhof, Hendrikus. *The Doctrine of the Holy Spirit*. Atlanta: John Knox, 1964.

———. *Christian Faith*. Translated by Sierd Woudstra. Rev. ed. Grand Rapids: Eerdmans, 1986.

———. *Christ The Meaning of History*. Grand Rapids: Baker, 1979.

———. *Two Hundred Years of Theology: Report of a Personal Journey*. Grand Rapids: Eerdmans, 1989.

Berkouwer, G. C. *Holy Scripture*. Translated by Jack Rogers. Grand Rapids: Eerdmans, 1975.

———. *General Revelation*. Grand Rapids: Eerdmans, 1955.

Berry, J. G. Review of *The Christian's Knowledge of God* in *Presbyterian Record* 66.2 (February 1941) 45.

Bevans, Stephen. *John Oman and His Doctrine of God*. Cambridge University Press, 1992.

Bland, Salem. *The New Christianity*. Toronto: University of Toronto Press, 1973.

Bloesch, Donald G. *The Essentials of Evangelical Theology*. Vols. I and II. San Francisco: Harper & Row, 1978 and 1979.

———. "Promise With Peril: A Response to James Olthuis." In *A Hermeneutics of Ultimacy: Peril or Promise?*, edited by James Olthuis, 61–69. Lanham, Md.: University Press of America, 1987.

Bolich, Gregory G. *Karl Barth and Evangelicalism*. Downers Grove, Ill.: InterVarsity, 1980.

Bromiley, Geoffrey W. *Introduction To The Theology of Karl Barth*. Grand Rapids: Eerdmans, 1979.

Brown, Colin. *Karl Barth and the Christian Message*. London: Tyndale, 1967.

Brunner, Emil. *Revelation and Reason*. Translated by Olive Wyon. Philadelphia: Westminster, 1946.

———. *The Mediator*. Translated by Olive Wyon. London: The Lutterworth, 1934.

———. *The Theology of Crisis*. New York: Charles Scribner's Sons, 1929.

———. *The Divine-Human Encounter*. Translated by Amandus William Loos. Philadelphia: Westminster, 1944.

Bryden, Kenneth. "Bryden the Social Critic." A Paper Presented at *The Bryden Symposium*, Knox College, May 1981.

Busch, Eberhard. *Karl Barth: His Life From Letters and Autobiographical Texts*. Translated by John Bowden. Philadelphia: Fortress, 1976.

Calvin, John. *Institutes of the Christian Religion*. Edited by John T. McNeill. The Library of Christian Classics 20, 21. Philadelphia: Westminster, 1960.

Cameron, Nigel de S., editor. *Dictionary of Scottish Church History and Theology*. Edinburgh: T. &. T. Clark, 1993.

Careless, J. M. S. *Brown of the Globe*. Vol. 1. Toronto: Macmillan, 1959.

Caven, William. "The Union of the Christian Churches." *The Westminster*, n.s. 1.1 (July 1902).

Chadwick, Owen. *The Secularization of the European Mind in the Nineteenth Century.* Cambridge University Press, 1975.

Chapman, J. Arundel. *The Theology of Karl Barth*. London: Epworth, 1931.

Charry, Ellen. *By The Renewing of Your Minds: The Pastoral Function of Christian Doctrine*. New York: Oxford University Press, 1997.

Childs, Brevard S. *Biblical Theology in Crisis*. Philadelphia: Westminster, 1970.

Choquette, Robert. *Canada's Religions*. Ottawa: University of Ottawa Press, 2004.

Clark, Gordon. *Karl Barth's Theological Method*. Philadelphia: Presbyterian and Reformed Publishing Co., 1963.

Clark, R. E. D. "John Wood Oman." In *The New International Dictionary of the Christian Church,* edited by J. D. Douglas, 730. Grand Rapids: Zondervan, 1978.

Clifford, N. Keith. "Charles Clayton Morrison and The United Church of Canada." *Canadian Journal of Theology* 15 (1969) 80–92.

———. *The Resistance to Church Union in Canada 1904–1939*. Vancouver: University of British Columbia Press, 1985.

Cochrane, A. C. *Eating and Drinking With Jesus*. Philadelphia: Westminster, 1974.

———. "Karl Barth and the Confessional Church." *The Presbyterian Student* 2.3 (February 1937) 8–9.

Cochrane, Charles. "Principal Bryden: Memorial Address." Knox College, June 4, 1952.

Coles, S. B. Review of *The Christian's Knowledge of God* in *Bible Christianity* (April–May 1948) 15–16.

Cone, James H. *God of The Oppressed*. New York: The Seabury, 1975.

Cook, Ramsay. *The Regenerators: Social Criticism in Late Victorian Canada*. Toronto: University of Toronto Press, 1985.

D., C. P. (name unknown) "The Book Table." A Review of *The Christian's Knowledge of God* in *The Intelligence-Leader* (July 25, 1941) 13.

Davies, Jenkin H. "The Ideas of Karl Barth." *Canadian Journal of Religious Thought* 7.4 (September–October 1930) 325–34.

Demarest, Bruce. *General Revelation: Historical Views and Contemporary Issues*. Grand Rapids: Zondervan, 1982.

Denney, James. *Studies in Theology*. London: Hodder and Stoughton, 1894.

———. *The Second Epistle to the Corinthians*. London: Hodder and Stoughton, 1894.

———. *The Death of Christ*. London: Hodder and Stoughton, 1903.

———. *The Atonement and the Modern Mind*. London: Hodder and Stoughton, 1903.

———. *Jesus and the Gospel*. London: Hodder and Stoughton, 1909.

———. *The Christian Doctrine of Reconciliation*. London: Hodder and Stoughton, 1917.

Dillistone, F. W. "The Present Theological Perplexity: Professor Bryden's Challenging Book." *The Canadian Churchman* (November 28, 1940) 678.

Dorrien, Gary. *The Barthian Revolt in Modern Theology*. Louisville, Kentucky: Westminster John Knox, 2000.

Douglas, George L. "Principal Walter W. Bryden: A Memorial Sermon Delivered To The Synod of Hamilton and London." Wednesday, April 30, 1952.

Douglas, J. D. "James Denney." In *The New International Dictionary of the Christian Church,* edited by J. D. Douglas, 293. Grand Rapids: Zondervan, 1978.

———. "T. M. Lindsay." In *The New International Dictionary of the Christian Church,* edited by J. D. Douglas, 597. Grand Rapids: Zondervan, 1978.

Doumerge, Emil. *Jean Calvin: Les hommes et les Choses de son Temps*. Lausanne: Georges Bridel & Cie Editeurs, 1910.

Dow, John. *This Is Our Faith: An Exposition of the Statement of the United Church of Canada*. Toronto: Board of Evangelism, United Church of Canada, 1943.

———. Review of *The Spirit of Jesus in St. Paul* in *Canadian Journal of Religious Thought* 4.1 (January–February 1927) 89–90.

Dowey, Edward A. *The Knowledge of God in Calvin's Theology*. New York and London: Columbia University Press, 1952.

Dulles, Avery. *Models of Revelation*. New York: Doubleday, 1985.

Fackre, Gabriel. *The Doctrine of Revelation: A Narrative Interpretation*. Edinburgh Studies in Constructive Theology. Grand Rapids: Eerdmans, 1997.

Fairweather, Eugene. "Christian Theology and the Bible." *Canadian Journal of Theology* 2.2 (1956) 65–75.

Farely, Edward. *Theologia: The Unity and Fragmentation of Theological Education*. Philadelphia: Fortress, 1983.

Farris, A. L. "The Fathers of 1925." In *Enkindled By The Word: Essays on Presbyterianism in Canada,* 59–82. Toronto: Presbyterian Publications, 1966. Reprinted in *The Tide of Time,* edited by John S. Moir, 95–124. Toronto: Knox College, 1978.

Fennell, W. O. "The Canadian Theological Society: An Anniversary Retrospective." *Studies in Religion* 14 (1985) 409–13.

Forstman, H. J. *Word and Spirit: Calvin's Doctrine of Biblical Authority*. Stanford: Stanford University Press, 1962.

Forsyth, P. T. *Positive Preaching and the Modern Mind*. New York: Hodder and Stoughton, 1907.

———. *The Person and Place of Jesus Christ*. London: Independent Press, 1948.

———. *The Work of Christ*. London: Hodder and Stoughton, 1949.

———. *The Principle of Authority*. London: Independent Press, 1952.

———. *The Church and The Sacraments*. London, 1953.

Fraser, Brian J. *The Social Uplifters: Presbyterian Progressives and The Social Gospel in Canada, 1875–1915*. Waterloo: Waterloo University Press, 1988.

———. *Church, College, and Clergy: A History of Theological Education at Knox College, Toronto, 1844–1994*. Montreal and Kingston: McGill-Queen's University Press, 1995.

———. "The Public Pieties of Canadian Presbyterians." In *Church and Canadian Culture,* edited by Robert E. VanderVennen, 87–104. Lanham: University Press of America, 1991.

———. "Bryden and The Church Thirty Years Later." A Paper Presented at *The Bryden Symposium*. Knox College, May 1981.

Frei, Hans. "The Doctrine of Revelation in the Thought of Karl Barth, 1909–1922, The Nature of Barth's Break with Liberalism." Ph.D. Dissertation, Yale University, 1956.

———. *The Eclipse of Biblical Narrative: A Study in Eighteenth and Nineteenth Century Hermeneutics*. New Haven: Yale University Press, 1974.

———. *Types of Christian Theology*. Edited by George Hunsinger and William Placher. New Haven: Yale University Press, 1992.

Gandier, Alfred. *The Doctrinal Basis of Union and Its Relation to the Historic Creeds*. Toronto: Ryerson, 1926.

Gauvreau, Michael. *The Evangelical Century: College and Creed in English Canada from the Great Revival to the Great Depression*. Montreal and Kingston: McGill-Queen's University Press, 1991.

George, Timothy. *Theology of the Reformers*. Nashville: Broadman, 1988.

Gilkey, Langdon. "Dissolution and Reconstruction in Theology." *Christian Century* 82.5 (February 3, 1965) 135–39.

———. "Cosmology, Ontology, and the Travail of Biblical Language." *Journal of Religion* 41 (1961) 194–205.

Gilson, Etienne. *The Spirit of Medieval Philosophy*. Translated by A. H. C. Downes. Oxford University Press, n.d. Reprinted Notre Dame: University of Notre Dame, 1991.

Godsey, John. "The Architecture of Karl Barth's Church Dogmatics." *Scottish Journal of Theology* 9 (March 1925) 236–50.

———. "Neo-orthodoxy." In *Encyclopedia of Religion*, edited by Mircea Eliade, 10:360ff. New York: Macmillan, 1986.

Grant, John Webster. "Blending Traditions: The United Church of Canada." *Canadian Journal of Theology* 9 (1963) 50–59.

———. *The Church in the Canadian Era*. Burlington: Welch, 1988.

Grave, S.A. *The Scottish Philosophy of Common Sense*. Oxford: Clarendon, 1960.

Grenz, Stanley J. and Olson, Roger E. *20th Century Theology*. Downers Grove, Ill.: InterVarsity, 1992.

Hall, Douglas John. *Thinking the Faith: Christian Theology in a North American Context*. Minneapolis: Augsburg, 1988.

———. *Remembered Voices: Reclaiming the Legacy of 'Neo-Orthodoxy.'* Louisville: Westminster John Knox,1998.

Handy, Robert T. *A History of the Church in the United States and Canada*. Oxford History of the Christian Church. Oxford: Oxford University Press, 1976.

Harland, Gordon. "God's Judging-Saving Word: The Legacy of Walter W. Bryden." *Touchstone: Journal on The United Church of Canada's Theology and Faith* 13.3 (September 1995).

Harvey, Van. *Handbook of Theological Terms*. New York: Macmillan, 1964.

———. *The Historian and the Believer*. New York: Macmillan, 1966.

Hay, J. C. "Allan L. Farris." In *The Tide of Time*, edited by John Moir. Toronto: Knox College, 1978.

Hay, William. *History of the Presbyterian Church in Lethbridge*. The Presbyterian Church Archives.

Helm, Paul. "James Orr." In *The New International Dictionary of the Christian Church*. Edited by J. D. Douglas, 734. Grand Rapids: Zondervan, 1978.

Hendry, George Stuart. *The Holy Spirit in Christian Theology*. Philadelphia: Westminster, 1965.

Henry, Carl F. H., editor. *Revelation and the Bible: Contemporary Evangelical Thought*. Grand Rapids: Baker, 1958.

Heron, A. I. C. *A Century of Protestant Theology*. London: Lutterworth, 1980.

Hesselink, I. John. *On Being Reformed*. Ann Arbor, Mich.: Servant, 1983.

Hick, John. *An Interpretation of Religion*. London: Macmillan, 1989.

Hordern, William. *The Case For A New Reformation Theology*. Philadelphia: Westminster, 1959.

Horton, Walter Marshall. *Realistic Theology*. New York: Harper & Brothers, 1934.

———. *Contemporary Continental Theology*. New York: Harper & Brothers, 1938.

Hoyle, Richard Birch. *The Teaching of Karl Barth*. London: SCM, 1930.

Hunsinger, George. *How To Read Karl Barth: The Shape of His Theology.* New York: Oxford University Press, 1991.

Hutchinson, William R. *The Modernist Impulse in American Protestantism.* Durham, N.C.: Duke University Press, 1992.

Jenkins, Philip. *The Next Christendom: The Coming of Global Christianity.* New York: Oxford University Press, 2002.

Jewett, Paul King. *Emil Brunner's Concept of Revelation.* London: James Clarke, 1954.

Johnson, William Stacey, and John Leith, editors. *Reformed Reader: A Sourcebook in Christian Theology.* Vol. 1. Louisville: Westminster John Knox, 1993.

Johnston, John. "Factors in the Formation of the Presbyterian Church in Canada in 1875." Ph.D. dissertation, McGill University, 1955.

Kantzer, Kenneth. "Calvin and the Holy Scriptures." In *Inspiration and Interpretation,* edited by John Walvoord. Grand Rapids: Eerdmans, 1957.

Kelsey, David. *The Uses of Scripture in Recent Theology.* Philadelphia: Fortress, 1975.

Kennedy, H. A. A. *St. Paul and The Mystery Religions.* London: Hodder and Stoughton, 1913.

———. A. *The Theology of the Epistles.* London: Duckworth, 1919.

———. A. *St. Paul's Conception of the Last Things.* London: Hodder and Stoughton, 1904.

Kierkegaard, Soren. *Training in Christianity.* Princeton: Princeton University Press, 1967.

Killen, R. Allan. "Canadian Ministerial Students Are Taught The Bible Has Discrepancies, Contradictions, Doubtful Morality, and Religious Myths." *The Christian Beacon* (April 3, 1947) 2.

Kilpatrick, T. B. *New Testament Evangelism.* Toronto: Westminster, 1911.

———. *The Redemption of Man.* Edinburgh: T. & T. Clark, 1920.

———. *Our Common Faith.* Toronto: Ryerson, 1928.

Klempa, William, editor. *What Does It Mean To Confess The Christian Faith.* Toronto: Committee on Church Doctrine, The Presbyterian Church in Canada, n.d.

———, editor. *The Burning Bush and a Few Acres of Snow.* Ottawa: Carleton University Press, 1994.

Kliever, Lonnie D. *H. Richard Niebuhr.* Makers of the Modern Theological Mind. Waco, Tex.: Word, 1977.

Kraemer, Hendrik. *The Christian Message in a Non-Christian World.* London: Edinburgh House, 1947.

Kraus, H. J. "Calvin's Exegetical Principles." *Interpretation* 31 (1977) 8–18.

Krusche, Werner. *Das Wirken des Heiligen Geistes nach Calvin.* Forschungen zur Kirchen- und Dogmengeschichte 7. Gottingen: Vandenhoeck & Ruprecht, 1957.

Kuyper, Abraham. *The Work of the Holy Spirit.* Translated by J. DeVries. New York: Funk and · Wagnalls, 1975.

Landon, F. *Western Ontario and the American Frontier.* Toronto: McClelland and Stewart, 1967.

Latourette, Kenneth Scott. *A History of Christianity, Volume 2: A.D. 1500—A.D. 1975.* New York: Harper & Row, 1975.

Lindbeck, George A. *The Nature of Doctrine: Religion and Theology in a Postliberal Age.* Philadelphia: Westminster, 1984.

Lindsay, T. M. *A History of the Reformation.* 2 Vols. Edinburgh: T. & T. Clark, 1907.

Leith, John H. *Introduction to the Reformed Tradition.* Atlanta: John Knox, 1977.

———. *John Calvin's Doctrine of the Christian Life.* Louisville: Westminster John Knox, 1989.

Line, John. "Barth and Barthianism." *Canadian Journal of Religious Thought* 6.2 (March–April 1929) 98–104.

Lowrie, Walter. *Our Concern With The Theology of Crisis.* Boston: Meador, 1932.

Machen, J. Gresham. *Christianity and Liberalism*. New York: Macmillan, 1923.

Mack, Barry. "Of Canadian Presbyterians and Guardian Angels." In *Amazing Grace: Evangelicalism in Australia, Britain, Canada and the United States,* edited by George A. Rawlyk and Mark A. Noll, 269–92. Grand Rapids: Baker, 1994.

Mackinnon, D.M. Review of *The Christian's Knowledge of God* in *Scottish Journal of Theology* 2 (1949) 208–10.

Mackintosh, H. R. *Types of Modern Theology*. London: Nisbet, 1937.

MacLeod, A. D. *Stanford Reid: An Evangelical Calvinist in the Academy*. Montreal and Kingston: McGill-Queen's University Press, 2004.

———. "The Formation of the Articles of Faith Committee: Ascendant Barthianism in the 1940s in the PCC." A paper presented to The Canadian Society of Presbyterian History, September 25, 004.

MacLeod, John. *Scottish Theology*. Edinburgh: Knox Press, 1943.

Marshall, David B. *Secularizing the Faith: Canadian Protestant Clergy and the Crisis of Belief.* Toronto: University of Toronto Press, 1992.

Marshall, I. Howard. "James Denney." In *Creative Minds in Contemporary Theology,* edited by P. E. Hughes, 203–36. Grand Rapids: Eerdmans, 1966.

Mc., R. J. (name unknown). Review of *The Christian's Knowledge of God* in *The Canadian Baptist* (December 1, 1941) 10.

McCasland, S. Vernon. Review of *The Christian's Knowledge of God* in *The Journal of Bible and Religion* (August 1941) 179–80.

McConnachie, John. *The Barthian Theology and the Man of Today*. London: Hodder and Stoughton, 1933.

———. "Religious Books of the Month." A Review of *The Christian's Knowledge of God* in *The British Weekly* (February 27, 1941) 218.

McCormack, Bruce L. *Karl Barth's Critically Realistic Dialectical Theology: Its Genesis and Development, 1909–1936*. Oxford: Clarendon, 1995.

McCullough, Donald. *The Trivialization of God: The Dangerous Illusion of a Manageable Deity*. Colorado Springs: NavPress, 1995.

McFadyen, John E. *The Interest of the Bible*. London: Hodder and Stoughton, 1922.

———. *Introduction to the Old Testament*. London: Hodder and Stoughton, 1905.

———. *A Guide To The Understanding of The Old Testament*. London: James Clarke, 1927.

———. *Old Testament Criticism and The Christian Church*. New York: Charles Scribner's Sons, 1903.

McKeown, W. J. "Memories of Dr. Bryden." *Presbyterian Record* 94.10 (October 1975) 8.

McKillop, A. B. *A Disciplined Mind: Critical Inquiry and Canadian Thought in the Victorian Era*. Montreal and Kingston: McGill-Queen's University Press, 1979.

McKim, Donald K. "Calvin's View of Scripture." In *Readings in Calvin's Theology*. Edited by Donald K. McKim. Grand Rapids: Baker, 1984.

———, editor. *How Karl Barth Changed My Mind*. Grand Rapids: Eerdmans, 1986.

McLaren, William D. *Our Growing Creed, or the Evangelical Faith as Developed and Reaffirmed by Current Thought*. Edinburgh: T. & T. Clark, 1912.

McLaren, William D. *The Unity of the Church and Church Unions*. Toronto: Presbyterian News Company, 1890.

McLelland, Joseph C. "Walter Bryden: 'By Circumstance and God.'" In *Called to Witness: Profiles of Canadian Presbyterians*, edited by W. S. Reid, 2:119–26. Toronto: Committee on History, The Presbyterian Church in Canada, 1980.

———. "The Natural Theology of Canada: Philosophy of Religion in Canadian Theological Education." Edited by Graham Brown. Toronto: United Church Publishing House, 1988.

McNeill, John T. *The Presbyterian Church in Canada, 1875–1925*. Toronto: The Presbyterian Church in Canada, 1925.

———. "The Significance of the Word of God for Calvin." *Church History* 28 (1959) 131–46.

———. *The History and Character of Calvinism*. New York: Oxford University Press, 1954.

Mikolaski, Samuel. *The Creative Theology of P. T. Forsyth*. Grand Rapids: Eerdmans, 1969.

Miller, Donald G., Browne Barr, and Robert S. Paul. *P. T. Forsyth: The Man, The Preachers' Theologian, Prophet of the 20th Century*. Pittsburgh Theological Monograph Series 36. Pittsburgh: Pickwick, 1981.

Moir, John S. *Enduring Witness: A History of the Presbyterian Church in Canada*. Hamilton, Ont.: Presbyterian Church in Canada, 1987.

———. *A History of Biblical Studies in Canada*. Society of Biblical Literature, Centennial Publications. Chico, Calif.: Scholars, 1982.

———. "'Who Pays The Piper . . .' Canadian Presbyterism and Church-State Relations." In *The Burning Bush and a Few Acres of Snow*, edited by William J. Klempa. Ottawa: Carleton University Press, 1994.

Moltmann, Jürgen. *The Church in the Power of the Spirit: A Contribution to Messianic Eschatology*. Translated by Margaret Kohl. New York: Harper & Row, 1977.

Morris, Leon. *I Believe in Revelation*. Grand Rapids: Eerdmans, 1976.

Mudge, Lewis. *One Church: Catholic and Reformed*. Philadelphia: Westminster, 1963.

Murray, John. *Calvin on Scripture and Divine Sovereignty*. Grand Rapids: Baker, 1960.

Nash, Arnold S., editor. *Protestant Theology in the Twentieth Century: Whence and Whither?* New York: Macmillan, 1951.

Newbigin, Lesslie. *The Gospel in a Pluralist Society*. Grand Rapids: Eerdmans, 1989.

Niebuhr, H. Richard. *The Meaning of Revelation*. New York: Macmillan, 1941.

Niesel, Wilhelm. *The Theology of Calvin*. Translated by H. Knight. Grand Rapids: Baker, 1980.

Noll, Mark A. *A History of Christianity in the United States and Canada*. Grand Rapids: Eerdmans, 1992.

———. "Common Sense Tradition and American Evangelical Thought." *American Quarterly* 37 (1985) 216–38.

Oman, John. *The Church and The Divine Order*. London: Hodder and Stoughton, 1911.

———. *The Natural and the Supernatural*. Cambridge: Cambridge University Press, 1931.

Orr, James. *The Christian View of God and The World*. Grand Rapids: Eerdmans, 1954.

Osterhaven, M. E. *The Spirit of the Reformed Tradition*. Grand Rapids: Eerdmans, 1971.

Packer, J. I. "Calvin's View of Scripture." In *God's Inerrant Word*, edited by John W. Montgomery. Minneapolis: Bethany Fellowship, 1974.

Pannenberg, Wolfhart, editor. *Revelation as History*. Translated by David Granskou. New York: Macmillan, 1968.

Parker, T. H. L. *The Doctrine of the Knowledge of God*. Edinburgh: Oliver and Boyd, 1952.

———. "Barth on Revelation." *Scottish Journal of Theology* 13 (1960) 366–82.

Parratt, J. K. "The Witness of the Holy Spirit: Calvin, the Puritans, and St. Paul." *Evangelical Quarterly* 41 (1969) 162–68.

Partee, C. "Calvin and Experience." *Scottish Journal of Theology* 26 (1973) 169–81.

Pauck, Wilhelm. *Karl Barth: Prophet of a New Christianity?* New York: Harper and Brothers, 1931.

———. *The Heritage of the Reformation*. Free Press, 1961.

Peddie, G. A. *The King of Kings: The Basis of Union of the Presbyterian Church in Canada, and its relationship to the present need of the Church for a Confession of Faith in Jesus Christ as Lord of Church and State*. Toronto: Age Publications, 1942.

Ramm, Bernard. *After Fundamentalism: The Future of Evangelical Theology.* San Francisco: Harper & Row, 1983.

Rawlyk, George, editor. *The Canadian Protestant Experience, 1760–1990.* Burlington: Welch, 1990.

Reid, J. K. S. *The Authority of Scripture: A Study of the Reformation and Post-Reformation Understanding of the Bible.* London: Methuen, 1957.

Reid, W. S, editor. *The Scottish Tradition in Canada.* Toronto: McClelland and Stewart, 1976.

Rennie, Ian S. "Conservatism in the Presbyterian Church in Canada and Beyond: An Introductory Exploration." In *Papers Presented To The Canadian Presbyterian History Society.* Toronto: October 1982.

Richmond, James. "Neo-orthodoxy." In *A Dictionary of Christian Theology,* edited by Alan Richardson, 228. Philadelphia: Westminster, 1969.

Ritchie, D. L. "Barth and Barthianism." *Canadian Journal of Religious Thought* 6.5 (September–October 1929) 317–25.

Robinson, James M., editor. *The Beginnings of Dialectical Theology.* Vol. 1. Richmond: John Knox, 1968.

Robinson, H. Wheeler. *The Christian Experience of the Holy Spirit.* London: James Nisbet, 1930.

Roberts, Richard H. *A Theology On Its Way? Essays on Karl Barth.* Edinburgh: T. & T. Clark, 1991.

Rodgers, John. *The Theology of P. T. Forsyth.* London: Independent Press, 1965.

Rogers, Jack B. "Creeds and Confessions." *Encyclopedia of the Reformed Faith,* edited by Donald K. McKim, 57–58. Louisville: Westminster John Knox, 1996.

———, and Donald K. McKim. *The Authority and Interpretation of the Bible.* San Francisco: Harper & Row, 1979.

Rolston, Holmes. *A Conservative Looks to Barth and Brunner.* Nashville: Cokesbury, 1933.

Runia, Klaas. *Karl Barth's Doctrine of Holy Scripture.* Grand Rapids: Eerdmans, 1962.

Sandeen, Ernest R. *The Roots of Fundamentalism.* Grand Rapids: Baker, 1970.

Schaff, Philip. *The Creeds of Christendom.* Vol. 2. New York: Harper and Brothers, 1877.

Schleiermacher, Friedrich D. E. *On Religion: Speeches To Its Cultured Despisers.* Translated by John Oman. New York: Harper & Row, 1958.

———. *The Christian Faith.* Edited and translated by H. R. Mackintosh and J. S. Stewart. Edinburgh: T. & T. Clark, 1928.

Scorgie, Glen G. *A Call for Continuity: The Theological Contribution of James Orr.* Macon, Ga.: Mercer University Press, 1988.

Sell, Alan P. F. *Defending and Declaring the Faith: Some Scottish Examples 1860–1920.* Exeter: Paternoster, 1992.

———. *Philosophical Idealism and Christian Belief.* New York: St. Martin's, 1995.

Shein, Louis. "Bryden The Churchman." A Paper Presented to *The Bryden Symposium,* Knox College, May 1981.

Sheppard, Gerald T. "How Do Neoorthodox and Post-Neoorthodox Theologians Approach The 'Doing of Theology' Today?," edited by J. D. Woodbridge and Thomas E. McComiskey, 437–59. Grand Rapids: Zondervan, 1991.

Silva, William Allen. "The Expression of Neo-orthodoxy in American Protestantism." Ph.D. Thesis, Yale University, 1988.

Smart, James D. "The Conflict Within The Church." *The Presbyterian Student* 2.3 (February 1937) 2–4.

———. "Defence and Counter-Attack." *The Presbyterian Student* 3.1 (December 1937) 5–9, 27.

———. "Is Karl Barth's Theology Extremist?" *The Presbyterian Student* 3.3 (March 1938) 8–14.

———. "The Death and Rebirth of Old Testament Theology." *Journal of Religion* 23 (1943) 1–11, 125–36.

———. "The Evangelist as Theologian." In *Separated Unto The Gospel,* edited by Donald V. Wade. Toronto: Burns and MacEachern, 1956.

———. *The Divided Mind of Modern Theology.* Philadelphia: Westminster, 1962.

———. *The Interpretation of Scripture.* Philadelphia: Westminster, 1962.

———. "Lest We Forget." *Presbyterian Record* 94.9 (September 1975) 6–7.

———. *The Past, Present, and Future of Biblical Theology.* Philadelphia: Westminster, 1979.

———. "Bryden the Theologian." A Paper Presented to *The Bryden Symposium,* Knox College, May 1981.

Smith, E. W. *The Creed of Presbyterians.* Toronto: Poole-Stewart, 1901.

Smith, Neil Gregor. "The Presbyterian Church in Canada: 1925–1963." In *A Short History of The Presbyterian Church in Canada,* 74–107. Toronto: Presbyterian Publications.

Stone, Ronald H. *Professor Reinhold Niebuhr: A Mentor To The Twentieth Century.* Louisville: Westminster John Knox, 1992.

Smith, Wilfrid Cantwell. *Towards A World Theology.* London: Macmillan, 1991.

Stackhouse, John G. Jr., *Canadian Evangelicalism in the Twentieth Century: An Introduction to Its Character.* Toronto: University of Toronto Press, 1993.

Sykes, S. W., editor. *Karl Barth: Centenary Essays.* Cambridge University Press, 1989.

Thiemann, Ronald. F. *Revelation and Theology: The Gospel as Narrated Promise.* Notre Dame: University of Notre Dame Press, 1985.

Thorne, C. G. "George Adam Smith." In *The New International Dictionary of The Christian Church,* edited by J. D. Douglas, 910. Grand Rapids: Zondervan, 1978.

Tillich, Paul. *Systematic Theology.* Vol. 1. Chicago: University of Chicago Press, 1951.

Torrance, Thomas F. *Karl Barth: An Introduction To His Early Theology, 1910–1931.* London: SCM, 1962.

———. *Karl Barth: Biblical and Evangelical Theologian.* Edinburgh: T. & T. Clark, 1990.

———. *Theological Science.* London: Oxford University Press, 1969.

———. *The Mediation of Christ.* Grand Rapids: Eerdmans, 1983.

———. *Reality and Evangelical Theology: A Fresh and Challenging Approach to Christian Revelation.* Philadelphia: Westminster, 1982.

Torrance, J. B. *Worship, Community, and the Triune God of Grace.* Downers Grove, Ill.: InterVarsity, 1996.

Tracy, David. *Blessed Rage For Order: The Pluralism in Theology.* New York: Seabury, 1975.

———. *The Analogical Imagination: Christian Theology and the Culture of Pluralism.* New York: Crossroad, 1981.

Tracy, F. "The Scottish Philosophy." *University of Toronto Quarterly* 2 (November 1895) 1–15.

Van Die, Marguerite. *An Evangelical Mind: Nathanael Burwash and the Methodist Tradition in Canada.* Kingston and Montreal: McGill-Queen's University Press, 1989.

Van Til, Cornelius. *Christianity and Barthianism.* Philadelphia: Presbyterian and Reformed Publishing, 1962.

Vaudry, Richard. *The Free Church in Victorian Canada.* Waterloo: Wilfrid Laurier University Press, 1994.

Vissers, John A. "W. W. Bryden and the Reformed Protestant Tradition in Canada." *Toronto Journal of Theology* 6 (1990) 70–85.

———. "Recovering the Reformation Conception of Revelation: Walter Williamson Bryden and Post-Union Canadian Presbyterianism." *The Burning Bush and a Few Acres of Snow.* Edited by William Klempa. Ottawa: Carleton University Press, 1994.

———. "The Holy Spirit and the Church in Modern Canadian Protestantism." *Semper Reformandum: Studies in Honour of Clark H. Pinnock,* edited by Stanley E. Porter and Anthony R. Cross. Carlisle: Paternoster, 2003.

Visser T'Hooft, W. A. "An Introduction To The Theology of Karl Barth." *Canadian Journal of Religious Thought* 8.1 (January–February 1931) 37–51.

Volf, Miroslav. *After Our Likeness: The Church as the Image of the Trinity.* Grand Rapids: Eerdmans, 1998.

Wade, Donald V. "The Theological Achievement of Walter Bryden." A Paper Presented to The Karl Barth Society of North America, Barth Colloquium, March 22, 1974, Toronto.

Warfield, B. B. *The Inspiration and Authority of the Bible.* Phillipsburg, N.J.: Presbyterian and Reformed Publishing Co., 1979.

———. *Calvin and Augustine.* Philadelphia: Presbyterian and Reformed Publishing House, 1956.

Watson, John. *The Interpretation of Religious Experience.* Vol. 2. Glasgow: Maclehose and Sons, 1912.

———. *Christianity and Idealism.* New York: Macmillan, 1897.

Webster, John B. *Eberhard Jüngel: An Introduction to His Theology.* Cambridge University Press, 1986.

Welch, Claude. *Protestant Thought in the Nineteenth Century.* 2 vols. New Haven: Yale University Press, 1972, 1985.

Wells, David, editor. *Reformed Theology in America.* Grand Rapids: Eerdmans, 1985.

Wendel, Francois. *Calvin: The Origins and Development of His Religious Thought.* Translated by Philip Mairet. New York: Collins, 1963.

Wilmer, Haddon. "P. T. Forsyth." In *The New International Dictionary of the Christian Church,* edited by J. D. Douglas, 382–83. Grand Rapids: Zondervan, 1978.

Wolterstorff, Nicholas. *Divine Discourse: Philosophical Reflections on the Claim that God Speaks.* New York: Cambridge University Press, 1995.

———. *Thomas Reid and the Story of Epistemology.* Cambridge University Press, 2001.

Wright, G. Ernest. *God Who Acts: Biblical Theology as Recital.* London: SCM, 1952.

———, and Reginald H. Fuller. *The Book of the Acts of God.* Garden City, N.Y.: Doubleday, 1957.

Zizoulas, John. *Being as Communion: Studies in Personhood and the Church.* Crestwood, N.Y.: St. Vladimir's Seminary Press, 1985.